Prism Press Books

Full Spanish and English text on same or facing pages

POCO / POCO   Adventures of a cactus wren in the Mexico City bird market. Story by Garry and Vesta Smith. Illustrated by Fred Crump Jr. 40 pages.

MOCHITO: The Story of an Ordinary Dog / MOCHITO: Historia de un perrito ordinario   Story by Nelly Canepari. Photographs by Jorge Schneider. Translated by Edith Rusconi Kaltovich. 40 pages.

LUIS / LUIS   Story of the Puerto Rican vacation of an 11-year-old Latino boy from Massachusetts. Written by John Getsinger, with photographs by the author. 48 pages.

A CARPET OF FLOWERS / UNA ALFOMBRA DE FLORES The story of how a blind boy's life is changed when he participates in a traditional village devotion honoring the Virgin of Guadelupe. By Elizabeth Borton de Trevino. Illustrated by Cyril Miles. 125 pages.

44 POEMS BY EDGAR ALLAN POE / 44 POEMAS DE EDGAR ALLAN POE   Translated by Raul Mariaca G. 175 pages.

UNA GALERIA IBERICA: Un Libro para colorear / AN IBERIAN GALLERY: A Coloring Book / UMA GALERIA IBERICA: Um livro para colorir   Illustrations by Elizabeth Wyant. Captions in Spanish, English, and Portuguese .

ALBERTO AND HIS MISSING SOCK / ALBERTO Y EL CALCETIN PERDIDO   Story by Barbara Ganz. Illustrated by Phyllis Noda. Translated by Agustina Santos del Favero. 40 pages.

Bilingual Schooling in the United States

HISTORY, RATIONALE, IMPLICATIONS, AND PLANNING

BY THEODORE ANDERSSON AND MILDRED BOYER

WITH A NEW FOREWORD AND SUPPLEMENTARY BIBLIOGRAPHY

by Francesco Cordasco

VOLUME ONE

Southwest Educational Development Laboratory, Austin, Texas 1970

Republished by Blaine Ethridge--Books, 1976

13977 Penrod Detroit, Michigan 48223

√

The Bilingual Task was performed by the Southwest Educational Development Laboratory pursuant to an amendment to the Laboratory's Title IV Contract (4-7-062113-3072) with the U. S. Office of Education. The Laboratory is a private non-profit corporation supported in part as a regional educational laboratory by funds from the United States Office of Education, Department of Health, Education, and Welfare. The opinions expressed in this publication do not necessarily reflect the position or policy of the Office of Education, and no official endorsement by the Office of Education should be inferred.

Library of Congress Cataloging in Publication Data

Andersson, Theodore, 1903-
Bilingual schooling in the United States.

"The bilingual task was performed by the Southwest Educational Development Laboratory."
Reprint of the 1970 ed. published by Southwest Educational Development Laboratory.
Bibliography: p.
1. Education, Bilingual--United States.
2. Bilingualism--Bibliography. I. Boyer, Mildred, 1926-
II. Southwest Educational Development Laboratory. III. Title.
[LC3731.A75 1976] 371.9'7 76-5907
ISBN 0-87917-050-6

TABLE OF CONTENTS

VOLUME I

NEW FOREWORD AND SUPPLEMENTAL BIBLIOGRAPHY

by FRANCESCO CORDASCO

Bilingual Schooling in the United States by Theodore Andersson and Mildred Boyer was an inevitable consequence of that vigorous and exciting period which followed the enactment of the Bilingual Education Act in 1967. President Lyndon B. Johnson signed the Act into law on January 2, 1968; and as Title VII of the Elementary and Secondary Education Act (enacted in 1965), the Bilingual Education Act furnished new perspectives, recognizing for special assistance, those children "who come from environments where the dominant language is other than English." In a nation in which it had been illegal in many states to teach in any language but English, the Bilingual Education Act was a revolutionary concept and, in the years since its passage, both its legislative history and funding have been attended by controversy:[2] yet, it can be safely affirmed that bilingual education (and the bicultural components which accompany it) are assured a continuing place in American education, even allowing for the many questions and concerns which still remain unresolved.[3]

Coming so soon after the enactment of the Bilingual Education Act, the Anderson/Boyer *Bilingual Schooling in the United States* is compendiously attentive to all the multifarious concerns which impinge on bilingualism: in a nation in which bilingualism had so long been neglected, it could hardly have been otherwise. Recognizing bilingualism as "a major, virtually untapped national resource," the study was designed to "reveal the promise of bilingual education and to serve as a guideline for those planning bilingual programs"; and the scope of the work was dimensionally defined to include "a history of bilingual schooling, both in the United States and in other parts of the world; alternative concepts of bilingual schooling; sample curriculum models; implications for education and society; and an outline of needs, as related to action and research." Andersson/Boyer saw their task as relatively uncomplicated:

> Non-English-speaking children are not the only ones who stand to profit from such a reform in our educational system. English-speaking children who are fortunate enough to live in a community in which another language is spoken have an unusual opportunity to learn this language. At the same time, they may also become sensitive to another culture and hence be better able to understand and interact with the different people around them.
>
> In the following chapters we hope to spell out this educational promise—by providing, both in the text and in the appendices, background information essential to the understanding of the complex subject of bilingual schooling; by suggesting a rationale; and by proposing guidelines for the development of bilingual programs to meet local needs and circumstances.
>
> The subject is so many-faceted and the relevant literature so extensive that we have not been able to digest it all. We prefer therefore that our readers consider our book as a preliminary effort, to be improved after more study and research. We invite criticisms, which we shall use or transmit to others, as may best serve the cause of bilingual education. (I, 4)

And *Bilingual Schooling in the United States* was patently congruent with those studies which Professors Andersson and Boyer had underway at the federally funded Southwest Educational Development Laboratory at Austin, Texas.

More than a ''preliminary effort,'' the Andersson/Boyer study is a major repository of information on bilingual education: in a strict sense, it is one of a handful of invaluable resources which furnishes guidance to the complex psychological, linguistic, and social interrelationships which are the components of bilingual/bicultural education. Essentially, the questions to which *Bilingual Schooling in the United States* addresses itself are very old issues, indeed, in American society: they are the ineluctable questions which surround ethnicity, language maintenance, and the twin processes of conflict and acculturation which are inevitable in as diverse a society as that in the United States. Taking the Bilingual Education Act as a centrifugal point of reference, Professors Andersson and Boyer distill out of the questions the thematic essences which must be pursued:

> Today we wear ''an ethnic coat of many colors, all but one strand of which has constantly been overlooked, denied, or degraded.'' The meeting of languages and the clash of cultures created tensions, which the Bilingual Education Act is designed to alleviate and can perhaps alleviate if it is expanded and adequately funded.
>
> The status of English as the official language of the United States has never been in doubt. The question which Joshua Fishman's book on *Language Loyalty in the United States* has raised and which the Bilingual Education Act now raises again is whether or not the official position of English leaves room for the maintenance of other languages and cultures. Stated in another way, what should be the attitude and policy of the 90 percent (native English speakers) toward the other ten percent of our population (native speakers of other languages)? These other languages surely do not constitute a threat to English. But are they a nuisance, or are they rather a resource which from a human and patriotic point of view ought to be conserved? These are fundamental questions, to which we shall return in later chapters.
>
> Over the years Americans' views toward newcomers have fluctuated. In the late nineteenth and twentieth centuries the older American stock found it gratifying to accept the view that the New World was the land of promise and America a melting pot, which received countless immigrants who came from some two dozen countries in Europe and spoke even more different languages. Tossed together and stirred up, they were supposed to undergo a delectable transformation and emerge as Americans, all essentially alike and all of course speaking American English. Actually, this is more myth than fact. As Glazer and Moynihan point out in their book, *Beyond the Melting Pot* (1963), the melting did not always take place. Immigrants to America did not cease being what they were and did not, except in rather superficial ways, become something different when they were naturalized as American citizens. Changes that occured were far less extensive and less structural than they were believed to be. In most cases a bicultural style developed which enabled American and ethnic identities to coexist and influence each other slowly over time. Even today we are regarded as one of the most multicultural nations in the world.
>
> Attempting to define what an American is is intriguing, but the task is not a simple one. Some impressive people have tried, more or less successfully: among others, Tocqueville, Lord Bryce, Count Keyserling, Mead, Brogan, Gorer, Commager, Riesman, and Montagu. (I, 2-3)

Bilingual Schooling in the United States, virtually by design, is an encyclopedic compendium on bilingual education: its two volume format (Volume I, ix, 292 pp.; Volume II, 328 pp., in large *octavo*) permitted largely unlimited contexts for theoretic, practical, and policy considerations, with a survey of vast bibliographical resources: and, for supporting studies, the inclusion of monographic appendices. Volume I includes the wide range of definitions of bilingual education, its historical backgrounds, rationale, program planning, needed research, and societal/educational implications, with tentatively formulated conclusions: the coverage is staggeringly comprehensive, and supports the proposals embodied in Professors Andersson and Boyer's epilogue:

> About some aspects of our study we feel confident; the evidence seems conclusive. Our past methods of educating children suffering linguistic handicaps in English have clearly been ineffective. The chief reasons for this seems to be that we have not taken advantage of the child's best instrument of learning—his mother tongue—and that we have failed to create in him a sense of dignity and confidence. In a word, we have not put first things first: We have thought it more important from the outset to teach the non-English-speaking child English than to educate him. We have in short been more interested in assimilating than in educating.
>
> Everyone agrees that in the education of American children English is indispensable. Those who do not know it must learn it. Disagreement comes over the order and method of learning. As we have seen, the mass of evidence shows that, everything being equal, children learn to read and write faster and better in their dominant tongue than they do in a second language. There is also ample evidence that children can learn to read and write a second language more easily and better if they have built confidence in themselves by having become literate first in their native tongue. If, in addition, their English-speaking playmates and teachers treat them with respect and affection, their understanding of themselves, of the meaning of their language, and of their cultural heritage will grow, as will their motivation for further learning.
>
> The new educational vista that the Bilingual Education Act opens is that it obviates the disintegrative choice that millions of "nonstandard" children have faced in our public schools: a choice between the language of their mothers and the language of their country and its schools. That mother-and-country has become cliché should not blind us to the fact that, especially in dealing with young children, we drive a wedge between them at our own peril. When certain identifiable ethnic groups among our people have been confronted with the choice, it has been the schools that have lost. But if the hopes extended by the Bilingual Education Act are realized, our ethnic children can not only maintain and develop their mother tongues but can also learn English better than they have in the past. Results of early bilingual schooling demonstrate that, when a child's learning is properly guided by competent teachers, he can acquire in both languages unaccented spoken command, grade-level literacy, and the means of continuing his education "toward the farthest edge of his talents and dreams." (I, 147)

Volume I also includes the invaluable bibliography which is an integral part of *Bilingual Schooling in the United States.* The bibliography (I, 151-243) includes books, articles, bibliographies, official documents, bulletins, dissertations, theses, manuals, papers, pamphlets, both published and unpublished, which Professors Andersson and Boyer and members of their staff had consulted. Many of its 870 entries are annotated, and the bibliography's use is further enhanced by a subject index (I, 247-276). Additionally, Volume I has a general index (I, 279-292) which further facilitates the volume's use.

The appendices in Volume II include the text of, and the guidelines for, the 1967 Bilingual Education Act; demographic data; notes on immigration legislation; William F. Mackey's detailed typology of bilingual education; a series of monographic essays on ethnic communities in the United States (*i.e.*, Mexican, Puerto Rican, Cuban, German, Italian, Polish, French, Norwegian, Japanese, Chinese, etc.); materials on Indians, Eskimos, and Aleuts; the status of Basque Americans; a list of bilingual programs operating in the United States as of May 1969; and a directory of persons and organizations identified with bilingualism, with notices of sources of teaching materials.

Bilingual Schooling in the United States was published in January 1970 by the U.S. Government Printing Office and distributed by the Superintendent of Documents. The print-order was necessarily small (governed by the limited federal funds appropriated for the study and its publication to the Southwest Educational Development Laboratory pursuant to an amendment to the Laboratory's Title IV contract with the U.S. Office of Education), and for some time the volumes have been out of print and generally unavailable. Its republication is intended to meet the continuing need for those academic libraries and agencies for which copies have been generally unobtainable. In the reprinting no changes have been made in the text of the study but I have added a supplemental bibliography.

At the historic *Hearings* in mid-1967 before the Congress (*Hearings* which were to culminate in the enactment of the Bilingual Education Act), I observed: "In its efforts to assimilate all of its charges, the American school assaulted (and, in consequence, very often destroyed) the cultural identity of the child; it forced him to leave his ancestral language at the schoolhouse door; it developed in the child a haunting ambivalence of language, of culture, of ethnicity, and of personal self-affirmation. It held up to its children mirrors in which they saw not themselves, but the stereotype middle-class, white, English-speaking child, who embodied the essence of what the American child was (or ought) to be. For the minority child, the images which the school fashioned were cruel deceptions. In the enforced acculturation, there was bitterness and confusion, but tragically, too, there was the rejection of the wellsprings of identity and, more often than not, the failure of achievement. The ghettoization of the European immigrant, in substance, is exactly analogous to the ghettoization of the Negro, Puerto Rican, and Mexican-American poor. A long time ago, Louis Wirth called attention to the vitality of the ghetto in its maintenance of the lifestyles, languages, and cultures of a minority people assaulted by the main institutions of a dominant society. The schools, if only because of the sensitivity of their role, measured their successes sparingly; for it increasingly became apparent that, if the schools truly were to be successful, they would have to build on the strengths which the children brought with them—on ancestral pride, on native language, and on the multiplicity of needs and identities which the community of the children afforded."[4] And these sentiments have been reaffirmed in a recently published insightful commentary on the current state of bilingual-bicultural education in the United States:

> One of the potential sources of greatness of the United States has always been the multilingual-multicultural character of its people. These diverse strains which make up the American nation should not be squandered or wilfully destroyed, but carefully cultivated and encouraged to thrive, so that each can make its contribution to the society. Bilingual-bicultural education—which in its varied manifestations in this country becomes multilingual-multicultural education—can add to the richness and the enduring strength of the United States by nurturing mother tongues and cultural diversity and by furthering understanding and respect for one another among persons who may have differing origins and points of view but who are always fundamentally more alike than they are different. For we all share the same basic hopes and desires and needs inherent in our common humanity.[5]

In the year of the American Bicentennial, it is singularly appropriate that *Bilingual Schooling in the United States* reappear: it is a reminder of our illustrious heritage.

FRANCESCO CORDASCO

REFERENCES

[1] Theodore Andersson and Mildred Boyer, *Bilingual Schooling in the United States,* 2 vols. (Washington: Government Printing Office, 1970). The study was undertaken by the Southwest Educational Development Laboratory (Austin, Texas) pursuant to an amendment to the Laboratory's federal Title IV contract (4-7-062113-3072) with the U.S. Office of Education. The Laboratory functioned as a private non-profit corporation supported in part as a regional educational laboratory by funds from the U.S. Office of Education. The study, upon its publication, included the legend-line: "The opinions expressed in this publication do not necessarily reflect the position or policy of the Office of Education, and no official endorsement by the Office of Education should be inferred."

[2] For the status of bilingual education legislation in the United States, see Hannah N. Geffert, *et al.*, *The Current Status of U.S. Bilingual Education Legislation* (Arlington, Virginia: Center for Applied Linguistics, 1975). The Bilingual Education Act was enacted for five years; however, its continuation was in doubt in early 1973 and it appeared that the Act would be a casualty of the reorganization of governmental departments during the Nixon tenure which resulted in the elimination of some "poverty" and educational programs. Congress chose to continue the Act on a one-year basis (1973-1974), supporting programs in operation but accepting no applications for new programs. In the summer of 1974 Congress passed (and President Gerald Ford signed) the *Education Amendments of 1974* (H.R. 69) which provided continuing financial support through 1978 for bilingual education programs of the type initiated under Title VII. The *Amendments* strengthened and extended the provisions for bilingual education, *e.g.*, in bilingual vocational training, adult bilingual education programs, fellowships for graduate study, etc. The text of the *Amendments* is available as Senate Report No. 93-1026, 93rd Congress, 2nd Session. A convenient repository for reference is *A Compilation of Federal Education Laws: As Amended Through December 31, 1974* [Prepared for the Use of the House Committee on Education and Labor and the Senate Committee on Labor and Public Welfare] (Washington: Government Printing Office, 1975). In 1974-1975, a total of 320 bilingual projects were funded in 41 states and territories, for which see, *Guide to Title VII ESEA Bilingual Bicultural Programs, 1974-1975* (Austin, Texas: Dissemination Center for Bilingual Bicultural Education, 1975). The 1974 *Amendments* (Section 105 of Title I) authorized under the amended Bilingual Education Act, $135 million for FY 1975, $140 million for FY 1976, $150 million for FY 1977, and $160 million for FY 1978. For FY 1975, $85 million was actually appropriated.

[3] Some of the unresolved problems are perceptively examined in A. Bruce Gaarder, "Bilingual Education: Central Questions and Concerns," *New York University Education Quarterly,* 6:1-6, Summer, 1975. "Enough has been written here to lead us to the centermost of all concerns: the goal or goals of bilingual education. Clearly there are three major ones, each in basic opposition to the others: 1. development of a more effective, more 'humane' one-way bridge to English; 2. more effective education for children whose mother tongue is not English, plus the longterm development and maintenance of that mother tongue; 3. provision of a source of jobs in education and of preferential treatment for members of the ethnic groups involved." (*loc. cit.*, p. 4) See also, Joshua A. Fishman, "Bilingual Education: What and Why?" in Joshua A. Fishman, ed., *Bilingual Education: An International Sociological Perspective* (Rowley, Mass.: Newbury House, 1976).

[4] *Hearings Before the General Subcommittee on Education of the Committee on Education and Labor.* House of Representatives, 90th Congress, 1st Session on H.R. 9840 and H.R. 10224, Bills to Amend the Elementary and Secondary Education Act of 1965 in Order to Assist Bilingual Education Programs (Washington: Government Printing Office, 1967), p. 271. With some changes, the text of my remarks appears in *School & Society,* 96:198-201, March 30, 1968.

[5] Francis Willard Von Maltitz, *Living and Learning in Two Languages: Bilingual-Bicultural Education in the United States* (New York: McGraw-Hill, 1975), p. 192.

SUPPLEMENTAL BIBLIOGRAPHY

A basic bibliography resource is William F. Mackey, *International Bibliography on Bilingualism* (Quebec: Les Presses de l'Université Laval, 1972), which is a computer print-out of an alphabetized and indexed checklist of 11,006 titles. Reference also should be made to Einar Haugen, *Bilingualism in the Americas: A Bibliography and Reference Guide* (University of Alabama Press, 1965), and the valuable bibliographies in Theodore Andersson and Mildred Boyer, *Bilingual Schooling in the United States,* 2 vols. (Austin, Texas: Southwest Educational Development Laboratory, 1970).

Major sources of continuing information are the CAL/ERIC Clearinghouse on Languages and Linguistics which is operated by the Center for Applied Linguistics (1611 North Kent Street, Arlington, Va., 22209); and the Dissemination and Assessment Center for Bilingual Education (6504 Tracor Lane, Austin, Texas, 78721) whose *Cartel: Annotated Bibliography of Bilingual Bicultural Materials* is a monthly listing providing project personnel with information about relevant materials in bilingual/bicultural education for their programs. Reference should be made to the publications catalogue of the Georgetown University (Washington, D.C., 20057) School of Languages and Linguistics, *e.g.*, sociolinguistics, general linguistics, and the School's "Working Papers on Languages and Linguistics," and "Round Table on Languages and Linguistics."

A variety of publications is available from the TESOL (Teachers of English to Speakers of Other Languages) Central Office (455 Nevils Building, Georgetown University, Washington, D.C., 20057). A valuable retrospective resource is Virginia F. Allen and Sidney Forman, *English As A Second Language: A Comprehensive Bibliography* (Columbia University, Teachers College Press [1966]) which is a listing by subject categories of the special collection (English As a Foreign or Second Language) in the Teachers College Library. Newbury House Publishers (68 Middle Road, Rowley, Mass., 01969) is a specialized resource of materials in applied linguistics, sociolinguistics, and bilingual education texts.

A number of journals should be consulted; particularly useful are *Florida FL Reporter; Human Organization; Journal of Verbal Learning and Verbal Behavior; Language Learning; Linguistic Reporter; The Modern Language Journal;* and *TESOL Quarterly.*

In the areas of poverty, socio-economic disadvantagement, the equality of educational opportunity and related concerns, reference may be made to Francesco Cordasco, *et al.*, *The Equality of Educational Opportunity: A Bibliography of Selected References* (Totowa, N.J.: Rowman and Littlefield, 1973); Francesco Cordasco, ed., *Toward Equal Educational Opportunity: The Report of the Select Committee on Equal Educational Opportunity, U.S. Senate* (New York: AMS Press, 1974), particularly Part V (Education of Language Minorities); and to Francesco Cordasco and David Alloway, eds., "Poverty in America: Economic Inequality, New Ideologies, and the Search for Educational Opportunity," *Journal of Human Relations* [Special Issue], vol. 20 (3rd Quarter, 1972), pp. 234-396, which includes articles on poverty contexts, minority responses to oppression, racial caste systems, the assimilation of Mexicans, and the educational neglect of Black, Puerto Rican, and Portuguese children.

Special note should be made of Harold B. Allen's *A Survey of the Teaching of English to Non-English Speakers in the United States* (Champaign, Illinois: National Council of Teachers of English, 1966). Known generally as the TENES report, Dr. Allen's data are still very useful. In a class by themselves are the valuable explorations of Basil Bernstein of the effect of class relationships upon the institutionalizing of elaborated codes in the school, *e.g.*, Basil Bernstein, *Class, Codes and Control* [Vol. I: *Theoretical Studies Towards a Sociology of Language;* Vol. II: *Applied Studies Towards a Sociology of Language;* Vol. III: *Towards a Theory of Educational Transmissions*] (London: Routledge & Kegan Paul, 1973-1975). Important bibliographical studies of the Center for Applied Linguistics should be noted: *A Bibliography of American Doctoral Dissertations in*

Linguistics, 1900-1964 (1968); *Reference List of Materials for English as a Second Language* (Three Parts, 1964, 1966, 1969); *Spanish and English of United States Hispanos: A Critical, Annotated, Linguistic Bibliography* (1975); and for native American Indian languages, the Center's *A Survey of the Current Teaching of North American Indian Languages in the United States and Canada* (1975). The Center has also published a *Vietnamese Refugee Education Series* (1975) which includes phrasebooks, cross-cultural materials, an annotated bibliography, a personnel resources directory, and a colloquium on the Vietnamese language.

Aarons, Alfred C., Barbara Y. Gordon, and William A. Stewart, eds. 'Linguistic-Cultural Differences and American Education.' *Florida FL Reporter*, vol. 7 (1969) (special anthology issue).

Abrahams, Roger D., and Rudolph C. Troike, eds. *Language and Cultural Diversity in American Education.* Englewood Cliffs, New Jersey: Prentice-Hall, 1972.

Adkins, Dorothy C. *Cross-Cultural Comparisons of the Motivation of Young Children to Achieve in School.* [ERIC ED 60 053]

Adkins, D. C., F. D. Payne, and B. L. Ballif. 'Motivation Factor Scores and Response Set Scores for 10 Ethnic Cultural Groups of Preschool Children.' *American Educational Research Journal*, vol. 9 (1972), pp. 557-72.

Agheyisi, Rebecca, and Joshua A. Fishman. 'Language Attitude Studies: A Brief Survey of Methodological Approaches.' *Anthropological Linguistics*, vol. 12 (1970), pp. 137-157.

Ainsworth, Len, and Gay Alford. *Responsive Environment Program for Spanish-American Children.* Evaluation Report, 1971-72. Lubbock, Texas: Adobe Educational Services, 1972. [ERIC ED 068 219]

Alatis, James E., ed. *Bilingualism and Language Contact: Anthropological, Linguistic, Psychological, and Sociological Aspects.* Monograph Series on Languages and Linguistics, 23. Washington: Georgetown University Press, 1970.

Alfaro, Manuel R., Jr., and Homer C. Hawkins. *The Chicano Migrant Child.* 1972. [ERIC ED 072 900]

Allen, Harold B. *Teaching English as a Second Language.* New York: McGraw-Hill, 1972.

Alloway, David N., and Francesco Cordasco. *Minorities and the American City: A Sociological Primer for Educators.* New York: David McKay, 1970.

Altus, David M. *American Indian Education: A Selected Bibliography.* Supplement No. 2. Washington: Superintendent of Documents, U.S. Government Printing Office, 1971. [ERIC ED 58 980]

Anastasi, Anne, and Cruz de Jesús. 'Language Development and Nonverbal IQ of Puerto Rican Children in New York City.' *Journal of Abnormal and Social Psychology*, vol. 48 (1953), pp. 357-66.

Andersson, Theodore, and Mildred Boyer. *Bilingual Schooling in the United States.* 2 vols. Austin, Texas: Southwest Educational Development Laboratory, 1970.

Anisfeld, Moshe. *Language and Cognition in the Young Child.* 1965. [ERIC ED 019 636]

Aquino, Federico. 'La Identidad Puertorriqueña y la Educación.' *Quimbamba,* June 1972 (Bilingual Education Quarterly).

Arciniega, T. A. *The Urban Mexican-American: A Socio-Cultural Profile.* 1971.

Arndt, Richard. *La Fortalecita: A Study of Low-Income (Urban) Mexican-Americans and Implications for Education.* Unpublished dissertation, University of New Mexico, 1970.

Arnold, Richard D., and Thommasine H. Taylor. 'Mexican-Americans and Language Learning.' *Childhood Education,* vol. 46 (1969), pp. 149-54.

[Aspira] *Hemos Trabajado Bien: A Report on the First National Conference of Puerto Ricans, Mexican-Americans and Educators on the Special Educational Needs of Puerto Rican Youth.* New York: Aspira, 1968.

Barclay, Lisa F. K. *The Comparative Efficacies of Spanish, English, and Bilingual Cognitive Verbal Instruction with Mexican-American Head Start Children.* Final Report. 1969. [ERIC ED 030 473]

Barik, H. C., and M. Swain. *Bilingual Education Project: Interim Report on the Spring 1972 Testing Program.* Toronto: Ontario Institute for Studies in Education, 1972.

Barker, George C. 'Social Functions of Language in a Mexican-American Community.' *Acta Americana,* vol. 5 (1947), pp. 185-202.

Barnes, F. *A Comparative Study of the Mental Ability of Indian Children.* M. A. Thesis, Stanford University, 1955.

Bebeau, D. E. 'Administration of a TOEFL Test to Sioux Indian High School Students.' *Journal of American Indian Education* vol. 9 (1969), pp. 7-16.

Bernal, Ernest M. *Concept-Learning Among Anglo, Black and Mexican-American Children Using Facilitation Strategies and Bilingual Techniques.* Unpublished dissertation, the University of Texas at Austin, 1971.

Bernbaum, Marcia. *Early Childhood Programs for Non-English Speaking Children.* Albany: The State Education Department, SUNY, 1972.

Biglin, J. E., *et al. A Study of Parental Attitudes and Values Towards Education on the Navajo and Hopi Reservations. Part I: A Summary of the Literature.* 1971 [ERIC ED 62 070 77]

'Bilingualism.' *The Center Forum,* vol. 4 (1969). [Entire issue devoted to programs and related matters.]

'Bilingualism and the Bilingual Child -- A Symposium.' *Modern Language Journal,* vol. 49 (March, April 1965).

Bilingualism in Education. Department of Education and Science. London: H. M. Stationery Office, 1965.

Bongers, Lael Shannon. *A Developmental Study of Time Perception and Time Perspective in Three Cultural Groups: Anglo-American, Indian-American and Mexican-American.* Unpublished dissertation, UCLA, 1971.

Bortin, Barbara H. *Bilingual Education Program Evaluation Report, Milwaukee Public Schools, 1969-70.* 1970 [ERIC ED 708]

Brannon, J. B. 'A Comparison of Syntactic Structures in the Speech of Three and Four Year Old Children.' *Language and Speech*, vol. 11 (1968), pp. 171-81.

Bright, William, ed. *Sociolinguistics: Proceedings of the UCLA Sociolinguistics Conference, 1964.* The Hague: Mouton, 1966.

Brisk, M. E. *The Spanish Syntax of the Pre-School Spanish American: The Case of New Mexican Five-Year-Old Children.* Unpublished dissertation, University of New Mexico, 1972.

Broman, Betty. 'The Spanish-Speaking Five Year Old.' *Childhood Education*, vol. 41 (1972), pp. 362-64.

Brooks, R., L. Brandt, and M. Wiener. 'Differential Response to Two Communication Channels: Socioeconomic Class Differences in Response to Verbal Reinforcers Communicated with and without Tonal Inflection.' *Child Development*, vol. 40 (1969), pp. 453-70.

Brophy, J. E. 'Mothers as Teachers of Their Own Preschool Children: The Influence of Socioeconomic Status and Task Structure on Teaching Specificity.' *Child Development*, vol. 41 (1970), pp. 79-94.

Brown, Marie L. S. *The Effect of Ethnicity on Visual-Perceptual Skills Related to Reading Readiness.* Unpublished dissertation, University of Colorado, 1971.

Brown, Roger. *A First Language: The Early Stages.* Cambridge, Mass.: Harvard University Press, 1973.

Brown, Roger, and Ursula Bellugi. 'Three Processes in the Child's Acquisition of Syntax.' *Language and Learning*, special issue of *Harvard Educational Review*, vol. 34 (1964), pp. 133-151.

Brussel, Charles B. *Disadvantaged Mexican-American Children and Early Educational Experience.* 1968 [ERIC ED 30 517]

Bryson, Juanita. *Comparison of Bilingual vs. Single Language Instruction in Concept Learning in Mexican-American Four Year Olds.* 1970 [ERIC ED 062 043]

Bucklin, L. Brice. *Anglo and Latin: The Cultural Difference.* 1970 [ERIC ED 44 977]

Bureau of Indian Affairs. *Bilingual Education for American Indians.* Washington: Bureau of Indian Affairs, 1971.

Bureau of Indian Affairs. *A Kindergarten Curriculum Guide for Indian Children: A Bilingual-Bicultural Approach.* 1970 [ERIC ED 65 236]

Burger, Henry C. *Ethno-Pedagogy: A Manual in Cultural Sensitivity with Techniques for Improving Cross-Cultural Teaching by Fitting Ethnic Patterns.* Albuquerque, N. M.: SWCEL, 1968.

Burma, John H. 'A Comparison of the Mexican-American Subculture with the Oscar Lewis Poverty Model.' In J. H. Burma, ed., *Mexican-Americans in the United States.* Cambridge, Mass.: Schenkman, 1970, pp. 17-28.

Burma, John H., ed. *Mexican-Americans in the United States.* Cambridge, Mass.: Schenkman, 1970.

Burma, John H. *Spanish-Speaking Groups in the United States.* Detroit: Blaine Ethridge, 1974. (originally, Duke University Press, 1954)

Canedo, Oscar Octavio. *Performance of Mexican-American Students on a Test of Verbal Intelligence.* Unpublished dissertation, International University, 1972.

Cannon, Garland. 'Bilingual Problems and Developments in the United States.' *PMLA*, vol. 86 (1971), pp. 452-58.

Cárdenas, Blandina, and José A. Cárdenas. 'Chicano -- Bright-Eyes, Bilingual, Brown, and Beautiful.' *Today's Education* [NEA Journal], February (1973), pp. 49-51.

Cárdenas, René. *Three Critical Factors that Inhibit Acculturation of Mexican-Americans.* Unpublished dissertation, University of California, Berkeley, 1970.

Carrow, Elizabeth. 'Auditory Comprehension of English by Monolingual and Bilingual Preschool Children.' *Journal of Speech and Hearing Research*, vol. 15 (1972), pp. 407-412.

Carrow, Elizabeth. 'Comprehension of English and Spanish by Preschool Mexican-American Children.' *Modern Language Journal*, vol. 55 (1971), pp. 299-306.

Carrow, Sister Mary Arthur. 'The Development of Auditory Comprehension of Language Structure in Children.' *Journal of Speech and Hearing Disorders*, vol. 33 (1968), pp. 105-108.

Caudill, William, and Lois Frost. *A Comparison of Maternal Care and Infant Behavior in Japanese-American, American, and Japanese Families.* 1971 [ERIC ED 57 153]

Cazden, Courtney B. 'The Hunt for the Independent Variables.' In Renira Huxley and Elizabeth Ingram, eds., *Language Acquisition Models and Methods.* New York: Academic Press, 1971, pp. 41-49.

Cazden, Courtney B., ed. *Language in Early Childhood Education.* Washington: National Association for the Education of Young Children, 1972.

Cazden, Courtney B. 'The Situation: A Neglected Source of Social Class Differences in Language Use.' *Journal of Social Issues*, vol. 26 (1970), pp. 35-59.

Cazden, Courtney B. 'Subcultural Differences in Child Language.' *Merrill-Palmer Quarterly*, vol. 12 (1966), pp. 185-219.

Cazden, Courtney B., and Vera John. 'Learning in American Indian Children.' In *Styles of Learning Among American Indians: An Outline for Research.* Washington: Center for Applied Linguistics, 1968.

Cazden, Courtney B., Vera John, and Dell Hymes, eds. *Functions of Language in the Classroom.* New York: Teachers College Press, 1972.

[Center for Applied Linguistics]. *Recommendations for Language Policy in Indian Education.* Arlington, Va.: Center for Applied Linguistics, 1973.

[Center for Applied Linguistics]. *Styles of Learning Among American Indians: An Outline for Research.* Washington: Center for Applied Linguistics, 1968.

[Certification] 'Proposed Guidelines for the Preparation and Certification of Teachers of Bilingual-Bicultural Education in the United States.' *Linguistic Reporter* (October, 1974).

Chafe, Wallace L. 'Estimates Regarding the Present Speakers of North American Indian Languages.' *International Journal of American Linguistics*, vol. 28 (1962), pp. 162-171.

Chilcott, John H., *et al. Handbook for Prima and Maricopa Indian Teacher Aides.* 1970 [ERIC ED 44 221]

Ching, D. C. 'Reading, Language Development, and the Bilingual Child: An Annotated Bibliography.' *Elementary English*, vol. 46 (1969), pp. 622-628.

Chomsky, Carol. *The Acquisition of Syntax in Children from Five to Ten.* Cambridge, Mass.: The M.I.T. Press, 1969.

Christiansen, T., and G. Livermore. 'A Comparison of Anglo-American and Spanish-American Children on the WISC.' *Journal of Social Psychology*, vol. 81 (1970), pp. 1-14.

Cintrón de Crespo, Patria. *Puerto Rican Women Teachers in New York, Self-Perception and Work Adjustment as Perceived in Themselves and by Others.* Ed. D. Report, New York: Columbia University Teachers College, 1965.

Cohen, Andrew D. *A Sociolinguistic Approach to Bilingual Education.* Rowley, Mass.: Newbury House, 1975.

Cohen, R., G. Fraenkel, and J. Brewer. 'Implications for 'Culture Conflict' from a Semantic Feature Analysis of the Lexicon of the Hard Core Poor.' *Linguistics*, vol. 44 (1968), pp. 11-21.

Cole, H. J. *A Comparison of Associative Learning Rates of Indian and White Adolescents.* Unpublished dissertation, the University of Oklahoma, 1971.

Cole, Michael, and Jerome S. Bruner. 'Cultural Differences and Inferences About Psychological Processes.' *American Psychologist*, October, 1971.

Coleman, James. *Equality of Educational Opportunity.* Washington: U.S. Government Printing Office, 1966.

Coombs, L. Madison. *The Indian Student Is Not Low Man on the Totem Pole.* Lawrence, Kansas: Haskell Institute Press, 1972.

Cooper, James G. *Perception of Self and Others as a Function of Ethnic Group Membership.* 1971 [ERIC ED 57 965]

Cooper, R. L. 'Two Contextualized Measures of Degree of Bilingualism.' *Modern Language Journal*, vol. 53 (1969), pp. 172-8.

Cordasco, Francesco. 'Another View of Poverty: Oscar Lewis' *La Vida.*' *Phylon: The Atlanta Review of Race & Culture,* vol. 29 (Spring 1968), pp. 88-92.

Cordasco, Francesco. 'The Challenge of the Non-English Speaking Child in the American School.' *School and Society,* vol. 96 (March 30, 1968), pp. 198-201.

Cordasco, Francesco. 'The Children of Immigrants in Schools: Historical Analogues of Educational Deprivation.' *Journal of Negro Education,* vol. 42 (Winter 1973) pp. 44-53.

Cordasco, Francesco. 'Educational Enlightenment out of Texas: Toward Bilingualism.' *Teachers College Record,* vol. 72 (May 1970), pp. 608-612. See also, F. Cordasco, 'The Bilingual Education Act,' *Phi Delta Kappan* (October 1969).

Cordasco, Francesco, advisory editor. *The Puerto Rican Experience.* 33 vols. New York: Arno Press/New York Times, 1975.

Cordasco, Francesco. 'Puerto Rican Pupils and American Education.' *School and Society,* vol. 95 (February 18, 1967), pp. 116-119.

Cordasco, Francesco. 'Teaching the Puerto Rican Experience,' in James A. Banks, ed., *Teaching Ethnic Studies: Concepts and Strategies.* (Washington: Council for the Social Studies, 1973), pp. 226-253.

Cordasco, Francesco, *et al. Puerto Ricans on the United States Mainland: A Bibliography of Reports, Texts, Critical Studies and Related Materials.* Totowa, N. J.: Rowman and Littlefield, 1972.

Cordasco, Francesco, and Eugene Bucchioni. *The Puerto Rican Community and Its Children on the Mainland: A Sourcebook for Teachers, Social Workers and Other Professionals.* Metuchen, N. J.: Scarecrow Press, 1972.

Cordasco, Francesco, and Eugene Bucchioni. *The Puerto Rican Experience: A Sociological Sourcebook.* Totowa, N. J. : Littlefield, Adams, 1973.

Cordasco, Francesco, and Eugene Bucchioni. 'A Staff Institute for Teachers of Puerto Rican Students.' *School and Society,* vol. 99 (Summer 1972).

Cordasco, Francesco, and Leonard Covello. *Studies of Puerto Rican Children in American Schools: A Preliminary Bibliography.* New York: Department of Labor Migration Division, Commonwealth of Puerto Rico, 1967. Also in *Education Libraries Bulletin,* Institute of Education, University of London, No. 31 (Spring 1968), pp. 7-33; and in *Journal of Human Relations,* vol. 16 (1968), pp. 264-285.

Cornejo, Ricardo. 'The Acquisition of Lexicon in the Speech of Bilingual Children,' in Paul Turner, ed., *Bilingualism in the South West.* Tucson: University of Arizona Press, 1973, pp. 67-93.

Cornejo, Ricardo. *Bilingualism: Study of the Lexicon of the Five-Year-Old Spanish-Speaking Children of Texas.* Unpublished dissertation, the University of Texas at Austin, 1969.

Cortés, Carlos E., advisory editor. *The Mexican American.* 21 vols. New York: Arno Press/New York Times, 1974.

Covello, Leonard. *The Social Background of the Italo-American School Child: A Study of the Southern Italian Family Mores and Their Effect on the School*

Situation in Italy and America. Edited and with an introduction by F. Cordasco. Leiden, The Netherlands: E. J. Brill, 1967; Totowa, N.J.: Rowman and Littlefield, 1972.

Crossland, F. *Minority Access to College.* Ford Foundation Report, New York: Schocken Books, 1971.

Darcy, N.T. 'Bilingualism and the Measurement of Intelligence: Review of a Decade of Research.' *Journal of Genetic Psychology*, vol. 103 (1963), pp.259-282.

Davidson, M. Ruth. *A Comparative Pilot Study of Two First-Grade Programs for Culturally-Deprived Mexican-American Children.* Unpublished dissertation, the University of Texas at Austin, 1967.

Del Campo, Philip E. *An Analysis of Selected Features in the Acculturation Process of the Mexican-American School Child.* Unpublished dissertation, International University, 1970.

Denzin, G. K. 'Genesis of Self in Early Childhood.' *Social Quarterly*, vol. 13 (1972), pp. 291-314.

Dickeman, Mildren. 'The Integrity of the Cherokee Student.' In Eleanor Leacock, ed., *The Culture of Poverty: A Critique.* New York: Simon and Schuster, 1971, pp. 140-79.

Diebold, A. Richard, Jr. *The Consequences of Early Bilingualism in Cognitive Development and Personality Formation.* 1966 [ERIC ED 020 491]

Dielman, T. E. 'Childrearing Antecedents of Early Child Personality Factors.' *Journal of Marriage and the Family*, vol. 34 (1972), pp. 431-6.

Di Lorenzo, L. G., and R. Salter. 'Evaluative Study of Prekindergarten Programs for Educationally Disadvantaged Children: Followup and Replication.' *Exceptional Children*, vol. 34 (1968), pp. 111-19.

Donofrio, R. M. *Situations and Language: A Socio- Linguistic Investigation.* Final Report. Washington: National Center for Research and Development, 1972 [ERIC ED 168 236]

Doob, C. F. 'Family Background and Peer Group Development in a Puerto Rican District.' *Sociological Quarterly*, vol. 11 (1970), pp. 523-32.

Drach, Kerry, Ben Kobashigawa, Carol Pfuderer, and Dan Slobin. *The Structure of Linguistic Input to Children.* Working Paper No. 14, Language Behavior Research Lab. Berkeley: University of California, 1969.

Dulay, Heide C. 'Goofing: An Indicator of Children's Second Language Learning Strategies.' *Language Learning*, vol. 22 (1972), pp. 235-52.

Dumont, Robert V., Jr. 'Learning English and How to be Silent: Studies in Sioux and Cherokee Classrooms.' In *Functions of Language in the Classroom.* C. B. Cazden, *et al.*, eds., New York: Teachers College Press, 1972, pp. 344-69.

Dumont, Robert V., Jr., and Murray L. Wax. 'Cherokee School Society and the Intercultural Classroom' *Human Organization*, vol. 28 (1969), pp. 217-26.

Duphiney, Lorna. *Oriental - Americans: An Annotated Bibliography.* 1972 [ERIC ED 60 136]

Dwyer, R. C., *et al.* 'Evaluation of Effectiveness of a Problem - Based Preschool Compensatory Program.' *Journal of Educational Research,* vol. 66 (1972), pp. 153-156.

Dyke, R. B., and H. A. Witkin. 'Family Experiences Related to the Development of Differentiation in Children.' *Child Development,* vol. 36 (1965), pp. 21-55.

Early Childhood and School - Age Intensive Education Program: Evaluation of the ESEA Compensatory Education Program of the San Francisco Unified School District. 1968 - 69 Evaluation Report, San Francisco Unified School District. 1970 [ERIC ED 041 066]

Eastman, Clyde. *Assessing Cultural Change in North - Central New Mexico.* 1972 [ERIC ED 63 070]

Edelman, Martin. 'The Contextualization of School Children's Bilingualism.' *Modern Language Journal,* vol. 53 (1969), pp. 179-82.

Edwards, J., and C. Stern. 'Comparison of Three Intervention Programs with Disadvantaged Preschool Children.' *Journal of Special Education,* vol. 4 (1970), pp. 205-14.

Eggan, Dorothy. 'Instruction and Affect in Hopi Cultural Continuity.' *Southwestern Journal of Anthropology,* vol. 12 (1956), pp. 347-70.

Engle, Patricia L. *The Use of Vernacular Languages in Education. Language Medium in Early School Years for Minority Language Groups.* Washington: Center for Applied Linguistics, 1975. (Bilingual Education Series, No. 3)

Engle, Patricia Lee. *The Use of the Vernacular Languages in Education: Revisited.* A Literature Review prepared for the Ford Foundation Office of Mexico, Central America and the Caribbean (mimeo.), 1973.

Epstein, Erwin, ed. *Politics and Education in Puerto Rico.* Metuchen, N. J.: Scarecrow Press, 1970.

Ervin-Tripp, Susan. *Becoming a Bilingual.* 1968 [ERIC ED 018 786]

Evans, J. S. *Word - Pair Discrimination and Imitation Abilities of Preschool Economically-Disadvantaged Native-Spanish-Speaking Children.* Unpublished dissertation, the University of Texas at Austin, 1971.

Evans, J. S., and T. E. Bangs. 'Effects of Preschool Language Training on Later Academic Achievement.' *Journal of Learning Disabilities,* vol. 5 (1972), pp. 585-92.

Farmer, G. L. *Education: The Dilemma of the Spanish-surname American.* Los Angeles: University of Southern California, 1968.

Fedder, Ruth, and Jacqueline Gabaldon. *No Longer Deprived: The Use of Minority Cultures and Languages in the Education of Disadvantaged Children and Their Teachers.* New York: Teachers College Press, 1970.

Feldman, Carol, and M. Shen. 'Some Language-Related Cognitive Advantages of Bilingual Five-Year-Olds.' *Journal of Genetic Psychology*, vol. 118 (1971), pp. 235-244.

Feldman, Carol F. *Concept Formation in Children: A Study Using Nonsense Stimuli and Free-Sort Task.* 1969 [ERIC ED 031 306]

Feldman, David H. *The Fixed Sequence Hypothesis: Ethnic Differences in the Development of Spatial Reasoning.* 1969 [ERIC ED 33 476]

Finocchiaro, Mary. *Teaching English as a Second Language.* Rev. ed. New York: Harper & Row, 1969.

Fisher, John C. 'Bilingualism in Puerto Rico: A History of Frustration.' *The English Record*, vol. 21 (April 1971), pp. 19-24.

Fishman, Joshua, *et al.* 'Bilingualism in the Barrio.' *Modern Language Journal*, vol. 53 (March, April 1969)

Fishman, Joshua A. *Language and Nationalism.* Rowley, Mass.: Newbury House, 1973.

Fishman, Joshua A. *Language Loyalty in the United States.* The Hague: Mouton, 1966.

Fishman, Joshua A. 'The Measurement and Description of Widespread and Relatively Stable Bilingualism.' *Modern Language Journal*, vol. 53 (1969), pp. 153-56.

Fishman, Joshua A. 'The Politics of Bilingual Education' In James E. Alatis, ed., *Bilingualism and Language Contact* (Georgetown University Round Table on Languages and Linguistics, 1970), Washington: Georgetown University Press, pp. 47-58.

Fishman, Joshua A., ed. *Readings in the Sociology of Language.* The Hague: Mouton, 1968.

Fishman, Joshua A. 'A Sociolinguistic Census of a Bilingual Neighborhood.' *American Journal of Sociology*, vol. 75 (1969), pp. 323-39.

Fishman, Joshua A. *Sociolinguistics: A Brief Introduction.* Rowley, Mass.: Newbury House, 1971.

Fishman, Joshua A., and Heriberto Casiano. 'Puerto Ricans in Our Press.' *Modern Language Journal*, vol. 53 (1969), pp. 157-62.

Fishman, Joshua A., Robert L. Cooper, and Roxana Ma, eds. *Bilingualism in the Barrio.* Language Science Monographs 7, Indiana University. The Hague: Mouton, 1971.

Fishman, Joshua A., and John Lovas. 'Bilingual Education in a Sociolinguistic Perspective.' *TESOL Quarterly*, vol. 4 (September 1970).

Fitzpatrick, Joseph. *Puerto Rican Americans: The Meaning of Migration to the Mainland.* Englewood Cliffs: Prentice-Hall, 1971.

Francescato, G. 'Theoretical and Practical Aspects of Child Bilingualism.' *Lingua Stile*, vol. 4 (1969).

Freed, S. A., and R. S. Freed. 'Technique for Studying Role Behavior.' *Ethnology*, vol. 10 (1971), pp. 107-21.

Gaarder, A. Bruce. 'Bilingual Education: Central Questions and Concerns.' *New York University Quarterly*, vol. 6 (Summer 1975), pp. 2-6.

[Gaarder, A. Bruce, Chairman] 'The Challenge of Bilingualism.' *Reports,* Northeast Conference on the Teaching of Foreign Languages, 1965, pp. 57-101.

Gaarder, A. Bruce. 'The First Seventy-Six Bilingual Education Projects.' In James E. Alatis, ed., *Bilingualism and Language Contact.* (Georgetown University Round Table on Languages and Linguistics, 1970). Washington: Georgetown University Press, 1970, pp. 163-178.

Gaarder, A. Bruce. 'Organization of the Bilingual School.' *Journal of Social Issues,* vol. 23 (1967), pp. 110-20.

Gabet, Yvonne Helen Y. *Birth-Order and Achievement in Anglo, Mexican-American and Black Americans.* Unpublished dissertation, University of Texas at Austin, 1971.

Garbarino, M. S. 'Seminole Girl: The Autobiography of a Young Woman Between Two Worlds.' *Transaction*, vol. 7 (1970), pp. 40-46.

Garcia, A. B., and B. J. Zimmerna. 'The Effect of Examiner Ethnicity and Language on the Performance of Bilingual Mexican-American First Graders.' *Journal of Social Psychology*, vol. 87 (1972), pp. 3-11.

Gardner, R. C. 'Attitudes and Motivation: Their Role in Second Language Acquisition.' *TESOL Quarterly*, vol. 2 (1968), pp. 141-150. [ERIC ED 024 035]

Geffert, Hannah N., *et al. The Current Status of U.S. Bilingual Education Legislation.* Washington: Center for Applied Linguistics, 1975. (Bilingual Education Series, No. 4)

Gerber, Malcolm. *Ethnicity and Measures of Educability: Differences among Rural Navajo, Pueblo, and Rural-Spanish-American First Graders on Measures of Learning Style, Hearing Vocabulary, Entry Skills, Motivation, and Home Environment Processes.* Unpublished dissertation, University of Southern California, 1968.

Gievins, J. W., A. R. Neville, and R. E. Davidson. 'Acquisition of Morphological Rules and Usage as a Function of Social Experience.' *Psychology of the School,* vol. 7 (1970), pp. 217-21.

Gill, Joseph. *A Handbook for Teachers of Sioux Indian Students.* Unpublished dissertation, University of South Dakota, 1971.

Goldman, R., and J. W. Sanders. 'Cultural Factors and Hearing.' *Exceptional Children*, vol. 35 (1969), pp. 489-90.

Gonzales, James Lee. *The Effects of Maternal Stimulation on Early Language Development of Mexican-American Children.* Unpublished dissertation, University of New Mexico, 1972.

González, Gustavo. 'The Acquisition of Questions in Texas Spanish: Age 2 - Age 5.' Arlington, Va.: Center for Applied Linguistics (mimeo.), 1973.

González, Gustavo. *The Acquisition of Spanish Grammar by Native Spanish Speakers.* Unpublished dissertation, University of Texas at Austin, 1970.

González, Gustavo. *The English of Spanish-Speaking Migrant Children: Preliminary Report.* Austin, Texas: SEDL, 1969.

González, Gustavo. *A Linguistic Profile of the Spanish-Speaking First-Grader in Corpus Christi.* M.A. thesis, University of Texas at Austin, 1968.

Gordon, Susan B. *Ethnic and Socioeconomic Influences on the Home Language Ex- of Children.* Albuquerque, N.M.: SWCEL, 1970.

Gordon, Susan. *The Relationship Between the English Language Abilities and Home Language Experiences of First Grade Children, from Three Ethnic Groups, of Varying Degrees of Bilingualism.* Unpublished dissertation, University of New Mexico, 1969.

Graves, Nancy B. *City, Country and Child Rearing: A Tricultural Study of Mother-Child Relationships in Varying Environments.* Unpublished dissertation, University of Colorado, 1971.

Grebler, Lee, J. W. More, and R. C. Guzman, *et al.* *The Mexican-American People.* New York: The Free Press, 1970.

Greenfield, L. 'Situational Measures of Normative Language Views in Relation to Person, Place and Topic among Puerto Ricans.' *Anthropos,* vol. 65 (1970), pp. 602-18.

Gumperz, John J., and Eduardo Hernández-Chavez. 'Bilingualism, Bidialectalis and Classroom Interaction.' In C. B. Cazden, *et al.*, eds., *Functions of Language in the Classroom.* New York: Teachers College Press, 1972, pp. 84-108.

Gumperz, John J., and Dell Hymes eds. *Directions in Sociolinguistics: The Ethnography of Communication.* New York: Holt, Rinehart & Winston, 1972.

Gumperz, John J., and Dell Hymes, eds. 'The Ethnography of Communication.' *American Antrhopologist,* vol. 66 (1964).

Gustafson, R. A. *The Self-concept of Mexican-American Youngsters and Related Environmental Characteristics. 1971* [ERIC ED 053 195]

Gutiérrez, Arturo Luis. 'The Implications of Early Childhood Education.' In *Proceedings of the National Conference on Bilingual Education, April 14-15, 1972.* Austin, Texas: Dissemination Center for Bilingual Bicultural Education. 1972, pp. 282-87.

Harkins, Arthur M., *et al.* *Indian Americans in Omaha and Lincoln.* 1970 [ERIC ED 47 860]

Harris, M. B., and W. C. Hassemer. 'Some Factors Affecting the Complexity of Children's Sentences, the Effects of Modeling, Age, Sex and Bilingualism.' *Journal of Experimental Child Psychology,* vol. 13 (1972), pp. 447-455.

Harvey, Curtis. 'General Descriptions of Bilingual Programs That Meet Students' Needs.' *Proceedings* (National Conference on Bilingual Education, April 14-15, 1972). Austin, Texas: Dissemination Center for Bilingual Bicultural Education, 1972, pp. 252-264.

Has, Peter Yuan. *An Analysis of Certain Learning Difficulties of Chinese Students in New York City.* Unpublished dissertation, New York University, 1955.

Havighurst, Robert J. *The National Study of American Indian Education.* Chicago: University of Chicago Press, 1970.

Hayes, John R., ed. *Cognition and the Development of Language.* New York: John Wiley & Sons, 1970.

Henderson, R. W. *Environmental Stimulation and Intellectual Development of Mexican-American Children.* Unpublished dissertation, University of Arizona, 1966.

Henderson, R. W., and G. C. Merritt. 'Environmental Backgrounds of Mexican-American Children with Different Potentials for School Success.' *Journal of Social Psychology*, vol. 75 (1969), pp. 101-106.

Hepner, E. M. *Self-Concepts, Values, and Needs of Mexican-American Underachievers (or Must the Mexican-American Child Adapt a Self-Concept that Fits the American School?)* 1970 [ERIC ED 048 954]

Hertzig, Margaret E. 'Aspects of Cognitive Style in Young Children of Differing Social and Ethnic Backgrounds.' In J. Hellmuth, ed., *Cognitive Studies II: Deficits in Cognition.* New York: Brunner/Mazel, Inc., 1971.

Hertzig, Margaret E., and Herbert G. Birch. 'Longitudinal Course of Measured Intelligence in Preschool Children of Different Social and Ethnic Backgrounds.' *American Journal of Orthopsychiatry*, vol. 41 (1971), pp. 416-26.

Hertzig, Margaret E., Herbert G. Birch, Alexander Thomas, and O. A. Mendez. *Class and Ethnic Differences in the Responsiveness of Preschool Children to Cognitive Demands.* Monograph of the Society for Research in Child Development, Serial No. 117 (1968).

Hickey, T. 'Bilingualism and the Measurement of Intelligence and Verbal Learning Abilities.' *Exceptional Children*, vol. 39 (1972), pp. 24-28.

Hilger, Sister Inez. *Arapaho Child Life and Its Cultural Background.* Smithsonian Institution, Bureau of American Ethnology, Bulletin 148. Washington: Government Printing Office, 1952.

Hilton, Darla C. *Investigation of Internalization and Phonological Rules in Monolingual and Bilingual Children.* Master's thesis, University of Texas at Austin, 1969.

Hurt, M., Jr., and S. P. Mishra. 'Reliability and Validity of the Metropolitan Achievement Tests for Mexican-American Children.' *Educational and Psychological Measurement*, vol. 30 (1970), pp. 989-92.

Huxley, Renira. 'Development of the Correct Use of Subject Personal Pronouns in Two Children.' In Giovanni B. Flores d'Arcais and William J. M. Lavelt, eds., *Advances in Psycholinguistics.* Amsterdam: North-Holland Publishing Co., 1970.

Hymes, Dell. 'Bilingual Education: Linguistic vs. Sociolinguistic Bases.' In James E. Alatis, ed., *Bilingualism and Language Contact* (Georgetown University Round Table on Language and Linguistics, 1970). Washington: Georgetown University Press, 1970, pp. 69-76.

Hymes, Dell, ed. *Language in Culture and Society: A Reader in Linguistics and Anthropology*. New York: Harper and Row, 1964.

Ianni, Francis A. J., and Edward Storey, eds. *Cultural Relevance, Educational Issues: A Reader in Anthropology and Education.* Boston: Little, Brown, 1971.

Ingram, D. 'Transitivity in Child Language.' *Language*, vol. 47 (1971), pp. 888-910.

Jakobovits, Leon A., and M. S. Miron. *Readings in the Psychology of Language.* Englewood Cliffs: Prentice-Hall, 1967.

Jampolsky, L. 'Advancement in Indian Education.' In *The Education of Indian Children in Canada.* Symposium by members of Indian Affairs Education. Toronto: Ryerson Press, 1965.

Jayagopal, R. *Problem Solving Abilities and Psychomotor Skills of Navajo Indians, Spanish Americans and Anglos in Junior High School.* Unpublished dissertation, University of New Mexico, 1970.

Jensen, Arthur R. 'Learning Abilities in Mexican-American and Anglo-American Children.' *California Journal of Educational Research*, vol. 12 (1961), pp. 147-159.

Jensen, Arthur R., and William D. Rohwer, Jr. *An Experimental Analysis of Learning Abilities in Culturally Disadvantaged Children.* 1970 [ERIC ED 43 690]

John, Vera P., and Vivian M. Horner. *Early Childhood Bilingual Education.* New York: The Modern Language Association of America, 1971.

Johnson, Colleen L. *The Japanese-American Family and Community in Honolulu: Generational Continuities in Ethnic Affiliation.* Unpublished dissertation, Syracuse University, 1972.

Johnson, D. L., and C.A. 'Comparison of Four Intelligence Tests Used with Culturally Disadvantaged Children.' *Psychological Reports*, vol. 28 (1971), pp. 209-210.

Jorstad, D. 'Psycholinguistic Learning Disabilities in Twenty Mexican-American Students.' *Journal of Learning Disabilities*, vol. 4 (1971), pp. 143-149.

Justin, Neal. 'Experiments in Bilingual Education.' *School & Society* (January 1970).

Justin, Neal. 'Mexican-American Achievement Hindered by Culture Conflict.' *Sociology and Social Research*, vol. 56 (1972), pp.271-9.

Kagan, Spencer, and Millard C. Madsen. 'Cooperation and Competition of Mexican-American and Anglo-American Children of Two Ages under Four Instructional Sets.' *Developmental Psychology*, vol. 5 (1971), pp. 32-39.

Kagan, Spencer, and Millard C. Madsen. 'Rivalry in Anglo-American and Mexican Children of Two Ages.' *Journal of Personality and Social Psychology*, vol. 24 (1972), pp. 214-220.

Karabinus, R. A., *et al.* 'Van Alystyne Picture Vocabulary Test Used with Six-Year-Old Mexican-American Children.' *Educational and Psychological Measurement*, vol. 29 (1969), pp. 935-939.

Karadenes, Mark. *A Comparison of Differences in Achievement and Learning Abilities between Anglo and Mexican-American Children when the Two Groups are Equated by Intelligence.* Unpublished dissertation, University of Virginia, 1971.

Karnes, M. B., J. A. Teska, and A. S. Hodgins. 'The Effects of Four Programs of Classroom Intervention on the Intellectual and Language Development of Four-Year-Old Disadvantaged Children.' *American Journal of Orthopsychia*, vol. 40 (1970), pp. 58-76.

Kashinsky, M., and M. Wiener. 'Tone in Communication and the Performance of Children from Two Socioeconomic Groups.' *Child Development*, vol. 40 (1969), pp. 1193-1202.

Kee, Daniel W., and William D. Rohwer, Jr. 'Elaboration and Learning Efficiency in Four Ethnic Groups.' Paper presented at the American Educational Research Association Conference, Chicago, 1972. [ERIC ED 63 084]

Kennedy, Edward, Sen. *Indian Education; Hearings before the Subcommittee on Indian Education of the Committee on Labor and Public Welfare, U.S. Senate.* Washington: U.S. Government Printing Office, 1969.

Kernan, Keith T. 'Semantic Relationships and the Child's Acquisition of Language.' *Anthropological Linguistics*, vol. 12 (1970), pp. 171-87.

Kershner, J. K. 'Ethnic Group Differences in Children's Ability to Reproduce Direction and Orientation.' *Journal of Social Psychology*, vol. 88 (1972), pp. 3-13.

Kessler, Carolyn. *The Acquisition of Syntax in Bilingual Children.* Washington: Georgetown University Press, 1971.

Keston, J. J. and C. A. Jiminez. ' A Study of the Performance on English and Spanish Editions of the Stanford-Binet Intelligence Test by Spanish-American Children.' *Journal of Genetic Psychology*, vol. 85 (1954), pp. 262-269.

Kiefer, W. Christie, *et al. Biculturalism: Psychological Costs and Profits.* 1970 [ERIC ED 47 054]

Killian, J. R. 'WISC, Illinois Test of Psycholinguistic Abilities, and Bender Visual-Motor Gestalt Test Performance on Spanish-American Kindergarten and First Grade School Children.' *Journal of Consulting and Clinical Psychology*, vol. 37 (1971), pp. 38-43.

Kimball, Solon T. 'Cultural Influences Shaping the Role of the Child.' In George D. Spindler, ed., *Education and Culture: Anthropological Approaches.* New York: Holt, Rinehart and Winston, 1963, pp. 268-83.

Kirk, S. A. 'Ethnic Differences in Psycholinguistic Abilities.' *Exceptional Children*, vol. 39 (1972), pp. 112-18.

Kitano, Harry H. L. *Japanese Americans: The Evolution of a Subculture.* Englewood Cliffs, N.J.: Prentice-Hall, 1969.

Kjolseth, Rolf. 'Bilingual Education Programs in the United States: For Assimilation or Pluralism?' in Bernard Spolsky, ed., *The Language Education of Minority Children.* Rowley, Mass.: Newbury House, 1972, pp. 94-121.

Kleinfeld, Judith S. *Cognitive Strengths of Eskimos and Implications for Education.* 1970 [ERIC ED 45 281]

Kleinfeld, Judith S. *Instructional Style and the Intellectual Performance of Indian and Eskimo Students. Final Report.* 1972 [ERIC ED 59 831]

Kleinfeld, Judith S. *Some Instructional Strategies for the Cross-Cultural Classroom.* Juneau: Alaska State Department of Education, 1971. [ERIC ED 059 001]

Kobrick, J. W. 'The Compelling Case for Bilingual Education.' *Saturday Review* (April 29, 1972).

Krear, Serafina. *Development of Pre-Reading Skills in a Second Language or Dialect.* 1971 [ERIC ED 60 754]

Krear, Serafina. 'The Role of the Mother Tongue at Home and at School in the Development of Bilingualism.' *English Language Teaching,* vol. 24 (1969), pp. 2-4.

Kuo, Eddie Chen-Yu. *Bilingual Socialization of Preschool Chinese Children in the Twin-Cities Area.* Unpublished dissertation, University of Minnesota, 1972.

Kuttner, R. E. 'Comparative Performance of Disadvantaged Ethnic and Racial Groups.' *Psychological Reports,* vol. 27 (1970), p. 372.

Kuzma, K. J., and C. Stern. 'Effects of Three Preschool Intervention Programs on the Development of Autonomy in Mexican-American and Negro Children.' *Journal of Special Education,* vol. 6 (1972), pp. 197-205.

Labov, William. 'Finding Out about Children's Language.' Paper presented to the Hawaii Council of Teachers of English, 1970.

Labov, William. 'The Logic of Nonstandard English.' In Alfred Aarons, *et al.*, eds., 'Linguistic-Cultural Differences and American Education.' *Florida FL Reporter,* vol. 7 (special anthology edition), 1969.

Labov, William, and Clarence Robins. 'A Note on the Relation of Reading Failure to Peer-Group Status in Urban Ghettos.' *TC Record,* vol. 70 (February), 1969.

Lamarche, Maurice M. *The Topic-Comment Pattern in the Development of English among Some Chinese Children Living in the United States.* Unpublished dissertation, Georgetown University, 1972.

Lambert, Wallace E., R. R. Gardner, R. Olton, and K. Tunstall. 'A Study of the Role of Attitudes and Motivation in Second-Language Learning.' In Joshua A. Fishman, ed., *Readings in the Sociology of Language.* The Hague: Mouton, 1968, pp. 473-91.

Lambert, Wallace E., J. Havelka, and C. Crosby. 'The Influence of Language Acquisition Contexts on Bilingualism.' *Journal of Abnormal and Social Psychology,* vol. 56 (1958), pp. 239-244.

Lambert, Wallace E., and Chris Rawlings. 'Bilingual Processing of Mixed-Language Associative Networks.' *Journal of Verbal Learning and Verbal Behavior,* vol. 8 (1969), pp. 604-9.

Lambert, Wallace E., and Y. Taguchi. 'Ethnic Cleavage Among Young Children.' *Journal of Abnormal and Social Psychology,* vol. 53 (1956), pp. 380-82.

Lambert, Wallace E., and Richard C. Tucker. *Bilingual Education of Children: The St. Lambert Experiment.* Rowley, Mass.: Newbury House, 1972.

Lampe, P. E. 'The Acculturation of Mexican-Americans in Public and Parochial Schools.' *Sociological Analysis,* vol. 36 (Spring 1975).

Landy, David. *Tropical Childhood. Cultural Transmission and Learning in a Puerto Rican Village.* New York: Harper and Row, 1965.

Lassey, William R., and Gerald Navratil. *The Agricultural Workforce and Rural Development: The Plight of the Migrant Worker.* 1971 [ERIC ED 59 797]

Lastra, Yolanda. 'El Hablar y la Educación de Niños de Origen Mexicano en Los Angeles.' Paper read at Fifth Symposium of the Inter-American Program of Linguistics and Language Teaching, São Paulo, Brazil, January 5-14, 1965.

Lemus-Serrano, Francisco. *Mother-Tongue Acquisition andIts Implications for the Learning of a Second Language.* Unpublished dissertation, Claremont Graduate School, 1972.

Lenneberg, Eric H., ed. *New Directions in the Study of Language.* Cambridge, Mass.: M.I.T. Press, 1964.

Lenneberg, Eric H. *Biological Foundations of Language.* New York: John Wiley and Sons, 1967.

Lenneberg, Eric H. 'The Biological Foundations of Language.' In Mark Lester, ed., *Readings in Applied Transformational Grammar.* New York: Holt, Rinehart and Winston, 1970.

Lenneberg, Eric H. 'The Capacity for Language Acquisition.' In Mark Lester, ed., *Readings in Applied Transformational Grammar.* New York: Holt, Rinehart and Winston, 1970.

Lenneberg, Eric H. 'On Explaining Language.' In Doris V. Gunderson, ed., *Language and Reading.* Washington: Center for Applied Linguistics, 1970.

Lesser, G. S., G. Fifer, and D. H. Clark. *Mental Abilities of Children in Different Social and Cultural Groups.* Monograph of the Society for Research in Child Development, Serial No. 102 (1965).

Levine, H. 'Bilingualism, Its Effect on Emotional and Social Development.' *Journal of Secondary Education,* vol. 44 (1969), pp. 69-73.

Le Vine, R. A. 'Cross-Cultural Study in Child Psychology.' In P. H. Mussen, ed., *Carmichael's Manual of Child Psychology,* vol. 2. New York: Wiley, 1970, pp. 559-614.

Lewis, Gordon K. *Puerto Rico: Freedom and Power in the Caribbean.* New York: Monthly Review Press, 1964.

Linton, Marigold. *Problems of Indian Children.* 1970 [ERIC ED 44 727]

Lombardi, Thomas D. 'Psycholinguistic Abilities of Papago Indian School Children.' *Exceptional Children,* vol. 36 (1970), pp. 485-93.

Long, Barbara H., and Edmund H. Henderson. 'Self-Social Concepts of Disadvantaged School Beginners.' *Journal of Genetic Psychology,* vol. 113 (1968), pp. 41-51.

Mace, Betty Jane. *A Linguistic Profile of Children Entering Seattle Public Schools Kindergartens in September, 1971, and Implications for Their Instruction.* Unpublished dissertation, University of Texas at Austin, 1972.

Mackey, William F. *Bilingual Education in a Binational School: A Study of Equal Language Maintenance Through Free Alternation.* Rowley, Mass.: Newbury House, 1972.

Mackey, William F. *Bilingualism as a World Problem.* Montreal: Harvest House, 1967.

Macnamara, John. 'The Cognitive Strategies of Language Learning.' In *Conference on Child Language, Preprints of Papers Presented at Conference, Chicago, Illinois, November 22-24.* Quebec: Laval University, International Center on Bilingualism, 1971, pp. 471-84.

Macnamara, John. 'The Effects of the Instructions in a Weaker Language.' *Journal of Social Issues,* vol. 23 (1967).

Madsen, Millard C. *Developmental and Cross-Cultural Differences in the Cooperative and Competitive Behavior of Young Children.* 1970. [ERIC ED 62 040]

Madsen, Millard C., and A. Shapira. 'Cooperative and Competitive Behavior of Urban Afro-American, Anglo-American, Mexican-American and Mexican Village Children.' *Developmental Psychology,* vol. 3 (1970), pp. 16-20.

Madsen, William. *Mexican-Americans of South Texas.* New York: Holt, Rinehart and Winston, 1964.

Maldonado Denis, Manual. *Puerto Rico: A Socio-Historic Interpretation.* New York: Random House, 1972.

Malkoc, Anna M., and A. H. Roberts. 'Bilingual Education: A Special Report from CAL-ERIC.' *Elementary English* (May 1970), pp. 713-725.

Manning, John C., and Frederick Brengelman. *Teaching English as a Second Language to Kindergarten Pupils Whose Native Language is Spanish.* Fresno, California: Fresno State College, 1965.

Manuel, Herschel T. 'Recruiting and Training Teachers for Spanish-Speaking Children in the South West.' *School and Society,* vol. 96 (March 30, 1968).

Margolis, Richard J. *The Losers: A Report on Puerto Ricans and the Public Schools.* New York: Aspira, 1968.

Marjoribanks, K. 'Ethnic and Environmental Influences on Mental Abilities.' *American Journal of Sociology,* vol. 78 (1972), pp. 323-37.

Martinez-Bernal, J. A. *Children's Acquisition of Spanish and English Morphology Systems and Noun Phrases.* Unpublished dissertation, Georgetown University, 1972.

Mazeika, E. J. *A Descriptive Analysis of the Language of a Bilingual Child.* Unpublished dissertation, University of Rochester, 1971.

McCarthy, Jacqueline. *A Study of the Leisure Activities of Taos Pueblo Indian Children.* Unpublished dissertation, North Texas State University, 1970.

McCauley, Margaret A. *A Study of Social Class and Assimilation in Relation to Puerto Rican Family Patterns.* Unpublished dissertation, Fordham University, 1972.

McConnell, F. 'Language Development and Cultural Disadvantagement.' *Exceptional Children,* vol. 35 (1969), pp. 597-606.

McNeill, David. *The Acquisition of Language: The Study of Developmental Psycholinguistics.* New York: Harper and Row, 1970.

McNeill, David. *The Development of Language.* 1967 [ERIC ED 017 921]

Melaragno, R. J., and G. Newark. 'A Pilot Study to Supply Evaluation-Revision Procedures in First-Grade Mexican-American Classrooms.' Technical Memorandum TM 3950/000/00. Santa Monica, California: Systems Development Corporation, May 17, 1968.

Mencher, Joan. *Child Rearing and Family Organization among Puerto Ricans in Eastville: El Barrio de Nueva York.* Unpublished dissertation, Columbia University, 1958.

Menyuk, Paula. 'Alternation of Rules in Children's Grammar.' *Journal of Verbal Learning and Verbal Behavior,* vol. 3 (1964), pp. 480-488.

Menyuk, Paula. *Sentences Children Use.* Cambridge, Mass.: M.I.T. Press, 1969.

Menyuk, Paula. 'Syntactic Rules Used by Children from Preschool Through First Grade.' *Child Development,* vol. 35 (1964), pp. 533-546.

Mexican-American Cultural Differences: A Brief Survey to Enhance Teacher-Pupil Understanding. 1969 [ERIC ED 41 665]

Mickelson, N. I., and C. G. Galloway. 'Cumulative Language Deficit among Indian Children.' *Exceptional Children,* vol. 36 (1969), pp. 187-90.

Mickey, Barbara H. *A Bibliography of Studies Concerning the Spanish-Speaking Population of the American Southwest.* 1969. [ERIC ED 42 548]

Middleton, John, ed. *From Child to Adult: Studies in the Anthropology of Education.* Garden City, New York: The Natural History Press, 1970.

Miller, Louise B., and Jean L. Dyer. *Four Preschool Programs: Their Dimensions and Effects.* 1972. [ERIC ED 69 411]

Miller, Max D. *Patterns of Relationships of Fluid and Crystallized Mental Abilities to Achievement in Different Ethnic Groups.* Unpublished dissertation, University of Houston, 1972.

Miller, M. R. 'The Language and Language Beliefs of Indian Children.' *Anthropological Linguistics,* vol. 12 (1970), pp. 51-61.

Mishra, S. P., and M. Hurt, Jr. 'Use of Metropolitan Readiness Tests with Mexican-American Children.' *California Journal of Educational Research,* vol. 21 (1970), pp. 182-187.

Moore, Joan W. *Mexican Americans.* Englewood Cliffs, N.J.: Prentice-Hall, 1970.

[Morrison, J. Cayce, director] *The Puerto Rican Study, 1953-1957.* New York: Board of Education, 1958. Reissued with an introductory essay by F. Cordasco (New York: Oriole Editions, 1972).

Mycue, E. *Testing in Spanish and the Subsequent Measurement of English Fluency.* Texas: Texas Women's University, 1968. [ERIC ED 026 193]

Nagy, Lois B. *Effectiveness of Speech and Language Therapy as an Integral Part of the Educational Program for Bilingual Children.* Unpublished dissertation, International University, 1972.

Natalicio, Diana. *Formation of the Plural in English: A Study of Native Speakers of English and Native Speakers of Spanish.* Unpublished dissertation, University of Texas at Austin, 1969.

Natalicio, Diana S., and Frederick Williams. *Repetition as an Oral Language Assessment Technique.* Austin: Center for Communication Research, University of Texas at Austin, 1971.

Nava, Julian. 'Cultural Barriers and Factors that Affect Learning by Spanish-Speaking Children.' In John H. Burma, ed., *Mexican-Americans in the United States.* Cambridge, Mass.: Shenkman, 1970, pp. 125-34.

Naylor, Gordon Hardy. *Learning Styles at Six Years in Two Ethnic Groups in a Disadvantaged Area.* Unpublished dissertation, University of Southern California, 1971.

Nichols, C. A. *Moral Education among the North American Indians.* New York: Bureau of Publications, Teachers College, Columbia University, 1930.

Nuñez, Louis. *Puerto Ricans and Education.* New York: Board of Education of the City of New York. Puerto Rican Heritage Lecture Series for Bilingual Professionals, May 17, 1971.

O'Donnell, R. C., Wm. Griffin, and R. C. Norris. *Syntax of Kindergarten and Elementary School Children: A Transformational Analysis.* Champaign, Illinois: NCTE, 1967.

Ohannessian, Sirarpi. *The Study of the Problems of Teaching English to American Indians.* Washington: Center for Applied Linguistics, 1967.

Olim, E. G. 'Maternal Language Styles and Cognitive Behavior.' *Journal of Special Education*, vol. 4 (1970), pp. 53-68.

Osborn, L. R. 'Rhetoric, Repetition, Silence: Traditional Requisites of Indian Communication.' *Journal of American Indian Education*, vol. 12 (1973), pp. 15-21.

Ott, Elizabeth H. *A Study of Levels of Fluency and Proficiency in Oral English of Spanish-Speaking School Beginners.* Unpublished dissertation, University of Texas at Austin, 1967.

Owen, George M., *et al. Nutrition Survey of White Mountain Apache Preschool Children.* 1970 [ERIC ED 46 508]

Padilla, Elena. *Up From Puerto Rico.* New York: Columbia University Press, 1958.

Paquita, Vivó, ed. *The Puerto Ricans: An Annotated Bibliography.* New York: R. R. Bowker, 1973.

Parisi, Domenico. 'Development of Syntactic Comprehension in Preschool Children as a Function of Socioeconomic Level.' *Developmental Psychology*, vol. 5 (1971), pp. 186-89.

Parisi, Domenico. 'Differences of Socio-Cultural Origin in the Linguistic Production of Pre-School Subjects.' *Rassegna Italiana di Linguista Applicata*, vol. 2 (1970), pp. 95-101.

Parisi, Domenico, and Francesco Antinucci. 'Lexical Competence.' In d'Arcais and Levelt, eds., *Advances in Psycholinguistics.* Amsterdam: North-Holland Pub. Co., 1970, pp. 197-210.

Parker, Ronald K., *et al. An Overview of Cognitive and Language Programs for 3, 4, and 5 Year Old Children.* 1970. [ERIC ED 70 534]

Paulston, Christina B. *Implications of Language Learning Theory for Language Planning: Concerns in Bilingual Education.* Washington: Center for Applied Linguistics, 1974. (Bilingual Education Series, No. 1)

Peak, E., and Wallace Lambert. 'The Relation of Bilingualism to Intelligence.' *Psychological Monographs: General and Applied,* vol. 126 (1962), pp. 1-23.

Pedreira, Antonio S. *Bibliografía Puertorriqueña, 1493-1930.* Madrid: Imprenta de Hernando, 1932; reissued with a foreword by F. Cordasco, New York: Burt Franklin, 1974.

Pelletier, Wilfred. 'Childhood in an Indian Village.' *Northian,* vol. 7 (1970), pp. 20-23.

Peñalosa, Fernando. 'The Changing Mexican-American in Southern California.' *Sociological and Social Research,* vol. 51 (1967), pp. 405-417.

Peñalosa, Fernando. *Chicano Multilingualism and Multiglossia.* [ERIC ED 56 590]

Penfield, Wilder. 'Conditioning the Uncommitted Cortex for Language Learning.' *Brain,* vol. 88 (1965), pp. 787-98.

Pettit, George A. *Primitive Education in North America.* University of California, Publications in American Archaeology and Ethnology 43, 1946.

Philips, Susan U. 'Acquisition of Rules for Appropriate Speech Usage.' In James E. Alatis, ed., *Bilingualism and Language Contact* (Georgetown University Round Table on Languages and Linguistics, 1970). Washington: Georgetown University Press, 1970, pp. 77-101.

Philips, Susan U. 'Participant Structures and Communicative Competence: Warm Springs Children in Community and Classroom.' In C. B. Cazden, *et al.*, eds., *Functions of Language in the Classroom.* New York: Teachers College Press, 1972, pp. 370-94.

Piaget, Jean. *The Language and Thought of the Child.* Cleveland: The World Publishing Co., 1955.

Pialorsi, Frank, ed. *Teaching the Bilingual: New Methods and Old Traditions.* Tucson University of Arizona Press, 1974.

Pineiro, Carlos Juan. 'Estudios Puertorriqueños II.' *Quimbamba,* June 1973 (Bilingual Education Quarterly).

Platoff, Joan C. *The Effect of Education and Race on the Language and Attitude Verbally Expressed by Mothers of Pre-School Children.* Unpublished dissertation, New York University.

Poulsen, M. K. *Automatic Patterning of Grammatical Structures and Auditory and Visual Stimuli as Related to Reading in Disadvantaged Mexican-American Children.* Unpublished dissertation, University of Southern California, 1971.

Proceedings. First Annual International Multilingual Multicultural Conference. San Diego, April 1-5, 1973. Austin, Texas: Dissemination Center for Bilingual Bicultural Education, 1973.

Proceedings. National Conference on Bilingual Education. April 14-15, 1972. Austin, Texas: Dissemination Center for Bilingual Bicultural Education, 1972.

Proshansky, Harold M. 'The Development of Intergroup Attitudes.' In L. and M. Hoffman, eds., *Review of Child Development Research,* Vol. 2. New York: Russell Sage Foundation, 1966, pp. 311-71.

Puidollars, Carmen. 'Nuestra Lengua Vernácula: Base para un Currículo al Enseñar Niños Puertorriqueños.' *Quimbamba,* June 1973. (Bilingual Education Quarterly)

Purdy, J. D. *Associative Learning Rates of Second, Fourth and Sixth Grade Indian and White Children Using a Paired-Associate Learning Task.* Unpublished dissertation, University of Oklahoma, 1968.

Quijano, Teresa. *A Cross-Cultural Study of Six Differences among First-Graders on a Verbal Test.* M.A. thesis, Texas Women's University, 1968. [ERIC ED 026 191]

Raffler Engel, W. von. 'Suprasentential and Substitution Tests in First Language Acquisition.' *Bollettino di Psicologia Applicata (1968).*

Raffler Engel, W. von. 'Videotape in Dialectology.' Paper presented to the International Conference on Methods in Dialectology, Charlottetown, P.E.I., July, 1972.

Ramírez de Arellano, Diana. *El Español: La Lengua de Puerto Rico--Aprecio y Defensa de Nuestra Lengua Materna en la Ciudad de Nueva York.* Puerto Rican Heritage Series for Bilingual Professionals. New York: Board of Education, 1971.

Rapier, J. L. 'Effects of Verbal Mediation upon the Learning of Mexican-American Children.' *California Journal of Educational Research,* vol. 18 (1967), pp. 40-48.

Reboussin, R., and J. W. Goldstein. 'Achievement Motivation in Navajo and White Students.' *American Anthropologist,* vol. 68 (1966), pp. 740-44.

Reinstein, Steven, and Judy Hoffman. 'Dialect Interaction Between Black and Puerto Rican Children in New York City: Implications for the Language Arts.' *Elementary English,* vol. 49 (1972), pp. 190-96.

Rivera, Carmen E. 'Administration, Supervision, and Implementation of a Bilingual Bicultural Curriculum.' *Proceedings* (National Conference on Bilingual Education, April 14-15, 1972). Austin, Texas: Dissemination Center for Bilingual Bicultural Education, 1972, pp. 105-120.

Robbins, Lynn. 'Economics, Household Composition and the Family Cycle: The Blackfeet Case.' In June Helm, ed., *Spanish-Speaking People in the United States.* Proceedings of the 1968 American Ethnological Society Meeting, 1968, pp. 196-215.

Rodríguez, Armando. 'The Mexican-American Disadvantaged? Ya Basta!' In Alfred Aarons, *et al.,* eds., 'Linguistic-Cultural Differences and American Education.' *Florida FL Reporter,* vol. 7 (1969) (special anthology issue).

Rohner, Ronald P. 'Factors Influencing the Academic Performance of Kwakiutl Children in Canada.' *Comparative Educational Review*, vol. 9 (1965), pp. 331-40.

Rosen, Carl L., and Phillip D. Ortego. 'Resources: Teaching Spanish-Speaking Childre *The Reading Teacher*, vol. 25 (1971), pp. 11-13.

Rosenblatt, J. *Cognitive Impulsivity in Mexican-American and Anglo-American Children.* Unpublished dissertation, University of Arizona, 1968.

Rosenthal, Alan G. *Pre-School Experience and Adjustment of Puerto Rican Children.* Unpublished dissertation, New York University, 1955.

Samuels, S. Jay. 'Psychological and Educational Considerations in Early Language Learning.' In F. Andre Paquette, ed., *New Dimensions in the Teaching of FLES.* New York: American Council on the Teaching of Foreign Languages, 1969.

Sanches, Mary. *Features in the Acquisition of Japanese Grammar.* Unpublished dissertation, Stanford University, 1968.

Sanches, Mary, and Ben Blount, eds. *Sociocultural Dimensions of Language Use.* New York: Academic Press, 1975.

Sandler, L., *et al.* 'Developmental Test Performance of Disadvantaged Children.' *Exceptional Children*, vol. 39 (1972), pp. 201-8.

Sapir, Edward. 'Language and Thinking.' In Charlton Laird and Robert M. Gorrell, eds., *Reading about Language.* New York: Harcourt Brace Jovanovich, 1971.

Sapir, Edward, and Morris Swadesh. 'American Indian Grammatical Categories.' *Word*, vol. 2 (1946), pp. 103-112.

Sasser, C. *Motor Development of the Kindergarten Spanish-Speaking Disadvantaged Child.* M. A. thesis, Texas Women's University, 1970. [ERIC ED 167 186]

Saville, Muriel R. 'Interference Phenomena in Language Teaching: Their Nature, Extent, and Significance in the Acquisition of Standard English.' *Elementary English*, March, 1971, pp. 396-405.

Saville, Muriel R. 'Linguistic and Attitudinal Correlates in Indian Education.' Paper presented at the American Educational Research Association Convention, Chicago 1972.

Saville-Troike, Muriel. 'Basing Practice on What We Know About Children's Language. In *Classroom Practices in ESL and Bilingual Education*, Vol. 1. Washington: Teachers of English to Speakers of Other Languages, 1973.

Saville-Troike, Muriel. *Bilingual Children: A Resource Document.* Washington: Center for Applied Linguistics, 1973. (Bilingual Education Series, No. 2)

Saville, Muriel R., and Rudolph C. Troike. *A Handbook of Bilingual Education.* Washington: Center for Applied Linguistics, 1971.

Say, Margaret Z., and William J. Meyer. *Effects of Early Day Care Experience on Subsequent Observed Program Behaviors.* 1970. [ERIC ED 68 149]

Schmidt, L., and J. Gallessich. 'Adjustment of Anglo-American and Mexican-America Pupils in Self-Contained and Team-Teaching Classrooms.' *Journal of Educational Psychology*, vol. 62 (1971), pp. 328-332.

Selected Characteristics of Persons and Families of Mexican, Puerto Rican, and Other Spanish Origin. 1972. [ERIC ED 70 546]

Serrano, Rodolfa G. 'The Language of the Four Year Old Chicano.' Paper presented at the Rocky Mountain Educational Research Association meeting, Boulder, Col., 1971. [ERIC ED 071 791]

Shaw, Jean W., and Maxine Schoggen. *Children Learning: Samples of Everyday Life of Children at Home.* 1969. [ERIC ED 33 763]

Sherk, John K. *A Word-Count of Spoken English of Culturally Disadvantaged Preschool and Elementary Pupils.* Kansas City: University of Missouri, 1973.

Shriner, T. H., and L. Miner. 'Morphological Structures in the Language of Disadvantaged and Advantaged Children.' *Journal of Speech and Hearing Research,* vol. 11 (1968), pp. 605-10.

Shuy, Roger W., and Ralph W. Fasold, eds. *Language Attitudes: Current Trends and Prospects.* Washington: Georgetown University Press, 1973. [Georgetown University School of Languages and Linguistics]

Siegel, Irving E., *et al. Psycho-Educational Intervention Beginning at Age Two: Reflections and Outcomes.* 1972. [ERIC ED 68 161]

Silberstein, R. *Risk-Taking Behavior in Pre-School Children from Three Ethnic Backgrounds.* UCLA: Center for Head Start Evaluation and Research, 1969. [ERIC ED 042 486]

Silen, Juan A. *We, the Puerto Rican People.* New York: Monthly Review Press, 1971.

Simirenko, A. *Socio-Economic Variables in the Acculturation Process: A Pilot Study of Two Washo Indian Communities.* Final Report. Reno: University of Nevada, 1966.

Siu, Ping Kee. *The Relationship Between Motivational Patterns and Academic Achievement in Minority Group Children.* Final Report. 1972. [ERIC ED 63 443]

Skoczylas, Rudolph V. *An Evaluation of Some Cognitive and Affective Aspects of a Spanish-English Bilingual Education Program.* Dissertation, University of New Mexico, 1972 [ERIC ED 066 990]

Skrabanek, R. L. 'Language Maintenance among Mexican-Americans.' *International Journal of Comparative Sociology,* vol. 11 (1970), pp. 272-82.

Slears, Brian. *Aptitude, Content and Method of Teaching Word Recognition with Young American Indian Children.* Unpublished dissertation, University of Minnesota, 1970.

Slobin, Dan I. 'Children and Language: They Learn the Same Way All Around the World.' *Psychology Today,* vol. 6 (1972), pp. 74-77 and 82.

Slobin, Dan I. 'Imitation and Grammatical Development in Children.' In N. S. Endler, L. R. Boulter, and H. Osser, eds., *Contemporary Issues in Developmental Psychology.* New York: Holt, Rinehart and Winston, 1967, pp. 437-43.

Smith, Frank, and G. A. Miller. *The Genesis of Language: A Psycholinguistic Approach.* Cambridge, Mass.: M.I.T. Press, 1966.

Smothergill, N. L., F. Olson, and S. G. Moore. 'The Effects of Manipulation of Teacher Communication Style in the Preschool.' *Child Development*, vol. 42 (1971), pp. 1229-39.

Soares, Anthony T., and Louise M. 'Self-Perceptions of Culturally Disadvantaged Children.' *American Educational Research Journal*, vol. 6 (1969), pp. 31-45.

Southern, Mara, and Walter T. Plant. 'Differential Cognitive Development within and between Racial and Ethnic Groups of Disadvantaged Preschool and Kindergarten Children.' *Journal of Genetic Psychology*, vol. 119 (1971), pp. 259-66.

Southwest Council for Bilingual Education. *Bilingual Education in Three Cultures.* Annual Conference Report. Las Cruces, N.M., 1968. [ERIC ED 027 515]

Southwest Council of Foreign Language Teachers. *Our Bilinguals—Social and Psychological Barriers, Linguistic and Pedagogical Barriers.* El Paso, 1965. [ERIC ED 019 899]

Spence, A. G., S. P. Mishra, and S. Ghozeil. 'Home Language and Performance in Standardized Tests.' *Elementary School Journal*, March 1971, pp. 309-413.

Spector, S. *Patterns of Difficulty in English in Bilingual Mexican-American Children.* 1972. [ERIC ED 066 083]

Spellman, C. M. *The Shift from Color to Form Preference in Young Children of Different Ethnic Background.* Unpublished dissertation, University of Texas at Austin, 1968.

Spolsky, Bernard, ed. *The Language Education of Minority Children: Selected Readings.* Rowley, Mass.: Newbury House, 1973.

Staples, R. 'Mexican-American Family: Its Modification over Time and Space.' *Phylon*, vol. 32 (1971), pp. 179-92.

Stedman, James M., and Russell L. Adams. 'Achievement as a Function of Language Competence, Behavior Adjustment and Sex in Young, Disadvantaged Mexican-American Children.' *Journal of Educational Psychology*, vol. 63 (1972), pp. 411-417.

Stedman, James M., and Richard E. McKenzie. 'Family Factors Related to Competence in Young Disadvantaged Mexican-American Children.' *Child Development*, vol. 42 (1971), pp. 1602-07.

Stern, Carolyn, and Diane Ruble. *Teaching New Concepts to Non-English Speaking Preschool Children.* UCLA, 1970. [ERIC ED 054 903]

Steward, Margaret S. *The Observation of Parents as Teachers of Preschool Children as a Function of Social Class, Ethnicity, and Cultural Distance between Parent and Child.* 1971. [ERIC ED 57 925]

Steward, Margaret and David. 'The Observation of Anglo-, Mexican-, and Chinese-American Mothers Teaching Their Young Sons.' *Child Development*, vol. 44 (1973), pp. 329-37.

Stodolsky, Susan S., and Gerald Lesser. 'Learning Patterns in the Disadvantaged.' *Harvard Educational Review*, vol. 37 (1967), pp. 546-93.

Sugarman, Susan. *A Description of Communicative Development in the Pre-Language Child.* Unpublished honors thesis, Hampshire College, 1973.

Suter, Larry E. *Selected Characteristics of Persona and Families of Mexican, Puerto Rican, and Other Spanish Origin: March 1971. Population Characteristics: Current Population Reports.* [ERIC ED 65 224]

Swain, Merrill. 'Bilingualism, Monolingualism, and Code Acquisition.' In *Conference on Child Language Preprints of Chicago Conference,* 1971. [ERIC ED 060 748]

Swanson, E., and R. DeBlassie. 'Interpreter Effects on the WISC Performance of First Grade Mexican-American Children.' *Measurement and Evaluation in Guidance,* vol. 4 (1971), pp. 172-175.

Swinney, J.S. *The Development of Education Among the Choctaw Indians.* M. A. thesis, Oklahoma A&M College, 1935.

Tagatz, G. E., *et al.* 'Effects of Ethnic Background, Response Option, Task Complexity and Sex on Information Processing in Concept Attainment.' *Journal of Experimental Education,* vol. 39 (1971), pp. 69-72.

Taylor, M. E. *Investigation of Parent Factors Affecting Achievement of Mexican-American Children.* Unpublished dissertation, University of Southern California, 1969.

Tharp, R., and A. Meadow. 'Changes in Marriage Roles Accompanying the Acculturation of the Mexican-American Wife.' *Journal of Marriage and the Family,* vol. 30 (1968), pp. 404-412.

Thomas, Elizabeth. *The Conceptualization Process in Advantaged and Disadvantaged Kindergarten Children.* Unpublished dissertation, University of Illinois.

Thomas, R. M. *Social Differences in the Classroom: Social-Class, Ethnic and Religious Problems.* New York: David McKay, 1965.

Thonis, Eleanor. *The Dual Language Process in Young Children.* 1971. [ERIC ED 061 812]

Topper, Martin D. *The Daily Life of a Traditional Navajo Household: An Ethnographic Study in Human Daily Activities.* Unpublished dissertation, Northwestern University, 1972.

Tremaine, Ruth V. *Syntax and Piagetian Operational Thought.* Washington: Georgetown University Press, 1975. [Georgetown University School of Language and Linguistics]

Tucker, C. A. 'The Chinese Immigrant's Language Handicap: Its Extent and Its Effects.' *Florida FL Reporter,* vol. 7 (1969).

Turner, Paul R., ed. *Bilingualism in the Southwest.* Tucson: University of Arizona Press, 1973.

Ulibarri, Horacio. *Interpretive Studies on Bilingual Education.* Washington: U.S. Office of Education, 1969.

United States. Cabinet Committee on Opportunity for the Spanish Speaking. *The Spanish Speaking in the United States: A Guide to Materials.* With a Foreword by F. Cordasco. Detroit: Blaine Ethridge, 1975. (Originally, G.P.O., 1971)

United States Bureau of the Census. *American Indians: 1970 Census of Population.* Washington: U.S. Department of Commerce, 1973.

United States Bureau of the Census. *U.S. Census of Population and Housing: Puerto Rican Population Survey Areas, Employment Profiles of Selected Low Income Areas.* Final Report PHC (3). Washington: U.S. Government Printing Office, 1972.

United States Commission on Civil Rights. *Report 1: Ethnic Isolation of Mexican Americans in the Public Schools of the Southwest.* Washington: U.S. Government Printing Office, 1971.

United States Commission on Civil Rights. *Report 2: The Unfinished Education.* Washington: U.S. Government Printing Office, 1971.

United States Commission on Civil Rights. *Report 3: The Excluded Student: Educational Practices Affecting Mexican Americans in the Southwest.* Washington: U.S. Government Printing Office, 1972.

United States Commission on Civil Rights. *Report 4: Mexican American Education in Texas: A Function of Wealth.* Washington: U.S. Government Printing Office, 1972.

United States Commission on Civil Rights. *Report 5: Teachers and Students: Differences in Teacher Interaction with Mexican American and Anglo Students.* Washington: U.S. Government Printing Office, 1972.

Valencia, Atilano A. *The Effects of Bilingual/Bicultural Education among Spanish-Speaking, English-Speaking and Sioux-Speaking Kindergarten Children.* A report of statistical findings and recommendations for Educational Unit No. 18. Scottsbluff, Nebraska. Albuquerque, N.M.: SWCEL, 1970.

Van Duyne, H. J., and G. Gutierrez. 'The Regulatory Function of Language in Bilin-Children.' *Journal of Educational Research,* vol. 66 (1972), pp. 122-4.

Vane, J. R., and W. M. Davis. 'Factors Related to the Effectiveness of Preschool Programs with Disadvantaged Children.' *Journal of Educational Research,* vol. 64 (1971), pp. 297-99.

Varo, Carlos. *Consideraciones Antropológicas y Politicas en Torno a la Enseñanza del 'Spanglish' en Nueva York.* Rio Piedras: Ediciones Librería Internacional, 1971.

Vásquez, Hector I. 'Puerto Rican Americans.' *National Elementary Principal,* vol. 50 (1970).

Voyat, Gilbert, and Stephen Silk. *Cross-Cultural Study of Cognitive Development on the Pine Ridge Indian Reservation.* The Pine Ridge Research Bulletin No. 11, 1970. [ERIC ED 070 541]

Wagenheim, Kal, with Olga Wagenheim. *The Puerto Ricans: A Documentary History.* New York: Praeger, 1973. See also the author's *Puerto Rico: A Profile* (Praeger, 1970), and *A Survey of Puerto Ricans on the U.S. Mainland in the 1970s* (Praeger, 1975).

Walker, Willard. 'An Experiment in Programmed Cross-Cultural Education: The Import of the Cherokee Primer for the Cherokee Community and for the Behavioral Sciences.' Unpublished manuscript, background paper for 1967 CAL Survey, 1965.

Wampler, H. *A Case Study of 12 Spanish-Speaking Primary Children Concerning School Achievement and Socialization.* Unpublished dissertation, Pennsylvania State University, 1972.

Wasserman, S. A. 'Values of Mexican-American, Negro, and Anglo Blue-Collar and White-Collar Children.' *Child Development,* vol. 42 (1971), pp. 1624-28.

Wax, Murray L., Stanley Diamond, and Fred O. Georing, eds. *Anthropological Perspectives on Education.* New York: Basic Books, 1971.

Wax, Murray L., Rosalie Wax, and R. V. Dumont, Jr. *Formal Education in an American Indian Community.* Supplement to *Social Problems* 11, No. 4, Society for the Study of Social Problems, Monograph No. 1, 1964.

Wax, Murray L., *et al. Indian Education in Eastern Oklahoma: A Report of Fieldwork among the Cherokee.* Final Report. 1969. [ERIC ED 029 741]

Wight, B. W., M. F. Sloniger, and J. P. Keeve. 'Cultural Deprivation: Operational Definition in Terms of Language Development.' *American Journal of Orthopsychiatry,* vol. 40 (1970), pp. 77-86.

Wilkinson, Andrew. *The Foundations of Language: Talking and Reading in Young Children.* New York: Oxford University Press, 1971.

Williams, Frederick, ed. *Language and Poverty: Perspectives on a Theme.* Chicago: Markham, 1970.

Williams, Frederick. *Psychological Correlates of Speech Characteristics: On Sounding 'Disadvantaged.'* Madison, Wis.: The University of Wisconsin, 1969.

Williams, George M. *Puerto Rican English: A Discussion of Eight Major Works Relevant to its Linguistic Description.* New York: Columbia University. [ERIC ED 051 709]

Witkin, H. A. 'A Cognitive-Style Approach to Cross-Cultural Research.' *International Journal of Psychology,* vol. 2 (1967), pp. 233-50.

Wolcott, Harry F. *A Kwakiutl Village and its School.* New York: Holt, Rinehart and Winston, 1967.

Worrall, Anita Denise. *Bilingualism and Cognitive Development.* Unpublished dissertation, University of Washington, 1970.

Young, Rodney W. 'Development of Semantic Categories in Spanish-English and Navajo-English Bilingual Children.' In *Conference on Child Language,* preprints of papers presented at Chicago conference, November, 1971, pp. 193-208. [ERIC ED 060 749]

Zamora, Gloria. 'Staff Development for Bilingual/Bicultural Programs—A Philosophical Base.' *Proceedings* (National Conference on Bilingual Education, April 14-15, 1972). Austin, Texas: Dissemination Center for Bilingual Bicultural Education, 1972, pp. 299-303.

FOREWORD

A major, virtually untapped national resource, bilingualism, is the subject of this monograph, *Bilingual Schooling in the United States*. This study is designed to reveal the promise of bilingual education and to serve as a guideline for those planning bilingual programs. The project was undertaken by the Southwest Educational Development Laboratory as a special task for the U. S. Office of Education under an amendment to its 1968 Title IV contract.

As specified in the contract Scope of Work, the monograph includes a history of bilingual schooling, both in the United States and in other parts of the world; alternative concepts of bilingual schooling; sample curriculum models; implications for education and society; and an outline of needs, as related to action and research.

Theodore Andersson and Mildred Boyer, authors of the monograph, made three extensive field trips to visit sites where bilingual programs are in progress. The first led through the Northwest as far north as Barrow, Alaska; the second was a tour of the Southwest and Hawaii; the third trip was from Dade County, Florida, north through Washington, New York, New England, and into Canada. In addition, almost all the bilingual programs in Texas were visited to obtain background material and knowledge of ongoing programs. Staff members of the Laboratory, Dr. Andersson and Dr. Boyer are on leave from the University of Texas at Austin. Dr. Andersson is the former Chairman of the Department of Romance Languages. Both he and Dr. Boyer are Professors of Spanish and Education.

The Laboratory accepted responsibility for conducting the study resulting in this report in accordance with policies of the Laboratory's Board of Directors governing acceptance of outside contracts and grants. These policies include criteria for judging relevance to the Laboratory's problem focus, program emphasis, and the degree to which the activity would extend and significantly enhance the accomplishment of the Laboratory's development objectives under its primary source of funding, Title IV, ESEA.

Bilingual Education is one of the basic learning systems now under development by the Laboratory. Instructional materials in both English and Spanish – including Oral Language (Science), Oral Language (Social Studies), Reading and Composition – have been designed and are being pilot tested with Mexican American children in Texas. The English portions of the materials are also being pilot tested with Puerto Rican children in New York City and with French-speaking children in Louisiana.

The ultimate product of the Laboratory's Bilingual Education Learning System is people – persons who are equally literate in two languages, who understand their own culture and other cultures, and who have career and life-style options open to them.

Edwin Hindsman
Executive Director

PREFACE

The many voices of America, the many languages, compose a symphony of beauty and strength in which all Americans may take pride. Mutual understanding of different languages and cultures is important in a nation which respects diversity and individuality while it works toward unity.

The Bilingual Education Act, introduced in the United States Senate in January, 1967, became Title VII of the Elementary and Secondary Education Act Amendments of 1967. It is intended to conserve our language resources and to advance the learning of the child, irrespective of language. It seeks to make *learning* the objective of the classroom, using other languages in addition to English to accomplish this objective.

The three million American school children from non-English speaking homes are entitled to full participation in our society, and bilingual education opens the door to that participation.

This study was conducted by the Southwest Educational Development Laboratory with support from the U.S. Office of Education to give guidance and direction to those interested in developing programs that may be eligible for support through the Bilingual Education Act, Title VII of the Elementary and Secondary Education Act.

This Act, passed by the Congress on January 2, 1968, had the bipartisan sponsorship in the U.S. Senate of the following:

Ralph Yarborough, Dem., Texas, sponsor; and Jacob Javits, Rep., New York; Robert Kennedy, Dem., New York; Thomas A. Kuchel, Rep., California; Joseph M. Montoya, Dem., New Mexico; John Tower, Rep., Texas; Harrison A. Williams, Jr., Dem., New Jersey; and George Murphy, Rep., California, co-sponsors.

Bilingual education legislation (H. R. 9840) was introduced in the U.S. House of Representatives by James Scheuer, New York, on May 10, 1967. This proposal became H.R. 13103 on September 25, 1967, and a modification of it was passed as an amendment to the Elementary and Secondary Education Act, and provided assistance in bilingual education.

Members of the H. R. 13103 Committee included:

Congressmen Carl D. Perkins, Dem., Kentucky; John Brademas, Dem., Indiana; Hugh L. Carey, Dem., New York; Lloyd Meeds, Dem., Washington; Gus Hawkins, Dem., California; Sam Gibbons, Dem., Florida; William D. Hathaway, Dem., Maine; and Congresswoman Mrs. Patsy T. Mink, Dem., Hawaii.

Also, Congressmen Alphonzo Bell, Rep., California; Frank Thompson, Dem., New Jersey; John H. Dent, Dem., Pennsylvania; Dominick V. Daniels, Dem., New Jersey; Phillip Burton, Dem., California; Jacob H. Gilbert, Dem., New York; Edward R. Roybal, Dem., California; Claude Pepper, Dem., Florida; Hastings Keith, Rep., Massachusetts.

Also, Bob Eckhardt, Dem., Texas; Spark M. Matsunaga, Dem., Hawaii; Morris K. Udall, Dem., Arizona; Chet Holifield, Dem., California; Michael A. Feighan, Dem., Ohio; and Roman C. Pucinski, Dem., Illinois.

ACKNOWLEDGMENTS

It is not merely in the usual sense of formal acknowledgments that we wish to stress either the contributions of a great many other people to this book or our own final responsibility for its shortcomings. So extensive are the contributions in a number of cases that they are in effect collaboration, and the reader will see, as authors either of separate appendices or of substantial passages in the text, the names of Einar Haugen, William F. Mackey, A. Bruce Gaarder, Sarah C. Gudschinsky, Heinz Kloss, Ernest F. Haden, Kai-yu Hsu, Mieko S. Han, and William A. Douglass; as well as those of our own stalwart staff, Carol Phillips, Joan Frost, Maurice Mizrahi, and Dorothy Kerr.

All these names might quite properly figure on the title page as co-authors if they had been given the opportunity of seeing and revising the final form the manuscript has taken. There too it would be equally just to name Wallace E. Lambert, Joshua A. Fishman, and Rudolph Troike, whose influence on us has been at least as great, though what we derived from them was more on the order of ubiquitous infusions of spirit and viewpoint than specific verbatim quotations.

Yet if the assistance we received has been extensive beyond our ability to convey, we must not imply over-all responsibility on the part of any but ourselves. Again this is more than usually true, because of the way in which the text has evolved during these past ten months. In October of 1968 a conference of distinguished advisers met with us for two days in Chicago. Their names appear on page 327. Our early conception of our task was tested there and in a variety of ways found wanting. From the greater insight gained as a result of that conference and from the travel, correspondence, consultation, and reading which occupied us during the intervening months, we prepared a full draft by April 1, 1969. Few of the original Chicago conferees were pressed into service again at this stage, but the April draft in turn underwent careful scrutiny. The ten readers who served as our official consultants in April are listed on page 325. In addition, some twenty others voluntarily read and criticized our work. Among these we are particularly indebted to Howard Lee Nostrand, Jacob Ornstein, Chester C. Christian, Jr., Severo Gómez, Horacio Ulibarrí, Thomas Carter, William Madsen, Robert Randall, and Susan Ervin-Tripp. The wealth, both in amount and in variety, of assistance that we received for bettering the draft literally overwhelmed us. Having unwisely scheduled only two weeks for revision on the basis of expected criticism, we found that what was needed was not minor correction: it was a complete reorganization of the book, which involved totally rewriting every chapter of our draft but one, "Planning a Bilingual Program." Now, six weeks later, we are just completing in haste the task of revision. The haste shows not only in imperfections of style such as disparities of tone and an unevenness in treating the multiple facets of our subject, but also in the excessive length of the total monograph. As Pascal said, we regret that there was not time to make it shorter. We regret also that we have not been able to submit this final draft again to those who so magnanimously worked for the improvement of the April version. Such a resubmission to these outstanding figures here and abroad would no doubt have made the present book far more acceptable, and we can only hope that we have not completely missed the mark in our effort to incorporate their contributions.

In acknowledging our indebtedness, we cannot fail to make particular mention of Dr. Vera P. John, who gave us not only her questionnaire for collecting data on known bilingual programs but also numerous completed forms and indications of further leads. Her forthcoming book describing in detail many of the Spanish and American Indian programs we have so briefly sketched will be a major contribution to the study of bilingual schooling in the United States.

In this connection we also wish to thank the many persons – some of them already old friends, but many others to whom we were simply importunate strangers – who have taken time they did not have to answer our letters, complete questionnaires, and gather data to which we had no other access; and to receive us personally with most memorable courtesy and kindness, from Alaska to Texas, from Hawaii to Florida and Maine, in Mexico and Canada, and at countless schools, universities, state and federal offices, private homes, and airports in between. It has been an extraordinary year and we do not forget what has been done to help us in this impossible undertaking, even though the list of our benefactors is too long to be recited here.

A special word of thanks is due to Muriel Saville, to whom we owe much of our initiation into the vast and varied world of the American Indian, particularly the Navajo. On our journey through New Mexico and Arizona she was our companion, fellow observer, and mentor. We profited greatly from this association.

To Evangelos Angelos Afendras, of the International Center for Research on Bilingualism, we wish to express our gratitude for his gracious preparation of an index classification system designed to make our index compatible with the international bibliography on bilingualism now being compiled at the Center in Quebec. The completion of this larger bibliography, and of the indexing being done by Dr. Afendras to make information retrieval from it possible even for those not trained in the specialized fields it crosses, are eagerly being awaited by students throughout the world.

Nor have local helpers been lacking. Among them we want to give our thanks especially to Martha Cotera, librarian of the Southwest Educational Development Laboratory, who found not only what we requested but often also material we would not have known to ask for; to Rachel Ortiz and her staff in the Laboratory's secretarial support center, who have patiently produced, refined, and replaced successive drafts of our work; to the art and printing staff; to Earl Martin, who volunteered a considerable amount of his time as research assistant and who organized the section of photographs; to Nina Cooper, our colleague at The University of Texas, who read and shortened some of the more verbose portions of the text; and certainly not least, to Anita Brewer and her staff, for their editorial work on the book as a whole: they have been a comfort and a stay to us in time of tribulation.

Finally, we are deeply grateful for the opportunity to have worked on this subject, which we consider to be replete with significance for our state and our nation. We therefore wish to make public our thanks to the U. S. Office of Education for its support of this contract, and most especially to Edwin Hindsman, Executive Director of the Southwest Educational Development Laboratory, for his invitation to undertake this task. If, as one of our advisers suggested, we were foolhardy to accept the unequal challenge, we cannot even now regret that we entered the lists.

Theodore Andersson
Mildred Boyer

Austin, Texas
July 1969

CHAPTER I

INTRODUCTION

On January 2, 1968, President Lyndon B. Johnson signed into law the Bilingual Education Act.[1] The President called attention to the significance of the new law in these words:

> *This bill authorizes a new effort to prevent dropouts; new programs for handicapped children; new planning help for rural schools. It also contains a special provision establishing bilingual education programs for children whose first language is not English. Thousands of children of Latin descent, young Indians, and others will get a better start – a better chance – in school....*
>
> *What this law means, is that we are now giving every child in America a better chance to touch his outermost limits – to reach the farthest edge of his talents and his dreams. We have begun a campaign to unlock the full potential of every boy and girl – regardless of his race or his region or his father's income.*[2]

Senator Ralph W. Yarborough of Texas, author of the first bilingual education bill ever introduced in either House of Congress, called it a "landmark" in education legislation.[3] The senior Senator from Texas deserves much credit for his work as Chairman of the Special Subcommittee on Bilingual Education in winning overwhelming congressional support for this innovative bill.

In the Foreword of the *Committee Print* of the Act Senator Wayne Morse of Oregon, Chairman of the Education Subcommittee, declared the enactment of this bill to be "of great significance to school systems of the country." He added, "such legislative authorization steps are, however, but initial moves. It is up to the teachers, the school administrators, and, above all, the parents of our school children working together to make these programs come to life in the classroom and on the campus. These programs should be fully funded to achieve their capabilities. They will be if teacher, administrator, and parent ask that they be, and can show that our children are benefited by the uses to which the funds are put."

The Bilingual Education Act (BEA) – passage of which would have been impossible as recently as five years ago, so rapidly is public opinion changing – was conceived primarily to meet the needs of "children who come from environments where the dominant language is other than English." It adds an important new chapter to the long story of this "nation of immigrants."[4]

The first, dim chapter of this story would relate, if only the facts were known, how the ancestors of our American Indians crossed the Bering Strait from northeast Asia and occupied the American continent. The Indians whom the Europeans found here on their arrival, numbering a million or so,[5] were at the beginning not greatly threatened by the small numbers of settlers. The fur trade with the whites even provided them with a period of unparalleled prosperity. Gradually, however, they were displaced by successive waves of pale-faced newcomers. Their loss of freedom, their inability to pursue their native ways of life, can never be made up to them, but the Bilingual Education Act at last recognizes their educational needs and suggests ways to meet them.[6]

To the Indians, America came increasingly to represent tragedy at the same time that it became the land of promise to growing numbers of Europeans, and later to Asians and Latin Americans, who were experiencing hunger, oppression, and hopelessness in their homelands. The trickle of immigration in the sixteenth, seventeenth, and eighteenth centuries–induced by such explorers as Ponce de León in Florida (1513); De Soto, discoverer of the Mississippi (1541); Coronado in New Mexico, Arizona, and Texas (1540-41); La Salle in Louisiana (1682); Father Junípero Serra, founder of the first California mission, in San Diego (1769); and Gálvez in Upper California (c. 1770) – swelled into torrents in the nineteenth and twentieth centuries.[7] To control this influx, laws limiting immigration were passed in 1917 and again in 1921 and 1924. After the mid-century point these laws were felt to be too restrictive and ethnically biased and were liberalized in 1952, 1958, and 1960. A new immigration law enacted in 1965 and effective in 1968 abolished the national origins quota system and authorized small increases in the annual quota numbers.[8]

Today we wear "an ethnic coat of many colors" (Nelson Brooks), all but one strand of which has constantly been overlooked, denied, or degraded" (Joshua Fishman). The meeting of languages and the clash of cultures created tensions, which the Bilingual Education Act is designed to alleviate and can perhaps alleviate if it is expanded and adequately funded.

The status of English as the official language of the United States has never been in doubt. The question which Joshua Fishman's book on *Language Loyalty in the United States* has raised and which the Bilingual Education Act now raises again is whether or not the official position of English leaves room for the maintenance of other languages and cultures. Stated in another way, what should be the attitude and policy of the 90 percent (native English speakers) toward the other ten percent of our population (native speakers of other languages)?[9] These other languages surely do not constitute a threat to English. But are they a nuisance, or are they rather a resource which from a human and patriotic point of view ought to be conserved? These are fundamental questions, to which we shall return in later chapters.

Over the years Americans' views toward newcomers have fluctuated. In the late nineteenth and twentieth centuries the older American stock found it gratifying to accept the view that the New World was the land of promise and America a melting pot, which received countless immigrants who came from some two dozen countries in Europe and spoke even more different languages. Tossed together and stirred up, they were supposed to undergo a delectable transformation and emerge as Americans, all essentially alike and all of course speaking American English. Actually, this is more myth than fact. As Glazer and Moynihan point out in their book, *Beyond the Melting Pot* (1963), the melting did not always take place. Immigrants to America did not cease being what they were and did not, except in rather superficial ways, become something different when they were naturalized as American citizens. Changes that occurred were far less extensive and less structural than they were believed to be. In most cases a bicultural style developed which enabled American and ethnic identities to coexist and influence each other slowly over time. (Fishman) Even today we are regarded as one of the most multicultural nations in the world.

Attempting to define what an American is is intriguing, but the task is not a simple one. Some impressive people have tried, more or less successfully: among others, Tocqueville, Lord Bryce, Count Keyserling, Mead, Brogan, Gorer, Commager, Riesman, and Montagu.[10]

The difficulty in accurately describing an American does not, of course, prevent us from forming ideas concerning our fellow countrymen. Early arrivals to our shores acquired the privileged position of first comers and with it a special cohesiveness. Their descendents are bound together by a common language and culture and they, like everyone else, are most comfortable with "their own kind of folk." It takes an effort to go out to meet speakers of other languages or representatives of other cultures. Members of new groups, all of them minorities, feel typically threatened or overwhelmed by the dominant group and are especially prone to seek comfort in association with *their* own. Language thus serves the double function of bringing members of ethnic groups closer together and of shutting out members of other groups. The question is how best to deal with this fact of life. Must people with different languages and cultures be suspicious and hostile toward one another? Or can they develop mutual tolerance, understanding, and respect?

English-speaking children in the United States naturally begin their formal schooling in their mother tongue, while children of Navajo, Chinese, Japanese, Eskimo, German, or any of half a hundred other language backgrounds are not encouraged to begin their formal learning in *their* mother tongue. English-speaking children profit from carefully prepared reading-readiness and reading programs while children with other language backgrounds have no such provisions for reading in their language. Not only do such practices leave them illiterate in their mother tongue, they also indirectly foster illiteracy in English by forcing them to read in English before they are ready. Developmental psychology is applied to the education of English-speaking children, but not to non-English-speaking children, whose needs are greater. The mediocre results that have been so well publicized of late should hardly surprise us.[11]

This wide-spread negative attitude toward the maintenance and cultivation of other languages spoken natively in American homes does not, for the most part, spring from deliberate perversity. Many, in fact, think it is considerate to urge non-English-speaking children to devote themselves singlemindedly to the learning of English. Many genuinely welcome Mexican Americans, for example, into the mainstream if they can "operate" in English and adopt enough of the ways of Anglo-Saxons to pass as "one of us."

The Spanish-surname American too has been conditioned by decades to realize that in fact he must learn English to compete successfully in a society that believes he must. The error comes in also believing that the maintenance and cultivation of Spanish will somehow interfere with his learning English. No wonder he is confused by recent changes in the story. Anglos have told him for generations that he should forget his Spanish and learn English; now he is told by these same people that learning to read and write in Spanish will make it easier to learn reading and writing in English. He is told, too, that not only can he compete with the English-speaking child in English; he can also excel him in Spanish. Thus he may be proud both of his inherited language and culture and of the official language and culture of his country. In fact he may one day find himself representing his country in another Spanish-speaking nation, provided his education has prepared him for such a role. This is the vista which Senator Ralph Yarborough and his colleagues in the United States Congress have opened up for countless children who had previously been doomed to educational underdevelopment.

Non-English-speaking children are not the only ones who stand to profit from such a reform in our educational system. English-speaking children who are fortunate enough to live in a community in which another language is spoken have an unusual opportunity to learn this language. At the same time, they may also become sensitive to another culture and hence be better able to understand and interact with the different people around them.

In the following chapters we hope to spell out this educational promise—by providing, both in the text and in the appendices, background information essential to the understanding of the complex subject of bilingual schooling; by suggesting a rationale; and by proposing guidelines for the development of bilingual programs to meet local needs and circumstances.

The subject is so many-faceted and the relevant literature so extensive that we have not been able to digest it all. We prefer therefore that our readers consider our book as a preliminary effort, to be improved after more study and research. We invite criticisms, which we shall use or transmit to others, as may best serve the cause of bilingual education.

NOTES

[1]In the House of Representatives the vote on the H. R. 7819 on May 24, 1967 was 294 in favor and 122 opposed. (See the *Congressional Record Daily Digest* for this date, p. D252.) The Senate approved this bill as amended on December 11, 1967, by a vote of 71 to 7. (See *Congressional Record*, December 11, 1967, S18, 357.) On December 15, 1967, the House and Senate agreed to a conference report. (See United States Congress, Senate, Committee on Labor and Public Welfare, *Committee Print, Elementary and Secondary Education Act Amendments of 1967 with Background Materials and Tables*, Prepared for the Subcommittee on Education of the Committee on Labor and Public Welfare, Washington: U. S. Government Printing Office, March 1968, p. 39.)

For easy reference the Bilingual Education Act (BEA) is printed as Appendix A of this monograph. Title VII of the Elementary and Secondary Education Act of 1965, as amended in 1967, is known as Public Law 90-247.

The BEA has been placed under the administration of Ralph Becker, Director of the Division of Plans and Supplementary Centers, Bureau of Elementary and Secondary Education, United States Office of Education.

[2]See *Committee Print*, footnote 1, pp. 40-41.

[3]*Congressional Record,* December 11, 1967, S18,352.

[4]John F. Kennedy, *A Nation of Immigrants* (1963).

[5]*Encyclopaedia Britannica,* 1965 edition, Vol. XII, "Indian, North American," p. 65. Using as a source James Mackey's "The Aboriginal Population of America North of Mexico," Smithsonian Miscellaneous Collection Vol. LXXX, No. 7 (1928), the Encyclopaedia authors cite the following estimated figures: United States (except Alaska), 849,000; Alaska, 773,000; British America, 221,000; Greenland, 10,000; approximate total, 1,153,000.

[6]Although American Indians, Eskimos, and Aleuts are by definition included in the target population of the BEA ("children who come from environments where the dominant language is other than English" and "in schools having a high concentration of such children from families (A) with incomes below $3,000 per year, or (B) receiving payments under a program of aid to families with dependent children under a State plan approved under Title IV of the Social Security Act"), and despite the fact that it was the intention of Congress that these groups should be served (See *Congressional Record*, December 11, 1967, S18,350.), the Act provides no direct way of extending its benefits to such children when they are enrolled in schools operated by the Bureau of Indian Affairs (BIA). To be sure, there is nothing, except possibly the lack of funds, to prevent the BIA from operating its own bilingual program.

[7]See Appendix C, Demographic Data, especially Table 8 and Table 1.

[8]See Appendix D, Immigration Legislation.

[9]For a tentative list of the twenty-five most numerous language groups in the U.S. as of 1960 see Appendix C, Demographic Data, Table 15.

[10]Alexis de Tocqueville, *De la démocratie en Amérique* (1835, 1840); James Bryce, *The American Commonwealth* (1888); Hermann Alexander Keyserling, *America Set Free* (1929); Margaret Mead, *And Keep Your Powder Dry: An Anthropologist Looks at America* (1942); Denis Brogan, *The American Character* (1944) and *American in the Modern World* (1960); Geoffrey Gorer, *The American People: A Study in National Character* (1948); Henry Steele Commager, *The American Mind: An Interpretation of American Thought and Character Since the 1880's* (1950); David Riesman, *The Lonely Crowd: A Study of the Changing American Character* (1950); Ashley Montagu, *The American Way of Life* (1967).

[11]One example is Senator Ralph Yarborough's statement made at the first session of the *Hearings Before the Special Subcommittee on Bilingual Education* of the Senate Committee on Labor and Public Welfare, held in Washington, D. C., on May 18, 1967 (pp. 1-2): "The failure of our schools to educate Spanish-speaking students is reflected in comparative dropout rates. In the five Southwestern States...Anglos 14 years of age and over have completed an average of 12 years of school compared with 8.1 years for Spanish-surname students. I regret to say that my own State of Texas ranks at the bottom, with a median of only 4.7 years of school completed by persons of Spanish surname, according to the 1960 census."

See also Appendix G.

CHAPTER II

DEFINITIONS

Bilingualism is for me the fundamental problem of linguistics....[1]
–*Roman Jakobson*

The terms "bilingual," "bilingualism," "bilingual schooling" seem to carry their meaning clearly within them. And yet a discussion involving any one of these words soon reveals the strikingly different concepts that people have of them.

Thinking primarily of the non-specialist reader, the distinguished scholar and authority on bilingualism, Einar Haugen, has prepared the following succinct definitions of "language," "dialect," "correctness," and "bilingualism."

Language. The word "language" is ambiguous and may easily be misunderstood. We exclude at once such meanings as "the language of flowers" or "the language of mathematics," where it refers to any code that is used for communication. As scientific linguists use the word, "language" is a specifically human form of communication in which sounds (or as a substitute for these, letters) are combined into words and sentences in order to convey meanings from one person to another. The capacity to perform this remarkable feat is inborn in every normal child, and within the first four years of this life he will quite inevitably acquire the sounds, the grammar, and the basic vocabulary of whatever language he hears around him. Being human, he will never acquire it in exactly the same form as it is used by those he hears it from, which is the reason that languages gradually change over time. In this scientific sense of language every human being has at least one language, his first language, sometimes called his mother tongue. He may go on to learn a second and a third later, or he may have two first languages, which he learns in his earliest childhood; in either case he is a "bilingual" by our definition, as will appear later. The main point is that no matter what the social status or the educational achievement of his environment, what he learns is a language in the strict scientific sense, just as an orchid and a dandelion and a tumbleweed are all plants, regardless of their social and economic value.

Dialect. It has long been recognized that there are many different languages in the world and that many of them (perhaps all) have branched off from each other by regular changes over long periods of time. Isolation has been the primary factor in this change, since people who communicate regularly tend to stay together in their language in order to make sure that they are understood. It is also well known that every language is spoken in a variety of dialects and that such dialect differences have been the beginning of all the different languages of the world that have branched off from one another. So English and German are by origin dialects of Germanic that grew into separate languages, just as Spanish and French are dialects of Latin; and, farther back, just as Latin and Germanic are dialects of a long-lost

Indo-European language. The differences that separate any two dialects of the same language may consist of differences in sounds, grammar, or vocabulary; as long as these are not great enough to make understanding impossible, we may still speak of them as dialects in the strictly linguistic sense. Each speaker has his own personal dialect, which is sometimes called an "idiolect," but in the main he shares with the fellow members of his community a dialect that is part of the cultural heritage of the community. To those whose first language it is, the dialect carries all the meanings and overtones of home, family, love, and friendship. It is the instrument of their thinking and feeling, their gateway to the world.

Correctness. Dialects differ not only in their linguistic structure but also in the attitudes which people hold towards them. Every dialect, no matter who speaks it, is objectively equally good for the expression of what its speakers have a need to express. Its sounds are equally easy to pronounce and its grammar equally easy to master for those who learn them as part of their first language. Its vocabulary reflects the cultural level of its speakers, and it can be expanded by training and education from the simple basic vocabulary of childhood to that of the most complex scientific and philosophical thought. Only a few dialects have been so expanded and made into standard languages for the use of whole nations, with standards of correctness which are imposed through the school systems. English and Spanish are among such standard languages. But in the general population common dialects of these languages continue to be spoken and serve as the daily medium of living communities. Any attitude that implies that these are "wrong" or "bad" is built on a standard of correctness which overlooks the validity of these dialects within their communities. A dialect that may be called "non-standard" or even "sub-standard" English or Spanish usually has long roots in history and is for those who use it a valid language, through which alone its users can express their full personalities. The importance of the mother tongue in instruction has only recently been recognized by many educators. They have overlooked that the mother tongue may for many children be the very "non-standard" dialect which the educators are trying to eliminate by teaching standard dialect. When the differences are not between one dialect and another, but between wholly distinct languages, the necessity of giving full consideration to this problem becomes even more pressing.

Bilingualism. There have been many attempts to produce an exact definition of bilingualism, but the only agreement among its various users is that it refers to the knowledge and use of two languages by the same persons. Some writers emphasize the *use* of the languages, e.g. Weinreich (1953), who defined bilingualism as "the practice of alternately using two languages" (similarly Mackey 1962, Brooks 1969). Since it is quite possible to be bilingual without using one of the two languages one knows, others have emphasized the *knowledge* or competence of the speakers, e.g., Haugen (1956), who defined a bilingual as "one who knows two languages" (so also Bloomfield, 1933, who spoke of "control of two languages"). Another difference in the use of the term is that some scholars extend it to include the mastery of more than two languages (in recognition of the fact that the phenomena involved are essentially similar), which is more precisely referred to as *multilingualism* or *polyglossy*. By contrast, one who knows only one language is called a *monolingual* or a *unilingual*.[2]

Within this framework, however, the major problem is that bilinguals differ widely both in their knowledge and in their use of the two languages they master. Knowledge may extend from a few scraps of language to the mastery possessed by a highly educated native speaker and writer. The usual definition has been a rather narrow one, summed up in Bloomfield's use of the term "native-like control" (1933); a German writer, Maximilian Braun,[3] demanded "active, completely equal mastery of two or more languages." Such bilinguals are rare, if they exist at all, and most students prefer a wider definition. In trying to set a lower limit, Haugen (1953) suggested that this be the ability of a speaker to "produce complete meaningful utterances in the other language." Diebold (1961) went a step further in including also a passive knowledge, which required the users only to *understand* speakers of another language, not to speak the language themselves.

Bilinguals may thus be classified according to their skill in their two languages along a more or less infinite scale. Broadly considered, there are bilinguals who have one dominant and one secondary language, while there are others who are reasonably balanced.[4] There are bilinguals who switch easily from one language to the other, and some who find it extremely difficult and confusing to do so. It is very common to find bilinguals who have specialized their use of the languages, so that they can speak of some topics in one and of others in the other.[5]

In considering bilingualism as a "problem" we must not forget that for millions of people throughout the world bilingualism is no problem at all. In many countries it is quite simply a way of life for all or some communities and occasions no particular comment; for educated persons in many countries it is a matter of course that one speaks and even writes more than one language. The problem arises only when a population through emigration or conquest becomes a part of a community where another language is spoken and this language is imposed on them through the school system or by other authorities. We may call this "asymmetrical bilingualism," an example of which is the topic of this book.

To Haugen's definitions, we add two other brief statements on the meaning of "dialect" and its relation to "standard."

> *All languages have dialects. The so-called "standard" is but itself a dialect, and in many language areas there are both regional standard dialects (e.g., London vs. San Francisco vs. Sydney, or Madrid vs. Mexico City vs. Buenos Aires), and non-standard dialects in the same areas, each with its regional hue. Furthermore, language is constantly changing, indeed nowhere faster than among speakers of "standard" dialects; and many of the features of present "non-standard" dialects simply represent survivals of elements which were once in "standard" use, rather than, as is so often erroneously assumed, "corruptions" of the standard. (Rudolph Troike)*

> *It might be easier for non-linguists to understand the adequacy of non-standard dialects if they were thought of in terms of* different dialects for

different purposes. *Every educated speaker of standard English uses the following varieties: formal written style for written reports, technical articles, and the like; formal spoken style for public speeches or lectures; informal written style for personal letters; informal colloquial spoken style for conversation with family and colleagues. For the speaker of non-standard English, the normal, adequate dialect for use in the beginning stages of education, is his own non-standard dialect. He needs to learn standard colloquial for use with possible employers, etc.; he needs to learn standard colloquial written style for business letters; he may eventually also need to control the more formal spoken and written styles and certainly he will need to understand them. (Sarah Gudschinsky)*

As Fishman puts it, individuals who have meaningful roles in a variety of milieus acquire competence in several varieties of language or dialect. It is a proper function of the school, not to destroy the learner's native dialect, but to assist him in acquiring such additional dialects or languages as may be of value to him.

The Description and Measurement of Bilingualism. For two decades or more linguists have become increasingly concerned with the description (definition) and measurement of bilingualism. In 1952 William F. Mackey, one of the leading students of bilingualism, wrote:[6] "The inadequacy of definition...is not the only theoretical drawback to the study of bilinguals. There is also the lack of any adequate system of classification and measurement. The problem of classification includes the following factors: levels of proficiency, similarity and differences between languages, the social function of each language, the effects, through bilingualism, of one language upon another." Writing on the same subject again in 1956, Mackey suggested that: "The solution to the problem of definition is to consider bilingualism (or multilingualism) not as an absolute but as a relative concept. The question should not be simply 'Is a person bilingual?' but rather 'How bilingual is he?'....Such a definition would put the subject on a more stable theoretical basis and would open the way to a systematic measurement of the *degree* of bilingualism. It would lead to classifications which would include the following divisions:

1. The number of languages involved....
2. The type of languages used....
3. Influence of one language upon another....
4. Degree of proficiency....
5. Vacillation....
6. Social function"[7]....

The Report on an *International Seminar on Bilingualism in Education* held in Aberystwyth, Wales, August 20–September 2, 1960, and sponsored by the United Kingdom National Commission for UNESCO–contributed further to the description of bilingualism.[8] The Report proposes the following key elements in the description of individual bilingualism, followed by charts for recording analytical observations under each heading:[9]

I. Number – i.e. the number of languages used by the individual (e.g. language A and language B).
II. Type – i.e. the linguistic relationship between language A and language B.
III. Function – i.e. the conditions of learning and use of the two languages.
IV. Degree – i.e. proficiency in each language.
V. Alternation – i.e. "switching" from one language to another.
VI. Interaction – i.e. the way in which the languages affect each other linguistically, namely by importation and substitution.

Encouraged by his colleagues at Aberystwyth, William Mackey prepared in 1962, *The Description of Bilingualism,*[10] in which he elaborated his earlier thinking into a general framework around the concepts of *degree, function, alternation,* and *interference.*

In June 1967 the Canadian National Commission for UNESCO sponsored at the University of Moncton, New Brunswick, an International Seminar on the Description and Measurement of Bilingualism. Publication of the report is now being awaited.

It may be inferred from the foregoing that the description of bilingualism is far from having found its definitive expression. It touches too many specialized disciplines. In the conclusion of *The Description of Bilingualism* Mackey provides an admirable persepective:

> *Bilingualism cannot be described within the science of linguistics; we must go beyond. Linguistics has been interested in bilingualism only in so far as it could be used as an explanation for changes in a language, since language, not the individual, is the proper concern of this science. Psychology has regarded bilingualism as an influence on mental processes. Sociology has treated bilingualism as an element in culture conflict. Pedagogy has been concerned with bilingualism in connection with school organization and media of instruction. For each of these disciplines bilingualism is incidental; it is treated as a special case or as an exception to the norm. Each discipline, pursuing its own particular interests in its own special way, will add from time to time to the growing literature on bilingualism (see bibliographies in Haugen, 1956, Weinreich, 1953, and Jones, 1960). But it seems to add little to our understanding of bilingualism as such, with its complex psychological, linguistic, and social interrelationships.*
>
> *What is needed, to begin with, is a perspective in which these interrelationships may be considered.*[11]

Bilingual Schooling or Bilingual Education. While such efforts at more nearly complete description move forward, what is bilingual schooling? We take as our working definition that of the Draft Guidelines to the Bilingual Education Program,[12] which seems sufficiently broad: "Bilingual education is instruction in *two languages* and the use of those two languages as mediums of instruction for any part of or all of the school curriculum. Study of the history and culture associated with a student's mother tongue is considered an integral part of *bilingual education.*"

Some Misconceptions. Finally, having sampled authoritative definitions and settled on those that seem adequate to the purposes of the Bilingual Education Act, we come to what appears to us to be misconceptions that need to be rectified.

Confusion of ESL (English as a Second Language) and Bilingual Education. One widely held misconception is that ESL is a form of bilingual education. As we shall see, ESL *is* an important component of bilingual education; but unless the home language is used as a medium for teaching a part or the whole of the curriculum, we believe education cannot properly be called bilingual.[13] To call ESL programs bilingual only causes confusion. Thus, for example, in a U.S. Office of Education report of Projects to Advance Creativity in Education (PACE) entitled "Bilingual Education Projects–SR-68-25 Projects Funded in FY 1966, FY 1967, and FY 1968," there are reported descriptions of selected planning and operational programs funded under Title III of the Elementary and Secondary Education Act. The foreword, dated August 12, 1968, defines bilingual education as "the use of two different languages, such as English and German, in the regular classroom educational process." In spite of the title of the document and in spite of the definition of bilingual education given, the list includes projects which are definitely *not* covered by the definition. Thus, "bilingual education" is used as an official label to designate not only ESL projects, but also a project for the transfer of student records by data processing equipment and general cultural awareness programs. Such indiscriminate use of the term renders it meaningless.

What's in a Name? Spanish-surname persons in the Southwest are frequently called bilinguals though they may have no knowledge of Spanish at all. Misclassification on the basis of name is likely to continue until we recognize that the term "bilingual" is inappropriate unless the person concerned does indeed have some knowledge of two languages. The "nationality" of his surname is an unreliable indicator of which language or languages an American speaks.

In California we were informed that the word "bilingual" has acquired a disparaging connotation ("uneducated"). We keep the term and use it in its technical sense, remembering, as Haugen has said above, that "in many countries [bilingualism] is quite simply a way of life...."

On the subject of definitions there is no easy stopping-place. Specialists in linguistics—especially psycholinguistics and sociolinguistics–in psychology, in sociology, in anthropology, and in education are all busily studying various forms of bilingualism, diglossia, and bilingual education. Each passing year will see the progressive refinement of terms and concepts. For our present purposes we believe that the definitions here given will serve as an adequate basis for the following study.

NOTES

[1]Indiana University, *Indiana University Publications in Anthropology and Linguistics*, Memoir 8, April 1953, p. GE 16.

[2]Editors' note: The term "monoglot" has also been used.

[3]*Göttingische Gelehrte Anzeigen*, Vol. 199 (1937), p. 115.

[4]Editors' note: As Haugen has pointed out in the preceding paragraph, balanced bilingualism or equilingualism–the perfect and equal control of two languages–is not only not a necessary condition of bilingualism but it is extremely rare and indeed all but imposible, at least for any length of time.

[5]"Diglossia" is a term which has become common since 1959, when Charles Ferguson first proposed it in connection with societal or national bilingualism. It refers to the presence within a society or country of two languages or dialects that serve different purposes and therefore maintain a high degree of stability. Like "bilingualism," the concept of "diglossia" is being constantly elaborated and refined by such linguists as John J. Gumperz (e.g., "Types of Linguistic Communities," *Anthropological Linguistics*, Vol. IV, No. 1, 1962, pp. 28-40; "Linguistic and Social Interaction in Two Communities," *American Anthropologist*, Vol. LXVI, Part 2, 1964, pp. 137-154; "On the Ethnology of Linguistic Change;" in William Bright, ed., *Sociolinguistics*, The Hague: Mouton and Co., 1966, pp. 27-38; "On the Linguistic Markers of Bilingual Communication," *The Journal of Social Issues*, Vol. XXIII, No. 2, April 1967, pp. 48-57); Joshua Fishman "Varieties of Ethnicity and Language Consciousness," *Monograph Series on Languages and Linguistics*, Vol. XVIII, Georgetown University, 1965, pp. 69-79; "Who Speaks What Language to Whom and When?" *Linguistique*, 1965, 2, pp. 67-88; "Language Maintenance and Language Shift; The American Immigrant Case Within a General Theoretical Prespective," *Sociologus*, Vol. XVI, 1965, pp. 19-38; "Some Contrasts Between Linguistically Homogeneous and Linguistically Heterogeneous Polities," *Sociological Inquiry*, Vol. XXXVI, 1966, pp. 146-158; "Bilingualism With or Without Diglossia; Diglossia With or Without Bilingualism," *The Journal of Social Issues*, Vol. XXIII, No. 2, April 1967, pp. 29-38. See also Fishman, ed., *Readings in the Sociology of Language*. The Hague: Mouton, 1968); and Heinz Kloss ("Types of Multilingual Communities: A Discussion of Ten Variables," *Sociological Inquiry,* Vol. XXXVI, No. 2, Spring 1966, pp. 135-145; "Bilingualism and Nationalism," *The Journal of Social Issues*, Vol. XXIII, No. 2, April 1967, pp. 37-47).

By way of clarification, the latter (Kloss) writes:

The concept of diglossia has emerged in two phases. As originally conceived by Ferguson in 1959, it referred to the presence, within a society or nation, of two closely and recognizably related languages or dialects (e.g., French and Creole in Haiti, standard German and Schwyzertütsch in Switzerland; Koranic and vernacular Arabic in Egypt) between which a definite and stable division of functions has taken place. In an article I published in 1966 I foresaw that an attempt would be made to apply the concept to the functional "division of labor" between unrelated languages and suggested to speak of "in-diglossia" in the case of kin-tongues (in keeping with the original concept of Ferguson) and of "out-diglossia" in the case of genetically unrelated (or only distantly related) languages (e.g., Spanish and Guaraní in Paraguay). (See Kloss, "Types of Multilingual Communities: A Discussion of Ten Variables," p. 138.)

The next year J. A. Fishman published his paper "Bilingualism With and Without Diglossia; Diglossia With and Without Bilingualism," wherein he broadened the concept of diglossia so as to cover what I had proposed to call "out-diglossia." But for this broader concept Fishman simply retained the original term "diglossia." Brilliant as his essay is, it inevitably leads to some terminological and even conceptual confusion, especially since Ferguson's unaltered essay has been reprinted (in Dell Hymes 1964, pp. 429-439) and his use of the term been followed by several authors.

[6]Pédagogie-Orientation (de l'Université Laval), Vol. II, No. 6 (1952), p. 137.

[7]"Toward a Redefinition of Bilingualism," *Journal of the Canadian Linguistic Association*, March 1956.

[8]London: Her Majesty's Stationery Office, 1965, p. 139.

[9]Ibid., pp. 166-171.

[10]*Canadian Journal of Linguistics*, Vol. VII, No. 2 (Spring 1962).

[11]Ibid., pp. 84-85.

[12]See Appendix B.

[13]See Appendices A and B, The Bilingual Education Act and Guidelines.

CHAPTER III

BILINGUAL SCHOOLING: AN HISTORICAL SAMPLING

There is probably not a nation in the world without some bilingual population, and bilingual schooling has also been widespread. But the origin and status of bilingualism in different countries, as well as the national policies underlying bilingual education, have varied so widely that care must be taken in interpreting the results. Clearly, we cannot assume that practices which have succeeded abroad under entirely different circumstances will necessarily succeed in the United States. They may, or they may not. On the other hand, we would be foolish indeed to ignore the experience of others in other settings. Without any attempt at complete coverage, we have therefore selected a few examples to lend perspective and to give us an orientation. Let us, however, begin with a review of the situation in the United States.[1]

Bilingual Schooling in the United States

The history of public bilingual schooling in our country divides itself into two main parts: pre-World War I and post-1963. Kloss (1942 and 1963), who has studied this subject in great detail, distinguishes in the first part two segments and two phases:[2]

First Segment: Public Elementary Schools

Phase I: 1839-1880

German was the only non-English tongue admitted as a medium of teaching except for French in Louisiana and, from 1848, Spanish in New Mexico. The heyday of the public bilingual school was before the Civil War.

Phase II: 1880-1917

There were German-English bilingual schools in Cincinnati; Indianapolis;[3] Baltimore; New Ulm, Minnesota; and in an unknown number of rural places. In other schools German was taught as a subject, but not used as a medium of instruction. Norwegian, Czech, Italian, Polish, and Dutch were also occasionally taught but not used as teaching mediums.[4]

Second Segment: Non-Public (Chiefly Parochial) Elementary Schools

Phase I: (Before 1800)

German schools flourished throughout the country.[5] Also this period saw the beginning of many French schools in New England and many Scandinavian and some Dutch schools in the Midwest. Many of these schools were not actually bilingual in their curricula; they were non-English schools where English was taught as a subject.

Phase II: (After 1880)

This period saw the multiplication of French and Scandinavian schools as well as the founding of numerous parochial schools especially for Catholic newcomers from Eastern and Southern Europe: e.g., Poles, Lithuanians, Slovaks.

Kloss has reminded us of the considerable number of non-public Franco-American schools in New England between the two World Wars. These included both elementary and secondary schools as well as colleges. Kloss also mentions the Chinese, and a considerably larger number of Japanese, afternoon schools in Hawaii and on the West Coast. For an account of other afternoon or all-day parochial schools of newer immigrant groups, the reader is referred to Fishman's chapter on education in his *Language Loyalty in the United States.*

Rebirth of Bilingual Schooling, Miami, 1963. In an effort to meet the educational needs of the children of the Cubans who pour into Miami at the rate of some 3,000 a month the Dade County, Florida, Schools undertook in 1963 a completely bilingual program in grades one, two, and three of the Coral Way School, Miami, with plans to move up one grade each year. The first director of this program was Dr. Pauline Rojas, who had had long experience in Puerto Rico. At first, participation was made voluntary and a few parents chose to have their children follow the all-English program. By the end of the first year, however, the bilingual program had won almost unanimous approval and it was no longer necessary to offer the unilingual option. Approximately half of the instruction is given in Spanish by competent Cuban teachers and half in English by American teachers. The American and Cuban teachers working in the same grade form a cooperative team and confer frequently in order to coordinate their teaching.[6] In addition to this notable bilingual program, which has now been extended to two other elementary schools, Dade County offers Spanish as a subject in every grade from one through twelve in all other Miami schools. To start with, there were equal numbers of English- and Spanish-speaking children in the Coral Way School, but now the balance is steadily shifting in the direction of the Cuban children. The socioeconomic level is also declining; for, as the Castro regime continues, more lower-income Cubans are seeking escape.

An evaluation of the achievement in the Coral Way School in language arts and arithmetic shows that the bilingual program is as effective as the regular program in English. Dr. Mabel Wilson Richardson, the evaluator, writes: "It must be noted here that, in addition to performing as well as the control group in the regular curriculum, the English-speaking pupils were learning a second language and the Spanish-speaking pupils were learning to read and write their native language."[7] The Dade County bilingual program has the distinction of being the first public elementary school program in this second period of bilingual schooling in the United States, and it is also widely considered as one of the best.

One year later, in 1964, two noteworthy programs were launched in Texas, one in the Nye School of the United Consolidated Independent School District in Webb County, outside of Laredo, and the other in the San Antonio Independent School District.

United Consolidated Program. An interested school board and an enthusiastic superintendent were responsible for the launching of this program in the first grades of Nye School, in which half the children are English speakers and half Spanish speakers. In 1965 the program was expanded into the second grades and in 1966 into the third grades. In 1966 too the other two elementary schools in this sparsely populated school district—with an area slightly greater than that of Delaware—began their bilingual programs in grade one and planned to move up one grade at a time. The teaching, in English and Spanish in all elementary school subjects, is done by bilingual teachers who are native speakers of Spanish and fluent also in English. They move without effort back and forth in Spanish and English, using each language about half of the time. In the fourth grade, where the self-contained classroom changes to the departmental organization, Spanish is continued as a subject one class period a day. An evaluation of learning in mathematics reveals that bilingual learning—for both Anglo and Mexican American children—gives better results than does learning in English alone. The enthusiasm of school board, administration, and teachers has enabled this program to prosper, to attract numerous visitors, and even to entice families to move into the district.[8]

San Antonio Independent School District Program. There are by now (1969) at least two other school districts in San Antonio that have bilingual programs, but the one in the San Antonio ISD is the oldest and best known in the city. It was begun in 1964, under the direction of Dr. Thomas D. Horn of the University of Texas at Austin, and has been carried forward chiefly by Dr. Elizabeth Ott of the Southwest Educational Development Laboratory. Originally it was a reading-readiness program in English for Spanish-speaking children in selected schools in neighborhoods which are all Mexican American. New materials were prepared and new teaching techniques were developed. These were used for thirty minutes in the morning and thirty in the afternoon, in English in one experimental stream and in Spanish in another. By 1967 the success of the program was sufficiently recognized to permit a somewhat greater emphasis on the use of Spanish, starting in grades one and two, and to designate it as a bilingual program. The teaching in Spanish is all done by native speakers, either the regular classroom teacher or another who exchanges with the regular teacher. The subject matter stresses the self-concept and includes language arts, science, and—recently—social studies. The relatively limited emphasis on the use of Spanish—some eighty minutes a day—suggests that, in contrast with Dade Cohnty and United Consolidated, this program is more concerned with transfer than it is with maintenance of Spanish as such. Spanish is used essentialy to build the self-concept of children and to facilitate their learning of English as the eventually exclusive medium of learning.[9]

Other Bilingual Programs in the United States.[10] Bilingual programs began in Pecos, New Mexico, and in Edinburg, Texas, in 1965. In 1966, similar programs started in the Harlandale Independent School District of San Antonio; in Del Rio, Texas; in Zapata, Texas, in Calexico, California; Marysville, California; and Rough Rock, Arizona. The following programs began in 1967: Las Cruces, New Mexico; Hoboken, New Jersey; Corpus Christi, Texas; Del Valle, Texas (Creedmoor School); and St. Croix, Virgin Islands.

This list, consisting almost exclusively of public elementary schools, is merely suggestive. With the exception of Navajo, taught along with English at the Rough Rock Demonstration School, the two languages concerned are Spanish and English. Approximately ninety percent of the BEA proposals submitted in 1968-1969, and of the projects funded, involved these two languages.

For further information on current bilingual programs we refer the reader to Appendix V, Bilingual Programs in the United States. Part I consists of programs known to have existed in May 1969, fifty-six in number, of which forty-nine were in preprimary or elementary grades, four in secondary schools, and three in colleges. A second list consists of the seventy-six projects which have been funded under Title VII, BEA, for 1969-1970. We have indicated with an asterisk fifteen projects which are continuations or transformations of programs in the first list.

Summary. Twelve years ago there was nowhere in the country any perceptible interest in organizing bilingual programs in public schools. And yet a potential must have existed, for soon after a successful program was launched in Miami, it was followed, as we have seen, by increasing numbers each year. We do not know exactly how to account for this rapid change in public temper. Did the relative success of FLES (foreign languages in the elementary school) suggest the bilingual pattern? Or was the example of such non-English medium schools as the Lycée Français in New York a cue? Or the bilingual schools in Latin America? Or should one instead seek the explanation in the tremendous changes taking place in our society, such as the Supreme Court Desegregation Decision of 1954 and the increasing search for identity and self-assertion on the part of ethnic groups and of low-income classes? Whatever the explanation, opinion has evolved rapidly and the American public now seems to be of a mind to give this experiment a new try.

Bilingualism and Bilingual Schooling in Other Parts of the World

In sampling bilingualism in other parts of the world we shall first consider Switzerland, the only officially plurilingual country we know of, then take up four officially bilingual nations: Belgium, Canada, Finland, and the Union of South Africa. Thereafter we shall see what can be learned from a selection of officially monolingual countries that have nevertheless to deal with minority languages.

Official Bilingualism and Multilingualism. Most countries in the world, however many languages may be spoken within their borders, have only one official language. A few are officially bilingual. And Switzerland occupies a unique position with three official languages—French, German, and Italian—and one additional nationally recognized language, Romansch.

Switzerland. Of Switzerland's three official languages, German is spoken by seventy-four percent of the population, French by twenty percent, and Italian by four percent. Romansch, which also enjoys national recognition, is spoken by one percent of the population. In addition, German-speaking Swiss have a language or dialect for intimate use in the home or among close friends, known as Swiss German or Schwyzertütsch. The contact of these various languages does not cause any notable friction. Switzerland's language policy is based on the "territorial principle": that is, in a given canton the language of the majority is official and speakers of other languages are expected to learn and use it. But a "personality principle" is used at the federal level, according to which any individual may be attended to in his own language, no matter where he lives. Individual Swiss citizens are not notably more bilingual or more plurilingual than other Europeans. Their elementary schooling takes place in their respective mother tongues, and a second language is learned at the beginning of the secondary school. Cases of teaching in and through more than one language in the Swiss elementary school have not been reported.[11]

Belgium. Popularly considered a bilingual country, Belgium is more accurately described as a combination of two officially unilingual areas separated by a fixed linguistic boundary, which crosses the middle of the country from east to west. The present language legislation dates back to 1963, at which time the government legally separated the country into the two areas (the territorial principle). In the northern area, only Dutch is available for administrative services and Dutch is the medium of instruction in all publicly supported elementary and secondary schools. To the South, only French is used, in the same fashion. Matters of national concern are announced bilingually. Brussels and the immediately surrounding area have both Dutch and French schools and are the only parts of the country to enjoy a special bilingual status. The hostility between the two language groups appears to be beyond immediate alleviation. The French-speaking Walloons of the South feel that since theirs is a language of international prestige they have little need to learn the other official language, Dutch. The Flemings, on the other hand, feel incensed by the attitude of the Walloons and do not see why the Flemings should carry the entire burden of communication, particularly since they are in the ascendency, both numerically (about sixty percent) and economically. Neither group seems to be motivated to learn two languages in order to build one unified bilingual nation. By resorting to the territorial principle the government hopes to maintain a degree of tranquillity in this sharply divided nation.[12]

Canada. Canada's two official tongues, English and French, are both international languages of prestige, but English speakers outnumber French speakers about two to one and have a great economic advantage. Canada's commonwealth status and proximity to the United States in addition tend to favor the English Canadians. For this reason, the pressure is greater on the French speakers to learn English than on the English speakers to learn French. Until five years ago, French-speaking Canadians were treated legally as a minority. At that time, the government created the Royal Commission on Bilingualism and Biculturalism, to study the thorny language question. This Commission, created on a temporary basis, produced or elicited 400 briefs by representatives of the two official languages as well as by different linguistic minorities, including Ukrainians, Poles, and Italians. One hundred research reports were also produced, which will be used by the Commission in preparing its official report of twelve volumes. At this writing, three volumes have been published: *A Preliminary Report of the Royal Commission on Bilingualism and Biculturalism*; Book I, *A General Introduction: The Official Languages*; and Book II, *Education.* Minorities other than the French-speaking are waiting for more adequate treatment of their problems in a later volume. These initial volumes, though they cannot be expected to satisfy all factions equally, represent an admirable effort at objectivity and scholarliness. They stand as a kind of model of what needs in the first instance to be done in countries where language and culture differences constitute serious problems.

A multilingual country like Canada[13] should be fertile ground for bilingual education, and indeed there are extensive efforts by language groups to maintain their languages and cultures in private schools. The two official languages are of course taught extensively in public schools, where the common pattern is to use the majority language of the particular province as the medium of instruction and to teach the other official language as a subject. Bilingual schooling in the sense defined by the Draft Guidelines to the Bilingual Education Program (Appendix B), that is, using two languages as mediums of instruction for part or all of the curriculum, is rare in Canada, as it is in most nations.

Worthy of note is the unusual case of Welland, a city of 40,000 located in southern Ontario, a few miles west of Niagara Falls. The 8,000 Franco-Ontarians living in Welland are completely isolated from the French-speaking communities living in the northern and eastern parts of the province. Nevertheless, thanks to the fact that the Welland public schools provide education for the French-Canadian children in their mother tongue, both French and English speakers of this small city have been able to preserve their own language and culture in educated form.

"Some of the French Canadian children in Welland are accommodated in French-language classes in English-language schools, but the majority of them attend schools in which all the pupils have French as their mother tongue."[14] In two such schools French is used as the exclusive medium of instruction in K through 6 as well as the medium of communication in the classroom and gymnasium and on the playground. In grade 3 English is introduced as a subject and continued through grade 6. Upon completion of grade 6 the children move to a "senior public school" (grades 7 and 8), where French continues to be the language of instruction for most subjects. "With the opening of Confederation Secondary School last September [1968], it became possible for the French Canadian children of Welland to continue their bilingual education throughout the secondary grades within the publicly supported school system."[15]

In thus emphasizing teaching French speakers in and through French the Welland schools do not neglect English but rather take advantage of the local circumstances.

> *Although English as a school subject is new to the Grade 3 French-speaking pupil of Welland, English as both a spoken and a written language is familiar. Except for the hours he spends in school, he is immersed in a predominantly English environment. Although French is the language of his family, he also hears English at home—whenever the radio or television set is turned on. In all probability there are English-language newspapers, magazines and books in his own home. In the streets of Welland, on buses, in restaurants and stores, the French-Canadian child hears English spoken and he sees that street signs, public notices, and advertisements are in English. There are English-language movies, comics, and children's magazines readily available. Although he has had no formal instruction in how to read or speak English, he does have some notion*

of the usefulness of English and it may be assumed that he has a greater motivation to become functionally bilingual than has his English-speaking counterpart living in some other Ontario town or city where French is rarely, if ever, seen or heard. The very factors which facilitate the acquisition of English as a second language by French-speaking children in Welland at the same time increase the difficulty of preserving and cultivating their mother tongue; English language and culture are ever-present and all-pervasive.[16]

In an effort to determine how successful this bilingual education for French-speaking children is, Giroux and Ellis, with the assistance of the Ontario Institute for Studies in Education, have measured reading achievement of grade 6 pupils in both French and English.[17]

In both speed and comprehension the reading achievement [in French] of the average grade 6 pupil in Welland is similar to that of the average grade 6 pupil in an urban area of the [French-speaking] province of Quebec....It was found that the average French-Canadian grade 6 pupil in Welland reads English with the speed and comprehension of an English-speaking Ontario child who is about eighteen months younger. After only three years of studying English as a school subject, the Welland pupils obtained a median score of 19, which is equivalent to a grade level of 4.7.[18]

In commenting on the possible relationship between French and English reading achievement, Giroux and Ellis conclude

that there is a tendency for pupils who earn high scores in the reading of French to also earn high scores in the reading of English and for pupils who earn low scores in the reading of French to also earn low scores in the reading of English. There is certainly no evidence that competence in reading one of the languages interferes with reading the other language.[19]

Another significant experiment is taking place in the middle-class English-speaking community of St. Lambert, located just across the St. Lawrence River from Montreal, in the Province of Quebec. The parents of the English-speaking children of a Protestant elementary school, having read about the results of recent research in early elementary school learning, contacted several staff members of McGill University, including Dr. Wilder Penfield, former Director of the Montreal Neurological Institute, and Professor of Psychology Wallace E. Lambert, head of a group of productive researchers in bilingualism. They discussed the possibility of an experiment in their school. In 1966-1967 one first-grade class was taught exclusively in French with the attendant testing and reserach supervised by Lambert.[20] The results were so satisfactory that it was decided to continue the experimentation for three years. In 1967-1968 the pilot experimental class was followed through grade 2, which remained all-French except for fifty minutes of instruction each day by a teacher of English. At the same time different experimental and control classes were started in the first grade.[21] And in 1968-1969 the project was expanded into the third grade and replicated in grades 1 and 2.[22]

For a summary conclusion we shall let the researchers speak for themsleves:

> *The results of this experiment to date indicate that the type of bilingual training offered these children is extremely effective, even more so than was originally expected. The similarity of the findings for two different sets of firstgrade classes, involving changes in teachers, methods of instruction and modes of testing and analysis, speaks well for the stability and generality of the effects produced by the experimental program. These effects demonstrate a very high level of skill in both the receptive and productive aspects of French, the language of instruction; a generally excellent command of all aspects of English, the home language of the children; and a high level of skill in a non-language subject matter, mathematics, taught through the foreign language only. The results for the second year of the French program, during which a minimum of training was given in English, show a general improvement in French and English language achievement and in mathematics so that the second year Experimental class performs as well as, and in some cases better than, either English or French control classes in most abilities examined. Impressive as the grade II results are, however, they should be considered as tentative until they are replicated with new sets of classes in 1969. Their significance will become clearer, too, as the scope of the research is broadened to include an examination of the impact of the experimental program on the ethnic attitudes of the children and their parents, relative to the control children and their parents. It would be surprising if a program of the sort offered the children did not affect their self-conceptions, since they have become progressively more bicultural, perhaps much more so than their parents.*
>
> *Finally, it is felt that plans should be made to study the effects of the same type of experimental program on English-speaking children from somewhat lower social-class backgrounds and on children with an even broader range of intelligence scores. To be of general value to a region or nation that is serious about developing a bilingual and bicultural citizenry, the children from working class backgrounds and those of limited intellectual endowment should be given every opportunity to capitalize on a program as promising as this one now appears to be. In other words, it should not be a program for the priviledged classes only. Similarly, it is hoped that certain French Canadian schools will see the obvious advantages of such a program for their children.*

Finland. For a capsule description of the harmonious bilingual situation in Finland we resort to the *Report* of the Royal Commission on Bilingualism and Biculturalism in Canada:[23]

In Finland, there are two main languages: Finnish and Swedish. The two languages have had many years' experience of association–for 600 years present–day Finland was part of the Kingdom of Sweden. Only in modern times, however, have they existed in a state of legal equality. Earlier, Swedish, as the language of learning, administration, the church, and commerce, had characterized the educated classes, and more particularly the civil service, the clergy, and the economic elite. From about 1840, the forces of Finnish nationalism began to gain momentum. The movement culminated in the 1919 Constitution. Both Finnish and Swedish were declared national languages of Finland, and citizens were guaranteed the right to use either language in their relations with the administrative authorities. Article 14 of the Constitution also provided that "care shall be taken that the rights [of both populations] shall be promoted by the state upon an identical basis."

This sweeping promise of equality is at first sight surprising, since the minority group who spoke Swedish accounted for only 11 percent of the population in 1919. Admittedly, they had formed 14 percent in 1880, but by 1960 this population had declined to 7 percent or 331,000 persons in a total population of 4,100,000. Yet, while the numerical strength of the Finnish-speaking citizens explains the comparative rapidity with which they established parity with those speaking Swedish, the past pre-eminence of the latter largely accounts for the present position of formal equality between the languages. Another factor is the usefulness of Swedish in increasing contacts between the Nordic countries: the status of Swedish is an affirmation of Finland's position as one of these countries.

Though it was not always so, language rarely seems to be a subject of serious discord in Finland nowadays. Given the smallness of the Swedish minority and the lack of widespread individual bilingualism (some 11 percent had a knowledge of the two languages in 1969), it is accepted on both sides that the equality spoken of by the Constitution should be implemented principally by regions. Such a territorial principle restricts an individual's right to receive services in his own language to certain defined districts. As the Swedish-speaking community is for the most part concentrated in the costal areas and in certain cities and towns rather than scattered across the country, this is not as great a restriction as it might first appear.

The commune is the unit of local government in Finland. It will be officially bilingual if it includes in its territory a linguistic minority of at least 10 percent of the population or at least 5,000 persons. If the proportion of the minority is smaller, the commune will be unilingual in the language of the majority, whether Finnish or Swedish. For administrative purposes, one or more communes may form a district; this will be unilingual if all the communes making it up are of the same language. But if there are bilingual communes or communes of different languages, the administrative district will be considered bilingual. School districts, whose boundaries do not necessarily coincide with those of administrative districts, are similarly organized: for more than a given number of students who speak Finnish or Swedish, an education in their own language must be assured.

This, in a very broad outline, is how the people of Finland have established linguistic equal partnership. By impartially subjecting minorities of both language groups to the territorial principal, on the basis of the most recently available census figures, they have met their constitutional requirement of official equality. Yet at the same time they have never lost sight of the practical limits imposed by the country's demography and history on the provision of equal service.[24]

Union of South Africa. In his Inaugural Address at the International Seminar on Bilingualism in Education, held in Aberystwyth, Wales, in 1960, Dr. E. G. Malherbe, Principal and Vice-Chancellor of the University of Natal, refers to his country as "the most bilingual country in the world today." He adds that "it has administratively applied bilingualism in schools in a more universal and thoroughgoing way than any other country I know of."[25] We shall use Malherbe as our main source of information on the Union of South Africa.[26]

When the four Provinces were united into the Union of South Africa in 1910, one of the main principles laid down in the Act of Union was that: "Both the English and Afrikaans languages shall be official languages of the Union and shall be treated on a footing of equality and possess and enjoy equal freedom and rights and privileges."

Every child in every school throughout the Union is taught both English and Afrikaans as languages, with the second language being started not later than one to two years after beginning school. The results of this official policy are reflected in the census figures, which show a steady rise in bilingualism amongst the white population of 7 years and over, during the last 40 years.

Afrikaans is a highly streamlined form of the 17th century Dutch brought to South Africa by its first permanent settlers. It is a very flexible medium of expression in all fields, technical as well as literary. It is able to draw on modern Dutch when necessary for technical terms, and uses it as supporting literature in the higher classes. In its short span of life as a language it has developed a literature in poetry and prose, the best of which compares favourably with that of older literatures. It has proved a very successful medium of instruction over the whole educational range from the kindergarten to the university. Its spelling is phonetic and can for that reason alone be learnt far more easily at school than English.

At present roughly 60 percent of the three million white population speak mostly Afrikaans at home, *and 40 percent English.*

In 1918 (i.e., 42 years ago) the percentage who could speak both English and Afrikaans was 42 percent. In 1921 it has risen to 51 percent; in 1926 to 58 percent; in 1936 to 64 percent; in 1946 to 69 percent; in 1951 to 73 percent. If one takes the age group of 10-64 years, the percentage is 78 percent bilingual. This was in 1951. (Today I am sure it must be over 80 percent.) The number who spoke Afrikaans only was 8 percent and English only was 14 percent....

Commenting on the organization of schools, Malherbe distinguishes between language as a subject and language as a medium:

(A) *Language as a subject:*

Though the regulations differ somewhat in the four Provinces, it can be assumed that all white and coloured children in South African schools are taught both official languages, English and Afrikaans, *as subjects.* All indigenous African pupils are taught their vernacular language as well as at least one of the official European languages. For the moment I shall limit my observations to schools for white pupils.

This is the general position in a nutshell as far as the legislative requirements are concerned.

Obviously the child begins to learn his first language as a subject right from the start. But as to *when and how* a beginning should be made with the study of the second language as a subject, this becomes a question of *educational method.*

According to the best educational theory in South Africa today, both official languages should be taught to all pupils *as subjects* right from the beginning. *But with the following important provisos*:

(i) The child must hear the second language first, then learn to speak it, then to read and write it.

(ii) The young child must under no circumstances learn to *read* or *write* the second language until it can do so in the first language. This is a necessary proviso, particularly where the one language is phonetic (e.g., Afrikaans) and the other (English) is not phonetic in its spelling.

(iii) It does not matter much how early in school life the child starts with the second language, provided that it follows the mode of acquisition of the first language in learning it. This is best achieved in free association with other children who speak the second language. And, failing the presence of such children, the second language should be introduced *conversationally* through games and other interesting experiences of intrinsically educational value to the child, e.g., simple stories from the field of history, geography, nature study, etc.

Used in this way, the language lesson (whether in the first or the second language) becomes ancillary to the other subjects, instead of being something sterile by itself....

(A) *Language as a medium:*

In South Africa the child must be taught at least up to the end of the primary school through the medium of the home language, i.e., the language which the child understands best. This is determined by the school inspector. Only in the Province of Natal does the parent have a choice in the matter.

The second language may be introduced as an additional medium beyond the primary stage. In Natal this may be done earlier.

The home (or family) language medium principle is more strongly entrenched in the educational enactments in South Africa than in any other bilingual country.

As an educational principle, the use of the child's home language as a medium of instruction, especially in the early stages, is sound. Education, to be effective, must utilise the child's own environment and experience as a foundation on which to build.

Malherbe then describes the various types of schools:

(1) *The unilingual or single-medium school:*

Here children with Afrikaans and English home languages respectively are segregated into separate schools, even though they live in the same community or town. Thus only one medium of instruction is used throughout the school, except when teaching the second language as a subject. The majority of schools in the larger towns and cities are of this type. This type of school organisation has led to the artificially "kraaling off" [separation] of children into two distinct and sometimes socially hostile groups, even where they come from homes and communities where both English and Afrikaans are currently spoken. This not only deprives children while at school of the benefit of associating on the playground with children of the other language group—thus diminishing the opportunities of hearing and using the second language—but has also had important social and political consequences. By accentuating language differences it has caused a set-back to the process of developing a corporate national feeling of South Africanism amongst the younger generation.

In general there are four different principles according to which the media of instruction are determined in bilingual (or trilingual) countries:

(a) the home;
(b) the religious allegiance;
(c) local geographical area;
(d) the political unit (the State).

A logical consequence of the separate-medium type of school organisation has been in fact that we have now four English-medium universities and four Afrikaans-medium universities....

(2) *Parallel classes:*

Here Afrikaans and English home language children go to the same school, but are taught in separate classes. The only time they will hear the second language spoken is in the language lesson and on the playground.

(3) *Dual medium:*

This takes several forms in practice (a) where some subjects are taught through Afrikaans and others through English medium to the same classes: (b) where both media are used alternatively: (i) in the same lesson, by repeating completely or partially in the one language what has been said in the other language, (ii) on successive days of the week. The situation in (b) is feasible only when the teacher is fully bilingual....

(4) *A combination of the parallel class and dual-medium system,* the former being more common in the lower classes and the latter more common in the upper classes.

Types (2), (3) and (4) are usually grouped together under the generic term *Bilingual School* to distinguish them from the single-medium school.

In 1938 I made a study of over 18,000 pupils in over 200 representative primary and secondary schools in South Africa to ascertain *inter alia* the effect which these various types of school organisation had on (a) their progress in their first and second languages respectively, and (b) their content subjects by using either or both first and second languages as a medium of instruction. (The results have been published in "The Bilingual School"–Longmans, 1946.)

In short it may be stated that where English and Afrikaans children attended the same school, either with the method of parallel classes or of dual medium, (a) they gained in proficiency in their second language over those in separate single-medium schools, while their first language was unimpaired; (b) by the time they reached Standard VI (i.e. the end of the primary school), they were in no way behind in their content subjects as a result of their second language being used as medium of instruction.

Bilingual or Plurilingual Countries Having One Official Language.

We have selected about a dozen countries in this category with the thought that they will suggest something of the diverse conditions–linguistic, cultural, political, etc.–which affect education. Not discovering any better procedure, we shall take them up in alphabetical order.

Ceylon. Ceylon, an independent nation within the British Commonwealth since 1948, has unresolved language and educational problems. The majority of the population are Sinhalese (about 6,000,000) and the largest of the minority groups are the Tamils (about 2,000,000). All others–Moors, Burghers, Malays, etc.–comprise less than 1,000,000. In 1961, after much discussion, Sinhalese was made the single official language of the country. As a result, the minority groups, especially the Tamils, feel that their best interests are not adequately protected, and there are frequent language disputes.[27]

China. In China, despite the presence of sometimes mutually incomprehensible languages or dialects, what may comprehensively be called Chinese is spoken by ninety-five percent of the population and ninety-five percent of all speakers of Chinese–some of whom are to be found in almost any part of the world, from Singapore to New York–live in China. The national language of China is Mandarin (or Kuo-yu), which is also one of the five official languages of the UN.[28]

There are eight subgroups of non-Chinese languages spoken by the ethnic minorities in China including Taiwan. Many of these languages never had any fully developed scripts until, interestingly, the advent of the People's Republic of China, whose policy approximated that of the USSR with regard to minority languages. The general thrust generated by Peking was to help the minority people either to perfect or to create written forms for their languages. The theory was that these people must first be helped to become literate in their own way to facilitate their education, and then along with improved education would come the incentive to join in the mainstream of Chinese society, to the extent of wanting to learn the national Chinese language in addition to their own. For example, in 1955, a script was developed for the Chuang Minority Nationals in Kwangsi Province, Southeast China, using the Latin alphabet as the basis.[29]

Within the subgroup of minority languages in Taiwan, nine different forms of speech have been identified, with a total of about 160,000 speakers.[30] The government of the Republic of China in Taiwan so far has encouraged only academic interest in studying these languages; there has been little activity to promote their use. (Kai-yu Hsu)

Faroe Islands. These Islands in the North Atlantic comprise a county of Denmark. The local language, Faroese, is one of six distinct written languages of Scandinavia. The written form of Faroese was developed about 1846 by V. U. Hammershaimb, and in 1912 the use of Faroese in schools and churches was to some extent authorized. Since 1938, teachers are free to use Faroese as the single language of instruction, reversing the trend of the preceding period.

Greenland. Greenland, which until 1953 was a Danish colony and which since that time has become an integral part of the realm, has a Danish-Greenlandish bilingual program in its elementary schools. Instruction in Greenlandish, the mother tongue of the Eskimos, is emphasized at the beginning and then Danish is added to the curriculum. It is generally considered that the Eskimos of Greenland receive a more suitable education than they do in Alaska or Northern Canada. However, the Danes are not satisfied and continue to study the problem.

India. India represents what is perhaps the most complex multilingual situation in the world. In the Census of 1961 "every individual was asked to give his mother tongue. A total of 1,652 different names of mother tongues were returned, of which 1,022 could firmly be classed as Indian languages."[31] Even though this multiplicity of tongues may be reduced to "twleve major languages of Indo-European or Dravidian origin,"[32] the problem of education is complicated. Addressing a Conference of Provincial Ministers of Education in 1949, Minister of Education Manlana Azad stated: "India is a vast country with many languages. We must accept unreservedly that all these languages are Indian languages and deserve equal treatment....What objection can there be if a minority in a particular province speak or learn in a language other than that of the majority....Even if our aim is unity, it cannot be achieved by compulsion or imposition....We should approach this problem with large-hearted generosity and try to meet the wishes of the minorities in a manner which will leave no ground for dissatisfaction or complaint."[33] This expresses an irreproachable sentiment, and to this day nearly all minority languages are used as mediums of instruction, at least in the lower forms of the schools. The trouble comes when national unity is sought, for Hindi, the national language, is spoken by only one-third of the population. As a medium for higher education it competes poorly with English, which also serves as the best medium of communication among well-educated Indians and as a link language with the world outside. After more than a decade of controversy a tolerable formula has been worked out. Recognizing the tendency of regional languages to become the mediums of university education, the Central Advisory Board proposed in 1962 "that any university adopting a regional language should continue to provide facilities for instruction in English and Hindi....The National Integration Council, while conceding that regional languages should become the media of university education, warmed to the theme of Hindi as the eventual, and English as the transitional link between universities....The link language formula satisfied everyone because it left open the question of timing."[34] This is the language policy today, reflected in a speech by Mrs. Ghandi on August 15 (the Indian national holiday), 1967, in which she said, "In the present-day world, we cannot afford to live in isolation. Therefore there should be three languages, regional, national, and international."[35]

Mexico, Guatemala, Peru,[36] *and Ecuador.* Monolingual Indian populations in these countries have been for many years a serious problem for any educational program. Increasingly in the past two decades, the governments of these countries have sponsored programs in which the Indian languages are used as mediums of instruction in the early grades of special schools, while at the same time the children are introduced to Spanish as their second and national language. The Summer Institute of Linguistics, whose teams of linguists are engaged in research in these languages, has assisted in such programs by cooperating in the development of writing systems, in the preparation of basic primers and readers, and in the vernacular side of teacher training. (Sarah Gudschinsky)

Paraguay. "In Paraguay, two languages, Spanish and Guaraní, have co-existed for the past three hundred years in relative equilibrium. A high percentage (52%) of the community is said to be bilingual and almost the entire community (92%) can speak the aboriginal language, Guaraní."[37] Rubin points out that "Paraguayans are unique in Latin America in the importance they give their aboriginal language, Guaraní. In all other...countries the Indian language is relegated to a secondary position–it is the language of the lower class or of the still extant aboriginal groups."[38]In Paraguay Guaraní is the language of intimacy, of love, of poetry, and of jokes.[39] The explanation for this unique situation is to be found in the close interaction between the Spanish conquerors and the Guaraníes from the very beginning. The latter were willing to collaborate with the Spaniards for their mutual protection, and a high percentage of Spanish-Guaraní households were established.[40] The children learned Guaraní from their mothers and from the servants, and Guaraní became quickly the language of the home. There is a high degree of loyalty to Guaraní, which is considered to be the national language *par excellence*, though Spanish is the official language and is also highly respected.[41] The fact that the two languages are used for different roles makes for the great stability of both.

Philippines. One of the earliest pieces of serious research on the effects of beginning education in the child's mother tongue was done in the Philippines in the late forties. The

Iloilo experiment demonstrated the superiority of this form of instruction.[42] Current experimentation in the use of two languages in the primary grades is being carried out under the sponsorship of the Language Study Center of the Philippine Normal College, Bonifacio P. Sibayan, Director.[43] In general the first two years of schooling are conducted in the child's home language, and the rest of the elementary school in Tagalog (Filipino, Pilipino), the official language, with English studied as a subject.

The Union of Soviet Socialist Republics (USSR). The European nation with the greatest variety of experiences in bilingual schooling is presumably the USSR. The Soviets were from the beginning committed to allow the ethnic minority groups considerable freedom in their educational planning. With some 200 distinct languages, spoken by about forty-five percent of the population, the USSR became the scene of extensive language-development. The principal languages were standardized, writing systems were developed for unwritten languages, and well over sixty languages began to be used in primary schools and in some instances past this level.[44]

In the 1930's a new policy was initiated, which emphasized the role of Russian in the Soviet communication network and limited the use of the minority tongues. The more important minority languages, however, continued to be used as mediums of instruction in primary and to a lesser extent in secondary schools.[45] It is reported that some 700 schools make some use of foreign languages like English, French, German, and Chinese as languages of instruction in various subjects.[46] Mackey adds that there are more than twenty Pedagogical Institutes for Foreign Language Teaching and at least four times this number of Special Language Schools in which, from the first grade, a foreign language is used almost exclusively as modern history and economic geography of the foreign country are taught in the foreign language.[47]

United Kingdom. As E. Glyn Lewis remarks in his chapter on "Bilingualism–Some Aspects of its History," there has been in Britain "a long, almost unbroken, tradition of bilingualism of one form or another over large areas of the country. Latin, of course, was a living language in these islands as it was on the continent....Latin was spoken by members of all classes of the Celtic population....It is probable that the Romanised Britons were bilingual exactly as the well-to-do-classes in Norman England a thousand years later."[48] Lewis continues: "In the 13th century French was spoken practically everywhere, certainly everywhere that mattered. It was the language of the court, and of society; it was the language of administration, of parliament, of the law courts, the church and monasteries. It was the language of schools, which forbade the speaking of English, much as Welsh was forbidden in Wales in the 19th century."[49]

In our day, the Celtic minority languages, having long since retreated to the edges of Great Britain, are struggling manfully to maintain themselves. Welsh-English bilingualism is still active in parts of Wales.[50]

The Constitution of Ireland lays down in the famous Article 8 that "1) the Irish language as the national language is the first official language. 2) The English language is recognised as a second official language. 3) Provision may, however, be made by law for the exclusive use of either of the said languages for any one of more official purposes, either throughout the State or in any part thereof."[51] Proponents of Irish-English bilingualism see it as the only way of maintaining the Irish language and culture. Others, while sympathetic to the desirability of maintaining the ancestral heritage, point out that Irish speakers account for only three percent of the population, according to the 1961 Census. Recent surveys show that "about 83 percent of the population did not believe that Irish could be restored as the most widely spoken language..."[52] Apparently the motivational factor is lacking. Even those who are sympathetic to the maintenance of Irish have little reason for optimism.

In Scotland Gaelic plays a feeble role in the schools.[53]

Summary

This cursory sampling of a dozen bilingual or plurilingual communities is intended to be more than suggestive. An American educator will perhaps detect among these foreign settings an occasional feature that matches the situation in his own bilingual community. He will probably have more questions than answers. Is bilingualism a good thing for a community or a nation? Should it be confined to the home and to use among intimate friends? Or should it be supported through instruction in the schools? How do languages relate to social roles? What are appropriate roles for the home language, for a second language, and for foreign languages? Are there essential differences between local languages and languages of wider communication? What makes some languages prestigious and others not? What determines community attitude toward a given language, toward bilingualism, toward bilingual schooling? How should majority and minority language groups interact? Does the power advantage of the majority or dominant group imply special responsibility toward the minority groups? How much do language problems and intergroup tensions result from ignorance—of the nature of language; the process of language learning; the inter-relationship of language, culture, and society, etc.? In the chapters that follow we cannot presume to give definitive answers to all of these questions, but we hope that the information we have gathered will be suggestive of some lines of thought.

NOTES

[1]The reader will find it useful to refer to the varied matter contained in the appendices. Especially relevant to this chapter are Appendix C, Demographic Data; Appendix J, From Egypt to America: A Multilingual's Story; and Appendices K through U, which contain basic information on a dozen different American ethnic groups.

We also call attention at the very outset to a basic book, Joshua A. Fishman's *Language Loyalty in the United States*, which should be within reach of every educator interested in bilingual schooling.

[2]In a personal communication to us, from which we quote and paraphrase.

[3]See Frances H. Ellis (1954) for a detailed account of the Indianapolis program between 1869 and 1919.

[4]Kloss (1942), pp. 615-682; Kloss (1963), pp. 95-109.

[5]Dr. Kloss has communicated to us a one-page tabulation, published under the title "Die Deutschamerikanische Schule" in *Jahrbach für Amerikastudien*, Vol. VII (1962), pp. 159-160, and which we reproduce herewith. Kloss writes:

In 1962, I published the following tabulation, giving data from 1900 (the figures were taken from Viereck, but the capital letters A, B. C have been added by me):

I. Enrollments in Programs with Highly Developed German Studies in Elementary Schools

Place	Private	Public[1]	Total	% of All Pupils
New Braunfels, Tex.	120	240 A	360	100
Tell City, Ind.	120	500 C	620	96
Belleville, Ill.	960	2,026 A	2,986	71
New Ulm, Minn.	330	575 A	905	90
Carlstadt, N.J.	122	486 C	608	95
Erie, Penn.	1,985	4,830 B	6,815	66
Milwaukee, Wisc.	10,525	21,190 B	31,715	62
Cincinnati, Ohio	10,700	17,287 A	27,987	50
Cleveland, Ohio	8,041	17,643 A	25,684	40
Evansville, Ind.	1,365	2,480 C	3,845	36
Hamilton, Ohio	450	1,017 C	1,467	32
Columbus, Ohio	1,580	3,980 A	5,560	22
Dayton, Ohio	1,320	2,203 A	3,523	25
Saginaw, Mich	250	1,130 A	1,380	33
Baltimore, Md.	7,250	8,450 A	15,700	16
Indianapolis, Ind.	1,861	4,537 A	6,398	18

II. Enrollment in Programs with Less Highly Developed German Studies in Elementary Schools

Place	Private	Public[1]	Total	% of All Pupils
New York, N.Y.	18,240	60,000 B	78,240	25
Buffalo, N.Y.	5,030	7,030 B	12,060	17
Hoboken, N.Y.	870	980 C	1,850	20
Sheboygan, Wisc.	1,870	744 C	2,614	55
Davenport, Iowa	430	3,400 C	3,830	56
Chicago, Ill.	25,340	31,768 B	57,108	19
Denver, Colo.	530	2,861 C	3,391	15
Lancaster, Pa.	980	580 A	1,560	25
Akron, Ohio	750	75 C	825	11
Toledo, Ohio	1,868	1,932 C	3,800	18
La Crosse, Wisc.	893	560 C	1,453	25
Houston, Tex.	350	816 C	1,166	20

[1]A=dual medium schools
B=German mere branch of study
C=precise status of German unknown

III. Secondary School Enrollment in Cities Where Public Elementary Schools Teach No German

Place	Private	Public[1]	Total	% of All Pupils
St. Louis, Mo.	16,850	148 B	16,998	17
Detroit, Mich.	7,180	250 B	7,430	15
Newark, N.J.	5,180	500 B	5,680	14
Louisville, Ky.	4,530	150 B	4,680	14
St. Paul, Minn.	2,180	443 B	2,623	9
Brooklyn, N.Y.	7,150	960 B	8,110	5
Allegheny, Pa.	2,560	150 B	2,710	11
Peoria, Ill.	1,020	150 B	1,170	12
Dubuque, Iowa	1,850	175 B	2,025	30
Rochester, N.Y.	2,180	448 B	2,628	9
Pittsburgh, Pa.	7,128	160 B	7,288	13

[1]A=dual medium schools
B=German mere branch of study
C=precise status of German unknown

[6]For a description of this and one other Spanish program in the Dade County Schools see Gaarder and Richardson (1968) and Bell (1969).

[7]Richardson (1968).

[8]See Texas Education Agency (1967).

[9]Ibid.

[10]Ibid. See also Appendix V, Bilingual Programs in the United States.

[11]For a brief report on Switzerland as a plurilingual state see Canada (1967), pp. 79-80. See also Welsh (1966).

[12]Ibid., pp. 77-79.

[13]See Canada (1965), p. 95. This table names the following languages or language groups, with numbers and percentages:

Language (groups)	Number of Speakers	Percentage of Population
German	563,713	3.09
Ukrainian	361,496	1.98
Italian	339,626	1.86
Dutch	170,177	0.93
Indian and Eskimo	166,531	0.91
Polish	161,720	0.88
Scandinavian	116,714	0.63
Jewish (Yiddish and Hebrew?)	82,442	0.45
Others, not stated	492,137	2.69
TOTAL	2,454,562	13.45

[14]Giroux and Ellis (1968), p. 2. Our description is based on this study, supplemented by a personal visit.

[15]Ibid.

[16]P. 3.

[17]The procedure is described on pp. 5ff.

[18]P. 6.

[19]P. 7.

[20]For a detailed report see Lambert and Macnamara (1969).

[21]Gratifying results are reported by Lambert, Just, and Segalowitz (1969).

[22]The authors had an opportunity to visit this school in April 1969 and were most favorably impressed by the interest expressed by several parents and the principal, by the skill and dedication of the teachers, by the performance of the children, and by the effective research collaboration of Lambert and his team.

[23]Canada (1967), pp. 75ff.

[24]For a much more detailed treatment of the Finnish situation the reader is referred to T. Miljan, *Bilingualism in Finland*, a research report submitted to the Royal Commission on Bilingualism and Biculturalism. See p. 211 of Book I, *General Introduction: The Official Languages*. Miljan reports, for example, that the normal pattern for a Finnish school child is to receive his education through his mother tongue and to study the second official language as a subject starting in grade 5. See also Wuorinen (1931).

[25]United Kingdom (1965), pp. 8ff.

[26]For another succinct description see Canada (1967), pp. 80-82. See also Aucamp (1926), and Malherbe (1946).

[27]See Macrae (1939).

[28]See also Appendix R, Chinese, by Kai-yu Hsu.

[29]American Consulate General in Hong Kong, "Survey of Mainland Press," No. 1068 (June 14, 1955), p. 1.

[30]Chung Lu-Sheng, *The Phonology of the National Language*, Taipei, 1966, pp. 10-12.

[31]Julian Dakin, et al. (1968), pp. 12-13. Our brief account is based on this chapter.

[32]Ibid., p. 16. Kloss states that there are fourteen (not twelve) official languages (including Sanscrit). See his "Problèmes linguistiques des Indes et de leurs minorités," in *Revue de Psychologie des Peuples*, Vol. XXL (1966), pp. 310-348.

[33]Ibid., p. 36.

[34]Ibid., p. 53.

[35]Ibid., p. 61.

[36]Burns (1968).

[37]Joan Rubin (1968), p. 14.

[38]Ibid., p. 21.

[39]Ibid., p. 16.

[40]Ibid., p. 23.

[41]Ibid., p. 21.

[42]Pedro T. Orata, "The Iloilo Experiment in Education Through the Vernacular," UNESCO, *The Use of Vernacular Languages in Education*, Paris, 1953, Monograph 8 on Fundamental Education, pp. 123-131

[43]Prator (1956).

Bonifacio P. Sibayan, "Some Problems of Bilingual Education in the Philippines. *Philippine Journal of Education*, Vol. XLV (1966).

---- "Language Planning in the Philippines." Paper read at the Thomas Jefferson Cultural Center. Mimeographed, 10 p. See also Sibayan (1968).

---- "Pilipino, English and the Vernaculars in Philippine Life," *The Catholic Teacher,* Vol. XIV (January 1969), pp. 1-12.

---- "Planned Multilingualism in the Philippines, In Thomas A. Sebeok, ed., *Current Trends in Linguistics*: Vol. VIII, *Linguistics in Oceania*, The Hague: Mouton & Co. (in press).

---- G. Richard Tucker, "An Assessment of Bilingual Education in Philippine Context." See interim report attached to correspondence with Work Page No. 1, Philippine Normal College Bilingual Experiment, 1968-1969.

[44]Eric Goldhagen (1968). See especially Jacob Ornstein's chapter entitled "Soviet Language Policy: Continuity and Change." See also Kreusler (1961).

[45]Ibid.

[46]H. H. Stern (1969), p. 82.

[47]Source: Xronika, *Inostrannije Jazyki v Skole*, 1960-1968.

[48]United Kingdom National Commission for UNESCO, *Bilingualism in Education*, London: Her Majesty's Stationery Office, 1965, p. 71.

[49]Ibid., pp. 72-73.

[50]Ministry of Education, "The Place of Welsh and English in the Schools of Wales," London: Her Majesty's Stationery Office, 1953. See also Jones (1966).

[51]See the chapter by Colmán L. O'Huallacháin, O. F. M., "Some Development in the Irish Republic: Language Teaching in Ireland," in Peter Strevens, ed., *Modern Languages in Great Britain and Ireland*, Strasbourg: AIDELA, 1967.

[52]Macnamara (1969), p. 17. See also Macnamara (1966).

[53]Scottish Council for Educational Research, *Gaelic-Speaking Children in Highland Schools*, London 1961.

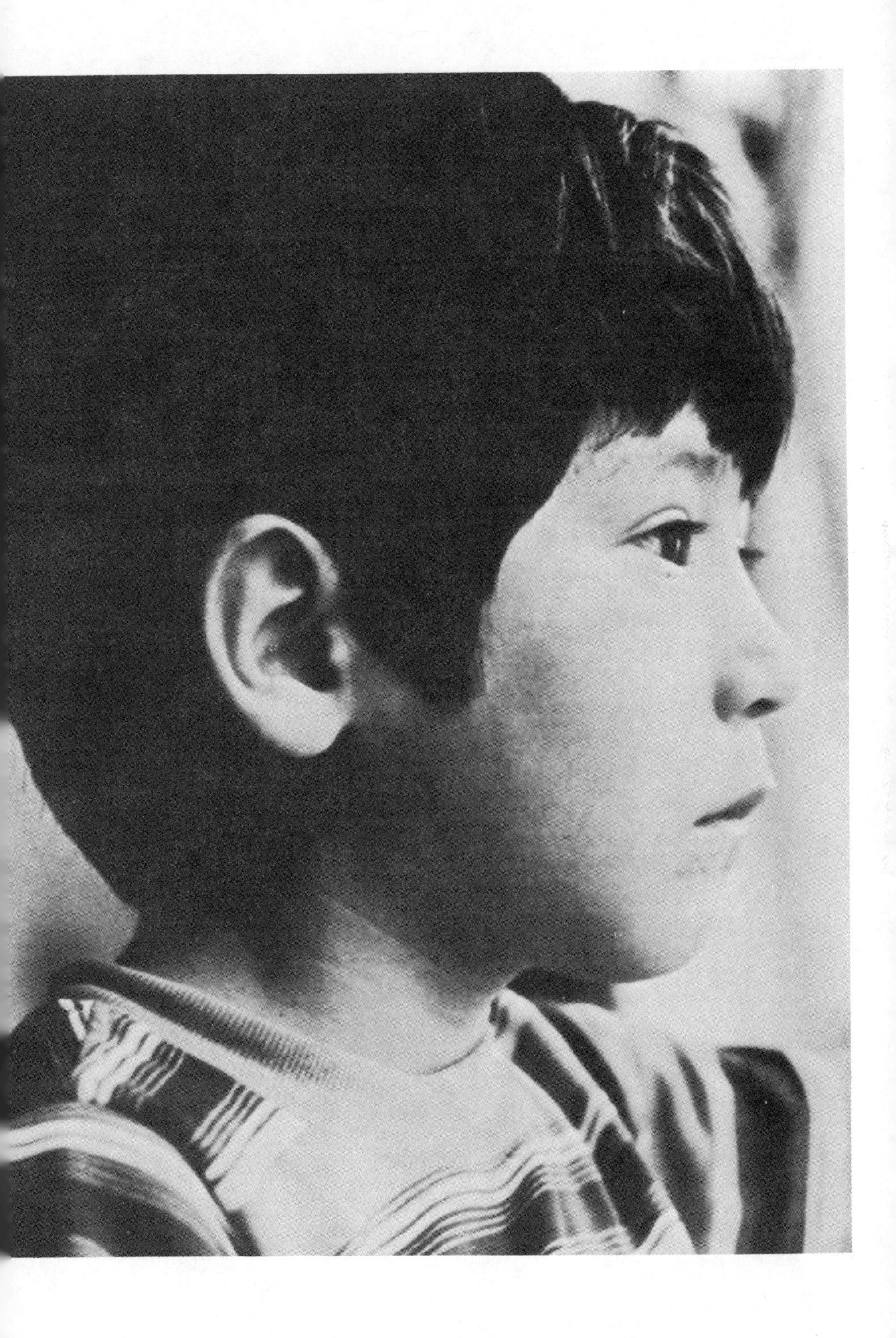

1. This first grader enters a foreign world

2. ...and begins to feel at home
3. A male teacher can enhance education
4. St. Sergius High School, New York City
   Russian-English bilingual education

5. Bilingual education reaches across races and cultures
   at Washington International School,
6. ...United Consolidated School, Laredo, Texas
7. ...The Bilingual School, P.S. 25, New York City
8. A ready answer in a familiar tongue

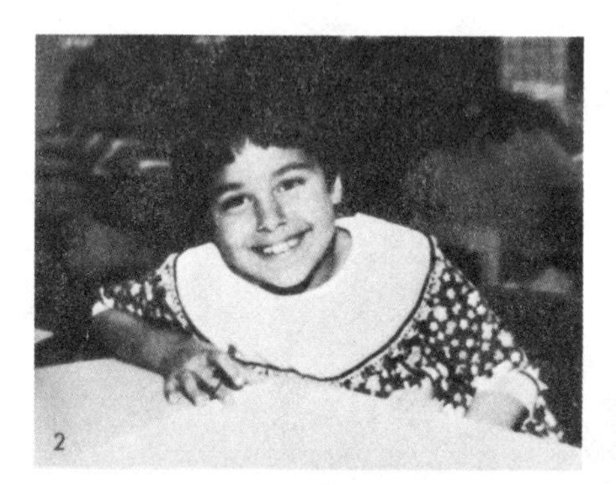

5

6

7

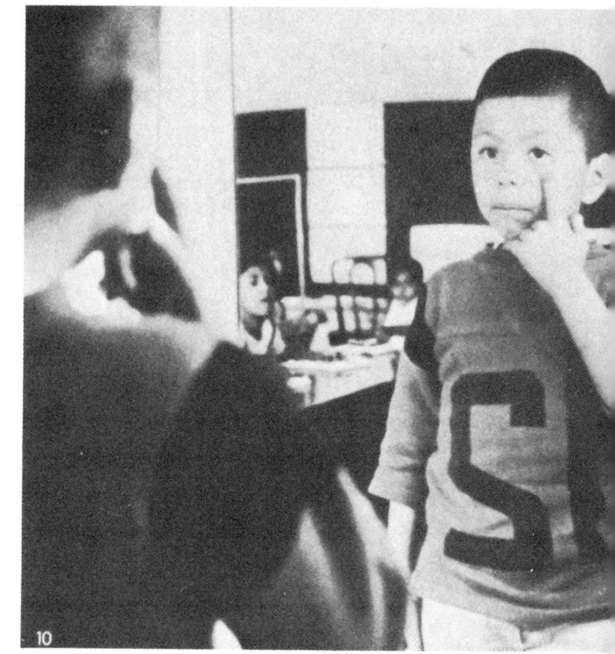

9. Garfield Elementary School Library, Del Rio, Texas, where half the books in Spanish is the aim.
10. Developing self-concept, the value of the individual (Southwest Educational Development Laboratory program: San Antonio, McAllen, etc.
11. Bilingual education is for native English-speaking children
12. ...and for newly arrived students from Mexico (Calexico Union High School, Calexico, Calif.)
13. It is implemented by cooperative planning
14. ....language labs
15. ...dramatization (Lowell Elementary School, San Diego, Calif.)

12

15

16. Rough Rock Demonstration School, Chinle, Arizona where Navajo children embrace two cultures
17. Interest leads to learning
18. And learning has room for dreams

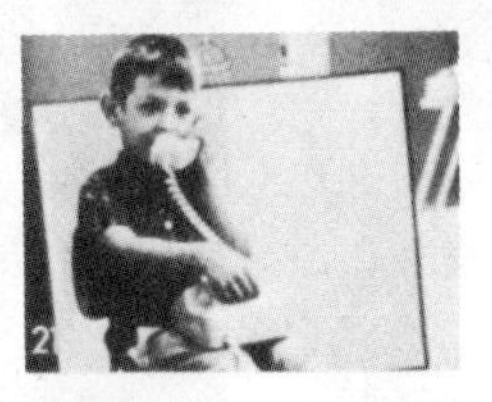

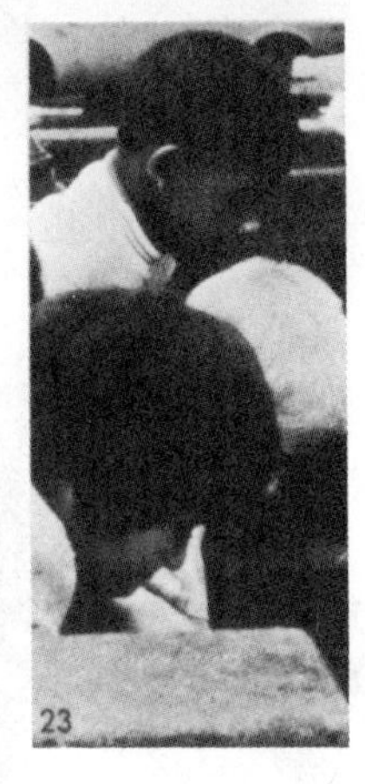

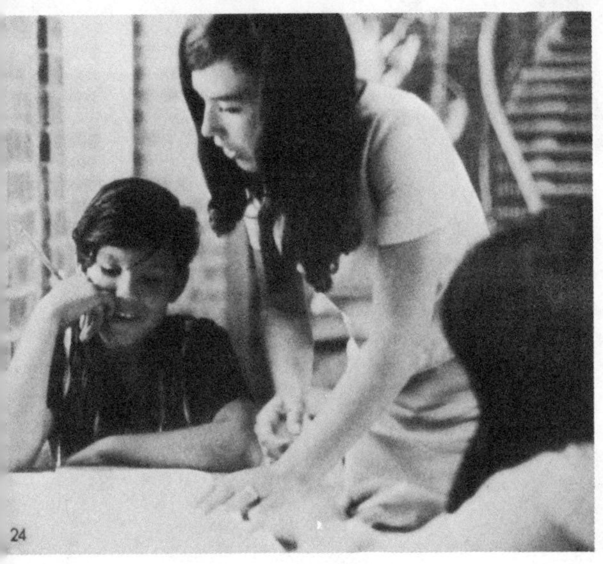

19. The bilingual teacher
20. Introducing bilingual education to the public via television
21. ...to a child through verbal play
22. Videotape helps the teacher learn
23. Common interests cross the barriers
24. A student tutor helps a child (Elbert Covell College, University of Pacific, Stockton, Calif.)

25. Two approaches to mathematics
26. But only one to a good hot meal
27. "How will they treat my children?"
28. At Mesilla Elementary School, Las Cruces, New Mexico, parent involvement helps provide an answer

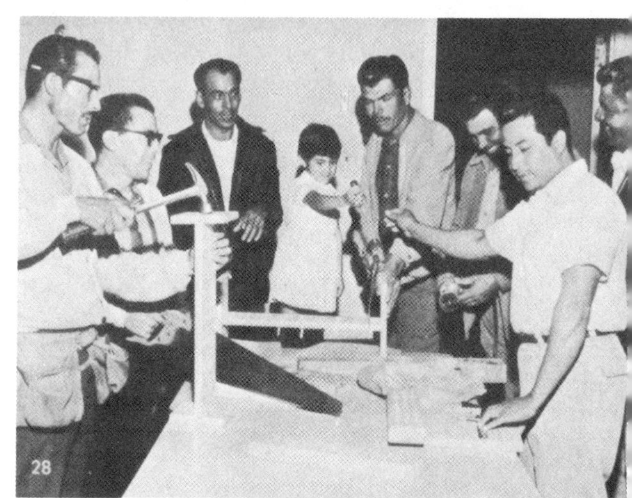

CHAPTER IV

A RATIONALE FOR BILINGUAL SCHOOLING

Current thinking about bilingual schooling is far from uniform, and the wise administrator and school board will seek information representing more than one point of view. Here are the basic questions that are being raised:

Is bilingualism desirable or undesirable? For the nation? For the individual child? If desirable, is it worth the trouble and expense?

Is Bilingualism Desirable or Undesirable for the Nation? This fundamental question comes down eventually to a value judgment, which cannot be pronounced either correct or incorrect except in terms of the particular time and circumstance of a specific nation. William A. Stewart describes two different policies:

1. *The eventual elimination, by education and decree, of all but one language, which remains to serve for both official and general purposes.*

2. *The recognition and preservation of important languages within the national scene, supplemented by universal use of one or more languages to serve for official purposes and for communication across language boundaries.* [1]

For the United States of America in this latter half of the twentieth century the question of desirability for the nation seems almost rhetorical. America's relations, official and unofficial, with almost every country in the world, involving diplomacy, trade, security, technical assistance, health, education, religion, and the arts, are steadily increasing. The success of these international relations often depends on the bilingual skills and cultural sensitiveness of American representatives both here and abroad.[2] In our country, as in every important nation, educated bilingualism is an accepted mark of the elite, a key which opens doors of opportunity far and wide. It seems clear to us that bilingualism is highly desirable for the nation.

Is Bilingualism Desirable or Undesirable for the Individual Child? If the individual child belongs to a high socioeconomic class, the answer is obvious. As in other countries, the elite considers knowledge of other languages essential for participation in international affairs. To argue that children of lower socioeconomic classes will never need to use other languages is in effect to deprive them of the opportunity to become eligible for such participation. In the case of American children who are born into a non-English language, not to give them the education needed to perfect their first language to the point of usefulness amounts to a virtual betrayal of the children's potential. As Bruce Gaarder has said,[3]

> *The most obvious anomaly—or asburdity—of our educational policy regarding foreign language learning is the fact that we spend perhaps a biliion*

dollars a year to teach languages—in the schools, the colleges and universities, the Foreign Service Institute, the Department of Defense, AID, USIA, CIA, etc. (and to a large extent to adults who are too old ever to master a new tongue)—yet virtually no part of the effort goes to maintain and to develop the competence of American children who speak the same languages natively. There are over four million native speakers of French or Spanish in our country and these two languages are the two most widely taught, yet they are the ones for which our Government recognizes the greatest unfilled need (at the levels, for example, of the Foreign Service of the Department of State and the program of lectures and technical specialists sent abroad under the Fulbright-Hays Act).

In the succeeding pages we shall speak of other advantages of bilingualism to the American child, of whatever social class; but the views already suggested leave us with but one conclusion: For the individual child, as for the nation, bilingualism is clearly desirable.

Is Bilingual Schooling Worth the Trouble and Expense? This is a question that each community must decide for itself, just as it must decide about other features of the education it wants for its children. Every school district, we suppose, wants *all* of its children to have *some* education, usually represented by the three R's, plus some acquaintance with the other subjects regularly included in the elementary school curriculum. Some children are considered to be entitled to more education than others. These are recognized by their ability to learn everything the school offers—and more. In their cases, the curriculum may be enriched by additional subjects—e.g., another language—or by greater depth in some of the common learnings.

In the average school setting languages other than English have usually been thought of as foreign, even though they may be the native languages of some of the school's children. Foreign languages have been on the periphery of American public education, generally not to be approached except as an extra or in high school, where they are not so much *learned* by the average student as *studied* for two years. Only the privileged child has an opportunity really to learn another language, either in the exceptional FLES (foreign language in the elementary school) program which enjoys the support of its community or from a "foreign" servant or playmates or from prolonged residence abroad. Many lower or middle-income communities think of other languages in the elementary grades as a frill which, with the rising cost of education, cannot be afforded.

If bilingual schooling is thought of merely as a form of foreign-language education, it already has one strike against it. In the following pages we shall hope to make it plain that though bilingual schooling does involve the learning of two languages, neither is foreign. The non-English-speaking child's home language is his native language, his mother tongue; and English is his second language, to be learned in a special way. As we hope to demonstrate, bilingual schooling is not exclusively either the learning of a "foreign" language or the learning of English—though both of these are involved—; it is rather a new way of conceiving of the whole range of education, especially for the non-English-speaking child who is just entering school. It necessitates rethinking the entire curriculum in terms of the child's best instruments for learning, of his readiness and motivation for learning the various subjects, and of his own identity and potential for growth and development.

It is clear that restructuring the whole educational process will involve both trouble and expense. The authors of this study cannot possibly decide for anyone whether the results promised by proposed educational changes will be worth while. Only after considering such evidence as we hope to adduce in the course of this study can a school district reasonably be expected to make a thoughtful and responsible decision. We make no secret of the fact that our study has led us to believe that certain basic changes in the policy and practice of education for our "bilingual" children *can* bring about significant improvements, not only for the children themselves but for our communities and our country as well.

Rationale

Need for Change. It is perhaps healthy to begin by acknowledging the potent need for change and improvement in the education of our non-English-speaking children. Throughout the length of our educational history we have been aware of this need. The Bureau of Indian Affairs in the Department of the Interior, the United States Office of Education, the State department of education in bilingual areas, and local school districts have all shown their concern by conducting studies and experiments on behalf of non-English-speaking children. We shall cite a single example from the abundant literature: "A Resolution Concerning the Education of Bilingual Children, El Paso, Texas, January 1966,"[4] This document, based on a Texas Education Agency report and on a study by sociologists Browning and McLemore of the University of Texas at Austin, points out such sobering facts as the following:

"The per capita median income of 'Anglos' in Texas in 1959 was $4,137, that of Spanish-surname Texans $2,019."

In 1955-1956 "the average Spanish-surname Texan was—spending three years in the first grade and was dropping out of school before reaching the fifth grade (4.7). This compares with 10.8 school years completed by 'all whites' (which includes Spanish-surname Texans) and 8.1 by 'non-whites' (primarily Negroes and Orientals)."

The Resolution passed by the Southwest Council of Foreign Language Teachers constitutes a capsule rationale for the bilingual education of all the poor of America whose English is non-functional. The reader is invited to see this short document at this point.

The Need for Identity. The non-English-speaking child who has typically lived the critical first five or six years of his life in a language and a culture different from those he encounters as he enters school inevitably suffers a culture shock. To be sure, most administrators and teachers try their best—in English—to make such a child feel comfortable and welcome. However, to the extent that English is the only medium of communication and the child's language is banned from the classroom and playground, he inevitably feels himself to be a stranger. Only as he succeeds in suppressing his language and natural way of behaving, and in assuming a new and unaccustomed role, does he feel the full warmth of approval. In subtle or not so subtle ways he is made to think that his language is inferior to English, that he is inferior to the English-speaking children in school, and that his parents are inferior to English speakers in the community.

His parents find themselves in a similar equivocal situation. Pride in their heritage and a natural sense of dignity make them want to maintain the ancestral language in the home. At the same time, many parents want to do all they can to help their children adjust to school and so they talk English as best they can in the home rather than their native language. Sometimes what results is a mixture of the two, with an inadequate hold on either. The fault here lies less with the parents than with the teacher and schools that misguide them.

The Best Medium for Learning. The school, as the agency whose task it is to organize the best possible education for all children, has an unusual opportunity today "to develop forward-looking approaches" through bilingual schooling. This can be done only if administrators and teachers understand clearly the basic principles involved. In addition to those already mentioned, educators have in recent years come to agree that the best medium, especially for the initial stages of a child's learning, is his dominant language. This was stated categorically by a group of international educators who met in Paris in 1951 to prepare a monograph on fundamental education. In their book, entitled *The Use of Vernacular Languages in Education,*[5] they say "It is axiomatic that the best medium for teaching a child is his mother tongue."[6] Similar findings have been reported by Nancy Modiano[7] following research with three Indian groups in Chiapas.[8] The Summer Institute of Linguistics, which has extensive experience in teaching literacy to so-called primitive peoples, has adopted as regular procedure the teaching of reading and writing first in the mother tongue and then in the national language.[9] In a foreword to the 1964 Bibliography of the Summer Institute of Linguistics in Peru Augusto Tamayo Vargas, Dean of the Faculty of Letters of the University of San Marcos in Lima expressed the satisfaction felt by Peruvians in educational government circles over the results obtained. His words have been translated from Spanish by Mary Ruth Wise.

> *The Summer Institute of Linguistics...has worked in Peru almost twenty years and in those years their work has been so fruitful that the name of the Institute is linked to the work of national literacy and to the spirit of bilingual teaching. For, the members of this Institute, who initiated their work in our country in 1945, have created alphabets for each of the tribal groups of the jungle thereby extending the possibility of reading and writing to isolated tribes; and thanks to their technical ability in teaching, the concept continues to spread that the diverse groups of humanity should receive their first education in their native tongue in order later to offer them the national language, Spanish, as a second mother tongue without losing the first.*

From these reports and others that could be cited educators are agreed that a child's mother tongue is the best normal instrument for learning, especially in the early stages of school, and that reading and writing in the first language should precede literacy in a second. This principle is respected in the educational policy of such bilingual countries as Canada, Finland, Belgium, Switzerland, and the Union of South Africa.[10]

Learning Through English. There is a widespread fear among non-English-speaking ethnic groups in the United States that by beginning their schooling in the home language their children will be retarded in their learning of English. Such evidence as there is points in the opposite direction. There are many examples of young children's ability to learn two or more languages at the same time, as we shall mention later in this chapter. Preliminary research indicates that, provided one of the languages is the mother tongue, children who learn through two languages tend to learn as well or better than those who learn through only one.[11]

First, Second, and Foreign Language. The organizer of a bilingual program in the United States needs to understand clearly the difference between the children's *home* language (also called first language, mother tongue, or vernacular), their *second* language (English), and *foreign* languages. The language into which a non-English-speaking child is born is normally the language which exercises the most important and the durable influence on him; it helps to fashion his basic style of speech and personality. For such a child in the United States, English is usually the second language. The teaching of English as a second language to children whose first language is not English requires a special approach, special techniques, special materials, and special understanding. ESL (English as a second language) techniques are used widely in areas where we have concentrations of non-English-speaking persons. The limited English thus acquired is not for quite some time a sufficient medium for the non-English-speaking child's total learning, but it should be an important component of a well-planned bilingual program.

For many non-English-speaking children in the United States, English may very well initially be altogether foreign, but it has become conventional to refer to it as a second language since it is used actively and officially, even in our bilingual areas. Social scientists tend now to restrict the term "foreign language" to languages not commonly spoken in a given community. Thus, for example, a Spanish-speaking American encounters his first language at birth, may not meet his second language (English) until he begins school at age six, and studies his first foreign language perhaps as a high school subject.

The Best Order for Learning Language Skills. Another important factor in planning a sound bilingual program is the proper ordering of language skills, usually called language arts by elementary-school educators. Just as a child first learns to hear, understand, and speak his own language and then learns to read and write it, so should he learn his second language in the same way.

What has not been sufficiently understood in the past is that a Spanish-speaking child who has lived his first five or six years in a Spanish-speaking family and community is "ready" to learn to read and write *in Spanish but not in English.* A teacher who fails to take advantage of his "readiness" and to teach him how to read and write his mother tongue without delay is missing a golden opportunity.

The Factor of Age. Recent research confirms what perceptive educators have long known, that the human infant is a surprising learner. "Psychologist Benjamin Bloom estimates that about 50 percent of mature intelligence is developed by age four and another 30 percent by age eight. Some psychologists doubt whether any amount of remedial work later on will enable a child to develop intellectually to his full potential if he does not receive the proper stimulation at the proper time–that is, very young."[12]

We cite this arresting quotation, for it underlines what is coming to be accepted more and more as a truism by educational theorists, namely, that formal schooling normally begins at an age when much of the learning potential of a child has already been lost. Realizing that the early-learning movement is accelerating rapidly, New York City school officials are experimenting with two-year-olds. "The earlier we get youngsters," says one administrator, "the better chances of their doing will in school later."[13] The results of early investigation are so promising that bilingual program planners would do well to include infants and preschool children in their designs.

Early Language Learning. We are coming to realize the unsuspected capacity of infants and young children for learning in general, but their extraordinary capacity for the learning of languages, both the mother tongue and other languages, has long been common knowledge.

We cannot explain how man developed language, thus setting himself apart from the other animals, and we never cease to wonder at the infant's skill in mastering his mother tongue. Less well known is the fact that the vocal noises which the infant enjoys producing far transcend the limits of the community language. After making a number of sample recordings of the vocalizations of a single infant in the first year of life, Charles Osgood observes that "within the data for the first two months of life may be found all of the speech sounds that the human vocal system can produce."[14] This fact has enormous implications for the proponents of bilingual schooling. Linguists are agreed that by the age of about five and one-half the average child has mastered most of the sound system and much of the basic structure of his language, as well as a sufficient vocabulary to participate fully in the activities of immediate concern to him.

Another indication of the child's fantastic learning power is the size of his vocabulary. Mary Katherine Smith, using the Seashore-Eckerson English Recognition Vocabulary Test, found that "for grade one, the average number of basic words known was 16,900, with a range from 5,500 to 48,800."[15] Henry D. Rinsland, using written sources supplemented by children's conversation, counted 5,099 different words used by first graders as an active vocabulary out of 353,874 running words.[16]

In learning additional languages, too, young children astonish adolescents and adults, who have so much difficulty acquiring their second language. A well-known example of children's plurilingualism in a multilingual societal setting is that cited by British psychologist J. W. Tomb: "It is common experience in the district in Bengal in which the writer resided to hear English children three or four years old who have been born in the country conversing freely at different times with their parents in English, with their *ayahs* (nurses) in Bengali, with the garden coolies in Santali, and with the house-servants in Hindustani, while their parents have learned with the aid of a *munshi* (teacher) and much laborious effort just sufficient Hindustani to comprehend what the house-servants are saying (provided they do not speak too quickly) and to issue simple orders to them connected with domestic affairs. It is even not unusual to see English parents in India unable to understand what their servants are saying to them in Hindustani and being driven in consequence to bring along an English child of four or five years old, if available, to act as interpreter."[17]

Missionary families are a particularly rich source of examples to illustrate children's language learning ability. "One American missionary family in Vietnam tells this story: When they went out to Vietnam, they were three, father, mother, and four-year-old daughter. Shortly after their arrival a son was born. The parents' work took them on extended trips to the interior of the country, at which times they left their children in the care of a Vietnamese housekeeper and a nursemaid. When the time came for the young son to talk, he did in fact talk, but in Vietnamese. Suddenly, the parents realized that they could not even communicate with their son except by using their daughter as an interpreter."[18]

According to Dr. Wilder Penfield, the distinguished former Director of the Montreal Nuerological Institute, "A child who is exposed to two or three languages during the ideal period for language learning pronounces each with the accent of his teacher. If he hears one language at home, another at school, and a third perhaps from a governess in a nursery, he is not aware that he is learning three languages at all. He is aware of the fact that to get what he wants from the governess he must speak one way and with the teacher he must speak in another way. He has not reasoned it out at all.

In his biography of the Canadian Prime Minister, Louis St. Laurent, Bruce Hutchison quotes the former Prime Minister as follows, "'I thought,' he used to say in later years, 'that everybody spoke to his father in French and his mother in English.'"[20]

From these examples, and from many others that could be found, educators may safely conclude that the learning of two languages does not constitute an undue expectation of children, especially very young children.[21]

Language and Culture. "Study of the history and culture associated with a student's mother tongue is considered an integral part of *bilingual education.*" This quotation from the Guidelines to the Bilingual Education Program emphasizes the relation of language to culture. Language is only one of the important parts of the characteristic behavior of a people bound together in one culture. It is closely connected with a particular way of feeling, thinking, and acting, and it is rooted in and reflects a commonly accepted set of values. Educators need to remember that a child born into a Spanish-speaking family in the Southwest, a Navajo child born on the reservation in Arizona, a Franco-American child born into a French-speaking family in Northern Maine, and a Chinese child born into a Cantonese-speaking family in San Francisco all enter different worlds, worlds which are organized and presented through the grid of the particular language that they hear about them and that they acquire. There is, therefore, an intimate relationship between the child, his family, his community, their language, and their view of the world. How to harmonize these with American English and with prevailing American culture patterns without damaging the self-image of a non-English-speaking child is the challenge. It is not a minor one.

Bilingualism, Biculturalism, and the Community. Bilingual education can provide one important means of building out of varied ethnic elements a harmonious and creative community. It is not enough for educators to understand the principles on which a solid bilingual program must be built; they must also create understanding throughout the community concerning the important connection between one's mother tongue, one's self-image, and one's heritage (both individual and group-cultural). One can hardly despise or depreciate any people's language without depreciating the people themselves. As forty-nine Scandinavian professors, assembled in 1962, so eloquently said: "L'extermination d'une langue, d'une culture et d'un peuple sont une seule et même chose."[22] (The extermination of a language, of a culture, and of a people are all one and the same thing.)

Wherever the vicious circle begins, it is the community as a whole or the nation as a whole that suffers the consequences. Both those responsible for the administration of the schools and those who exert leadership in the community must search their consciences before deciding what kind of education to provide. The non-English-speaking child who at the beginning of school is unable to acquire literacy in English in competition with his English-speaking classmates and who is not permitted to acquire it in his own language makes a poor beginning that he may never be able to overcome. Frustrated and discouraged, he seeks the first opportunity to drop out of school; and if he finds a job at all it will be the lowest paying job. He will be laid off first, will remain unemployed longest, and is least able to adapt to changing occupational requirements.

The Bilingual Education Act was conceived to rectify certain obvious educational defects of the past. But educational discrimination is but one aspect of the ills which characterize our still far from perfect society; and the building of a better education system, resting on a full recognition of many languages and cultures can be expected to make only a modest start toward our full knowledge and acceptance of ourselves for the vast multifarious unhomogeneous nation that we are.

To summarize, a rationale for bilingual schooling in the United States rests on the following proposition:

1. American schooling has not met the needs of children coming from homes where non-English languages are spoken; a radical improvement is therefore urgently needed.
2. Such improvement must first of all maintain and strengthen the sense of identity of children entering the school from such homes.
3. The self-image and sense of dignity of families that speak other languages must also be preserved and strengthened.
4. The child's mother tongue is not only an essential part of his sense of identity; it is also his best instrument for learning, especially in the early stages.
5. Preliminary evidence indicates that initial learning through a child's non-English home language does not hinder learning in English or other school subjects.
6. Differences among first, second, and foreign languages need to be understood if learning through them is to be sequenced effectively.
7. The best order of the learning of basic skills in a language–whether first or second–needs to be understood and respected if best results are to be obtained; this order is normally, especially for children: listening comprehension, speaking, reading, and writing.
8. Young children have an impressive learning capacity; especially in the case of language learning, the young child learns more easily and better than adolescents of adults the sound system, the basic structure, and vocabulary of a language.
9. Closely related to bilingualism is biculturalism, which should be an integral part of bilingual instruction.
10. Bilingual education holds the promise of helping to harmonize various ethnic elements in a community into a mutually respectful and creative pluralistic society.

Another Rationale

We have represented a brief rationale in the form of a Resolution Concerning the Education of Bilingual Children and have sketched the main points which we consider essential to its understanding. We want in conclusion to present another viewpoint, that of A. Bruce Gaarder, a trilingual whose study of bilingual education has been long and intense. The statement which he presented to Senator Yarborough's Special Subcommittee on Bilingual Education on May 18, 1967 is a complete rationale in itself. We reproduce it herewith except for one paragraph, which we have quoted earlier in this chapter.

Prepared Statement of A. Bruce Gaarder,
Chief, Basic Studies Branch,
Division of College Programs, Bureau of
Educational Personnel Development,
U. S. Office of Education[23]

Mr. Chairman and members of the subcommittee, there were in 1960 about five million persons of school age (6-18) in the United States who had a non-English mother tongue. It is reliably estimated that over three million of this group did in fact retain the use of that tongue. In this group of school children who still use the non-English mother tongue, there are 1.75 million Spanish-speakers, about 77,000 American Indians, and slightly over a million from some 30 additional language groups: French, German, Polish, Czech, Yiddish, Ukrainian, and many others. The situation is not known to have changed notably since 1960. These are the children we are concerned with, plus another million or so in the same category under six years of age and soon to enter the schools. They are necessarily and unavoidably bilingual children.

Bilingualism can be either a great asset or a great liability. In our schools millions of these youngsters have been cheated or damaged or both by well-intentioned but ill-informed educational policies which have made of their bilingualism an ugly disadvantage in their lives. The object of this testimony is to show the nature of the damage that has been done and suggest how it can be remedied in the future.

Bilingual education means the use of both English and another language—usually the child's mother tongue—as mediums of instruction in the schools. It is not "foreign language teaching" but rather the use of each language to teach all of the school curriculum (except, of course, the other language itself). There are five main reasons which support bilingual education. The first three apply to the child's years in the elementary school:

1. Children who enter school with less competence in English than monolingual English-speaking children will probably become retarded in their school work to the extent of their deficiency in English, if English is the sole medium of instruction. On the other hand, the bilingual child's conceptual development and acquisition of other experience and information could proceed at a normal rate if the mother tongue were used as an alternate medium of instruction. Retardation is not likely if there is only one or very few non-English-speaking children in an entire school. It is almost inevitable if the non-English language is spoken by large groups of children.
2. Non-English-speaking children come from non-English-speaking homes. The use of the child's mother tongue by some of the teachers and as a school language is necessary if there is to be a strong, mutually reinforcing relationship between the home and the school.
3. Language is the most important exteriorization or manifestation of the self, of the human personality. If the school, the all-powerful school, rejects the mother tongue of an entire group of children, it can be expected to affect seriously and adversely those children's concept of their parents, their homes, and of themselves.

The other two reasons apply when the bilingual child becomes an adult:

4. If he has not achieved reasonable literacy in his mother tongue—ability to read, write, and speak it accurately—it will be virtually useless to him for any technical or professional work where language matters. Thus, his unique potential career advantage, his bilingualism, will have been destroyed.
5. Our people's native competence in Spanish and French and Czech and all the other languages and the cultural heritage each language transmits are a national resource

that we need badly and must conserve by every reasonable means.

I will return later to most of these points.

There is a vast body of writing by educators who believe that bilingualism is a handicap. The evidence seems at first glance to be obvious and incontrovertible. There is a clear, direct chain relationship between language competence, formal education, and economic status among Americans whose mother tongue is not English. The children speak Spanish, or Navajo, or French, and they do poorly in school: therefore, (so goes the argument) their bilingualism is to blame. Many researchers have established a decided correlation between bilingualism and low marks on intelligence tests, but what no research has shown is that bilingualism, per se, is a *cause* of low performance on intelligence tests. On the contrary, studies which have attempted to take into account all of the factors which enter the relationship show that it is not the fact of bilingualism but *how* and *to what extent* and *under what conditions* the two languages are taught that make the difference. (If this were not true, how could one explain the fact that the governing and intellectual elite in all countries have sought to give their children bilingual or even multi-lingual education?) Much of the literature on bilingualism does not deal at all with bilingual education. Rather it shows the unfortunate results when the child's mother tongue is ignored, deplored or otherwise degraded.

The McGill University psychologists, Lambert and Peale (now Anisfeld) have shown that if the bilingualism is "balanced." i.e., if there has been something like equal, normal, literacy developed in the two languages, bilingual 19-year-olds in Montreal are markedly superior to monolinguals on verbal and non-verbal tests of intelligence and appear to have greater mental flexibility, a superiority in concept formation, and a more diversified set of mental abilities. It is their judgment that there is no evidence that the supposed "handicap" of bilingualism is *caused* by bilingualsim, per se, and that "it would be more fruitful to seek that cause in the inadequacy of the measuring instrument and in other variables such as socioeconomic status, attitude toward the two languages, and educational policy and practice regarding the teaching of both languages."

There is an educational axiom, accepted virtually everywhere else in the world, that "the best medium for teaching a child is his mother tongue." What happens when the mother tongue is so used? A recent study made in Chiapas, Mexico, by Dr. N. Modiano for the New York University School of Education shows the results that can be expected. The Modiano research examined the hypothesis (implicit in current educational policies throughout the United States) that children of linguistic minorities learn to read English with greater comprehension when all reading instruction is offered through English than when they first learn to read in their non-English mother tongue.

The investigation involved all students attending 26 schools in three Indian *municipios* in Chiapas. All students were native speakers of either Tzeltal or Tzotzil, two of the indigenous languages of Mexico. Thirteen were Federal or State schools in which all reading instruction was offered in Spanish. Thirteen were National Indian Institute schools in which literacy was developed in the mother tongue prior to being attempted in Spanish. The purpose of the study was to determine which group of schools produced the greater measure of literacy (specifically, greater reading comprehension) in the national language, Spanish.

Two indications of reading comprehension were obtained. First, all teachers were asked to designate "all of your students who are able to understand what they read in Spanish." Approximately 20 percent of the students in the all-Spanish Federal and State schools were nominated by their teachers as being able to understand what they were asked to read in Spanish. Approximately 37 percent of the students in the bilingual Institute schools were nominated by their teachers as being able to understand what they read in Spanish. The difference favors the bilingual approach beyond the .001 level of probability.

Then, a carefully devised group reading comprehension test was administered to all of the selected children. The children's average score in State and Federal schools was 41.59; in the bilingual institute schools it was 50.30. The difference between these means was found to be significant at beyond the .01 level of probability. Within each of the three *municipios* mean scores in Institute schools were higher than in Federal and State schools. Thus, not only did the teachers using the bilingual approach nominate more of their students for testing, but their judgment was confirmed by the fact that their students scored significantly higher on the group test of reading comprehension.

In Puerto Rico, in 1925, the International Institute of Teachers College, Columbia University, made a study of the educational system on that island, where English was the major medium of instruction despite the fact that the children's mother tongue is Spanish. The Columbia University group undertook a testing program to measure pupil achievement in all grades and particularly to explore the relative effectiveness of learning through each of the two language mediums. To test reading, arithmetic, information, language, and spelling they used the Stanford Achievement Test in its regular English version and in a Spanish version modified to fit Puerto Rican conditions. Over 69,000 tests were given.

The results were displayed on charts so as to reveal graphically any significant difference between achievement through English and achievement through Spanish. Both of these could be compared on the same charts with the average achievement of children in schools in the continental United States. I will summarize the findings in two sentences:

1. In comparison with children in the continental United States, the Puerto Ricans' achievement through English showed them to be markedly retarded.
2. The Puerto Rican children's achievement through Spanish was, by and large, markedly superior to that of continental United States children, who were using their own mother tongue, English.

The Columbia University reserachers, explaining the astonishing fact that those elementary school children in Puerto Rico—poverty-stricken, backward, "benighted," beautiful

Puerto Rico—achieved more through Spanish than continental United States children did through English, came to the following conclusion, one with extraordinary implications for us here:

Spanish is much more easily learned as a native language than is English.

The facility with which Spanish is learned makes possible the early introduction of content into the primary curriculum.

Every effort should be made to maintain it and to take the fullest advantage of it as a medium of school instruction.

What they were actually saying is that because Spanish has a much better writing system than English (i.e., the writing system matches the sound system) speakers of Spanish can master reading and writing very quickly and can begin to acquire information from the printed page more easily and at an earlier age.

The conclusion is, in sum, that if the Spanish-speaking children of our Southwest were given all of their schooling through both Spanish and English, there is a strong likelihood that not only would their so-called handicap of bilingualism disappear, but *they would have a decided advantage over their English-speaking schoolmates, at least in elementary school, because of the excellence of the Spanish writing system*. There are no "reading problems," as we know them, among school children in Spanish-speaking countries.

And their English could be better too, but that's another story.

American Samoa, with about 20,000 people, is an example of what is meant when children, in communities which have a high degree of linguistic solidarity, are required to study through a language not their own. In American Samoa the home language of the native people is Samoan, and they cling to it tenaciously, even to the extent of providing their children both after-school and weekend instruction in Samoan. In 1963 the Science Research Associates high school placement tests were given to 535 graduates of Samoan junior high schools, i.e., pupils who had completed the ninth grade. The median grade placement score was 5.8, i.e., close to the end of the fifth grade. Only 21 of the 535 pupils scored 9.0, i.e., in the ninth grade, or better. Most of the 21 had studied in the United States or had other unusual advantages. The author of one report judged that one obstacle to the learning of English was the Samoan's pride in their own culture.

. . . .

The establishment of bilingual education programs in our schools could be expected to increase and improve, rather than lessen, emphasis on the proper teaching of English to children who speak another mother tongue. Under our present policy, which supports the ethnocentric illusion that English is not a "foreign" language for anyone in this country, it is almost always taught as if the bilingual child already knew English. Our failure to recognize the mother tongue and thus to present English *as a second language* helps to produce "functional illiteracy" in almost three out of every four Spanish speakers in Texas.

In a bilingual education program, English would be taught from the child's first day in school but his concept development, his acquisition of information and experience—in sum, his total *education*—would not depend on his imperfect knowledge of English. Bilingual education permits making a clear distinction between education and language, i.e., between the content of education and the vehicle through which it is acquired.

I use the example of two window panes, the green-tinted Spanish one and the blue-tinted English one, both looking out on the same world, the same reality. We tell the little child who has just entered the first grade, "You have two windows onto the world, the Spanish one and the English one. Unfortunately, your English window hasn't been built yet, but we're going to work on it as fast as we can and in a few years, maybe, it'll be as clear and bright as your Spanish window. Meantime, even if you don't see much, keep on trying to look out the space where the blue one will be. And stay away from the green one! It's against our educational policy to look through anything tinted green!"

The influx of Spanish-speaking Cuban refugee children into Florida in recent years brought about the establishment of two model bilingual education programs in the Dade County (Miami) public schools. The first is essentially a period a day of Spanish language arts instruction at all grade levels for native speakers of Spanish. It was established, according to educators, there, "because it did not seem right not to do something to maintain and develop these children's native language." The second program is a model bilingual public elementary school (Coral Way) which is now finishing its fourth year of operation. This highly successful school provides us with information on three points of great importance in the present context:

1. At the fifth grade level the children have been found—insofar as this can be determined by achievement testing—to be able to learn equally well through either of their two languages. (This is a level of achievement that cannot be expected in even our best college-level foreign language programs.)
2. Since half of the children are Cubans and half begin as monolingual speakers of English, each learning the other's language and his own, it is apparent that a truly comprehensive bilingual education program can serve not only the non-English mother tongue children *who must necessarily become bilingual*, but also the ordinary monolingual American child who speaks nothing but English and *whose parents want him to become bilingual.*
3. The strength of the program lies in the high quality of the teachers of both languages (all of them native and highly trained speakers of the language in which they teach) and the fullness of the support they get from the school administration and the community. The implications of these three points are momentous.

RECOMMENDATIONS

That comprehensive programs of bilingual education in self-selected schools and for self-selected pupils at all grade levels be supported.

2. That the opportunity to profit from bilingual education be extended to children of all non-English-speaking groups. All are now losers under our present educational one-language policy: at worst they become hopelessly retarded in school; at best they lose the advantage of mastery of their mother tongue.

3. That adequate provision be made for training and otherwise securing teachers capable of using the non-English tongue as a medium of instruction.

4. That there be provisions for cooperative efforts by the public schools and the non-English ethnic organizations which have thus far worked unaided and unrecognized to maintain two-language competence in their children.

5. That provision be made for safeguarding the quality of the bilingual education programs which receive Federal financial assistance.

NOTES

[1]"An Outline of Linguistic Typologies for Describing Multilingualism," in *Study of the Role of Second Languages in Asia, Africa, and Latin America*. Center for Applied Linguistics, Washington, D. C., 1962, p. 15.

[2]See for example William R. Parker, *The National Interest and Foreign Languages*, 3rd ed., Washington, D. C.: U. S. Government Printing Office, 1961.

[3]United States Congress. Senate. *Bilingual Education*. Hearings...., p. 54.

[4]See Appendix G.

[5]UNESCO (1953).

[6]Ibid., p. 11.

[7]"National or Mother Language in Beginning Reading: A Comparative Study," *Research in the Teaching of English*, Vol. I., No. 2 (Spring 1968), pp. 32-43.

[8]See Bruce Gaarder's account of this significant experiment later in this chapter.

[9]Dr. Benjamin F. Elson, Director of the Summer Institute of Linguistics, reported at the Chicago Conference that the SIL works with some 430 aboriginal and minority group languages (30 in the United States and Canada) in 20 countries. The usual procedure is (1) to make a linguistic and cultural study, (2) to devise alphabets and produce primers and readers (including a translation of the New Testament), and (3) to organize educational programs in cooperation with the government, beginning with literacy in the local language and moving to literacy in the national language.

[10]Joshua Fishman reminds us, however, that in most schools a variety of the mother tongue is used which is different from that spoken in the home (e.g., High German rather than Swiss German in the German parts of Switzerland and French French rather than Canadian French in French Canada).

[11]Mabel Wilson Richardson (1968) reports as follows concerning the Coral Way School in Miami: "The bilingual program of study was relatively as effective for both English and Spanish-speaking subjects as the regular curriculum in achieving progress in the language arts and in arithmetic....

"It must be noted here that, in addition to performing as well as the control group in the regular curriculum, the English-speaking pupils were learning a second language and the Spanish-speaking pupils were learning to read and write their native language."

Bertha Alicia Gámez Treviño (1968) found that children in the Nye School, United Consolidated Independent School District, outside Laredo, Texas, both English-speaking and

Spanish-speaking, learn mathematics better bilingually (in English and Spanish) than they do in English alone.

[12]Carnegie Corporation of New York, *Carnegie Quarterly*, Vol. XVII, No. 1 (Winter 1969), p. 1.

[13]*Newsweek*, January 29, 1968, p. 48.

[14]Osgood, *Method and Theory in Experimental Psychology,* p. 684.

[15]"Measurement of the Size of General English Vocabulary Through the Elementary Grades and High School." *Genetic Psychology Monograph*, Vol. XXIV, Second Half (November 1941), pp. 343-344.

[16]*A Basic Vocabulary of Elementary School Children*, p. 12.

[17]"On the Intuitive Capacity of Children to Understand Spoken Languages," *British Journal of Psychology*, Vol. XVI, Part 1 (July 1925), p. 52.

[18]Theodore Andersson, *Foreign Languages in the Elementary School: A Struggle Against Mediocrity*, p. 42.

[19]Penfield, Wilder, G. and Lamar Roberts, *Speech and Brain-Mechanisms*, Princeton, New Jersey: Princeton University Press, 1959, p. 253.

[20]*Mr. Prime Minister, 1876-1964*, p. 288.

[21]For similar findings in school settings see Mildred R. Donoghue, "Foreign Languages in the Elementary School: Effects and Instructional Arrangements According to Research," *ERIC Focus Reports on the Teaching of Foreign Languages*, No. 3, 1969 MLA/ACTFL Materials Center, 62 Fifth Avenue, New York, New York 10011.

[22]Naert, Pierre, and Halldór Halldórsson, et al., "Appel d'un ensemble de profusseurs des universités scandinaves en faveur de groupes ethniques et de langues menacées de disparition," *Revue de psychologie des Peuples,* Vol. XVII, (1962), p. 355.

[23]United States Congress. Senate. *Bilingual Education*. Hearings Before the Special Subcommittee on Bilingual Education of the Committee on Labor and Public Welfare, United States Senate, Ninetieth Congress, First Session, on S. 428, A Bill to Amend the Elementary and Secondary Education Act of 1965 in Order to Provide Assistance to Local Educational Agencies in Establishing Bilingual American Education Programs, and to Provide Certain Other Assistance to Promote Such Programs. Part 1, May 18, 19, 26, 29, and 31, 1967. Printed for the use of the Committee on Labor and Public Welfare. Washington, D. C.: United States Government Printing Office, 1967, pp. 51-55.

CHAPTER V

PLANNING A BILINGUAL PROGRAM

The present chapter is addressed primarily to the local school board, the school administration, and the teaching staff, in a community that has a concentration of non-English speakers in its population. These non-English speakers represent both a responsibility and a potential educational resource. Just how the local education agency meets this responsibility and exploits this resource depends on the attitude and conscience of the community. Some ethnic groups, whatever their true feelings, make little display of interest in maintaining their mother tongue; others are clamoring for this right. The question of whether or not to establish a program of bilingual schooling should be faced by the board and the superintendent without waiting for the community to take the initiative and, most certainly, before they are forced to do so by public pressure.

Study Committee

Once the school board is convinced that there is in the community a strong potential for bilingual education, a suitable first step is to appoint a broadly representative committee to study the feasibility of such schooling. This committee should include educators and laymen, representatives of both ethnic groups, enthusiastic proponents of bilingual schooling and complete skeptics, and able persons with open minds, willing to consider evidence. Depending on the local situation, the board may wish to invite the cooperation of the city council and representative civic or ethnic organizations. Care must be taken to insure a serious, non-partisan study and to avoid a political power struggle.

In instructing the committee the board ought to request a comprehensive study of the local non-English-speaking population, including number of speakers, socioeconomic distribution, educational achievement of various age groups, and attitude toward education. As it begins its study, the committee may wish to take a sampling of public opinion to serve as a guide in its deliberations. It may be necessary to explain to the public the basic issues concerning bilingual education and thus provide a basis for an objective expression of public opinion at the conclusion of the study. In addition to doing a good deal of background reading, the committee will want to visit representative bilingual programs and consult knowledgeable educators. In its final report the committee should assay the potential public support for bilingual schooling, the cost of a program, the sources of financial support, and the availability of adequate instructional resources.

If, after all the evidence has been considered, the committee reports a negative attitude on the part of the community, the school board may simply want to accept the report and await a more favorable occasion.

Advisory Committee

If, on the other hand, the committee recommends a bilingual program as desirable and the school board concurs in this finding, several steps are indicated which would lead ultimately to the implementation of this recommendation. The first of these is the appointment of an advisory committee on bilingual schooling, which, like the study committee, should consist of both educators and laymen and representatives of both the English and non-English groups. It might even be possible to convert the study committee into an advisory committee or at least to retain certain members on the new board. The advisory committee's function would be threefold. (1) Beginning where the study committee has left off, it would assist the school administration in defining the goals of a bilingual program in such a way as best to serve the needs and aspirations of the community; and periodically it should review and, if necessary, redefine these goals. (2) It should help interpret the program to the community and thus assure the school administration of maximal public support. (3) It should be sensitive to doubts in the community and should itself raise questions, when needed, concerning the conduct of the program.

Program Coordinator

A natural next step is the appointment of a program coordinator. Such a coordinator should be a bilingual educator, either a native speaker of the ethnic language of the community who also has a good command of English or a native speaker of English who has a good command of the non-English language and a sympathetic understanding of the culture of the community. He should also be sensitive to public relations and to the demands of the position, realizing that it will involve children, schools, curriculum design, evaluation, and research. His training should have included work in sociology, linguistics, anthropology, and psychology. And, adds one of our collaborators, he should have a tendency to be lucky in the things he undertakes to do.

The coordinator's responsibility is to implement the basic policy which has been determined by the school board and the school administration as a result of the findings of the study committee and the recommendations of the advisory committee. For maximum efficiency, the coordinator and the teaching staff should, from the beginning, participate in the planning and preparation of a bilingual program. If the coordinator and bilingual teachers are not already on the staff as plans are taking shape, they should be appointed at the earliest possible moment.

As soon as the coordinator has become familiar with the situation and has won the confidence of his colleagues, both above and below him in the hierarchy, he should take more initiative in proposing possible improvements in the program. Questions to be reconsidered frequently are the following: (1) Are the goals of the program soundly based? (2) Is the community kept informed, and are parents and other volunteers invited to participate in the program? (3) Can the program be improved? What are the best teaching arrangements? What are the best materials, in English and in the other language? Is the program experimentally designed? Are plans for evaluation adequate? Is there primary concern for quality?

A special word of caution is advisable on this last point. It is natural that once the school administration, teaching staff, and community are enthusiastic about the prospect of a bilingual program they should want to extend it to as many children as possible. Bilingual schooling is for most communities a totally new undertaking. Initial mistakes are inevitable and ample provision should be made for their easy correction, because a major failure could have profound repercussions in the community. As between quantity and quality, the latter is by all odds to be preferred. Therefore, the school authorities may wish to limit the initial operation to preschool or to preschool and first grade. They may decide to do this on a pilot basis in one school first. However it is done, the matter of quality should be carefully controlled.

Another task for which the coordinator is primarily responsible is the recruitment of bilingual teachers; teacher aides; and specialists in curriculum design, materials development, and evaluation. Bilingual librarians, nurses, guidance counselors, and public relations specialists will also be needed, but these can be shared with other parts of the school program.

The bilingual staff, or as many of them as can be appointed in advance, will need a long period for the preparation of the program–from six months to a year, at least. During this period arrangements for housing the program will have to be completed; personnel appointments made; a complete curriculum designed; plans for evaluation made; library orders processed; materials selected, adapted, or created for teaching and testing; and much more. Parents and as many volunteers as can be interested should be involved in plans and preparations.

There might well be a place for such volunteers in producing a body of written material in the ethnic language, writing down oral literature and folklore, and the like. There may be a special place for the older generation, to produce in writing (or on tape so that it can be transcribed) some of the wisdom of the cultural group and autobiographical material which gives something of the local history.

One minor but significant contribution would consist of sheets, a booklet, or an anthology of literature written by authors belonging to the non-English group. The contents might range from poems and short stories to documents of local relevance, e.g., letters written a century ago and the like. Spicing bilingual instruction with local and regional compositions written in the non-English language can be an effective means of awakening ethnic pride and of removing the reproach that this particular language is bound up with "foreignness."[1]

Full information should be planned for the news media, a newsletter prepared, and descriptive statements of the program written for distribution to inquirers. On the coordinator too will fall the main burden for making personal visits to key people in the community, giving public talks, appearing on TV programs, keeping in close touch with the advisory committee, and much more.

The principle of accountability to the public should be established early and maintained throughout the program.

Having made these preparations, the school administration is ready for its first year of operation, which should be clearly labeled experimental. Every effort should be exerted to maintain flexibility, so that changes may be made with a minimum of disruption. At the end of the first year, following a complete evaluation—which at this early stage can only be indicative, not conclusive—a decision should be made whether to continue the program on an experimental basis for a second year, to declare the experimental period over, or to abandon the project altogether.

Since planning should not stop with the launching of a program, let us consider in some detail a few of the elements of the program we have already mentioned.

Public Information

The most basic need is to foster a positive public attitude. A public that does not believe in bilingual schooling will not support it, and the public cannot be expected to believe without having the *facts* and some interpreting. Public information is therefore an important and continuing need of any successful program.

The bilingual coordinator can perhaps undertake this reporting function if the school system is small. In a large school system a special information officer would have to be appointed to assume this responsibility.

The need of reporting is especially acute in the case of a bilingual community. As John M. Hickman has remarked in an article, "Wherever there is bilingualism there will always be a certain degree of separation between knowledge and conduct...."[1a] In such a situation the information officer serves not only as the interpreter of the program to the public but also of one ethnic group to the other.

A satisfactory technique for handling information naturally includes two-way communication. More important even than getting accurate information to the public is listening for public reaction. Suggestions, criticisms, and complaints can be helpful if they are carefully studied by the competent authorities and responsible replies are made either to the individual critics or to the public at large.

Parental Involvement

Some of the most successful and secure programs we have observed are those in which parents are most intimately involved. At the same time we have heard complaints that non-English-speaking parents will not attend PTA meetings or other school activities. There are of course reasons for this. The school administration, bilingual coordinator and staff, and the advisory committee can perhaps overcome this reticence by analyzing the situation and taking the proper measures. We are told that meetings held on Sunday afternoon and conducted in the language of the parents are often successful. Real involvement can be achieved by listening carefully to what the parents have to say and by giving them a chance to make classroom supplies with their own hands according to specifications provided by the teachers. These can include charts, simple kinds of educational toys, blocks, bean-bags, pencil or crayon holders, etc.

Each school system will need to evolve its own system for encouraging parental participation and then communicate its techniques to others.

Preparation of Teachers and Teacher Aides

Vigorous action is needed to increase the number and improve the preparation of teachers and teacher aides. Teachers who have had little or no opportunity for a formal education in their own language naturally lack confidence in the classroom. When sufficiently motivated, they can make up in part for this lack of opportunity by studying privately, by attending special local courses of instruction, or by spending summers or a year in a university, preferably in a country of the language concerned. Information on how to get financial support should be an early concern of the bilingual coordinator, the advisory committee, and the school administration.

The steady supply of competent bilingual teachers is the responsibility of teacher-preparing institutions, but local school administrators can do two things to assure good cooperation with colleges and universities that supply them teachers. They can specify in detail the kinds of competencies needed in their teachers, and they can report their evaluations of teachers to the institutions that prepared them. The need in bilingual programs of various kinds of specialists, and in much greater numbers than heretofore, makes it particularly desirable for local school systems and preparing institutions to maintain a close working relationship.

Until such time as teacher-preparing institutions, in cooperation with the United States Office of Education, can develop programs capable of producing competent bilingual teachers in sufficient numbers, other measures will have to be adopted. One of these, which has already been tried on a limited scale, is that of using foreign teachers. Whether arranged on an exchange basis or not, the best use of foreign teachers should be studied and procedures should be developed for increasing the use of this promising source of competent teachers.

The recruitment, training, and further education of teacher aides also deserves high priority. Some teacher aides show considerable potential for becoming good teachers but are deterred from pursuing their education for economic reasons. If a system could be worked out for encouraging them and providing instruction or the means of self-instruction, some could in time qualify for a degree and a teacher certificate.

In the preparation of bilingual teachers—especially when the only bilinguals available are not highly educated—it is useful to provide very complete teacher's guides. In the case of beginning primers step-by-step instructions should be given to the teacher. These instructions, of course, provide a minimum, not a maximum. They can give assurance to the insecure teacher who is just beginning; it would be expected, however, that he would amplify the material in the guidebook as he gains confidence.

These are short-range measures. Long-range measures, designed to erase the shortage of qualified teachers, would consist of a program throughout the grades for identifying vocations suitable for bilinguals. These might include, among others, bilingual secretaries, social workers, telephone operators, nurses, translators, and, especially, bilingual teachers. Such fields as technical assistance, international business, and diplomacy are other possibilities. There is no reason, however, to avoid featuring the teacher among "community helpers" in the early grades. And children can occasionally be given an opportunity to play the role of teacher. As children think about what they want to do or be, the teacher can tactfully include his own profession among the many other possibilities. The personal satisfaction of the teacher and the social contribution he makes need not be emphaiszed more than those of the artist, the musician, the physician, the engineer, the foreign correspondent, the inventor, etc., but neither should they be minimized. Perhaps the most satisfactory procedure would be to plan cooperatively with the whole staff for the systematic and attractive featuring of a broad range of professions and occupations.

Since all children are exposed to teaching throughout their impressionable years, some say no special steps need to be taken to interest children in teaching; that the only thing necessary to spark their interest is for the teaching which the children observe to be as interesting as possible.

The obvious conclusion is that both approaches might be used with profit.

Objectives

Once the bilingual coordinator has secured a complete staff of bilingual teachers, he and they, working as a close-knit team, face their main task: defining objectives, planning the curriculum, and deciding on evaluation procedures.

Staff members may have inherited from the administration and advisory committee a list of objectives, but they cannot be expected to implement these objectives without scrutinizing them critically. The selected goals must be acceptable not only to the school board, the administration, and the advisory committee—representing the community—but also must be ones that the staff can believe in and will find possible to attain.

A statement of objectives should include the following features, in addition to the usual academic achievements:

1. Expected outcomes for the non-English-speaking child in his native language, in English, and in his attitudes toward both cultures.
2. Expected outcomes for the English-speaking child in English, in the non-English language, and in his attitudes toward both cultures.

The great difficulty is to state objectives clearly and in measurable terms. Language objectives, for example, may be subdivided into listening comprehension, speaking, reading, and writing. For each of these a concrete level of achievement might be indicated at each grade level. Despite the fact that they are intended for adults, the Modern Language Association Statement of Qualifications for Foreign Language Teachers[2] and the State Department Foreign Service Institute[3] definition of levels of language proficiency would be helpful guides in defining competency in the basic language skills in non-English languages. Similar guides and tests exist for English as a second language.[4] Other concrete measures of language proficiency involve vocabulary and structure counts.

The concrete measurement of cultural attitudes presents a much greater problem, but some work has been done on attitude scales.[4a] These scales can serve as guides in defining attitude objectives and in testing attitudes.

Similarly, for the rest of the curriculum, whether taught unilingually or bilingually, specific objectives should be stated in concrete terms. A statement of objectives presumably already exists, for those parts of the program which are taught in English only, but it will have to be changed because of the bilingual situation. For subjects taught in the non-English language it will be necessary to state both objectives and proposed methods of evaluating achievement. These objectives and methods will be different for English speakers and non-English speakers at various grade levels.

The Curriculum

Even if a school system is lucky enough to afford a curriculum specialist for the bilingual program, share one with the rest of the school program, or have at its disposal the services of a specialist from a neighboring university or regional educational laboratory or service center, the designing and frequent revision of the bilingual curriculum are of constant concern to the coordinator and the teaching staff.

Having agreed on the basic teaching medium—either English alone, with the other language as a temporary bridge, or both English and the other language—the entire staff will need to design one or more curricula to achieve their stated goals.[5] The advisory committee may be helpful in developing curricula; in any case it should be kept informed of progress in this as in other areas.

The main criteria to be observed in planning the curriculum are the stated objectives, the cultures and sub-cultures of the community, the needs and aspirations of the community, the age of the children, their socioeconomic background, their stage of educational advancement, the balance between their two languages, the differences between the two languages, the best order of learning, and motivation. These factors are so complex that they call for a real curriculum specialist or, better, close collaboration among various specialists. For this reason, each school district that undertakes a bilingual program should realize it is working in a relatively new field. It is not enough to solve the local curricular problem and then throw away the key to the solution. The *way* problems are solved is important, not only locally but for others pursuing the same goals. A careful record should be kept of the procedure—the questions posed and tentative answers given, as well as the final solution and the rationale used. If we are to have a minimum of wasted effort and duplication in this new educational venture, program designers engaged in developing similar curricula must maintain close communication.

Materials. Among the factors listed above under curriculum one of the most important is motivation. A child who is interested is more likely to learn than one who is not. Interest depends on the teacher and his success in making his teaching relevant, on the materials he uses, and on the value the child places on education. All three are related and almost inseparable. In the planning and production of materials, special action is needed. One of the most important criteria for selecting, adapting, or creating materials is their potential for catching and holding the interest of children. This is more fundamental than such factors as vocabulary range and grammatical difficulty, although these too should receive attention, secondarily. Children *may* learn from fascinating but inefficiently constructed materials; they will probably *not* learn much, in spite of superb engineering, if their interest is not held captive.

Early Childhood Learning. Special action is needed in the area of early childhood learning. Since very young children are known to be avid learners, the bilingual staff should consider the appropriateness of a readiness program for non-English-speaking children from birth to school age. One model would be the Carnegie sponsored program in Ypsilanti, Michigan, which provides teachers who go the the homes to tutor mothers and infants. Even if teachers cannot be made available to teach in the homes, materials and instructions prepared for non-English-speaking parents to use in the home promises to be of great benefit. These materials could be designed for both passive and active learning. Children should have the opportunity to play with a variety of toys, to listen to and make music, to look at and make pictures, to recognize and make the letters of the alphabet, and, if so inclined, to read and write. Suggestions to parents about what to watch for in the growth and development of children or even concerning health and nutrition can have adirect educational benefit. Joshua Lederberg, writing in the *Washington Post* of Sunday, April 6, 1969, on "The Jensen Study: Genetics of Intelligence," states that "In New York City, women of low socioeconomic status were given vitamin and mineral supplements during pregnancy. These women gave birth to children who, at four years of age, averaged eight points higher in IQ than a control group of children whose mothers have been given placebos during pregnancy." It is tempting to speculate on the benefits that might result from a relatively minor expenditure for modest educational materials in the home, as well as improved nutrition, and the early collaboration of parents in preparing their children for school.

Experimentation and Evaluation

Any school district of a certain size should perhaps appoint a research specialist who can design experiments to answer some of the many questiosn we have about bilingual schooling. As things are presently organized in schools, teachers have no time for experimentation, whether or not they are interested in it. It is unreasonable to expect *every* teacher to become research conscious, but would it not be productive when specialists are not available to identify those teachers who have a taste for experimentation and free them to pursue this interest?

One of the easiest ways to liberate interested teachers is to provide them with assistants who can collect the milk money, keep the attendance records, deal with the school photographer and other salesmen, help the children with their snowsuits, monitor the playground and the bathroom, and take care of a thousand and one other chores which at present take an incredible portion of a teacher's time. Interested parents of any ethnic background could be exceedingly useful in performing these duties, and perhaps find pride in sharing in the educational process.

The school system can also collaborate with a neighboring university or regional laboratory which has resources for research. A fine example of the fruit of such a collaboration is work conducted in McGill University by a team headed by Wallace E. Lambert in conjunction with an experimental program in the early grades of the St. Lambert Elementary School, just outside of Montreal. The first report will shortly appear[6] and the second, by W. E. Lambert, M. Just, and N. Segalowitz, titled "Some Cognitive Consequences of Following the Curricula of Grades One and Two in a Foreign Language," is in mimeograph form.

Experimentation depends on testing; but even if one is not interested in experimentation, evaluation is an indispensable part of a bilingual, or any other, program. Without testing, a teacher cannot determine whether he and the children have achieved the stated aims of a program. Educators are pretty well agreed, however, that at no point in this basic educational process have we reached total agreement as to procedure. Aims are frequently not stated in measurable terms. In teaching, teachers tend to lose sight of their aims. And rare indeed is the teacher whose testing really measures to what extent he has taught what needed to be learned.

This being so, a person responsible for testing is an indispensable member of the bilingual team—to be shared, if necessary, with other parts of the program. The great need is for the most advanced thinking about evaluation to be communicated to the bilingual staff so that the statement of aims, the teaching, and the testing may all be correlated.

Let us remark, in conclusion, that these modest suggestions are offered in the hope that they will be helpful to those responsible for planning a bilingual program. They are meant in addition to suggest some often overlooked needs of a program which administrators may wish to consider as they prepare proposals.

NOTES

[1]See Heinz Kloss, "German as an Immigrant, Indigenous, Second, and Foreign Language in the United States," *The German Language in America,* Dr. Glenn G. Gilbert, Ed. To be published by The University of Texas Press, Austin, 1970.

[1a]John M. Hickman, "Barreras Lingüísticas y Socioculturales a la Communicación."

[2]See Appendix H.

[3]For further information write to the Director, School of Foreign Languages, Foreign Service Institute, Department of State, Washington, D. C.

[4]For information write to the Center for Applied Linguistics, 1717 Massachusetts Avenue, N. W., Washington, D. C. 20036.

[5]See Chapter VI.

[6]W. E. Lambert and J. Macnamara, "Some Cognitive Consequences of Following a First-Grade Curriculum in a Second Language," *Journal of Educational Psychology*, 1969, in press.

CHAPTER VI

THE PROGRAM

Objectives

The objectives of a bilingual program are:

To plan and prepare the program in such a way as to gain the understanding and active support of all segments of the community.

To create in both school and community a situation which will enable all children–E-speaking and X-speaking–to "touch their outermost limits" of learning.

Specifically,

To plan and conduct the program in such a way that either language, or both, is used for most effective learning in any part of the curriculum.

To encourage all children, each at his own best rate, to cultivate their first language fully: to develop skill in all the language arts–listening comprehension, speaking, memorizing, reading, and writing.

To encourage all children to develop fully their second language, each at his own best rate of learning.

To enable all children to gain a sympathetic understanding of their own history and culture and of the history and culture of the other ethnic group.

In summary,

To give all children the opportunity to become fully articulate and literate and broadly educated in two languages and sensitive to two cultures.

The purposes are plain enough. The question is: Are they attainable, and are they worth the trouble and expense? Assuming affirmative answers, five main areas need to be considered.

I. *Content or Subject Matter*

In which language should each subject be taught? Should some or all be taught in both? How should sectioning be handled? Does it make a difference what the "other" language and culture is? Should the content be affected by bilingual schooling? If so, in what way?

II. *Time*

What time patterns are supportable under the Bilingual Education Act (BEA)? Should the program ultimately aim toward half the school time in each language–half in English (E) and half in the other language spoken in the community (X)? Or in the long run should English receive most or even all of the time in the school day? In either case, which language should carry the heavier load in the earliest stages, the child's dominant language or the language he stands in need of acquiring?

III. *Methods and Materials*

How can everything be gotten in? Should instruction be duplicated? To what extent are materials available and adequate in X, through the full range of subjects and levels, for children who speak this language better than English? What is there in English for children who speak another language, and how good is it? Are there suitable materials for native English-speakers seeking a bicultural education? What use can be made of current "foreign language" materials? What about materials from abroad? To what degree must availability of materials shape the program? What are the chances that "teacher-made" materials will justify the time and effort that go into them? What if the other language one is dealing with is unwritten?

IV. *Teachers*

What are the proper qualifications for teachers in a bilingual program? What are the advantages and disadvantages of using one bilingual as the teacher? Of using teams, on the "one teacher–one language" principle? How can local bilingual teachers and aides who received all their formal education through English be used best to promote bilingual education? What are the pros and cons of foreign teachers? Looking to the future, how should teachers for bilingual programs be trained?

V. *Evaluation*

What instruments are there to evaluate a) candidates for teaching positions; b) children's linguistic, conceptual, and attitudinal status, both on entering and at various points along the way; c) achievement in each content area in the appropriate language or languages at each grade level; d) effectiveness–separately and together–of materials, teaching, and program design in moving toward the community's goals for its children's education? How can the means for revision be built into a program?

In trying to cope with these questions, there is apparently no really good place to start. The complexity of the picture is enormous–so great in fact that one would be tempted to give it up altogether except for the fact that here and there, in various circumstances, true bilingual-bicultural education *does take place*, and we have glimpsed it now and again with our own eyes. The result, when it happens, is to our minds so worth striving for that it dignifies whatever efforts we make to set our children on that path.

So, then, to the grubby details! The five topics we have named above are all inextricably intertwined. We, the authors, will say what we can on various aspects of the problems. We will at times express our biases, and we will often expose our ignorance (oftener than we mean to, no doubt). What we cannot do is offer any town or city a whole, organized plan: that must be done by every community for itself.

I. *Content or Subject Matter*

In each separate curricular area, planners must decide not only which language or languages will be unicultural or bicultural in content. Borrowing a schematic idea from William F. Mackey's "A Typology of Bilingual Education,"[1] we can represent these possible language and content choices thus:

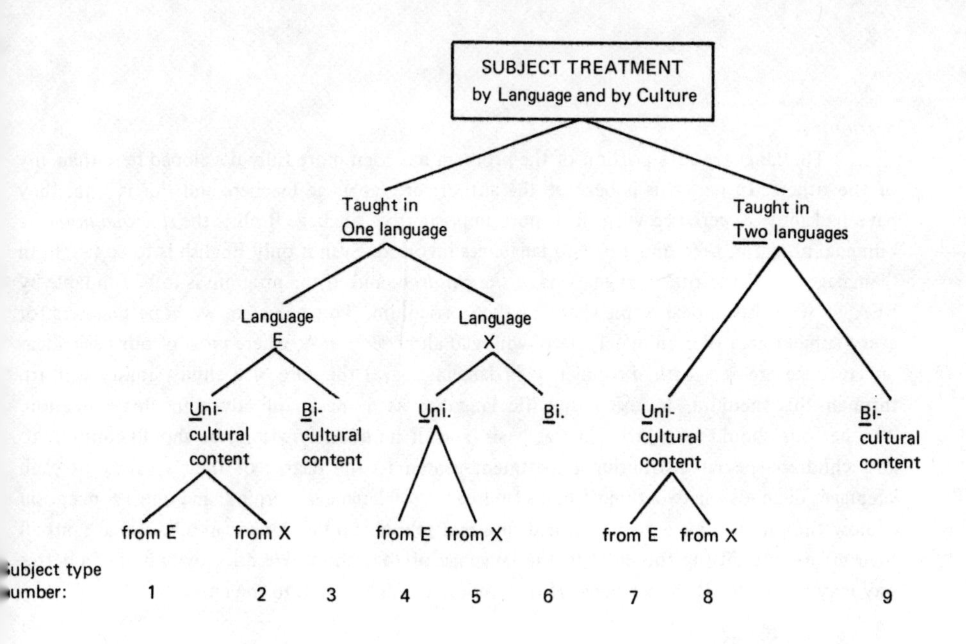

One illustration (not necessarily one we recommend) of each of these types follows:

1. Standard American mathematics curriculum, taught in English only.

2. French mathematics curriculum, translated into English and taught in E only. The obverse of number 1.

3. Social studies with bicultural (E and X) content, but taught in E only.

4. Standard American social studies, unicultural in content, translated into Portuguese and taught in Portuguese only.

5. Spanish language arts, taught in Spanish only.

6. Social studies with bicultural (E and X) content, but taught in X only. The obverse of number 3.

7. Standard American science curriculum; original in E, plus a version in X translated from E. Children study the same unicultural content in both language versions.

8. French mathematics curriculum; original in French plus a translated version in E. Children study the same unicultural content in both languages. The obverse of number 7.

9. Social studies with bicultural (E and X) content; independent but compatible versions in E and in X (not duplications). Children study bicultural content in both language versions. The effect of number 9 can sometimes be achieved within the child (if not within the school's teaching) if he studies a subject both by number 1 and by number 5.[2]

In considering these various possibilities, it will sometimes make less difference how one decides for a single subject than how the overall pattern takes shape. Overall distributions will be discussed in the section on Time.

Sectioning

The language arts portion of the program has been more fully developed here than any of the others. In part this is because the authors are language teachers and this is what they have had most experience with. But more importantly, language itself is the *sine qua non* of a bilingual program; there must be two languages involved. Even if only English is to be taught in "language arts," the other language is *in the children*; and, if the program is to be fundable by BEA, it will also appear somewhere in the curriculum. This being so, we hope planners for every subject area of a bilingual school will read all of section A, where most of our basic ideas on language are set forth. Proficiency in language is at the core of a child's ability to learn through this medium, to use a specific language as a means of advancing his education. Whether one should sectionize on this basis, and, if he does, how long he should continue to give children special instructional treatment geared to the degree of their mastery of each language, depends on two things: one's philsosphy of language learning, and one's conception of how the philosophy is to be applied in a real school. So far, American schools have put all their effort into fitting the child to the language of the school. We ask now whether a better way may not be to fit the language of the school, at least in part, to the child.

A. *Language Arts*

Language arts, in a bilingual school, should be treated either as one subject or as two, depending on whether only English is taught, or both English (E) and another language (X).

English language arts for children who are dominant in E can take the form of either type 3 or type 1. We prefer 3 because it is bicultural.

English language arts for X-dominant children takes one of the same forms (type 3 or type 1), but to these children E is a second language. To the extent that it is sectioned, taught in a different way, such English language arts is commonly called ESL (English as a second language). Although the use of highly structured materials is one approach that is widely known and used—and identified, sometimes erroneously, with "linguistic" principles—this approach is not the only means of teaching English as a second language. The term ESL is therefore at times ambiguous.

Language arts may also include the teaching of X as a subject. When this happens, X language arts can take forms paralleling those just described for English:

X language arts for X-dominant children (here type 6 or type 5).

X language arts for English-speaking children (again type 6 or type 5). These programs are the closest to what is now called FLES (foreign language in the elementary school); but in a bilingual program they should take on greatly expanded meaning, as we will see. As between type 6 and type 5, we again prefer the bicultural type 6.

In order to make a clear distinction between dominant language and weaker or second language, we will discuss these various language arts programs in this order; that is, we will talk first of E and X as "mother tongues," and then of each as a second language.

The Child's First Language

Language is the bed-rock of American elementary education, and once we come to realize its function in a young child's earliest experiences in school, we are well on the way to understanding what bilingual education can mean.

The first distinction to be made, as far as the school is concerned, is what language the child understands; or, if he knows two or more, which one he understands best. This is using what Mackey calls a "wide-mesh screen"[3] and it should not be cluttered at this point by judgments about "correctness" and "non-correctness." For most immediate purposes, it will be well to assume that one language is stronger or "dominant" in the child when he enters schools. It is also well to proceed on the assumption that the child can and does talk: referring to him as alingual[4] will usually only cloud the issue.

A second distinction is needed, to denote two different *kinds* of languages that may be involved along with English in bilingual schooling in the United States. This is not to set relative values on the languages as such. Every native tongue used anywhere in the world is central to each of its speakers' very being. Every language is reducible to writing, and every one is expandable to incorporate the means for expressing every object and every thought known to have existed among humankind. And beyond actual and potential use of every tongue to its own native speakers, there is something more: our needs as a human race. Somehow, in a manner not yet understood, the wisdom and the ways of peoples who have used each language through the ages cling to the language itself, as oil does to a clay pot. Mankind's problems are not yet solved, and until they are we can ill afford the loss of a single vessel where other ways of being are stored, or even remotely remembered.

Yet in planning bilingual programs beginning from where we are, there are certain differences to be seen. On the one hand there are the languages of wider communication,[5] such as Spanish, French, and Portuguese; and on the other hand the more local languages, such as Navajo, Hopi, and the Eskimo tongues.[6] Which one of these kinds of languages one is dealing with can affect the program in various ways: in selection of which subjects to teach through X, in how far up the grades to plan using X as a medium, in availability of materials, and in possible sources of teachers. To the extent that this distinction seems useful, we will try to bear it in mind in the discussions that follow.

1. *Language Arts, Dominant E*

Program plans and content for the English-speaking child are already under way, and there is little point in describing them here. English teachers know the range, from pre-reading to advanced literature, both oral and written. The one important extra dimension suggested by bilingual schooling is that adaptations in content may be desirable, especially if the school aims to be bicultural as well as bilingual. In dominant-E language arts, the teacher should of course adhere to language arts criteria of quality and developmental usefulness, but within this framework he can contribute greatly to furthering the aims of bilingual-bicultural education. One example might mean taking specific measures to include more high-quality material with—for instance—social studies content. Fine and effective use of language is not, after all, limited to the field of *belles lettres;* and broadening the horizons of this subject to overlap the rest of the curriculum would go far toward answering the crucial question of over-all time—how to get everything in.[7] A more obvious example of how the language arts teacher can advance the program is in the realm of purely imaginative oral and written literature. The teacher must choose, and his choices should be consciously affected by the kind of attitudes and values, as well as tastes, that he wishes to instill in the children. This is especially important at the primary and intermediate levels. In the opinion of the authors, ethnocentrism in any subject area—especially if it is benign or unconscious—can scuttle a bilingual program.

2. *Language Arts, Dominant X*

The normal English-speaking child, on his first day at school, brings with him a certain amount of linguistic equipment. So standard, so fully expected is this equipment that we tend to forget there is any other way for a child of that age to *be*. This six-year-old understands when he is spoken to (in English, of course), and he may or may not talk (again, in English, of course). If he doesn't talk we don't call him alingual; we don't summon a speech therapist or a remedial teacher; we simply say he is shy. He is a perfectly normal first-grader whose dominant language is English, and we accept him and take him from there. What we seem at times to be incredibly dense about is that it is *just* as normal to speak something *other* than English. Billions of people all over the earth do it, including millions of children in the United States. The six-year-olds in this group are the perfect counterparts of the kind of child described above: they understand the language in which they have grown up to the age of six, and they talk or don't talk as they think the circumstances require. The difference—the *only* difference worth discussing from the language arts point of view at this moment—is that the dominant language of these latter children is not English, but X. What then should be the objectives of language arts in X, when X is the children's dominant language?

(2a) *When Dominant X Is a Language of Wider Communication*

When an English-speaking child starts to school, we build (quite sanely, for once) on what he has: the ability to understand his language at his age level when he hears it, and to speak it to his own purposes. We put reading and writing at the beginning of his school program because we think of them as the foundations of all the rest of his formal education, among the most useful tools for acquiring knowledge, and "the door to the whole of the literature and culture connected with his language" (Sarah Gudschinsky).

A child whose dominant tongue is any other of the world's languages of wider communication deserves an opportunity to learn reading and writing in his language for the same reasons; and just as in the case of the English-speaker, reading and writing in the dominant tongue (now X) should be the prime objective of his first year at school. These great languages have venerable traditions, and all educated people recognize their inherent value. Any child who brings to school a six-year old's mastery of one of them comes equipped with a learning tool that millions of adults strive vainly to acquire later in life. To ignore the child's priceless possession, to despise it through our own ignorance, or to truncate its natural development and refinement by denying its use as a medium of formal instruction is, in the writers' view, not only short-sighted and inefficient; it is an educational crime.

The reasons for learning to read have much in common, whether it be in English or in one of the other major languages. Teaching young native speakers how to do it will also share some features, but not necessarily all. The following is Sarah Gudschinsky's statement, in a personal communication to us, of what a reading-readiness program in the dominant language does or should consist of:

> 1) an understanding of what reading is (through the experience of being read to, and the experience of seeing one's own utterance written by someone else and read back);
>
> 2) aural-oral skills (including specifically the ability to focus on the phonemes of one's own language; this might include producing words which begin with the same sound, words which rhyme, etc.);
>
> 3) visual skills (including particularly the ability to discriminate visually the shapes of letters);
>
> 4) manual skills (including the control of pencil and paper, and perhaps also chalk or crayon);
>
> 5) development of adult or nearly adult control of the structure of the language of instruction, and sufficient vocabulary (and experiences represented by such vocabulary) to read with understanding the material of instruction.
>
> In an active school program of reading-readiness, point 1 is most essential for children who come from illiterate or semi-literate homes and who have not been read to as a part of normal home activity....Point 5 is of less importance for children who come from a rich home environment but is a vital part of schooling for children who come from a disadvantaged background....
>
> What is important, it seems to me, is that any reading-readiness program focus on those particular points which the pupils need. It should never be a rigid mechanical program apart from such needs.

But even if a staff is generally agreed on these points, it is not to be expected that *specific* reading-readiness techniques either can or should be transferred *en bloc* from our way of applying them in English, to the teaching of dominant-X children to read in X. Ways of approaching literacy vary from language to language,[8] and the traditional techniques of competent X teachers in other countries should not be lightly dismissed even if at first blush they seem wrong to us. There may be strong connections between the means and the ends that are not immediately apparent. This is the kind of area in which one's faith in biculturalism gets tested. Further investigation may be in order, and exchanges of experiences will often be mutually enlightening; meanwhile the X-speaking teacher of X cannot be overridden with impunity.

We said earlier that reading should ordinarily be learned first in the dominant language.[9] This means that Spanish or French or Portuguese literacy would precede reading in English for children who speak these respective languages better. The acquisition of their second language, English, is discussed in another section.

Once the children have begun to read, it is just as important for them as for E-speakers to have high-quality materials to read. Selection should strike a balance between the best that exists elsewhere in this particular language, and the best written by immigrants or their descendants in this country, so that the scope and status of the language, both in the world at large and in their own nation, are faithfully represented to the children. Here, as in the dominant-E section, the possibilities for dovetailing with social studies should be exploited: if the literary quality at all allows, very local history and autobiography written in X, as well as locally-set imaginative literature in X, should be included in the curriculum. In all these areas special care must be taken not to give a lopsided picture which teaches the children that their dominant X is really only a language for another place or an earlier time. These subtle lessons, so deeply learned, are probably taught more by the kinds of readings we *expose* children to than by what we say about them.

It is perhaps appropriate to say here a few words about the use of memorization. Memorizing is the process of adding to one's personal store striking utterances and literary gems in prose or verse. Reciting to oneself or to others such remembered pieces or paraphrasing well-known passages can be a constant source of pleasure, both individual and social. The French poet André Spire has called this rolling of poetry on one's tongue a "muscular pleasure." In addition, it is of course an intellectual and esthetic pleasure, one which to our loss is more cultivated by other nations than by us. Having X-speaking children memorize and recite passages in X for their assembled parents is a good way to cement school-parent relations.

The role of the library should not be forgotten.

It should especially be kept in mind that in other parts of the world there are myriads of people whose entire education, indeed whose whole life, is carried on exclusively in the language of the children we are discussing here. The possibilities, therefore, of use, cultivation and enjoyment of the language arts in these languages by bilingual American children are limited only by the children's own vision—a vision for which the school itself, as an agent of our society, is largely responsibile.

(2b) *Language Arts When Dominant X Is a More Local Language*

What we sweepingly call "more local languages" are not in reality a very homogeneous group at all.[10] Their chief characteristic in common, as far as language arts teaching is concerned, is that they are not like those we have been talking about above: full curricula using them as the exclusive medium of instruction are nowhere in existence, either here or abroad. The effect of this is that course planners have few and in some cases no extant models even to depart from.

Some of the languages have been written for a long time—well in a few cases, less well in others. Cherokee has a writing system dating back to the remarkable Sequoyah, and in the 1830's an estimated 90 percent of the Cherokee Nation were literate in their native tongue.[11] At the other extreme of this particular scale are the as yet unwritten languages. In between, Navajo, Hopi, and others are in various stages, with one or more systems of writing more or less generally agreed upon.

In such circumstances, that is, where dominant X is local, what are the legitimate aims for X language arts as taught to native X-speakers in a bilingual school? They probably include these:[12]

1) The children should first be introduced to reading, and in the language they know best.

2) Familiarity with indigenous literature should be encouraged. Although these languages have no great quantity of written literature, it might well be among the aims of a bilingual program to expand the children's knowledge of their language's oral literature, to provide the people with this same body of literature in print, and in general to encourage further production.

* * * * *

The Child's Second Language

What do we mean when we speak of teaching English? The average American, when he hears the term "English teacher," ponders very little over the fact that what we call "English teaching" is a super-structure built on a relatively solid oral control of this language. When we speak of teaching English in school, we usually mean either honing off the rough spots that could in some contexts work to our own disadvantage; or, more recently, trying to *add* a generally advantageous dialect to the one we talk and want to keep on talking at home and with friends.

This is dominant-language teaching in school. It is not at all the same thing as teaching someone who doesn't already speak the language in question. Learners of the latter type seem to fall into two easily distinguishable groups: the baby who doesn't yet speak any language;[13] and the learner of whatever age who is learning his *second* language.[14] But the truth of the matter is that nobody knows for sure whether these kinds of learners really *are* two groups—whether there are two radically different processes of language-learning, or simply minor differences in essentially one process. If there are two, we do not know where the line of demarcation between them is: Is it age (physical, psychological, or both)? Or is it something else?

"Teaching" a baby to talk is in some respects like "teaching" him to walk. It consists mainly in encouraging him as he tries to do these things, in a setting where they are done naturally by other people and not primarily for the purpose of serving as models for the baby. The child overhears language in virtually its full range, and he sees the mobility of those around him. Whether an awareness of the utility of talking and walking is somehow innate in him or whether it is commmunicated to him by his observations, we do not know.[15] In other words, we do not know whether consciously or unconsciously we "teach" babies to walk and to talk. What we do know is that they *begin to do them* under certain natural conditions.

Beyond that, agreement dwindles rapidly. People concerned with helping children or adults acquire a second language are handicapped by this fundamental uncertainty. In dealing with very young children the question is particularly puzzling, for while older people may perhaps be "taught" an intellectualized approximation of a second language, perhaps the brain of the young child can operate best with little or no interference, or consciousness of "teacher."

If the teacher concentrates the child's attention too much on the mechanics, structure, or patterns of his second language, she may have quite the wrong effect. One is reminded of the centipede who got along admirably until his teacher tried to teach him to analyze the order in which he put his feet down.

On the other hand, if the teacher is oblivious to possible interferences from the first language; if she fails to see that the relative order of certain learnings may help or hinder the child; if she is not aware that the range of language the child hears will be severely limited unless she purposely arranges otherwise—then she may not be teaching at all, and the child would perhaps learn just as much of the second language, just as fast and well, in the company of any other adult whom he liked as well and spent as much time with. Probably he would learn more, because the context would in most cases be less circumscribed than that of a schoolroom.

It surely must be clear that if organized education makes any sense at all—a hypothesis not always entirely beyond question—the best approach to second language teaching for very young children must be somewhere between these two extremes, and it must surely include "the ability to get the child sufficiently involved in significant activities (such as survival or play or the search for adult approval) where language is an unavoidable tool of access" (Bruce Gaarder).[16]

Literacy in a Second Language

What we have just been saying refers to getting a child to the point of being able to understand and talk his second language with fair competence. Reading it and writing it should follow this stage, not precede. As we suggested earlier, having learned to read in one's dominant language greatly facilitates learning to read in a second, particularly if the learner knows how to speak the second. The learner who goes through the sequence here recommended has already grasped the concept of sound-symbol relationship in his dominant tongue, and he has "learned how to learn from books" (Gaarder). Other features, such as left-to-rightness, may or may not transfer depending on the degree of similarity between the two writing systems. Sarah Gudschinsky, in connection with her previously quoted statement on reading-readiness, cites the following features as they apply to second-language reading:

> *Points 3 and 4 [visual skills and manual skills] are vital prerequisites for the first reading experience, but do not have to be repeated for a second language. Point 2 [audiolingual skills] may indeed, however, be as necessary for a second language as for a first one. In effect, for the second language, it would be a matter of learning to recognize and reproduce the phonemes of that language....[Point 5, development of control of the structure and sufficient vocabulary to read with understanding, is] obviously the essential part of a readiness program for children who are about to learn to read a language which they do not yet speak adequately.*

3. *Language Arts, E for Dominant-X Children*

The following description of an English language arts program for Alaska natives, written by Lee M. Salisbury of the University of Alaska, illustrates how many things *can* go wrong.

> *By the time the native child reaches the age of seven, his cultural and language patterns have been set, and his parents are required by law to send him to school. Until this time he is likely to speak only his own local dialect of Indian, Aleut, or Eskimo or, if his parents have had some formal schooling, he may speak a kind of halting English.*
>
> *He now enters a completely foreign setting—a Western classroom. His teacher is likely to be a Caucasian who knows little or nothing about his*

cultural background. He is taught to read the Dick and Jane *series. Many things confuse him: Dick and Jane are two* gussuk* *[Eskimo term for "white person." Derived from the Russian Cossack.] children who play together. Yet, he knows that boys and girls do not play together and do not share toys. They have a dog named Spot who comes indoors and does not work. They have a father who leaves for some mysterious place called "office" each day and never brings any food home with him. He drives a machine called an automobile on a hard-covered road called a street which has a policeman on each corner. These policemen always smile, wear funny clothing, and spend their time helping children to cross the street. Why do these children need this help? Dick and Jane's mother spends a lot of time in the kitchen cooking a strange food called "cookies" on a stove which has no flame in it, but the most bewildering part is yet to come. One day they drive out to the country, which is a place where Dick and Jane's grandparents are kept. They do not live with the family and they are so glad to see Dick and Jane that one is certain that they have been ostricized from the rest of the family for some terrible reason. The old people live on something called a "farm" which is a place where many strange animals are kept: a peculiar beast called a "cow," some odd-looking birds called "chickens," and a "horse" which looks like a deformed moose....*

So it is not surprising that 60 percent of the native youngsters never reach the eighth grade.[17]

Even after the dominant-X children learn to speak the sounds of English and to read aloud from a written page, the course will still be inadequate if it is unicultural to this extreme. In this case, it has the further disadvantage of being trivial. Why should anyone want to read this kind of thing even once, let alone the number of times a beginner usually goes over his primer, in his second language or in his first? Anything that we oblige a child to repeat almost to the point of memorization should be intrinsically *worth* being memorized. Otherwise we may waste his time at the same time that we dull his mind. A third shortcoming in the program described by Salisbury is that—in Alaska as elsewhere—it is rarely supplemented or offset by any language arts course at all in the child's native X. The school fails.

Parents also fail, sometimes under pressure from the school, as the following experience of Sarah Gudschinsky illustrates:

I have seen Mazatec [Amerindian language of Mexico] children in a Mazatec village who were forbidden by their parents to speak and to force their children to use only Spanish in all contacts. Where the parental edict has been strong enough, the children fail to learn enough Mazatec to function successfully in a Mazatec environment. However, they do not have enough Spanish contact to learn an effective control of Spanish. The result is a lack of useful language sufficient, probably, to stunt all intellectual growth....If our attempts to force non-English speakers to abandon their mother tongue were more efficient, it would be in danger of producing an increasing population that could not use effectively any language.

English as a second language is a complex and growing field, and any teacher or administrator of children who study English as their weaker language should keep himself informed of developments. TESOL (Teachers of English to Speakers of Other Languages) is a relatively young but already very active organization and is an excellent source of information. The Center for Applied Linguistics is another valuable source of ESL information and publications.[18] A third is the National Council of Teachers of English (NCTE), whose booklet called *Language and Language Learning* (Albert H. Marckwardt, ed.) makes fine reading in this field for expert and beginner alike.

4. *Language Arts, X for Dominant–E Children*

The chief American resources in this area are the MLA (Modern Language Association of America), the various associations of teachers of specific languages (American Association of Teachers of Spanish and Portuguese, of French, etc.) and especially the new ACTFL (American Council on the Teaching of Foreign Languages.)[19] Traditionally the MLA has been oriented toward European languages, but both MLA and ACTFL now have broader scopes. Still, the stress of most professional language-teaching organizations has so far been on teaching in situations where there is little or no interaction with American native-speakers of the languages concerned. Bruce Gaarder speaks of the striking disparity between the "little academic world of foreign language teacher bilingualism" in the United States and the "great world of Spanish-speaking children in our schools, many of whom are disadvantaged precisely because of school policies which give no role to their mother tongue in their education."[20] While academia is awakening to the existence of this gap, the X-teacher would do well tokeep up also with TESOL developments in his search for workable approaches, though the societal contexts are obviously not identical for E and for X as second languages in the United States.

Whatever language the specific X may be, in a program that hopes for BEA support the community and the school have by definition a certain concentration of speakers of that language very near at hand. Except in the few cases where an X population has very recently immigrated *en masse* to this country (e.g., the influx of Portuguese-speakers from the Azores and Cape Verde Islands to the Providence-New Bedford-Fall River area), these children and their language can hardly be called "foreign." The significance of this is that the language in no case ought to be *treated* as foreign, isolated in the classroom. It should be accepted clearly for what it is: a language that known, visible, and audible people live in, people that can be talked to, played with, and worked with. "Foreign" language teachers in the past have rarely made use of live resources in their own communities, and this undoubtedly has been a major factor in the languages' having remained *foreign*.

Objectives in second-language language arts will be affected by the status (in Mackey's sense) of the particular X. If it is a language of wider communication, there are virtually no upper limits to what one can aspire to. Children who acquire these as second languages can further their studies of them through university levels here or abroad and can cultivate their bilingual taste for language arts throughout their lives.

If X is a local language, objectives will stress other kinds of values. E-speaking learners should still give first priority to the spoken language, then literacy, and so on from there. The order is important. Again there are no upper limits to what can be done in language arts as far as the oral language is concerned; written limitations will depend on the language itself, that is, on its stage of development in this dimension.

Finally, we would like to underline the *arts* of language arts, whether in English or in X. "Too often, I fear, the teacher's tenuous control of the classroom situation must be attributed to his assuming the role of language policeman" (Ross J. Waddell). His task should be rather to show that in every language *bien parler c'est se respecter* –there is the ideal of speaking or writing well; and the achievement of that ideal brings with it self-respect.

B. Social Studies

Each of us has his own little private conviction of rightness, and almost by definition the Utopian condition of which we all dream is that in which all people finally see the error of their ways and agree with us.

And underlying pratically all our attempts to bring agreement is the assumption that agreement is brought about by changing people's minds–other people's.

–S. I. Hayakawa[21]

Given the temper of our times, it is hardly an exaggeration to say that social studies in the United States have not in the past accorded much dignitv to diversity. Somehow we need to learn to see differences in a better light.[22]

The most important decision of all for social studies in a bilingual program is whether the course is to be bicultural or unicultural in content and perspective. If one goes the unicultural route, however many languages he uses, he appears to the authors to be headed for trouble. If the one cultural base being used in this subject is E, as in types 1, 4, and 7, the teacher fails to give the X-speakers's X culture its due,with the likely result that the learner will be either alienated, hostile, or defeated. If the unicultural base in social studies is X, as in types 2, 5, and 8, there is the possibility of setting up a polarization in the learner, especially if he is still very young. When he is older it may matter less.

The bicultural treatment (types 3, 6, and 9) seems by all odds to offer the better possibility in this sensitive subject area,[23] both for E-speakers and for X-speakers. Once this choice has been made, decisions about language (2) of instruction can be made on other grounds: the relative qualifications of teachers available, the overall balance one wishes to strike between the two languages, etc.

Along with language itself, this subject matter is one of the two most crucial for the success of a bilingual program. And unless the X-speakers of the community have for some reason consciously and resolutely turned their backs on their own past, as some Jewish Germans did on German culture after Hitler, a bilingual program that is not bicultural in social studies runs a very serious risk of failing.

It has been said that the hardest problem is this: how to give positive reinforcement to children without giving positive reinforcement to wrong answers.[24] Presumably this problem can only be solved when the whole society—or at least the school—can guilelessly convince the child that what is in question does not touch his own value as a person, nor the value of his family, his language, or his culture. Only then can he fully apply his mind to the questions that face us all.

Where to find materials for this bicultural or multicultural approach is another matter. Solutions here are needed desperately and now, and the broadened viewpoints that social science can offer should affect every subject in the school curriculum.

C. *Science and Mathematics*

Increasingly, science and mathematics are becoming international in content. Specialists at the top of these fields, perhaps more than any others, share symbolic systems that to a certain extent communicate across languages. Advances are being made rapidly and it is quite clear that no national, ethnic, or linguistic group can feel it has a monopoly on the potential for breakthroughs.

At the same time, there is some evidence that school children of certain linguistic and/or ethnic backgrounds tend to perform better in these school subjects than other children do. An international study measuring school performance in mathematics seemed to show that young Japanese children perform unusually well.[25] Another investigation, which compared both verbal and spatial abilities of three ethnic groups in New York, showed a spatial superiority for the Chinese over the other two groups tested.[26] Whether these differences are inherent in linguistic or other cultural factors, or whether they are purely accidental or the products of different methodologies in teaching, no one seems yet to know.

With this question still unanswered, certainly planners will want to select the best methodology and materials they can find; and if a choice has to be made of one language in which to teach these subjects, the language with the best materials may be the determining factor. This could result in a program of either type 1 or type 5; for example, for the French-speakers of New England, either a United States mathematics course (type 1) or a course from France (type 5), depending on which course the planners judge to be better in itself.

Another procedure is the one used in mathematics by the Toronto French school;[27] that is, dividing the time allotted to mathematics, and teaching type 1 *plus* type 5, or in effect treating it as *two* subjects: English mathematics and French mathematics. The children are taught both the Nuffield program in English and the Dienes program in French. Tested by the Metropolitan Achievement Tests (through English only), these children showed mean grade equivalents for every grade (1-6) at least one full year beyond grade level, both in arithmetic and in problem-solving.

Although the use of this combination pattern might not produce such spectacular results in schools whose children were not middle-class and highly motivated, both the fact of the accomplishment and the program-types involved are provocative. The two courses selected differ in philosophy or methodology. "It is suspected that the Dienes approach provides greater depth and perhaps rigidity and the Nuffield perhaps greater flexibility, but some real shallowness as well...."[28] Thus the two complement each other, offering the child the variety of avenues he may need, whereas "the use of a single type of learning experience to teach a concept is likely to produce a learning block, according to Bruner and Dienes."[29]

This is the essence of bilingual-bicultural education: not to block the child's learning by accidental limits imposed by any one culture or its language. All those enrolled in the Toronto French School take both mathematics programs, and the combination "works well for both the bright and the slow children."[30]

Problem: Is it the combination of methods that accounts for this success, or is it the combination of language-culture complexes?

Answer: Unknown.

But some tenuous light may be shed on the problem just cited by Bertha Treviño's study[31] of third graders at Nye Elementary School, United Consolidated Independent School District outside Laredo. Here the program pattern was type 7: English mathematics materials were translated into Spanish, and all children were taught this unicultural material through both mediums. Comparison was made with achievement at the same level the year *before*, when the same materials were taught to all in English only. The total amount of time allotted to mathematics was constant. In all cases—that is, for both X-speakers and E-speakers—children bilingually taught performed better than those who had been taught unilingually. This does not mean that they knew the same things as before, but now in two languages; it means they knew *more*. There was a bonus that came from somewhere: 2+2 equaled 5.

The experiences at Toronto and at Nye lead one to hypothesize that either two languages, or two different approaches to learning, can offer alternatives the child can profit from. When he is given both kinds of alternatives the potential for benefits increases accordingly.

Bicultural content is not a term that seems to have the same kind of meaning in mathematics and science as in social studies, language, or art. As we said at the beginning of this section, the deep content in mathematics and science seems to be headed for internationalism. On the surface, though, and especially with little children, differences do matter in that the practical application of problems and experiments needs to be attuned to the life the child finds around him. Casting an arithmetic problem in terms of bushels of tomatoes as opposed to bushels of mangos is not a cultural question of arithmetic *content*; it is simply an appropriate clothing to make the problem seem real. The answer should come out the same for tomatoes and for mangos. Yet we should beware of assuming that such surface differences are the only ones that might affect the learner. The Navajo understanding of the physical world is quite different from the Western European scientific tradition (which itself is not terribly old), Navajo means of classification are different, and spatial relations are differently conceived. The sensible approach seems to be to have the child learn both "sciences" side by side. Whatever our opinions of this idea or that in either system, both are a part of the history of science; and there have been cases of former "scientific" notions believed to be long dead that have proved instead to be insights into a deeper truth.

D. *Art and Music*

In the approach one should take toward art and music in a bilingual school, the first order of priority is to be sure that they are taught by people who love and feel the subjects. That there are different styles associated with different cultures is certain. But a really good teacher of either art or music is quite apt to be multicultural in his tastes already, even before the question of bilingual schooling arises. This is the kind of teacher that should be sought, even at considerable cost in effort and money. Whether the planners feel that for overall balance the need is for an X-speaker, an E-speaker, or a bilingual is a matter of secondary importance for these subjects.

Art and music are the areas in which we have perhaps achieved greatest intercultural tolerance. Talented and attractive teachers in these subjects can help transform tolerance into understanding, and from there open the possibility of multicultural appreciation.

E. *Health and Physical Education*

Most Americans are inclined to think that their ideas about health and physical education are scientifically based, and that the objective in these school subjects is to build good habits that will keep our children healthier throughout their lives. We give very little thought to the cultural biases woven into the fabric of our notions about good habits. Some cultures hold that eating raw vegetables is harmful; most American school dieticians think it is virtually essential. Some people believe bathing every day is bad for the skin; others consider it at least socially desirable, and probably healthy as well.

The fact is that many of the "good habits" we recommend to our children are not based on definite knowledge at all, but on our own culture's opinions–as of now. The rapidity with which science is changing the answers in our textbooks should give us more pause than it does, should make us leave more room for different views on the part of others around us today as well as room to change our own views gracefully tomorrow, if need be. One framework for this roomleaving seems to be to present more of those things we wish to inculcate in our young as our *opinions* or our *best judgment*. Children will learn just as well, and both they and their erstwhile mentors will be spared if what we thought was The Truth is later discovered to be erroneous. Remember thalidomide?

This approach could well be used in health, in our discussions of the human body, its needs, and its care. Similar latitude would not be amiss in the area of physical education. Children of different cultural backgrounds may have culturally-based feelings about participating in certain kinds of games. We saw above[32] that small Eskimo boys and girls are unaccustomed to playing together. Certain kinds of dance are approved by some cultures and disapproved by others. It makes little sense for us to say whether it is "better" for children to follow one pattern or the other in these respects, and it is possible to do real harm by obliging children to violate their cultural patterns.

On the positive side, especially in physical education, there are the riches of variety that can derive from taking into account two or more cultures' conceptions of play and their ideals of physical prowess.

Two special areas offer the physical education teacher opportunities to contribute in important ways to a bilingual-bicultural program: role-playing and kinesics. Kinesics has recently been discovered by second-language teachers as a powerful reinforcement to verbal learning.[33] Children whose classroom use of a second language is supplemented by kinetic association on the playground will have their learning greatly reinforced in the process. A child who experiences "Run! Jump! It's my turn to bat!" in the real world knows the meaning of these words in a way the schoolroom can usually only suggest. This argues for playground use, either mixed or at successive times, of both languages the child is attempting to control. If the E- and X-speakers are of about equal numbers, a mixture of the languages with one bilingual teacher is quite feasible and life-like. If the groups are of very unequal size, the majority language is likely to take over. In this case, it may be better to have two "unilingual" teachers alternate, so that an adult's weight is added now to one language, now to the other. If kinesics is to be fully exploited for the purposes described, the language arts teacher and the physical education teacher should be aware of each other's programs and of the help each can draw from the other.

Role-playing is a device that has been suggested as one possible way of handling some of the conflicts that arise in the minds of children faced with two cultures and their respective value systems. One example might be the conflicting attitudes toward competition between relatives or close friends as seen in Hispanic culture when compared with Anglo. Anglo-style games, played only in English, may be used to illustrate how brothers and friends can compete fiercely with each other in a way accepted and even postively enjoyed by all. Hispanic games, played in Spanish, can point up the value of alliance with brother or friend, the precedence these relationships take over the need of an individual to win. One way to bridge the gap is to have a bilingual teacher who can serve in this world of play as a model of biculturalism, acting now one part and now the other as the several games require, while all the children see. Children who are reluctant to join games they sense are antagonistic to their cultural style should not be forced or over-encouraged until they are ready. But the teacher who is able to participate in both kinds of games without losing his essential identity and integrity is a living lesson in how two cultures can combine in one human without the betrayal of one's self.

F. *Coda*

The traditional "subjects" of the elementary school curriculum are purely theoretical in their separateness one from the other. Life is not divided into these discrete compartments; nor is reality; nor are the children that bilingual schooling is meant to serve. If every teacher would make the effort to understand what his fellow-workers are about, and to fit his own specialization into the whole, multiculturalism could begin where it should: at home.

II. *Time*

The preceding section, on Content, has been an attempt to see each subject area separately in its dual relationship to language of instruction and to cultural focus. This section will deal with the instructional program as a whole, with respect to the amount of time allotted to each language.

William F. Mackey's "A Typology of Bilingual Education," which he has generously allowed us to append here *in toto* in its first published form,[34] analyzes the multiple relationships that may occur when one views the school in the contexts of the child's home and family, the community or immediate area, and the nation. The possible combinations are about 250, "Ranging from the unilingual education of bilingual children in unilingual communities to the bilingual education of unilingual children in bilingual communities."

Within this complex, Mackey identifies ten types of "curriculum patterns" or what we prefer to call patterns of school time (reserving the term curriculum to refer to content or subject matter). Mackey's orientation is international. If we apply his thinking to the United States alone, the patterns may be illustrated as follows:[35]

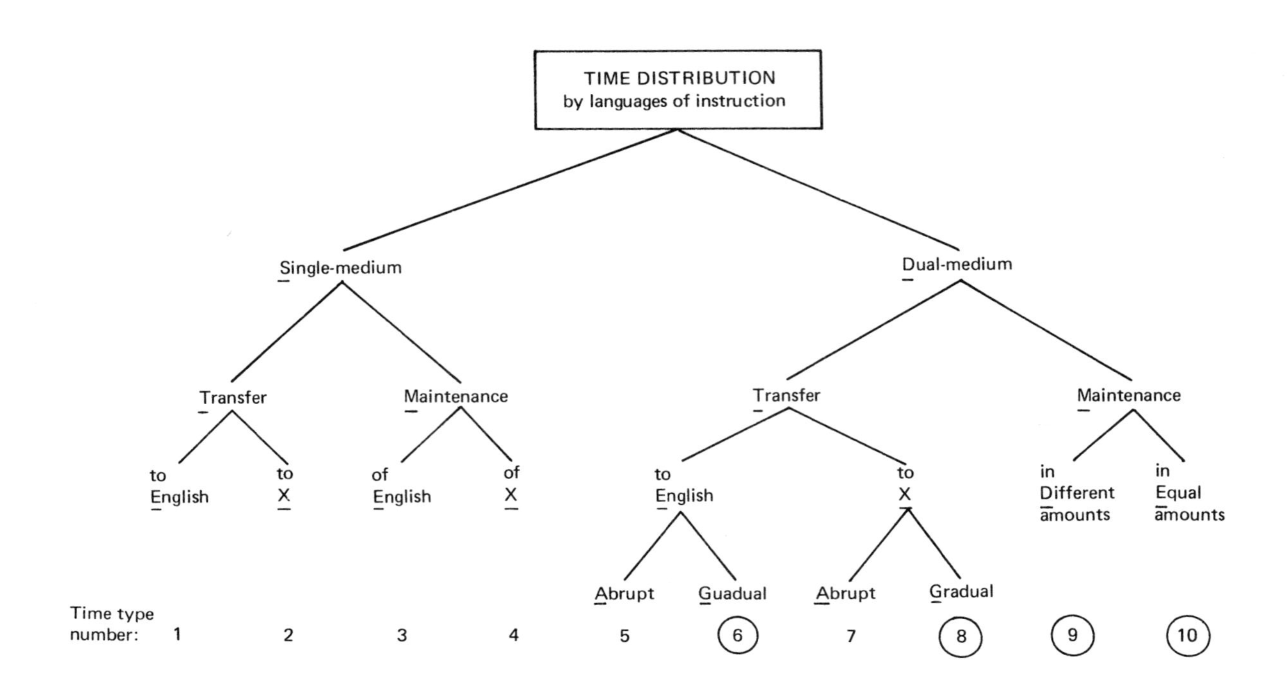
TIME DISTRIBUTION
by languages of instruction
Single-medium
Dual-medium
Transfer
Maintenance
Transfer
Maintenance
to English
to X
of English
of X
to English
to X
in Different amounts
in Equal amounts
Abrupt
Guadual
Abrupt
Gradual
Time type number:
1
2
3
4
5
6
7
8
9
10

It should be clearly understood that we are focusing now on the *entire school program* of a year or any other unit, such as primary grades. The discussion here does not refer to the language of *single* subject-matters, whose various possible patterns we treated above, in our section on Content.

Of the ten patterns just delineated, only the four that are circled appear to be fundable under the BEA and its Guidelines as they now stand. It will perhaps be well to explain our reasoning at this point because: 1) our interpretation is in no sense official; and 2) both the Guidelines and the Act are presumably subject to change through normal channels.

Types 1-4 are unilingual; they are therefore not fundable because the Guidelines specify that instruction must be in two languages.

Types 5 and 7, by virtue of the abruptness of their shift from one language to the other, are not fundable because at no particular point do they use both languages for instruction. For example, a program altogether in X in grades K-2, if it then shifts abruptly and totally to English, does not seem to meet the Guidelines' requirement at any grade level.

This leaves us with four basic patterns that could be funded: nos. 6, 8, 9, and 10. Each type represents not a fixed, absolute distribution of time but a *way* of distributing, so that the characteristics stylized here can differ in degree on being fitted to an actual school setting. They can also differ somewhat in form, for, within each of the patterns we believe are fundable, some subjects may be taught in one language and some in another (Complementary); or some or all may be taught in both languages to the same child (Overlapping), as we saw in our drawing on subject-matter treatment.[36] If there is overlap, it may take the form of using both languages for a subject during two periods of the same day (Simultaneous); or the whole course—say mathematics—may be taught in X for a certain period of time, followed by a period in E, and X again, and so on (Alternating).

Expanding the dual-medium section of the time distribution drawing, we can show these further distinctions. Then we will give an example of each.

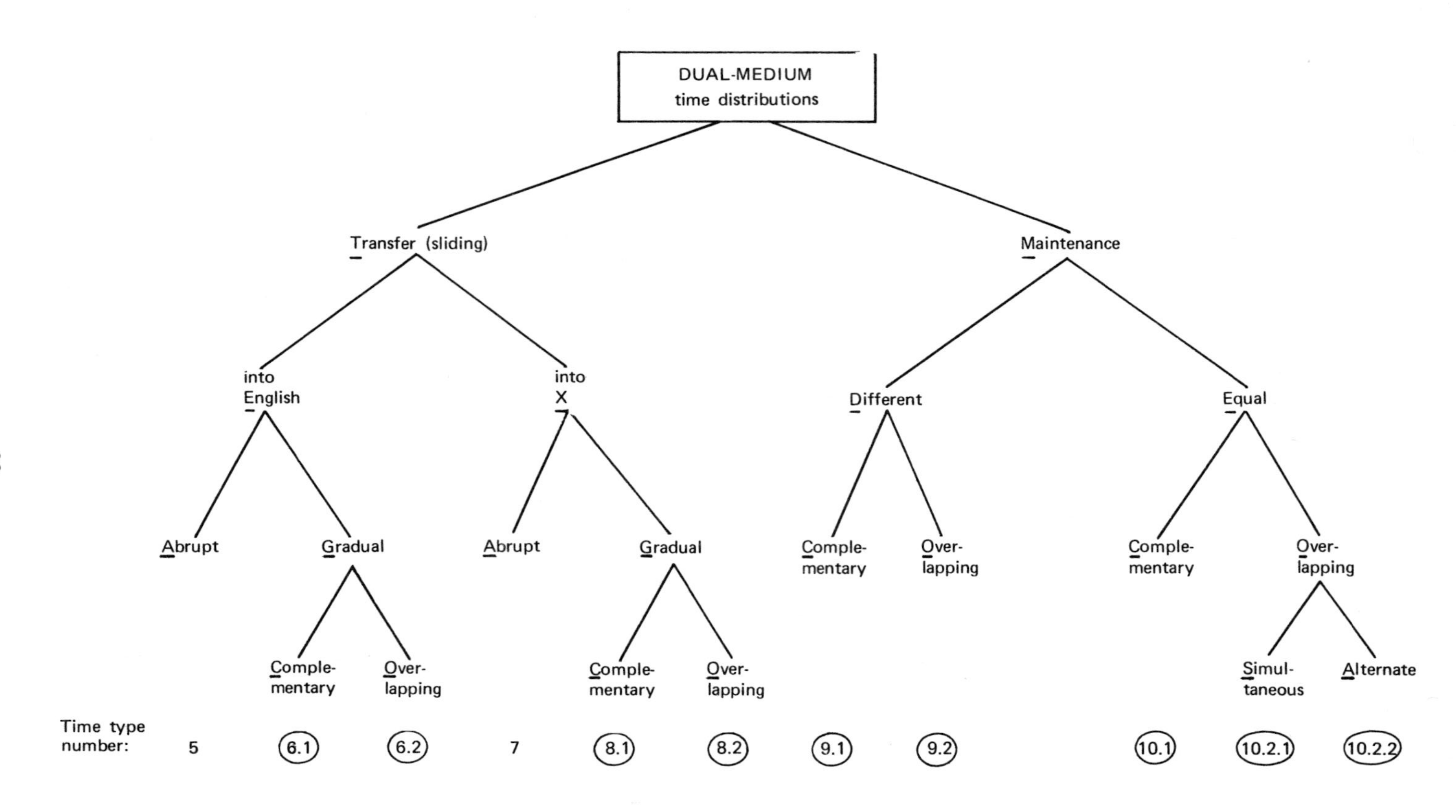
DUAL-MEDIUM
time distributions
Transfer (sliding)
Maintenance
into English
into X
Different
Equal
Abrupt
Gradual
Abrupt
Gradual
Comple-mentary
Over-lapping
Comple-mentary
Over-lapping
Comple-mentary
Over-lapping
Comple-mentary
Over-lapping
Simul-taneous
Alternate
Time type number:
5
6.1
6.2
7
8.1
8.2
9.1
9.2
10.1
10.2.1
10.2.2

CURRENTLY FUNDABLE
UNDER BEA

Description	For X-speakers	For X-Speakers, E-Speakers, or Both	Limitations on Funding
Dual-medium gradual transfer to English: 6.1 - Complementary distribution of subjects between languages E (English) and X (other). 6.2 - Overlapping distribution of subjects in E and X.	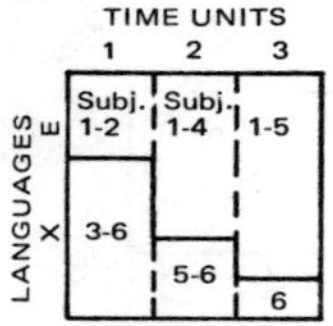 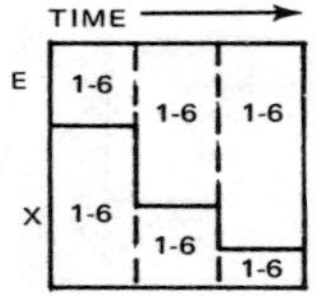 TIME UNITS 1 2 3; LANGUAGES E: Subj. 1-2, Subj. 1-4, 1-5; X: 3-6, 5-6, 6 TIME →; E: 1-6, 1-6, 1-6; X: 1-6, 1-6, 1-6		BEA funding ends when instruction through X ends. Number of subjects in each language and *rate* of transfer are illustrative only.
Dual-medium gradual transfer to X: 8.1 - Complementary distribution of subjects between E and X. 8.2 - Overlapping distribution of subjects in E and X.		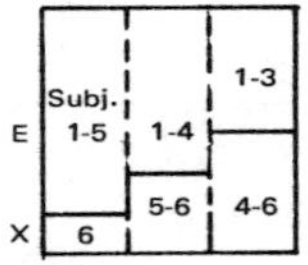 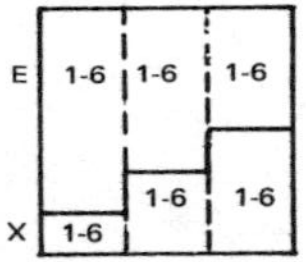 E: Subj. 1-5, 1-4, 1-3; X: 6, 5-6, 4-6 E: 1-6, 1-6, 1-6; X: 1-6, 1-6, 1-6	Maximum fundable amount of X on an *increasing* basis is presumably 50%. Number of subjects in each language and rate of transfer are illustrative only.

Description	X-Speakers	X-Speakers, E-Speakers, or Both.	Limitations
Dual-medium maintenance of both X and E, in different amounts of time:			Maximum X for *X-speakers*, up to but not including 100 percent, probably expected to decrease later to maximum of 50; maximum X for *E-Speakers,* up to 50 percent.
9.1 - Complementary distribution of subjects in E and X.	E: 1-2 X: Subjects 3-6	E: Subjects 1-4 X: 5-6	Portions of time shown in these 4 examples are illustrative only, but are *unequal.*
9.2 - Overlapping distribution of subjects in E and X.	E: 1-6 X: Subjects 1-6	E: Subjects 1-6 X: 1-6	See also types 10.1, 10.2.1, and 10.2.2 below, in which *equal* time is allowed for each language.

		E-Speakers, or Both.	
Dual-medium maintenance of both E and X, in equal amounts of time:			
10.1 - Complementary distribution of subjects in E and X.		E: Subjects 1-3 X: 4-6	
10.2 - Overlapping distribution of subjects in E and X.			
10.2.1 - Simultaneous timing.		F: Subjects 1-6 X: 1-6	A variation on type 10.2.1 is what is known as "mixed" use of both languages in all subjects, throughout the day. We may call this 10.2.1a: E X E X E X X E X E X E E X E X E X X E X E X E E X E X E X X E X E X E
10.22 - Alternate time units entirely in E, then X, etc. (e.g., by month, semester, year).		TIME UNITS 1: Subj. 1-6 in X 2: 1-6 in E 3: 1-6 in X 4: 1-6 in E 5: 1-6 in X 6: 1-6 in E	Length of alternating time units in 10.2.2 is not fixed by Act or Guidelines but presumably must be short enough to avoid confusion of this type with unilingual schooling.

As we have indicated, all the blocks shown above are abstractions. They may represent entire school programs, or they may be conceived as segments that can be combined in various orders and for varying periods of time. One block may be appropriate for all or part of the X-speaking children while at the same point in time another type is better suited to the educational needs of E-speakers in various stages of advancement toward bilingualism. For this reason the school may wish to design two or more tracks that move in the direction of merging. An example of such a design is Bruce Gaarder's much more detailed chart showing the time distribution pattern of Coral Way Elementary School. (See reproduction of this chart.[37])

Programs for X-Speaking Children

Again we refer our reader to Mackey's typology, especially to section 1 and 3, on "The Learner in the Home" and "The Community in the Nation." Of the five types of learners identified there, the prime beneficiaries of the BEA are:

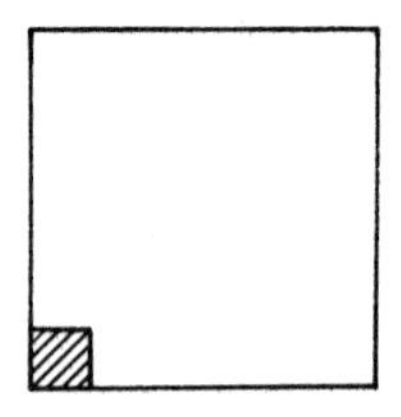

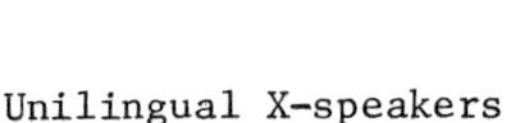

Unilingual X-speakers

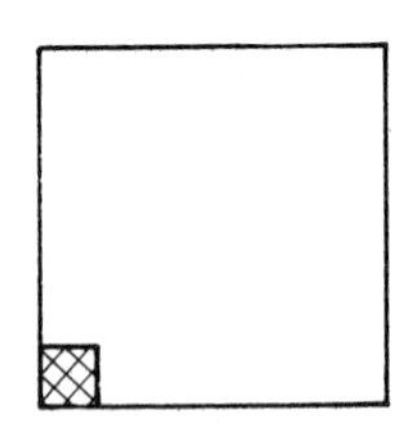

Bilinguals (in X and E, to whatever extent, but especially if X is dominant)

Yet not only American *children*, but also American communities or regions may be described as either essentially unilingual (in E), or more or less bilingual in E and X. Although there are other possibilities, there are the most common ones in our country today.

The kind and degree of language reinforcement which each child receives in the normal course of his life at home and in the community should figure heavily in determining how his school program can most fruitfully be distributed between English and X. Yet in introducing the dimensions of home and community, we cannot fail to stress that, if at all possible, program decisions should be made on educational, not political, grounds.

Two of the educational factors that should be given especially careful consideration are:

(1) the child's linguistic past—his readiness to receive the education he needs, through the medium of X, or E, or of both; and

(2) the child's context—the social and psychological impact that he can be expected to experience as a result of the particular school program in which he is placed.

The widely differing backgrounds of our X-speaking children give very different meaning to these two factors as they apply to different individuals and groups. There are immigrant children and children whose forbears have been here for centuries; there are urban children and rural children and migrant children; children of parents with proud educated heritages and children to whose ancestors books have been virtually unknown for generations; there are Eskimos in tiny villages, and French-speaking blacks in Louisiana, and Basque sheepherders scattered across the wide expanses of the West; there are the millions of Spanish-speakers of the Southwest, Florida, and New York, and the 267 Supai Indians who live on the floor of the Grand Canyon. It would be idle for us to try to determine here the exact formulas that would fit all these cases, but every X-speaking child has both background and surroundings. They cannot reasonably be ignored.

* * * * *

It may nonetheless be useful to elaborate on some situations in which various combinations might be put into operation. What follows is set forth in that spirit, and it should not be construed as in any way prescriptive.

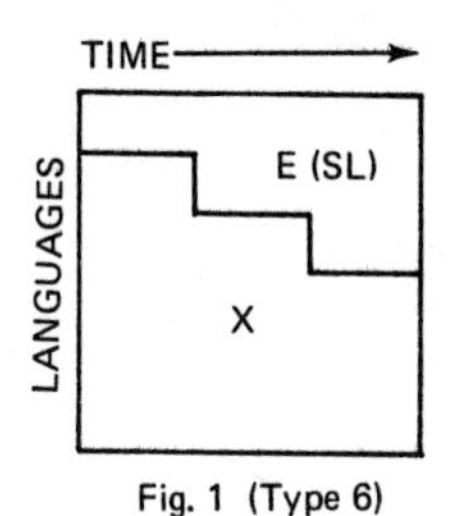

Fig. 1 (Type 6)

In this sketch, X is the child's stronger language—for example, Spanish or Navajo—and English is his second language. The figure shows how one group of planners might propose to arrange the first stage of this child's formal schooling. How long this portion should last is not indicated. Let us imagine that we are thinking of Nursery (N) or Kindergarten (K) through grade 3. The program shown here emphasizes the child's need first to establish himself firmly in school in his own language, X. It assumes that it would be to the child's advantage to spend the major portion of his early schooling in X. But E is gradually introduced and increased, for it is the language which in the long run will carry at least half the instructional load in his education. *How* E and X are to be used has been spoken of in our section on Content. Now we are concerned with the *how much*.

The beginning shown in Fig. 1 might be followed by any one of various programs, again depending on what is judged to be in the children's best interest. So, for example, children of Cuban or Puerto Rican families who now live in a bilingual-bicultural community in the United

States might profitably carry on the use of each language halftime through the elementary or secondary schools (Fig 2). Here the second block would represent, say grades 4-6 (or 8 or 12). This combination is roughly the time distribution of the Coral Way Elementary School in Miami, and the goal of the Bilingual School in New York City.[38]

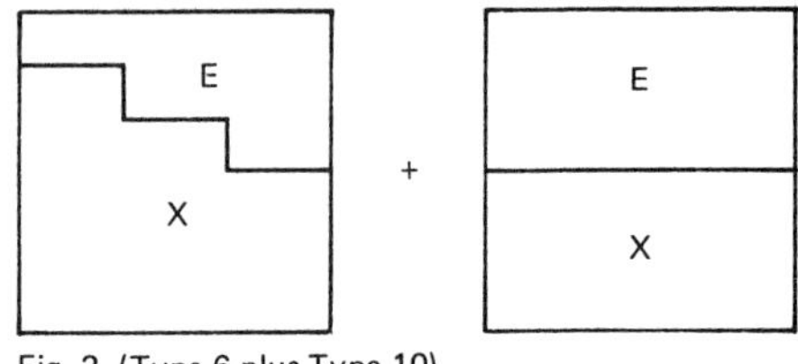

Fig. 2 (Type 6 plus Type 10)

A second kind of follow-up might be used in an area where the accident of birthplace has made literacy in X locally less strong. The loss of vigor in the literate tradition has in most cases been the direct result of our unilingualizing school policies, which have too often turned bilingualism into a personal liability; for example, among the Franco-Americans in parts of New England, or for the Spanish-speaking in parts of the Southwest. Although there are a few communities in these same areas that remain strong, that prefer and are following the pattern already described, others might choose to, or have to, aim at a program like this:

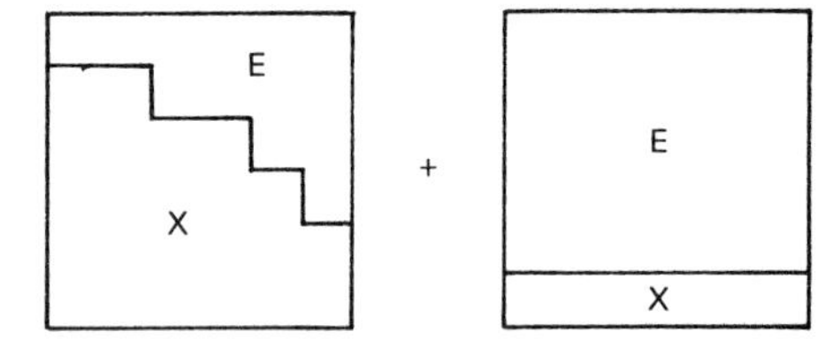

Fig. 3 (Type 6 plus Type 9)

Such a choice might not actually reflect the community's preference about the relative time given to each language. It might be based merely on inability to do more because of inadequate staff or materials, for example. If such is the case, a modest start might be in order while the necessary further provisions are being made. Then the school could move into fuller use of X, as in Fig. 2.

A third follow-up can be conceived for still other cases. In these situations, for one reason or another a total transfer to E is thought to be best or necessary for the X children. If, for example, educational materials are non-existent in X and none are foreseeable in the future (Supai might be an example.) Or if unexpected historical events place the schools in situations that require crash programs for short periods until provisions can be made for fuller use of X in the education of X-speakers.[39] Or if the X-speaking people themselves resolutely determine to have their children transfer totally into unilingual schooling in E. They have this right, and Fig. 4 shows a means to such an end. BEA funding would presumably cease at the asterisk (*) in any of these cases.

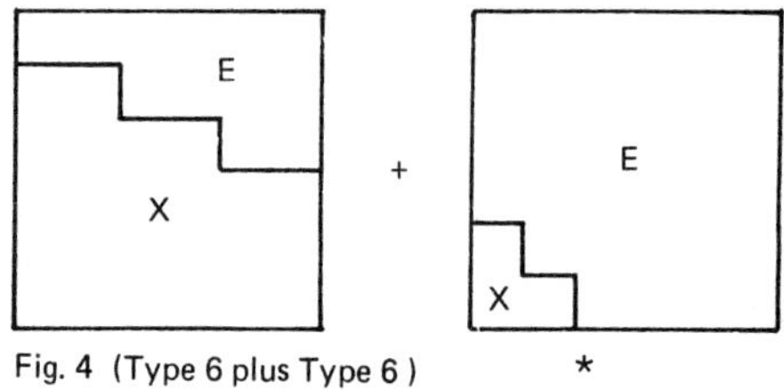

Fig. 4 (Type 6 plus Type 6)

* * * * *

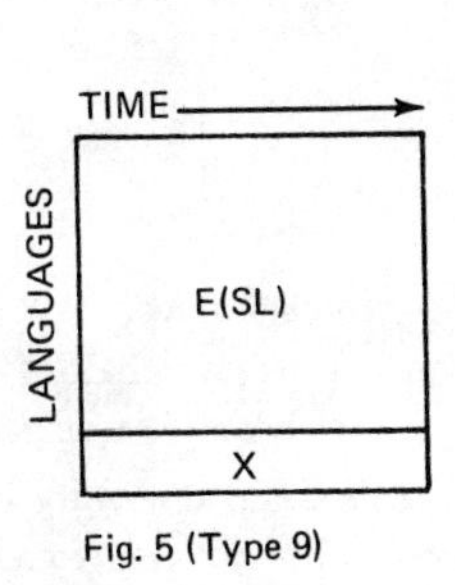

Fig. 5 (Type 9)

An entirely different approach is represented by programs *beginning* as in Fig. 5. Unlike Fig. 1, Fig. 5 stresses the importance, at this stage, of virtual immersion of the child in his second language (here English); it also minimizes his need for school use of X. This approach is supported by some who feel it is in the child's best interest to capitalize while he can on the ability to acquire another tongue with native-like pronunciation: an ability belonging almost exclusively to the very young. But Fig. 5 will also appeal to those whose aim is to delete X eventually altogether.

Depending on one's philosophy, therefore, or upon one's assessment of the relative importance of the several needs of children in a specific community, proposed follow-ups to Fig. 5 may range all the way from total use of E (Fig. 6) to greater use of X (Fig. 7)—possibly up to 50 percent.

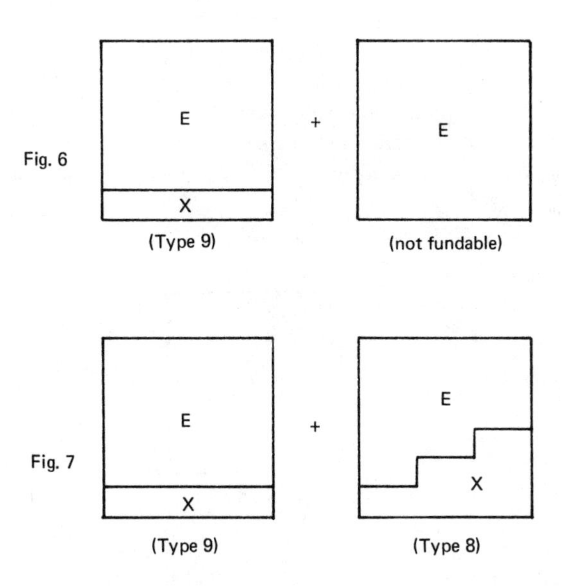

Again the choice should be made in consideration of what promises most for the children's total good, both in childhood and in the years beyond.

* * * * *

A middle ground between the two beginnings shown (in Fig. 1 and Fig. 5) is any one of the forms of Type 10, where each language is given half of the school time from the start (Fig. 8). Many communities find this the most convenient way of recognizing both *language* needs and *psychological or social* needs. If this balance is truly in keeping with the requirements of the children and is not merely an administrative convenience, it may indeed be ideal. It certainly appears to be the easiest to schedule; but it involves some hard decisions about distributing subjects between the two languages or teaching them all in both.

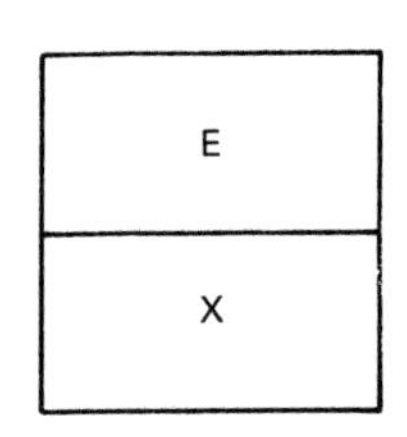

Fig. 8 (Type 10)

Programs for Children Whose Dominant Language Is English

"In an area eligible for a Title VII project, children from environments where the dominant language is English are eligible to participate when their participation is such as to enhance the effectiveness of the program." So say the Guidelines of the BEA. But even before this provision was made, a number of communities had seen the desirability of bilingual schooling for E-speaking children as well as for those dominant in X. Though E-speakers have usually not had the language-centered learning difficulties that plague many X-speakers,[40] other reasons for advocating bilingual education abound. It is a happy circumstance indeed that the BEA provides the means of encouraging programs whose benefits may be expected to redound in two directions, both to and from each group in a bilingual community. The authors would recommend that future revisions of the BEA lend greater support to programs where two-way efforts at bilingualism and biculturalism are among the highest aims.

Meanwhile, highly suggestive for planners are programs for E-speakers going even as far as this:

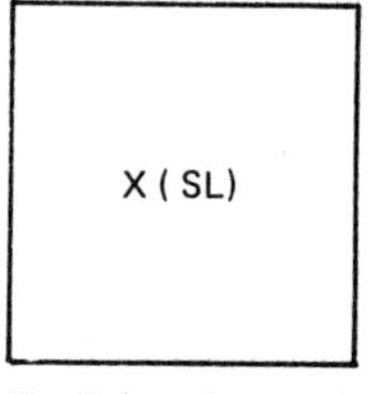

Fig. 9 (not fundable)

Here X is a second language for the children but is used exclusively for the entire first stage. An example, though not in this country, is the St. Lambert School near the bilingual city of

Montreal, a public elementary school where middle-class E-speaking children are taught entirely in French in K and grade 1. Thereafter, E is added and gradually increased toward half (as in Fig. 1, except that now X is the second language, not E).[41]

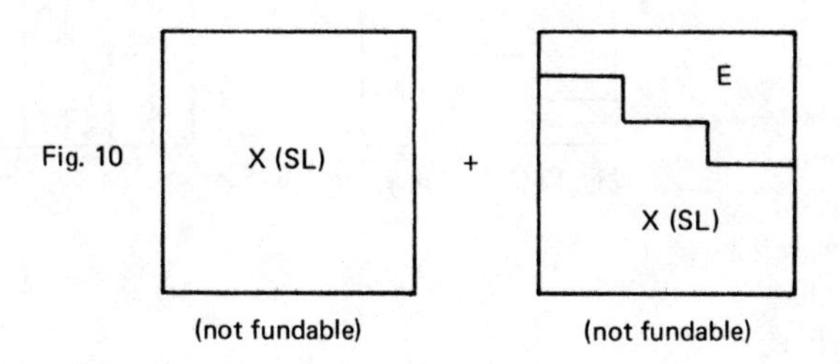

Fig. 10

Fundable patterns of X for E-speakers in bilingual areas range all the way from the type shown in Fig. 11 to a minimum as shown in Fig. 12.

Fig. 11 (Type 10)

Fig. 12 (Type 9)

Planners should be conscious of the problems that beset an XSL program of the limited dimensions shown in Fig. 12. Witness the average FLES (foreign language in the elementary school) program or the typical high school "foreign language" course, where X is so frequently treated in a vacuum. The direct and indirect benefits of XSL depend primarily on interaction with X-speaking peers. Without them, XSL tends to become academic (in the worst sense of the word). The smaller the amount of school time devoted to XSL, the more academic it usually becomes.

* * * * *

Programs designed for E-speaking children need not, of course, exactly parallel those for speakers of X. But if a community is seriously interested in educating children from *both* home backgrounds bilingually, the authors strongly recommend that the E group begin X(SL) from the very beginning of school and that instruction in X be made available (not obligatory) throughout the entire school program. Seemingly the optimum distribution for E children is that used at Coral Way School (Fig. 13), with this program extending throughout the school (grades 1-6). This is the full counterpart of the program of the Spanish-speaking children in that school, as seen in Fig. 2 above.

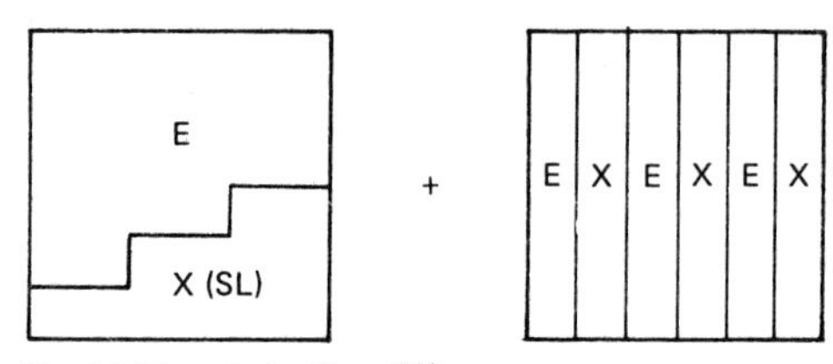

Fig. 13 (Type 8 plus Type 10)

* * * * *

"Mixed" Use of Two Languages

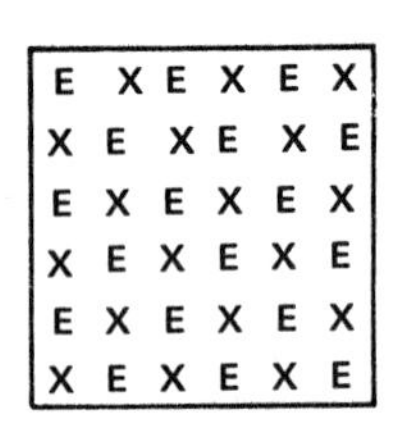

Fig. 14 (Type 10)

A few words may be in order about the unique time pattern in which bilingual teachers "mix" the languages or move freely from one to the other throughout the day. The goal is to achieve a 50-50 time distribution equivalent to that in other forms of Type 10 (see 10.1, 10.2.1, and 10.2.2).

This unfettered arrangement has two very great attractions: it mixes all children from the start, and it requires only one set of teachers. Examples can be seen in grades 1-3 in Nye School of the United Consolidated Independent School District outside Laredo, Texas; and in grade 1 of the John F. Kennedy Community School in West Berlin. The possibilities for equal treatment in all subject areas seem to be much greater in N and K, with progressively more problems as one moves up through the grades.

The chief difficulty, as far as time itself is concerned, is in actually achieving the desired time distribution in all subjects and activities. It is hard to keep track of how much each language is really used for what. In addition, the bilingual teacher is almost inevitably stronger in E in some domains and in X in others, and this is likely to tip the balance now one way and now the other. Special kinds of questions for achievement testing thus arise.

III. Methods and Materials

Both methods and materials have been touched on incidentally elsewhere in this chapter, particularly with respect to specific subject matters. But some of the most troublesome questions still remain. One of them is this: how to get everything in.

Time and again teachers and administrators will be forced to ask themselves what they really *want* to get in, and how badly they want it. This is the fundamental question. Be it said at the outset that the easiest solution is to forget about bilingual and bicultural education altogether; or if not that, to give only token recognition to the X language and culture. This is the easiest, we say; yet we have seen in the educational results of the past how far short of being satisfactory has been our policy of pouring all children into the same mold.

Any other system that we, the authors, know anything about takes more effort, more thought, and usually more money. No way around it. But there do seem to be ways of accomplishing this better education without taking more of the children's time. The three best ideas about this seem to be: (1) to split the total time for a subject between the two languages; (2) to allot some subjects to one language and some to the other; or (3) a combination of these two approaches: one system for some subjects, the other for the rest.[42]

Splitting the Time. This idea usually frightens a teacher, especially if there is the prospect of using a team-teaching approach in which one teacher has half the day in one language and his opposite number has the other half day. He immediately sees that this cuts in half his time for each subject he teaches. He needs to be reminded that, although this is true, the subject itself is not receiving any less time, for the child gets an equal amount of instruction from another teacher of the same subject.

All teaching involves repetition. In this case much of the repetition comes through the other language. This change of medium, it is supposed, works to make the repetition more effective, for we know that repetition should rarely be used verbatim. Teaching requires that the same thing be said over and over and over again, but in different ways, until the ideas are fully mastered. Using two languages can in itself combat boredom at the same time that it holds out the possibility of giving the child new perspectives on the subject he is studying.

Splitting the time can also be an antidote to laziness or "tuning out" on the part of some children, especially if the two-teacher system is used. Here the demands of each teacher are independent (the team will undoubtedly compare notes, but the children will have little consciousness of this behind-the-scenes operation),[43] and the child knows he needs the approval of each one.

Each teacher should therefore act as if everything the child learned in a specific subject depended on his own portion of the day, but comfort himself in his dark hours by realizing there is a counterpart he can rely on. His own work will always be supplemented by another teacher who is trying too.

The Coral Way School has recently devised a new system of grade-reporting which would appear to have advantages in this area as well as in others. Formerly the two teachers of a child conferred, and, at the end of each grading period they compromised on a grade for each subject. This had the disadvantage of obscuring the difference between *subject* strength or weakness and *language* strength or weakness. Under the new system there will be a grade for mathematics in Spanish and one for mathematics in English, etc. By looking at all the grades in both languages, both parent and school can tell whether the child's problem areas are related to a specific subject matter or to one or the other of the languages.

It is a part of our system that we require children to perform for grades. Under the arrangement proposed, we believe this aspect of the system could be turned to greater benefits for the child himself. One teacher may be able to keep all the children attentive and interested all the time, but unfortunately such master teachers are rare. Two teachers, each with half the total time for a school subject, seem much more likely than one to be able to make profitable use of the grade-reward system.

Whether the teaching is done by a team or by a single bilingual teacher, we are assuming that the instruction given in the two languages will not be carbon-copy. As we see it, translation or near-translation involves three major hazards in a bilingual program if the same child gets both versions. First, it is boring. Hardly anything more damaging could be said about elementary school instruction. Only the most phenomenal child will learn from something that bores him. Second, if the child knows he will get the same thing sooner or later in his own best language, he will tend to wait for that, and not reach for the second language. And third, materials that are translated for this purpose are almost invariably unicultural in content. We will not belabor this point, hoping instead that the reasons underlying our preference for a bicultural or multicultural outlook have already been made clear.

If one bilingual teacher is chosen rather than a team, the arguments of the preceding paragraph would suggest that he seriously consider setting aside specific portions of time for each language, rather than "mixing" them freely throughout the day.[44] Such a division does have what some teachers consider to be a drawback: a child's interest and curiosity may at a certain moment suggest a question that he hesitates to voice if the language being used at the time is his weaker means of communication. The loss can be minimized if children are made to feel that the division between the portions of the day is not inviolable – that there is never a time when the use of their mother tongue would be morally wrong – and only that the goal is to use each language at its own separate time. This attitude, developed in children, will help them to come to see that there are times and places when each language in turn is preferable to any other, and to develop a sense of which situations are which, and why. In the process, however, such instruction would require that no teacher in a bilingual school, at least through the primary grades, be 100 percent unilingual. It is not only children who must make room for other styles of life, but adults as well.

Finally, we should say that most of what has just preceded has taken for granted an equal split in time (Program Type 10.2.1.). Unequal splits are also possible (Types 6.2, 8.2, and 9.2). Under these arrangements one language is the main load-bearer, and the other, in a smaller amount of time, tries to reinforce the learning of the whole curriculum. This presents obvious difficulties for the teacher using the language with the smaller amount of time, but judicious emphasis, either on what is most needed or on what the children show special interest and talent for, can make the program valuable. In these cases of unequal split, it is especially important that the child's attention not be focused unduly on the language itself as a subject, but on the things that can be learned *through* that language.[45]

Allotting the Time by Subjects. The main questions, if it is decided to allot some subjects to English and others to X, are: which ones? and on what basis? There seems to be a fair amount of agreement. Language arts obviously go to their respective languages. Art, music, physical education, recess, lunch, assemblies, parties, field trips, and athletic contests – all these can be in either language or both. These are features of school that are close to life itself and, as Fishman points out,[46] *laissez-faire* used to be a part of the American mystique. Let us see if we can revitalize this value in our rapidly solidifying culture. Quick before it hardens!

Two criteria may help in making the other decisions, if not all subjects are to be learned bilingually by the child.

1) Those things considered to be the areas of highest achievement of each culture might be taught to the child in that culture's language. Especially for X-speaking children, outstanding aspects of the X culture should be available to them in their dominant tongue. Thus a people's history and its own cultural patterns should be seen from the inside, in X, by X-speaking children. Meanwhile, the E version of this same subject matter should not be so uniculturally E as to omit the X achievements, even if they are dealt with in somewhat less detail there.

2) Courses that may be expected to be of particular occupational utility to the child should be available to him in his dominant language. Children from the X side have natural advantages, if they are properly schooled, in becoming bilingual secretaries (very very few now have the literate skills for this), customs and immigration officials, international airline or other business employees, interpreters and translators for various governmental agencies, teachers of the X language or of other subjects in bilingual schools; "...no plan will be successful that does not open the door for the pupils into satisfying jobs in the American culture as it exists in the last half of the twentieth century."[47] Program planners should look at the region around them and ask themselves what special opportunities there are for educated bilinguals, not stopping with blue-collar jobs. What would be the opportunities in law, for example, or in medicine? It is not a mistake to look that far ahead in trying to determine what should be offered in which language in the elementary school. Nor should the present narrowness of subsequent educational facilities in X be too heavily weighed. As our whole society expands, opportunities for both education and work will certainly expand as well: it seems certain we can never be an island unto ourselves again.

We have been speaking of allotting subjects to languages on a more or less ongoing basis (Program Types 10.1, 9.1, 8.1, or 6.1). This can also be done by rotation, so that the children are not left with all their formal education in some subjects in E, and in other subjects in X. One way of offsetting this, especially after the point at which subjects are departmentalized, is to have a subject taught in E at one grade level and in X at the next. For example, if a school has two social studies teachers for grades 4-6, and one teacher can teach social studies in X at these three grades, the children who study that subject in X at grade 4 can pursue it in E at grade 5, and back to X in grade 6. The other teacher has a similarly rotating student body. Exceptions can be made for individual children as the need arises. This kind of leap-frogging from one year to the next is not as impractical as it may at first sound; most teachers spend a period at the first of each year in review. In this system, "review" would in part be a recapping of previously learned material by adding the necessary vocabulary and terminology to cover the new concepts acquired the year before.

Combinations. Combinations of time-splitting and subject-allotting are also possible, as we have suggested, and variations can be worked out best at each local scene. One example should suffice. If mathematics in E seems to be generally a great problem for X speakers, the X children might split their mathematics time between X and E even if E children study mathematics only in E. The point is that there is no reason to make all children follow precisely the same pattern: the idea is to help them *learn*. If, however, they can learn in two languages, bilingualism becomes an asset, not a liability. Arthur Jensen has noted that the two most reliable indices of socio-economic status are occupation and educational achievement. Beyond economics and beyond the number of grades completed lies the intellectual status of competence across cultures. We believe this kind of education is the finest that a community can offer, to any or all of its children.

Methodology in Early Stages. Contemporary views differ on what teaching method is most appropriate to early childhood. Stated in a greatly over-simplified way, some authorities stress freedom and play as the best avenues for learning, while others emphasize the economy of a highly structured approach, with teaching materials and procedures planned out in much detail. A third view is a synthesis of the first and second: it accepts the motivational validity of play, and it assumes this is not necessarily in conflict with order based on purely linguistic concerns.

In speaking of methodologies for a bilingual child or program, language teachers and others must constantly remind themselves that it is not language alone that the child must learn. It is everything that goes into his school education. The primary factor is who and what the child is, *apart* from the school. His particular background can tell us, if we listen hard enough, both what he wants to preserve of that non-school self and what the school may add that will benefit him.[48]

Ideally such diagnosis would be done on an absolutely individual basis. We are far from accomplishing such a dreamed-of education for each individual child, but the least we can do is to take cognizance of the large groups among us that bring different things with them to the school. This means that we should not expect to find one methodology that will work best with all cultural groups. Some cultures teach their children personal pride with high achievement; others teach theirs that personal victories should not be permitted to single out an individual from his fellows. In teaching the children of these two backgrounds, it would first of all seem essential that the teacher know thoroughly the framework of values within which his pupils live and work; and second, that he proceed in such a way as to help each child, rather than setting him at odds with his family or with the children of the other cultural group. The fact that all the children go to the same school does not mean there is no variety in their cultural milieu outside. Thus it may be entirely reasonable to have two very different methodologies being used in one school.

The teacher must be especially flexible in the presence of an X-speaking child. While respecting the child's native dialect, he must tactfully add or expand a standard form of X, and at the same time initiate the child into E. Also, while respecting the values of the X culture, he must teach sufficient understanding of E cultural values to enable the child to feel at home in both the X stream and the E stream. This is very far from being an easy task.

We agree with Zintz, Ulibarrí, and Miller that "the child whose cultural heritage is different from the school culture is in need of special educational services that will bridge the cultural barriers and meet his language needs before he can take advantage of the course of study with which he is apt to be confronted."[49] The authors spell out some of the values that the dominant culture teaches, values with which any child in an American school needs to become familiar:

1. He must climb the ladder of success, and in order to do this he must place a high value on competitive achievement.

2. He must learn time orientation that will be precise to the hour and minute, and he must also learn to place a high value on looking to the future.

3. He must accept the teachers' reiteration that there is a scientific explanation for all natural phenomena.

4. He must become accustomed to change and must anticipate change. (The dominant culture teaches that "change," in and of itself, is good and desirable!)

5. He must trade his shy, quiet, reserved, and anonymous behavior for socially approved aggressive, competitive behavior.

6. He must somehow be brought to understand that he can, with some independence, shape his own destiny, as opposed to the tradition of remaining an anonymous member of his society.[50]

These are new and in part alien concepts to some of the children in our schools, yet we wish to register serious doubts about a good bit of what passes for "concept development" among children with little or no English. On the whole, children come to school with their own culture's concepts already formed or forming in their minds. Too often teachers and materials writers think that they have *no* concepts, or proceed as if they had none. This can be quite damaging, for it fails to recognize that the child's mind is not simply a *tabula rasa:* he is being presented two different and sometimes positively conflicting value systems. As Sarah Gudschinsky comments,

> *...teachers are inclined to expect as "concept development" in a non-English speaker the simple memorizing and parroting of words for which the child has in fact no meaning. (Without doubt we do this with the English-speaking child as well. An immediate illustration which comes to mind is a Sunday school class which I taught on Easter Sunday of this year. Asked: what is Easter for? the children answered readily "It is the day when Jesus rose from the dead." Pressed for an explanation of the phrase "rose from the dead," however, the children had no realistic idea whatsoever of what these words mean. It was a shocking surprise to them when we discussed the Easter event in terms of a modern setting in which a corpse pushes up the lid of his coffin and climbs out.)*
>
> *It has been drawn to my attention that in Australia the Aborigines reach a ceiling in their education in English which is at least in part due to the fact that they have a great deal of English vocabulary that they can read and use in answering test questions but for which they actually have no real world meaning at all.*
>
> *It seems to me that this is an important element in the notion of teaching a second language to children, and in the notion of concept development.*
>
> *Another point ... is that it is not easy to give a person a new concept if that new concept is in conflict with something he already knows. In this connection the cross-cultural studies are exceedingly important. Unless the teacher understands what the child has already learned from his own culture, he will find it very difficult to give him new ideas which match the second culture.*[51]

Methodology of Second Language Teaching. Within this much larger picture is the methodology of teaching the second language as such, where there are again differences in contemporary ideas. The basis for some of these differences has been discussed in our section on Content, under "The Child's Second Language." Bruce Gaarder, speaking of second language teaching, writes as follows:

> *The teacher-learning cannot be left to chance or to the teacher's ingenuity.... The* structuring *comes outside of class, when the course of study is being laid down. It consists of the careful selection, in advance, of situations, experiences, activities,* and most especially teacher-pupil talk, *which guarantee complete coverage and re-coverage of the desired lexicon and structures and concepts, but which, in the classroom, make language the means of natural access to those situations, experiences, and activities. In other words, the child's attention should not be focused on language and the teacher's use of language should not be restricted or made inauthentic. The* structuring *should not be* apparent *to anyone, but the curriculum-makers know it's there.*[52]

Toward Merging. How far up the grades one has to go before all children are able to merge successfully without regard to language is not known, and there will always be individual differences. Two points should perhaps be made about the idea of merging:

1) All instruction in and through the child's weaker or second language (SL) should aim toward the eventual use of this language as if it were not weaker. That is, teachers should strive to bring ESL to E (ESLE), and XSL to X (XSLX) as rapidly as possible. The sooner this can be accomplished, the better. Children will profit in their SL by maximum interaction with native-speaking peers, and teachers will have their instructional planning reduced from two streams to one. This applies whether one is speaking of the language as a subject or as a medium for teaching other subjects. As soon as any child can join a section not marked SL, he should be transferred into the regular E or X section for that part of the day. Transfer of this kind should be highlighted as a mark of excellence, whichever language the child is "graduating" in.

2) The X child should not be forced to "graduate" before he is ready, especially from ESL language arts. The effect of pressing him too hard would be to abandon him too soon to competition he cannot meet. ESL language arts will probably be the last subject in which he can successfully join the rest of the E students in common instruction through E. By the same token XSL language arts will probably last longest for E students striving to join the X stream.

Materials

The identification, annotation, and evaluation of instructional materials in such a way as to be useful for

(1) each age and interest level, and
(2) each difficulty range, in
(3) each subject area, for
(4) each culture or subculture, and
(5) each linguistic group

is a task clearly beyond the scope of this monograph. Aside from the fact that the present writers do not have the various kinds of specialized knowledge to do the work that needs to be done in this field, it seems doubtful that a single listing for all these variables could be made quickly enough, or kept up to date well enough, to make such a project feasible. There is both a dearth of materials and a wealth of materials, depending on what one is looking for and what criteria he is trying to meet. Rather than naming specific sets of materials or individual books in one language or the other, therefore, we offer the reader a few thoughts on these subjects: finding existing materials that are usable or adaptable and creating materials, teacher made or otherwise. We have also indicated some sources of materials in Appendix W.

Finding Out What Exists. Unfortunately, many teachers and administrators who are new to the field of bilingual schooling conclude all too quickly that no materials, or no suitable materials, exist for their particular situation. This may indeed be true, particularly in the local languages. "Of the nearly 300 American Indian languages and dialects extant, only roughly 40 percent have more than 100 speakers. In the case of about 55 percent of these languages, the remaining speakers are of advanced age."[53] Instructional materials for these small groups are few and far between. At the other extreme there is the case of Spanish, whose abundance of visual and written material existing for the nearly 200 million Spanish speakers in various parts of the world has hardly had its surface scratched by our experimenters in bilingual schooling. This is not to suggest that every book written in an X language is immediately ready for use in the schools of this country. There are questions of commercial availability and supply; of standards of editing, printing, and binding; of uniculturalism from the X side, especially regarding national allegiance and religion. In some instances there is the need for diplomatic and cultural agreements between our countries to make use or adaptation possible. But the *creation* of materials is an arduous path, filled with pitfalls even for experienced travelers. We advise that, whenever it is at all possible, existing materials be tried first, and adapted as necessary. Let us survey the field briefly.

Materials for teaching English as a second language are in great supply, especially in the language arts sense. Materials in English for other subjects, specifically designed for those learning it as a second language, are much less common. Some ESL materials have been designed with a specific dominant-language background in mind, to teach, say, English to Spanish speakers. Writers of such books concentrate on specific points at which the Spanish and English language systems differ. Other writers attribute less importance to the learner's "language of departure" and stress each part of English structure or sound as they judge best. In selecting a set of materials, the bilingual program planner should be aware of the population the writers themselves had in mind. Such a factor might not preclude their usefulness for a different population, but it should be borne in mind.

To our knowledge, the best sources of information on materials for ESL–both titles and evaluations– are the Center for Applied Linguistics and TESOL. (See Appendix W, Directory: Sources of Materials). Inquiries should state the age of the learners, their linguistic and cultural background, and the difficulty level sought.

The subject of materials in the other languages makes a much less neat package. For Indian and Eskimo languages, the Center for Applied Linguistics is again probably the best source of information, but the Summer Institute of Linguistics (See Appendix W, Directory) is also extremely helpful. This organization has developed literacy materials and textbooks in numerous languages, even for very small groups of speakers, and its *Bibliography*[54] should not be overlooked by those concerned with local tongues.

For languages of wider communication other than English, the most general source of information is the MLA (Modern Language Association) and its organizational "child," the young but vigorous ACTFL (American Council for the Teaching of Foreign Languages), located at the same address. (See Appendix W, Directory.) In 1962, the MLA issued an annotated *Selective List of Materials* which included guidelines or criteria for judging numerous categories of materials, whether printed, audiovisual, or combinations. This list was updated with *Supplements* for various languages in 1964 (see Appendix W, Directory). Most of the items listed were judged with respect to their suitability for E speakers learning X as a foreign language. A few, however, were reviewed with an eye to their usefulness either to a native speaker of X attempting to further his general education through X, or to an E speaker in a more high-powered X course of the kind a full-blown bilingual program might need. Also included with each of these lists is a directory of publishers, some American and some foreign.

In the case of Spanish, another ambitious effort has been undertaken, this time by Books for the People Fund, Inc., whose director, Mrs. Marietta Daniels Shepard, can be contacted at the Pan American Union in Washington, D. C. Mrs. Shepard is guiding a staff of trained personnel in the collection of printed Spanish material on all subjects for use by children of various ages, whether as regular school texts or for general reading. The materials sent by publishers are reviewed for quality of content and for physical makeup. Only books available in quantities of at least 100 copies are considered. Those judged suitable for use by schools in this country except for binding are rebound sturdily. Translation from other languages are included if they meet the criteria otherwise. The items that have been accepted as recommendable are listed then in the bulletin of *Proyecto Leer*, whose editor is Martha Tomé. At present this bulletin is issued free, at about quarterly intervals. It seems to the authors of this monograph that *Proyecto Leer* deserves broad support, both from schools searching for texts and library books and from those in position to give financial aid. The work thus far has been done almost altogether on a volunteer basis. *Proyecto Leer* comes closer than any other center, that we know about, to being a possible clearinghouse for the entire spectrum of needed materials in print for Spanish. Since 90 percent of the programs funded by the BEA this year are for this one language, a major push to expand such services seems to be in order.

Efforts are already under way to try to arrange for use in the United States of schoolbooks published by the Republic of Mexico, either with or without adaptation. Also being investigated is the possibility that the AID/ROCAP texts in Spanish may become available here. These elementary-school texts in reading, language, mathematics, science, and social studies are being cooperatively produced by writing teams representing the six Central American countries and were initially planned for use there. Their appropriateness for use in our own bilingual schools, and their availability, are being explored. Again Mrs. Shepard is perhaps the best source of information.

Worthy of mention too are the French Cultural Services, which, like most foreign governmental services, are ready to help locate sources of materials and other professional information.

The important point to remember is that there are organizations that may quite properly be called upon to assume the primary responsibility for collecting, reviewing, evaluating, and publicizing materials. This work should be done by disinterested professional groups, with whom reputable publishers have shown that they know how to cooperate fully. If schools find themselves without information on the matter of materials, the authors suggest that they not delay in making their needs known to appropriate organizations—those we have mentioned and any of the others that may be expected to have the interests of particular groups of X children at heart (see Appendix W, Directory: Organizations).

An important question to decide is whether adopted or adapted materials *can* be made to fit the objectives of a program or whether their use will produce outcomes that will seriously alter the objectives. In our opinion the danger is not great provided one is aware of the problem. One bilingual program in Texas considered some Mexican materials but found them nationalistically oriented. They decided to refer the matter to the school board, which very sensibly suggested, "Use them by all means. Whenever the Mexican flag is waved, just wave the American flag, and go right on."

Creating Materials

> It is imperative to determine how long in the school life of the learner a language can be *maintained* as a medium of instruction. The availability of suitable reading matter is perhaps the most significant single measure which could be used to help answer this important question. If we are going to start with programs likely to succeed, it is more important to make use of what is available than to invest heavily in the preparation of expensive low-circulation materials which may never be used.[55]

To this *caveat* the authors would like to add that "inexpensive" school texts, produced by a single author, can turn out to be just as costly in the long run if individuals all across the country are working single-handedly or naively. Good textbooks for language study prepared by a sole author have become almost an anomaly. People in this field have come to realize more and more the variety of talents and skills involved, and the rarity of finding all the necessary wisdom and ability within one person. In this respect *Modern Spanish* was a kind of trail-blazer in 1959.[56] Textbook companies, regional service centers, and regional educational laboratories have all seen the value of applying teams of specialists (including classroom teachers) to production. Anyone, or any group, about to embark on a maiden voyage in materials-writing would probably find it instructive to consult with someone who has been involved in such a team undertaking, before plans are too firmly made.

Creation or Redesigning of a Writing System. But what if the X is an unwritten language, or one whose writing system is not very good? All languages were originally unwritten (except constructed languages like Esperanto) and the fact that some remain so today is unrelated to their essence as living languages and to their crucial significance to their native speakers' lives. Yet without written forms, these languages can have only a limited role in present-day American schooling. Any language that is to survive long as a medium of instruction in American education must have or acquire a viable writing system and a considerable body of writing on a variety of subjects.

Most of the major writing systems known in the world today have been the products of centuries of slow adaptation of symbol to sound (alphabets) or idea (ideograms or pictographs).[57] That there is a relatively consistent relationship between these arbitrarily shaped graphic symbols and human speech or thought is the first thing a beginner must learn about reading.

Some writing systems—the so-called "phonetic" or phonemic ones—are thought to be better than others for the purposes of learning how to read. Some systems have had a vast network of machinery invented for their use in print, or are compatible with one of these networks. Others are not so favored. Cherokee, for example. We are told that there is only one typewriter in existence that can mechanically produce the Cherokee symbols.[58] Serious attempts to produce instructional materials in appropriate quantities are naturally hindered by such a situation. Yet whether this linguistically sound alphabet should be abandoned in favor of another less precise one in the interest of ease of dissemination is not a question that should be decided by innocents.

> *It may not be quite so obvious to point out, in connection with modern spelling, that the objects of a good spelling system are two-fold. A speaker of the language should be able to pronounce correctly any sequence of letters that he may meet even if they were previously unknown, and secondarily, to be able to spell any phonemic sequence, again even if previously unknown. Most modern systems, such as Spanish, French, or Hungarian fulfill the first aim fairly well, and fail primarily in the second. The peculiar badness of the English system lies in the fact that it fails about equally in both. How badly it fails was once illustrated for me by the difficulty an Oriental student encountered in transliterating his name into English. The sequence of English phonemes was /čuw/. He could have chosen* Chew, Choo, *or* Chue, *but instead chose* Chough*–about the worst spelling which is possible.*[59]

The greatest single source of contemporary expertise in the field of invention of writing systems is the Summer Institute of Linguistics. A perusal of the *Bibliography of the Summer Institute of Linguistics 1935-1968* (compiled by Alan C. Wares, Santa Ana, California, 1968) suggests the nature and variety of the problems and also provides clues to some of the individuals who might appropriately be called upon to work on a specific language under educational development. This is a task of considerable complexity and certainly not one for amateurs.

Exclusively Oral Use of X. As we remarked above, no language can play an important role in present-day American schooling if it does not have a written form. The same can be said of the language that *can* be written and read but is in fact dealt with only orally by the community's school. Our educational system puts a tremendous premium on literacy, and it is not accidental that learning to read and write are among the bed-rock objectives of the first grade. If all this effort is devoted to literacy in E, the school is powerfully defining X, whether intentionally or unconsciously, as useless for the real business of education. The effects of this judgment can range from the sobering to the devastating and positively pernicious, depending on the actual measure of "development" the child's language has achieved on a world-wide scale. For the Supai on the floor of the Grand Canyon, it probably represents the cold truth of his tribe's place in today's world; but for the Spanish-speaking son of a migrant tomato-picker or the daughter of a Franco-American potato farmer it is misrepresentation of the grossest order.

Yet the Supai are not to be forgotten. However few there are, each of those children is one human life. How to square this basic fact with the press of other Americans who may be in less dire need but come in much greater numbers is a question with no easy solution. One hope is that public funds and private sacrifice can combine to attack the problem from both ends. The Summer Institute of Linguistics, otherwise known as the Wycliffe Bible Translators, works primarily with peoples too few in numbers to attract much public attention; yet these linguistic analysts are among the best trained in the world. Their work is interdenominational, but primarily religious and humanitarian in its motives. If one sees bilingual schooling as related to the health of our nation, these workers deserve their country's high regard. Public honor for noble service is a form of reward that should not be permitted to go out of style, and individual sacrifices will continue to be needed, even as we seek the public funds that will be required to help integrate the lives of larger masses of X speakers among us.

IV. *Teachers and Teacher Aides*

In this section we propose to discuss the role of teachers and teacher aides in a bilingual program under such headings as the special role of the teacher aide, English-medium teachers, teachers of English as a second language, X-medium teachers, the teacher's role, qualifications, inservice training, preservice training, recruitment and selection of teachers, and the use of foreign teachers. Not included in this section are other specialized personnel, such as librarians, guidance counselors, attendance officers, and nurses, important though they are.

The Special Role of Teacher Aides

Following the passage of the Elementary and Secondary Education Act of 1965, which authorized the use of teacher aides under Title I, they have been employed very commonly in bilingual areas. Girls who have completed two or three years of college and whose education has been interrupted for financial reasons, and housewives who can arrange their domestic chores in such a way as to be free during the school day, are frequently used as aides.

There are no academic qualifications required. More important than these are personal qualities and satisfaction with this kind of work. A cheerful disposition, a gentle touch, willingness to follow instructions, fondness for children, these are some of characteristics looked for in teacher aides.

It is the teacher who decides exactly how the aide shall be used, and the possibilities vary all the way from doing chores to overseeing seat work or even conducting group reading. The hope is that some aides will find this work so gratifying that they will make the effort necessary to continue schooling and ultimately get their degree and teaching certificate and help swell the ranks of teachers.

Study and research are needed to determine best ways to use teacher aides. Originally used to relieve the classroom teacher of such chores as taking attendance, collecting milk money, helping children with their snowsuits, supervising play, and gathering supplies, they have come to play a special role in the bilingual setting, by bringing to the classroom another language. If the teacher is a monolingual English speaker, an X-speaking aide serves as a link between X-speaking children and the E-speaking school environment. An E-speaking aide can likewise supplement the teaching of an X-speaking teacher. In either case the aide is a link between the school and the community.

English-Medium Teachers

Unilingual speakers of English are by no means unneeded in a bilingual program, but about their qualifications to teach in English to native English speakers, which have been set by a long tradition, we shall have nothing special to say except that they should have a sympathetic understanding of bilingual schooling.

English-speaking teachers assigned to teach any subject to children whose first language is *not* English do require special training, for English as a second language (ESL) poses special problems. Teachers' failure to realize that for X-speaking children English is not a native language has placed these children at a great disadvantage. The pioneering efforts of such men as C. C. Fries date back some twenty-five years, but only in the last decade has an understanding of ESL begun to penetrate the ranks of teachers. There are several organizations that can help the teacher of children who use English as a second language, such as the National Council of Teachers of English; the Center for Applied Linguistics; and since 1966, an organization called TESOL (Teachers of English to Sperkers of Other Languages), which publishes the TESOL QUARTERLY. There are also several universities which specialize in preparing ESL teachers, e.g., the University of Michigan, UCLA, Georgetown University, and the University of Texas. The Education Professions Development Act (EPDA) sponsors institutes for teachers of ESL, among others.

X-Medium Teachers

When X is a language of wider communication, e.g., Arabic, French, Chinese, German, Italian, Japanese, Portuguese, Russian, and Spanish, it coincides with what schools or universities have long taught *as foreign languages*. Teacher-preparing institutions have traditionally trained teachers of at least some of these languages, but they have not focused on their teaching *as non-foreign languages*, as is required in bilingual programs.

When X is a local language, e.g., Navajo, Hopi, Cherokee, Basque, Eskimo, and Samoan, we are even less well equipped to prepare the needed teachers. As happened in World War II, when we were caught short of linguistically competent personnel, our present sudden need of qualified teachers for bilingual programs finds us woefully unprepared.

Teachers for Indian and Eskimo Children

Whether the schools for these children are operated by the BIA, by a state, or by a local school district, they face the most difficult task of all in providing really adequate instruction.[60] History has been against these children so that they are generally forgotten and in many, many cases miserably deprived. At none of the levels where their education is provided for is there remotely enough money to do what is needed, and what is needed will be much more expensive than an ordinary or even good school program for most other children. Apart from the problem of instructional materials, which in the main have still to be produced, the supply of trained teachers coming from these ethnic and linguistic groups themselves is virtually nil. Indian education is under severe scrutiny already, and sweeping changes are in order. Some of them are already begun especially by the BIA in cooperation with the Center for Applied Linguistics.[61] It is imperative that in our zeal to see wrongs righted at once we not trample these tender sprouts of a new planting. American know-how has not yet invented instant harvest.

The Role of the Teacher in the Bilingual Program

One Teacher, Two Languages. What are the advantages of using one teacher to teach in two languages, as compared with those of using two or more teachers, each of whom uses one language? We shall assume for purposes of this discussion of the teacher's role that it makes no essential difference whether the X language is local or one of wider communication.

The ideal of the self-contained classroom, though not held so exclusively today as it was a few years ago, still appeals to many. The mother-substitute role of the teacher, which is a part of this concept, is especially applicable to the nursery, kindergarten, and primary grades, where the child still feels dependent on the teacher.

The use of a single bilingual teacher, rather than two or more, will appear as a great advantage to those who regard the self-contained classroom as desirable. In such a situation one teacher has exclusive responsibility for the children, can get to know each one intimately, and can plan the program in a unified and coherent fashion. Even when an aide is present, the latter plays only a subordinate and self-effacing role and is entirely subject to the directives of the teacher.

In such a situation the bilingual teacher enjoys a degree of freedom in deciding the relative use of the two languages and in implementing directives received from the principal and the bilingual coordinator.

Two or More Teachers, Each Using One Language. Perhaps the most obvious advantage of this "team" arrangement is that it makes possible the use of a native, unaccented speaker of English to teach in English and of a native, unaccented speaker of X to teach in X. In addition each teacher can presumably represent and interpret one culture better than two. Teachers serve as models to children, who learn more by imitation and analogy than by prescription. This is particularly applicable to the learning of pronunication and of cultural values. Authenticity—in speech and in cultural representation—is of prime importance.

Team teaching recommends itself also because often "two heads are better than one." In planning complex daily programs two or more teachers who collaborate harmoniously can tap greater resources than one and should find stimulation in such collaboration. Teachers with different cultural and educational backgrounds can learn a great deal from one another, which they can then pass on to the children.

The phrase "two or more" requires a word of explanation. In addition to the common pattern, in which one teacher does all of the teaching in English and another teacher does all of the teaching in X, though not necessarily in the same subjects, it is possible to add to the team other specialists in certain curricular subjects, such as art, music, health, and physical education, who can teach in either language and help with the planning. We suggest that the school librarian would also make an invaluable addition to such an instructional team.

One Teacher or Two? The single bilingual teacher pattern is perhaps easier and safer. It is clearly easier to translate ideas from one head into a unified and coherent lesson plan than to take the time necessary to reconcile varied points of view and to convert them into a mutually satisfactory plan of action. It is safer because dangers lurk in team teaching in the form of possible clashes of views and of personality.

Despite the advantages of the single bilingual teacher and the hazards of the teaching team, we see three significant advantages in the latter. (1) It gives greater assurance that the children will learn an authentic native accent in both languages and will acquire a more authentic understanding of both cultures. (2) It holds the promise of a more interesting and varied program of learning activities. (3) It is in its very format an example of cross-cultural education.

Qualifications

There is, so far as we know, no official definition of the qualifications of an X-medium teacher when X is the home language of the school children. Fortunately, however, the Statement of Qualifications of Teachers of Foreign Languages,[62] prepared by a group of modern foreign language teachers under the sponsorship of the Modern Language Association of America, are largely applicable. Teacher qualifications in several areas–listening comprehension, speaking, reading, writing, applied linguistics, culture and civilization, and professional preparation are defined in precise terms, which can be measured by the Modern Language Association Foreign Language Proficiency Tests. The first four tests would be used no matter what subject is to be taught through X, and the last three have particular significance for teachers of X as a second language.

In addition, we have two valuable unofficial statements of qualifications of teachers for programs of bilingual education, of which we quote one.[63]

> *The teacher should be a literate native speaker of the standard dialect and if possible of the student's variant of the language. For work at the high school level and above, the teacher should have learned through the medium of the second language the subject matter to be taught. This is essential because of the impossibility of improvising or translating extemporaneously the special terminology and phraseology that are inseparable from each academic discipline and professional field. The teacher's competence could be determined and his certification based on the results of proficiency tests such as those prepared by the Modern Language Association for the five common languages and distributed by the Educational Testing Service. For languages lacking such standardized tests, certification could be based on the report of a state examining committee.*
>
> *Experience with Franco-Americans has shown that while the ideal mother tongue teacher is a member of the same ethnic group as his students, his effectiveness depends as much upon his Americanness and modernity as upon his pedagogy and linguistic competence. Students do not sympathize readily with a teacher who is foreign to American language and culture and too prone to praise "Old Country" values and customs.*
>
> *The mother tongue teacher must, above all, know how to cope with dialectal variations, without disparagement of the student's idiolect and free of the misconception that the parents' speech is a serious impediment to learning.*

All teachers of young children should be thoroughly familiar with the process of child growth and development.

Despite the great concentrations of X speakers in the United States, which would seem to constitute a large reservoir of bilingual teachers, the truth is that most of these X speakers are undereducated in their language and almost entirely untrained for this specialized task. Even those among them who are already teachers have usually received their education and their teacher training in English, not in X. Suddenly called on to teach bilingually, they often feel unequal to the task.

Take the case of native speakers of Spanish in the Southwest and consider their preparation to teach bilingually. Typically, they spent their first six years in a Spanish-speaking home and neighborhood; and when they entered school, they were required to neglect their dominant language, Spanish, and to try to learn through their weaker language, English.[64] Deprived in the elementary grades of the opportunity to become literate in their native language, Spanish speakers are permitted in high school to elect an elementary course in Spanish. By this time they have lost interest and are resigned to the tag of "underachievers" which the school assigns them. If they bring themselves to take a high-school course in Spanish, they find the course designed for English speakers. Like them, the Spanish speaker needs to learn how to read and write, but unlike them he already has an audiolingual control of the language. The learning problems of English speakers and Spanish speakers are radically different, and yet they are put together in one class and treated alike. The result for the Spanish speaker, once again, is frustration. In college the speaker of Spanish encounters the same mass-production procedures. When, exceptionally, he is offered special sections planned to meet his particular needs, it is already too late. He feels hopeless or fears the amount of work that would be required of him if he is to make up for twelve years of miseducation.

Bruce Gaarder points out the adverse effect that this unfortunate language policy has had on the Spanish speaker: "If he has not achieved reasonable literacy in his mother tongue–ability to read, write, and speak it accurately–it will be virtually useless to him for any technical or professional work where language matters. Thus, his unique potential career advantage, his bilingualism, will have been destroyed."[65]

From this lugubrious sketch of the education of the Spanish speakers of the Southwest we conclude that, though there is potentially an ample supply of bilingual teachers, the actual supply is severely limited. Recent arrivals from Cuba and Puerto Rico in Florida and the New York area represent very different educational backgrounds and can more readily be called into service.

Immediately available, even in the Southwest, is a small number of potential teachers from the following sources: A few have learned to read and write in their homes because their parents required them to, out of respect for the ancestral language and culture. A few others have taught themselves to read and write, often before school age, and have continued to read.

And still others have resolved later in their schooling to make up for lost time. Individuals and families who have thus compensated for the deficiencies of schools and colleges naturally deserve the highest praise, but these exceptional initiatives cannot even come close to supplying our total need of bilingual teachers.

The insufficient education in Spanish of many Southwestern Spanish-surname teachers leaves them with deficiencies that they are well aware of. In fact they sometimes exaggerate their shortcomings. Let us examine what steps could be taken to convert these potential bilingual teachers into fully qualified ones.

What Can They Do to Upgrade Their Spanish? The first necessity is for them to understand the state of their Spanish—both its strong and weak points. To acquire such an understanding, it may be necessary to do some basic reading on the nature of language and on the process of language learning,[66] possibly to request a phonetic and syntactic analysis by a linguist, and to measure one's proficiency by taking all or part of the MLA FL Proficiency Tests for Teachers and Advanced Students.

Many a Spanish speaker, conscious of his lack of academic study in the language, underestimates the great advantage he has over those who have academic knowledge alone. For example, the native speaker of Spanish, though he may never have had any formal schooling in it, has complete control of the sound system and of the structure of the language, as it is used in his locale. He can communicate with ease and fluency with other Spanish speakers in his community. In fact, he can understand and be understood by Spanish speakers from any part of the Hispanic world. Dialectal differences in lexicon, in structure, in pronunciation very rarely constitue a serious obstacle to communication.

At the same time many Spanish speakers *do* have some shortcomings. The most common are: lack of skill in reading and writing, lack of vocabulary beyond immediate needs, lack of control of some levels of expression, lack of formal knowledge of grammar, and inexperience with dialects of other regions.

Some of these defects can gradually be eliminated by the individual himself if he has enough desire and will to work. For example, one can teach oneself how to read—or how to read better—by simply reserving a certain amount of time for reading every day. By keeping a dictionary at hand as one reads, one can gradually increase one's vocabulary. It is also perfectly possible to "learn grammar" by studying a grammar book. Writing, stylistic levels, and dialectal variation are harder to learn by oneself though even here it is possible to learn much by observing various speakers and studying various styles encountered in one's reading. Certain aspects of writing, for example, can be self taught. Spelling, including the use of written accents, can readily be learned from any good grammar or dictionary once its importance as an indicator of literacy has been acknowledged.

Inservice Training. Most school systems are willing to organize inservice workshops to assist teachers in improving their qualifications. Neighboring colleges and universities can help by offering courses in response to specific needs. And the Education Professions Development Act (EPDA) provides for summer and year-long institutes for the same purpose. Yet teacher-preparing institutions have done relatively little so far to train speakers of X languages to teach in their first language. In the summer of 1961 Gérard Brault directed at Bowdoin College the first institute for native speakers of French.[67] In 1962 George Ayer of the University of Texas at Austin directed an institute for native speakers of Spanish, and in the summer of 1968 one of the present writers, Theodore Andersson, directed—also in Austin—an institute for native Spanish-speaking elementary-school teachers planning to teach in bilingual programs. Several bilingual institutes are being held as this monograph goes to press, and their number will surely increase each year, with growing attention to curricular areas other than language arts.

Preservice Training. Teacher-preparing institutions are traditionally responsible for the education of teachers of non-English languages for all levels, but they have not been able to fill today's needs, either in quantity or in quality. Can bilingual education, which renews hopes once again for effective language and cultural education, succeed where previous ventures have failed?

Colleges and universities provide only faint prospects of success. Despite the statement of Teacher Qualifications, the availability of Tests for Teachers and Advanced Students, and the elaboration of Guidelines for the Preparation of Teachers,[68] there has been only slight improvement in the number and quality of language teachers produced in our country. Only a few universities have tried to implement the Guidelines, and fewer still have addressed themselves to the task of how to supply enough competent teachers for the bilingual programs which are growing by geometrical progression.

The few that are making resolute efforts to help meet the need deserve much credit. We have already mentioned examples of universities that specialize in the training of ESL teachers; many of the teachers so trained, however, are foreigners preparing to return to their respective countries to teach English. Another praiseworthy enterprise is that called Teacher Excellence for Economically Deprived and Culturally Differentiated Americans, directed by Dr. Guy C. Pryor of Our Lady of the Lake College, San Antonio, Texas. This is a teacher training program especially designed for prospective bilingual teachers who, without the help provided by this program, would not be able to go to college. A similar program under the direction of Dr. Dorothy Hurst Mills is in operation in Chapman College, Orange, California. By way of further examples, the University of Alaska is deeply concerned with the Eskimos, Alaskan Indians, and Aleuts; Northern Arizona University at Flagstaff is developing teaching materials for Hopi and Navajo; the University of Hawaii is a natural center for Japanese, Chinese, Korean, Philippine, Malaysian, and Samoan studies, among others.

Transforming Potential into Supply. We have in New York, Chicago, Miami, and the Southwest vast numbers of authentic speakers of Spanish, many of whom could if interested become teachers. It would take a resolute effort on their part, for many have not had the kind of education that would immediately enable them to enter the teaching ranks. But they already have some qualifications which most present teachers of Spanish can never acquire. Their speech is authentic, and in many ways they also think, feel, and act like Hispanics; that is, they can represent Hispanic culture authentically. What they don't know they can learn with patience, interest, and hard work.

"What is the place in foreign language teaching for a person who would teach his mother tongue?" inquire Bruce Gaarder and his Committee. "Opinion has it that such persons are often weak in methodology, often fail to understand the young American learner. Too, there is a current illusion that the N-EMT [non-English mother tongue] speaker's deviations from the 'standard' dialect are more grievous and less acceptable in the classroom than the 'pure' (untainted by ethnicity and social class distinctions) rash of errors which mark the tongue and pen of many teachers to whom the foreign language is still foreign. The authors of this report believe that the potentials of the native speaker and of the non-native speaker are equally high as language teachers, and that facilities are now available to make them equally competent."[69]

Given this situation, one wonders why teacher-preparing institutions do not organize special programs that would attract more of these promising young people into preparing themselves as fully qualified bilingual teachers.[70] Use of the MLA Foreign Language Proficiency Tests would help teacher trainers to determine quickly in what areas candidates need further training. By exempting them from further work in areas in which they can demonstrate adequate knowledge and skill, and by guiding them in areas where help is needed, teacher trainers could turn out competent teachers in a minimum of time.[71]

Some state departments of education have been sensitive to the need of developing effective procedures for certifying teachers on the basis of tested proficiency in lieu of course credits. New York State was the first, in May 1963, to use the MLA Teacher Proficiency Tests for this purpose. Other states using a similar procedure are Pennsylvania, West Virginia, Delaware, New Hampshire, Connecticut, and California.[72]

Recruitment and Selection of Bilingual Teachers. From the present sparse but hopefully increasing supply the superintendent of schools, the director of personnel, the coordinator of the bilingual program, and the school principal must make their selection of teachers. They are presumably all experienced in judging character, personality, and academic credentials. But unless they are native speakers of X or have themselves received a sound education in X, they have an inadequate basis for judging a candidate's qualifications in X. Under these circumstances they would be well advised to require that prospective teachers submit scores on the MLA FL Proficiency Test for Teachers and Advanced Students. Such scores provide a profile, revealing in which areas a candidate is strong or weak. In the case of weaknesses the superintendents may wish to prescribe remedial work and a re-examination at the end of a year.

The wide use of these tests would also enable school districts to identify for preparing institutions weaknesses in their teacher preparation program, thus laying the groundwork for a standardization and improvement of preservice training.

The Use of Foreign Teachers. Some years will be required to increase the educational opportunities for the many speakers of Spanish, French, Portuguese, Chinese, and Japanese who may wish in the future to qualify for a teaching position in a bilingual program. How to staff these programs in the meantime is a problem. One tempting solution is to use teachers that we might recruit in Spain, Spanish America, Cuba, Puerto Rico, the Philippines, France, French Canada, Portugal, Brazil, Taiwan, and Japan, who would be relatively well educated, trained to teach, and highly motivated. The availability of the MLA Teacher Proficiency Tests can greatly facilitate such an arrangement. But using these new recruits would be a delicate matter. The whole summer preceding the beginning of teaching should be used for orientation of the foreign teachers and as an opportunity for native and foreign teachers to get acquainted and to plan together. In addition, preparations should be made with great care to prevent the cultural shock which would be only natural as foreign teachers are transplanted into an entirely new setting. Once there are signs of cultural shock, it is too late to remedy the situation. For this reason someone must be designated in advance–from the staff or, better, from the community–to take measures to prevent a feeling of disorientation. The very challenge of making a foreign teacher feel at home and of learning another point of view is a valuable part of intercultural education.

V. *Evaluation*

We suggest that a program of evaluation should include teacher qualifications, children's learning, and the total effectiveness of the bilingual program.

Teacher Qualifications. We assume that present procedures for appraising the English-speaking teacher's qualifications to teach English-speaking children are adequate. The English-speaking teacher who teaches ESL or other subjects to X-speaking children needs to have special knowledge and skills, as yet undefined, for which special tests do not yet exist. It is to be hoped that the National Council of Teachers of English, Teachers of English to Speakers of Other Languages (TESOL), the Center for Applied Linguistics, or some other organization will, following the example of the Modern Language Association, undertake to prepare a statement of qualifications and the development of suitable evaluation instruments.

For teachers who will teach in the X language, we have already stated that tests exist in five languages (French, German, Italian, Russian, Spanish) for measuring listening comprehension, writing, applied linguistics, culture and civilization, and professional preparation.[73] Before beginning his teaching, such a teacher should as a matter of course take the Modern Language Association Foreign Language Proficiency Tests for Teachers and Advanced Students and make his scores a part of his credentials. Periodically, and on a voluntary basis, as he improves his knowledge and skill in this area, he may wish to retake the tests and update his scores.

As a quality control every five years or so a school board may wish to require its ESL and X-language teachers to take new tests and record their scores.

Children's Learning. At the beginning of each school year diagnostic tests should be used to determine the relative strength of the children's two languages. Classroom teachers can do this informally, but in most cases normed tests are preferable.[74] In this way it will be possible to record the factor of language balance each year.

The regular annual testing (in English), which is a traditional school procedure, should of course be continued. Any new tests which are introduced to complement the regular tests should avoid overlapping, so that total testing time is not excessive.

Beginning toward the end of the first year of a bilingual program, tests in the X language, parallel to the standard achievement tests in English, should be administered and the scores recorded and analyzed. Such tests will need to be developed and carefully adapted to the language usage of the particular area.

The Commonwealth of Puerto Rico has contracted with the Educational Testing Service for the development of tests in Spanish. Reading tests in Spanish have already been produced on four levels to cover grades K through 12. The plan is now to develop tests in

Spanish in the various other subjects of the curriculum.

It is perhaps worth pointing out a natural difficulty here. A teacher who teaches, say, social studies in X may be tempted to deviate quite far from the English course of study—perhaps justifiably so—and may therefore wish to test the children's achievement in a way to parallel his teaching closely. The results may or may not correlate with those on a version of the standardized achievement tests translated into X.. Although traditional tests should not be allowed to throttle innovation, neither should they be abandoned thoughtlessly, for results on these tests necessarily serve as a baseline for demonstrating whether children's achievement improves after a bilingual program is introduced. The most incontrovertible way of answering severe critics is often a superior set of scores on tests not designed specifically for the new program on trial.

In-course testing should naturally be done bilingually wherever appropriate, that is, wherever the teaching is done bilingually.

The testing discussed up to this point has to do primarily with children's cognitive learning. Perhaps even more important would be evaluation in the affective area since successful cognitive learning depends largely on children's motivation and attitude. The presence of two ethnic groups makes it particularly important to observe and appraise the children's cross-cultural behavior. As soon as satisfactory instruments are developed,[75] this kind of appraisal should be made annually as a regular part of the total evaluation. In judging children's attitudes and motivation it is essential to keep careful records of attendance and participation in various activities.

The Total Effectiveness of the Bilingual Program. At the end of each year of a bilingual program, at each grade level, and in all subjects taught in the X language or bilingually, the children's achievement should be compared with the corresponding achievement before the inception of the bilingual program.[76]

The classroom teacher is in the best position to judge certain aspects of the program. He should therefore be asked at the end of each year, after using whatever measures he finds suitable, to report in writing his evaluation of the children's progress and of the program design and materials.

Still another valuable piece of evidence is the annual report of the school principal. He is often in a position to evaluate the children's achievement and behavior as compared with former years, and to appraise the morale and effectiveness of the teachers, as well as to judge the overall design of the bilingual program.

Another important means of evaluating total effectiveness is the educational audit suggested by the staff of the U.S. Office of Education. According to their proposal, an impartial evaluator or team of evaluators would visit the program and consider such factors as planning and administration; community support; performance of the school board, school administration, teachers, parents, and children; testing and teachers' and principals' evaluation; and a comparison of the program's outcomes with the stated objectives. The written report of such evaluators would be a token of accountability to the public.

The kinds of evaluation we have suggested involve a great deal of extra work. Who is to do this extra work? Clearly some special provision must be made, for staff members who are already working full time cannot be expected to undertake this additional chore. The normal solution would be the appointment of a testing coordinator who, with one or more assistants as needed, would take responsibility for planning and conducting the evaluation program, for recording and analyzing the results, and for communicating significant outcomes to the superintendent, the school board, and the information officer.

Since tests are in some cases not available or not entirely satisfactory, the school authorities may wish to contract for the services of universities, education service centers, regional educational laboratories, or national testing organizations for the development of needed instruments.

NOTES

[1]Mackey's *Typology* is printed in full in Appendix E. It will be referred to further in our section on Time.

[2]An example is given below, in the discussion on mathematics.

[3]See section 4.1.1 of his *Typology*.

[4]There may be some children who do not speak at all, in any language. We urge that the term *alingual* be reserved for this specific abnormality, and that it not be applied to children who simply do not talk in a teacher's presence, or to those whose grammar and vocabulary do not meet someone's preconceived "standard."

[5]A term used by Charles A. Ferguson in *Study of the Role of Second Languages in Asia, Africa, and Latin America*, Frank A. Rice, ed.

[6]These local languages of America all sometimes go under the general name of Amerindian tongues, but genetically the differences among them are in some cases as vast as the differences among, for example, Indo-European languages.

[7]We are indebted to Ross J. Waddell for this reminder.

[8]See for example Charles Ferguson, "Variant Approaches to the Acquisition of Literacy" (1968).

[9]There are striking cases in which this order is not followed and yet there is no apparent disadvantage to the children. In St. Lambert Elementary School outside Montreal, E-speaking children are taught to read first in French. In the Hamilton School in Mexico City, the children are taught to read English before their native Spanish. In that same city Spanish--speaking Jewish children in the J. L. Peretz School read in both Yiddish and Hebrew before they do in their dominant language, Spanish. All these cases are atypical, however–or at least not representative of the kind of children for whom the BEA was written–for they are all middle-class or above, none are limited in their ability to speak the national language, and all are very highly motivated by some special factors (religion, economic, or cultural). Further, there is no certainty that the children in the schools mentioned would not have learned literacy even faster if they had been taught in their strongest language first.

[10]See section 4.2 on "The Status of the Languages" in Mackey's *Typology*, Appendix E.

[11]We have read with profit the informative unpublished paper by Willard Walker entitled "An Experiment in Programmed Cross-Cultural Education: The Import of the Cherokee Primer for the Cherokee Community and for the Behavioral Sciences" (March 1965, 12 pages mimeographed). Walker says (p. 3), in connection with literacy in Cherokee, that "by the 1880's the Western Cherokee had a higher *English* [emphasis added] literacy level than the white populations of either Texas or Arkansas." It would be interesting to know whether these Cherokees who outstripped the whites in reading English had previously learned to read through the less bizarre spelling system of their native Cherokee, where one symbol stands consistently for one syllable.

[12]These ideas are based on a communication from Sarah Gudschinsky.

[13]There is abundant literature on early language learning, e.g., François Gouin, *L'art d'enseigner et d'étudier les langues* (1880); Charles E. Osgood, *Method and Theory of Experimental Psychology* (1953), Chapter 16, "Language Behavior;" Wilder G. Penfield and Lamar Roberts, *Speech and Brain Mechanisms* (1959); Ruth Hirsch Weir, *Language in the Crib* (1962); Ursula Bellugi and Roger W. Brown, *The Acquisition of Language* (1964); Eric H. Lenneberg, *Biological Foundations of Language* (1967).

[14]The following are a sampling of the extensive bibliography on this subject: Jules Ronjat, *Le développement du langage observé chez un enfant bilingue* (1913); Werner F. Leopold, *Speech Development of a Bilingual Child* (1939-1949); Désiré Tits, *Le mécanisme d'une langue se substituant à la langue maternelle chez un enfant espangol âgé de six ans* (1948); Modern Language Association of America, "Childhood and Second Language Learning (1956); Theodore Andersson, "The Optimum Age for Beginning the Study of Modern Languages" (1960); H. H. Stern, ed., *Languages and the Young School Child* (1969).

[15]The question is explored by Noam Chomsky, among others, in "Language and the Mind" (1968).

[16]See also Gaarder's remarks on second language learning under Methods and Materials (Methodology in Early Stages), p. 106.

[17]Salisbury, "Cross-Cultural Communication and Dramatic Ritual" (1967), pp. 82-83.

[18]See, for example, Sirarpi Ohannessian, ed., et al, *Reference Lists of Materials for English as a Second Language,* 1964-1966. Sirarpi Ohannessian is Director of the CAL English for Speakers of Other Languages Program.

[19]The American Council on the Teaching of Foreign Languages (ACTFL) is a good general source of information on the existence and addresses of various groups of language teachers. See our Directory for ACTFL's address.

[20]Letter by Gaarder dated February 25, 2969, in his capacity as member of the Executive Council of the American Association of Teachers of Spanish and Portuguese. See also his cogent chapter entitled "Bilingualism" in Walsh (1969).

[21]In Martin Mayer, *Where, When and Why: Social Studies in American Schools*; New York, Harper & Row, 1963.

[22]From notes on an oral presentation by Dr. Dell Felder, Social Studies Program Director, Southwest Educational Development Laboratory.

[23]Just how complex bicultural education can be is suggested by Wayne H. Holtzman, "Cross-Cultural Studies in Psychology" (1968) and Holtzman, Díaz-Guerrero, Swartz, and Lara Tapia, "Cross-Cultural Longitudinal Research on Child Development" (1968). Complicating factors in such cross-cultural studies as the one here described–comparing 300 Mexican children between six and thirteen years of age with a like distribution of American children–are national differences, language differences, and subcultural differences, not to mention the complexity of individual behavioral differences. Despite the difficulties, the authors emphasize the importance of such research if we are to overcome ethnocentrism.

[24]Dell Felder. See note 17.

[25]This two-volume work entitled *International Study of Achievement in Mathematics* (New York: John Wiley & Sons, Inc., 1967) was edited by Torsten Husen. But its findings have been questioned by at least one reviewer. S. S. Willoughby, ("Who Won the International Contest?) in *Arithmetic Teacher*, Vol. 15, pp. 623-629, November 1968, explains why he feels the study showed neither superiority on the part of the Japanese nor inferiority on the part of any other group. His review also points up some of the difficulties involved in cross-national research.

[26]Lesser, et al. (1965).

[27]Giles, "Mathematics in Bilingualism–a Pragmatic Approach" (1969).

[28]Ibid., p. 22.

[29]Ibid.

[30]Ibid., p. 26.

[31]Treviño (1968).

[32]In the quote from Lee Salisbury under Language Arts, E for Dominant-X Children. See note 17.

[33]Asher (1965).

[34]See Appendix E.

[35]A comparison with Professor Mackey's original drawing in his section 2.6 will make plain our adjustments. In an effort to be specific we have changed his A(cculturation) and I(rredentism) to E(nglish) and X (any other language spoken natively in the Unites States). Hoping to make this drawing quickly understandable to the reader who has not read Mackey in full, we have also added a few words to the various labels, and we have replaced his C(omplete) by A(brupt) to indicate non-gradual change. Further, his definition of the DDM category (his section 2.6.7) is reinterpreted by us. See the note that follows.

[36]In distinguishing between "Different" and "Equal," Mackey does not speak of allotment of *time* for each language, as we have, but rather of *subjects* treated in each one. We have preempted his Different-Equal to refer to time only, in order to make room for the question of complementary or overlapping assignment of subjects at the next level below.

[37]Reproduced from Gaarder, "Organization of the Bilingual School," (1967):

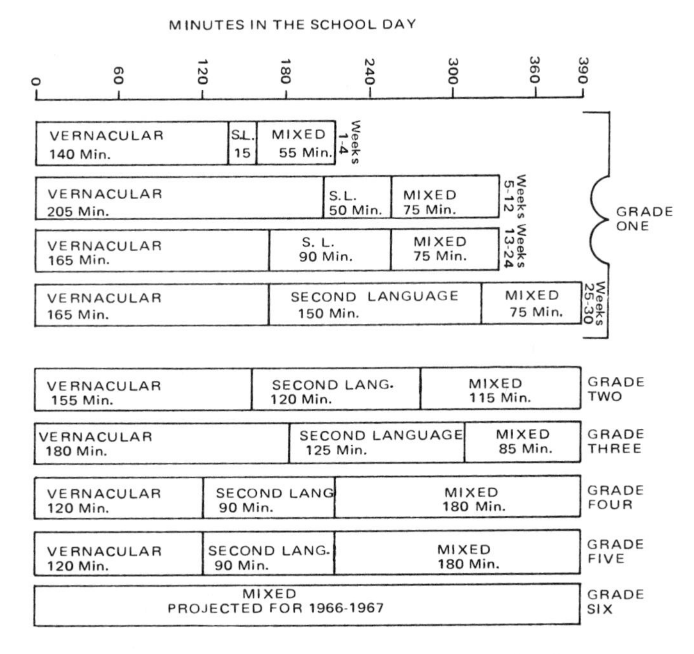

TIME DISTRIBUTION PATTERN—Coral Way Elementary School

VERNACULAR and SECOND LANGUAGE (S. L.) mean the use of these as mediums of instruction. MIXED in grades 1-3 means physical education, art and music only. In grades 4-6 MIXED also means combined classes of Anglos and Cubans alternating 3 weeks of each grading period working through English only, and 3 weeks working through Spanish only, in all subjects.

[38]La Fontaine and Pagan (1969).

[39]Mackey and Noonan (1952) describe how Polish refugee children were absorbed into the British schools after World War II. An experiment was made to find the quickest and best way of preparing the Polish speakers to continue their schooling in the new medium of English.

[40]Except in areas where bidialectalism in E seriously hampers communication or otherwise sets up hindrances to learning in school. This is a field that is increasingly attracting attention. A four-day conference on Social Dialectology and Its Pedagogical Implications is planned for November 1969, under sponsorship of the Center for Applied Linguistics. "An orientation in the study of the stratification of languages toward social, rather than regional, differences represents a new trend in linguistics....Roger W. Shuy will be chairman." (*The Linguistic Reporter*, Vol. II, no. 1, February 1969, pp. 5-6.) Shuy is general editor of the Urban Language Series, published by the Center for Applied Linguistics, containing so far five volumes (1966-69). See also William A. Stewart, *Non-Standard Speech and the Teaching of English*, Language Information Series no. 2; Washington: Center for Applied Linguistics, 1964.

[41]See Lambert and Macnamara (1969, in press); and Lambert, Just, and Segalowitz (1969).

[42]"Splitting" and "allotting" as used here refer to whether a subject is to be taught in two languages or in one, as in our section on Content.

[43]We feel impelled to urge that the operation *should* be behind the scenes. A thing that has appalled us, on visits to numerous classrooms, is the frequency with which teachers have spoken to us, as visitors, about the children–in the hearing of the children–in ways that were derogatory or that could cause some children to feel shame, about their background, their parents, their "disadvantage." We think the things children are apt to remember longest about an adult's attitude are those that he reveals when not talking directly to the children.

[44]This pattern is shown in Figure 14 of the section on Time. Some of its advantages are discussed there.

[45]See Gaarder et al. (1965), pp. 79-81.

[46]Fishman (1965), *Language Loyalty....*

[47]Sarah Gudschinsky's reminder of these opportunities is gratefully acknowledged.

[48]For illustrations of such cultural differences between home and school see Center for Applied Linguistics (1969).

[49]Zintz (1969), p. 3.

[50]Ibid.

[51]From a personal communication from Sarah Gudschinsky.

[52]From a personal communication to the authors. See also his "Beyond Grammar and Beyond Drills" (1967).

[53]Gaarder et al. (1965), pp. 58-59.

[54]Wares (1968).

[55]From a personal communication from William F. Mackey.

[56]This college beginners' text was planned by a conference of experienced textbook writers, sponsored by the Modern Language Association, written by a team of specialists, criticized by a large advisory committee, and financially supported by a foundation.

[57]Archibald A. Hill ("The Typology of Writing Systems," in *Papers in Linguistics in Honor of Leon Dostert*, William M. Austin, ed.; Mouton, The Hague, 1967; pp. 92-99) offers a modern and sophisticated means of classification.

[58]This machine, according to our reports, is located in Tahlequah, Oklahoma.

[59]Hill, op. cit., p. 98.

[60]See Appendix S on Indians, Eskimos, and Aleuts.

[61]See Ohannessian (1969) for specific recommendations on recruitment and training of teachers of Navajos.

[62]See Appendix H.

[63]Prepared by A. Bruce Gaarder, Chairman, Working Committee II, responsibile for a Report on "The Challenge of Bilingualism," published under the title *Foreign Language Teaching: Challenge to the Profession*, p. 85, Reports of the Working Committees, Northeast Conference on the Teaching of Foreign Languages, 1965, edited by G. Reginald Bishop, Jr., and available from The Materials Center, Modern Language Association, 62 Fifth Avenue, New York, New York, 10011, for $2.50.

The second is contained in C. L. Ainsworth, Ed., *Teachers and Counselors for Mexican American Children*. Austin, Texas: Southwest Educational Development Corporation, 1969, pp. 57-60.

[64]For a general treatment of this subject see Macnamara, "The Effects of Instruction in a Weaker Language" (1967).

[65]From a statement by A. Bruce Gaarder in: United States Congress. Senate. *Bilingual Education Program. Hearings...* (1967), p. 52.

[66]For example, Robert A. Hall, Jr., *Linguistics and Your Language*, (1960).

[67]Brault (1962).

[68]Drafted by the Modern Language Association in collaboration with the National Association of State Directors of Teacher Education and Certification. See Appendix I.

[69]See Gaarder, et al. (1965), p. 92.

[70]An example of such a program, which might serve as a model, is cited by Gaarder et al., pp. 90-91.

[71]For details see Gaarder et all. (1965), pp. 86-92.

[72]Gaarder et al. (1965) further explains the use of these tests and provides, pp. 86-99, a basis for interpreting scores.

[73]See Starr (1962) in our bibliography.

[74]Such tests are under development by the Southwest Educational Development Laboratory at Austin, Texas. See also Hoffman (1934), Lambert (1955), Macnamara (1967), Mackey (1967), Savard (1968), and Fishman et al. (1968). For excerpts from the latter see Fishman et al. (1969).

[75]See Hoffman (1945), Pryor (1966), and Lambert et al. (1966).

[76]For examples of this kind of evaluation see Richardson (1968), Treviño (1968), and Giles (1969) in our bibliography.

CHAPTER VII

NEEDED ACTION AND RESEARCH

"What is needed," William Mackey reminds us,[1] "is an overall research policy with a framework of interrelated projects of investigation into the problem of bilingual education in the United States." Bilingual schooling is still in its infancy, and it is too early to speculate about ways in which a comprehensive research policy may be elaborated. Many organizations have an interest in such a policy. For example, the United States Office of Education Bureau of Research is planning a research conference (June 27-28, 1969) as this book goes to press. The Center for Applied Linguistics, which is the ERIC Clearinghouse for Linguistics (including bilingualism), has sponsored numerous research planning conferences, especially those having to do with English as a Second Language and the education of American Indians. Among the regional educational development laboratories engaged in bilingual research and development are the Southwest Educational Cooperative Laboratory of Albuquerque and the Southwest Educational Development Laboratory of Austin. There are also numerous regional education service centers which are active in preparing teaching and testing materials. The Northeast Conference on the Teaching of Foreign Languages has published (1965) an excellent summary report, "The Challenge of Bilingualism." The Southwest Council for Bilingual Education (formerly the Southwest Council on the Teaching of Foreign Languages) has published several research oriented reports. ACTFL (American Council on the Teaching of Foreign Languages) takes an active interest in bilingualism, as does TESOL (Teachers of English to Speakers of Other Languages). Still other organizations interested in bilingualism are the Bureau of Indian Affairs of the Department of the Interior and several state departments of education. For example, the Texas Education Agency has a Department of International and Bilingual Education under the direction of an assistant commissioner of education. And, finally, there is the International Center for Research on Bilingualism at Laval University in Quebec directed by William F. Mackey. It remains to be seen whether these various organizations, each with its legitimate interest, can somehow be brought together into an overall plan for cooperative and non-overlapping research. Surely the need is urgent and time is pressing.

A. *National Needs*

Certain kinds of research and action should be carried on at a national level to ensure as broad a base as possible and to prevent unnecessary duplication and atomization of effort.

Broad Base of Support. Before the tax-paying public will be willing to underwrite the additional cost of bilingual education, it needs evidence that bilingual education is worth the investment. Comparisons of the effectiveness of learning through one or two languages have begun,[2] but such studies need to be replicated and expanded and widely diffused. Case studies of persons who have profited from knowing more than one language need to be carefully assembled and publicized. The assistance of the media is needed to help educate the public to the importance of beginning language learning at an early age and to the value of diversity for American life.

Modifications of State and Federal Laws. Citizenship requirements for teachers should be reviewed with the purpose of making possible the short-term use of foreign exchange teachers.

Bilingual programs have been hampered in many states by laws prohibiting classroom instruction in non-English languages. Several states have already amended their laws to allow teaching in two languages. Other states with similar constraints may wish to amend laws which prevent bilingual education from being introduced in their schools.

The Bilingual Education Act may need to be amended in the light of experience. As written, it fulfills two functions: First, it is part of anti-poverty legislation, and, second, it supports educational innovation. Congress may wish to consider evidence submitted to it by knowledgeable individuals or groups before deciding whether or not to change the relative emphasis of these two factors. For either purpose, it is hoped that Congress may in the future find it possible to bring the appropriations closer to the funds authorized.

Identification of Models. A small number of "models" or exemplary programs should be selected as specimens of different program types. These programs should be provided with sufficient funds to make it possible for them (1) to disseminate full documentation as well as succinct brochures on their operations; and (2) to augment their staffs and to make whatever physical adjustments are indicated, to accommodate large numbers of visitors and observers. Otherwise, successful programs are drowned by their own success. Contracts to serve as "models" should be for long enough terms (three to five years) to justify the added expenditures and to provide some stability to the school systems rendering this service.

Program Design Experimentation. Mackey's typology provides the groundwork for pursuing rational lines of experimentation in design. All the existing bilingual programs in our country should be canvassed to collect the needed data. Based on these actual programs any required adjustments in his instrument should be made. It will then be possible to study the relative effectiveness of different program design in specific kinds of circumstances, and to provide information to communities that are seeking reasonable avenues of change.

Curriculum Materials. As mentioned earlier, materials, whether plentiful, as they are in some languages, or scarce, as they are in many, constitute a challenging problem.

The range of material needs is enormous, and yet it ought not to be overwhelming once the decision is reached that the work must be done. The first order of priority is for a full set of instructional materials in all curricular subjects for each major linguistic group, beginning with the earliest levels and proceeding through grade twelve. In languages such as French or Spanish, provision should be made for immediate importation of suitable texts, even though such books will be imperfectly suited to an American population. Difficulties of procurement from abroad may have to be overcome. In any case, material will have to be evaluated and, if selected, adapted for local use. In this task regional or national organizations can be of assistance. School systems are urged to call on regional education service centers or laboratories or on one of their national professional organizations for help, first in developing criteria and then in evaluating materials.[3] This is a field in which some centralization would be advantageous, for the importation, selection, and possible adaptation of suitable materials is a very large undertaking for a local school administration. Spanish alone is likely to yield more than a dozen sets. Some of the languages involved may be taught as second languages in certain bilingual countries. If so, materials used in those countries may be suitable to bilingual minorities in the United States.

Considering the age, motivation, and purpose of the learner, should materials be based on vocabulary count, structure, analysis, situation, and/or interest? These are questions basic to the construction of a rational curriculum and therefore deserve extensive research.

Materials will have to be developed for languages or curricular areas where they are lacking. Individual teachers may be identified who have a special gift for preparing materials, and such teachers should be all means be freed to work in the area of their talents. It is the opinion of the present writers, however, that an individual teacher or, indeed, teams of local teachers can rarely be expected to produce materials which are of professional quality. It is to be hoped that professional organizations will come forward and take the initiative in organizing the vast cooperative effort necessary to establish criteria and to create quality materials.

Subordinate to this preparation of main-line materials, there should be changes made to salvage as many young minds as possible by introducing instruction in the mother tongue at various levels throughout the school system. For example, the elaboration of a complete set of materials for grades K to 12 in Spanish should not preclude immediate selection of materials to be used at the junior or senior high school levels for youngsters who were born too early to reap the full benefits of this new procedure.

The relationship between good and inspiring education and bilingual education needs to be explored. It would be unreasonable to claim that any given curricular innovation will be sufficient to cure the fundamental ill of irrelevance in education, but bilingual schooling could be an effective contribution to combat irrelevance.

The process of preparing or borrowing and adapting materials from other countries will, hopefully, broaden the horizon of our professional educators and pave the way for improving our materials as a result of the borrowed ideas. Even a cursory examination of a second-grade Chilean book, for example, showed us that Chilean children of seven years of age are advanced far beyond their United States counterparts in reading material considered suitable for second graders. R. J. Waddell, an experienced elementary-school principal, describes present readers as trivia resulting from an obsessive control of vocabulary. Research designed to compare the effectiveness of these readers with those containing stories of classical content might be illuminating. Waddell thinks the latter would have high interest value for young children and would be strongly motivating. If, on the other hand, the difference in achievement level expected of a seven-year-old is attributable to the greater ease with which one learns to read Spanish, the possibilities of using this language as the primary route to an educated mind among our own Spanish-English bilinguals ought to be evident.

Experience and research have shown that bilingual children have not made adequate progress with typical educational materials currently in use; typical books in use are more abstract than we realize, requiring considerable knowledge of both American culture and the English language. New materials suitable to the child's linguistic development, language skills, cultural background, age, and interests need to be investigated. Since some minorities, including some bilingual children, tend to score higher on performance tests of ability than on verbal tests, we should explore the possibility of reaching the children with non-verbal performance-oriented learning materials, those emphasizing learning by seeing, doing, and participating.[4]

Comparative Cultural Studies. In communities where two ethnic groups live together it is essential, if they are to understand each other, that sound and tactful comparisons of their value systems be made.[5] Such comparisons of cultural differences should first be made for the salient features of cultures as a whole on as broad a base as possible. For example, a comparison should be made in broad terms between "Anglo" and "Hispanic" values. Specific variations in either culture, as it manifests itself in a given locale, could be seen in better perspective by local workers if an overall framework were sketched out first. Such a task of cultural comparison is exceedingly difficult, especially with those cultures identified with "languages of wider communication." Local districts with limited resources can hardly be expected to make the fine adjustments needed if no working model has been drafted. Our schools and communities are in a state of crisis, and it is incumbent on the best minds among our social scientists, as well as on all others with usable expertise, to make some proposals, however imperfect.

We cite only a few examples. It has been suggested that different cultures emphasize different styles of learning. To what extent does our undifferentiated school technology need to be modified to take into account these different learning styles so that particular ethnic groups can achieve optimum learning? (Rudolph Troike)

Role identification for different cultures also needs explanation before it can be used advantageously as a tool by the teacher. The appropriateness of various emotional climates in the classroom, depending on different cultural backgrounds, needs to be made explicit. Social patterns, leadership models, and optimal grouping patterns for each culture should be suggested.

Linguistic Studies. Detailed linguistic analyses of English and each of the other native languages in an American bilingual program should be undertaken to provide critically-needed information for curricular decisions about sequence and methods of presentation. Also, we need much more information on the English and non-English language development of the children of non-English-speaking parents. (Rudolph Troike)

Beyond what age is it difficult to master more than one language without accent? It has been supposed that age ten, approximately, is the critical age, but an extensive survey of persons who have been born to another language and who have transferred to an English-speaking environment at various ages would be desirable.

Integrated Studies of the Bilingual Child. Although a considerable amount of study has been devoted to the development of the child of the majority culture, little has been done to identify the special characteristics of the bilingual learner. With regard to mental growth, not only the bilingual's linguistic patterns but also his acquired concepts need research because they have been conditioned by his cultural background. What is the total effect of exposure to two cultures? There is some evidence to indicate that bilingual children do not learn concepts in the same way or at the same rate as the majority culture child. We need to research both the cause and the effect.

There is increasing research evidence that the younger the child, the greater his learning potential. This provides a rich field for investigation of early learning in the home. Will the planting of appropriate English and non-English books in the home result in earlier learning of reading? Will listening to selected music have a beneficial attitudinal effect? Will an early opportunity to work with art materials yield positive effects later? Should not the bilingual potential of Head Start programs be tested experimentally?

Testing. Teaching and testing are always two sides of the same coin. Each needs to be considered in connection with the other, and each needs to be constantly improved. Due in part to the difference in goals and objectives of local schools with minority groups and of national test publishers, standardized tests generally do not give an accurate measure of the achievement of bilingual children. Linguistic and cultural differences need to be considered in developing additional instruments more appropriate for measuring the achievement of the populations.

More work is needed on attitudinal testing, since the development of positive attitudes toward self and others is essential both for teachers and for children of minority groups who must adjust to their environment.

The validity of present occupational aptitude tests when applied to minority group children needs careful study.

Teachers. In every state, certification of teachers needs to be closely scrutinized. Simply stated, persons who are qualified to teach should be certified, and those that are not, should not. Chief offenders of this rule are (1) universities and colleges that recommend certification of individuals who have simply collected the requisite number of grade points in an approved combination of college courses without regard to their total preparedness to teach, and (2) school systems that continue to accept such paper-prepared products without reporting back to the colleges their inadequateness for the jobs to be done. School administrators on close terms with their preparing institutions should make their needs known directly. Colleges are prone to believe they are doing well unless told otherwise. If this is not productive, school administrators should inform the state education agency, in its certification capacity, of specific areas of weakness in newly-trained teachers. State institutions, in particular, can quite reasonably be required to pay special attention to the specific educational needs of the states that support them.

State agencies should take whatever measures are required to make it possible for qualified persons to be certified, with or without credits from institutions. Ways of judging qualifications of bilingual teachers have been devised, as we explained in Chapter IV, The Program. Such means are useless, however, if they are not implemented.

B. *Local Needs*

Although educators in bilingual education need a broad consciousness of what is involved and many kinds of scholars will be needed to do special tasks at regional and national levels, the eventual focus should be on the individual child who is in school in any one of the many bilingual areas of the United States – primarily the non-English-speaking and secondarily the English-speaking child. This is where action and research come together, and it is the most difficult plane of all.

We have seen what expertise is needed for comparison of cultural and linguistic differences in abstract, general terms. Let no one think the adaptation of the general – when it is prepared – to one local situation is any less exacting. This is perhaps where our educational system encounters its greatest difficulties today. We have put our efforts in efficient, economical style, into the nation as a whole, expecting adjustments to take place where they are called for. Instead, the very power of our efficiency has begun to overrule us. We find ourselves being reshaped to fit the norm, rather than altering the norms to fit our own legitimate differences. Having been extraordinarily successful in establishing our unity, we must now shift our weight and begin to emphasize our diversity, lest we lose it. We must consider the uniqueness of every local school district. What action and research are needed, at this level, to improve the education of all our children?

Local Survey and Analysis. Essential to a carefully planned bilingual program is a comprehensive survey to determine who the pre-school and school-age children of the community are. When completed, the survey should reveal the economic, social, political, linguistic, and cultural status of the community as a whole as well as how individual children and families fit into the total community picture. Such a report should be prepared by competent specialists, and should certainly involve social scientists (from sociology and anthropology, political science, economics, and history) and linguists (those knowledgeable about X in its multiple facets and varieties, and those specialized in English). These data and interpretations should then be reviewed by persons responsible for school planning, in consultation with the disciplinary specialists, to find ways of fitting the parts of this mosaic together into one or more plans for changes in the schools.

Nor can the community be expected to remain static. Provision needs to be made, therefore, for periodic reassessment of who the current school children are and of what their educational needs and aspirations are.

We cannot go into detail here about the kinds of studies that should be done in depth in each community with a bilingual population, but a few suggestions may illustrate.

What is the size of the local children's active and passive vocabulary at age six? The Seashore-Eckerson technique should be applied not only to English but also to other languages spoken by the children so that fruitful comparisons can be made.

Among many minority groups (Germans, Italians, and Norwegians, for example), the children, though bilingual, do not speak the "standard language." Research into the local dialect and expecially into the differences between it and the textbook standard or so-called "cultivated usage" will pinpoint likely trouble spots and will help determine teaching strategies. This applies to English as well as to the local X.

How do local mores of the English- and X-speaking populations differ from those considered nationally to be "typical" for that culture? If there are presumed conflicts between them, which of these conflicts are not in effect locally? What additional differences, not foreseen nationally, exist in this particular community?

What community problems does the community itself want its children to be educated to solve?

In conclusion, it is obvious that we have not comprehensively outlined the needed action and research, or perhaps even been conscious of all the facets. We conclude this section therefore by repeating the statement with which we began: "What is needed is an overall research policy with a framework of interrelated projects of investigation into the problem of bilingual education in the United States."

NOTES

[1]In a personal communication to us.

[2]See Richardson (1968) and Treviño (1968).

[3]See for example the *MLA Selective List of Materials* (1962) and especially Appendix 2: Criteria for the Evaluation of Materials, pp. 143-153.

[4]See Jensen (1961, 1968).

[5]See, for example, G. Reginald Bishop Jr., ed., *Culture in Language Learning: Reports of the Working Committees: Northeast Conference on the Teaching of Foreign Languages, 1960;* Robert Lado, *Linguistics Across Cultures: Applied Linguistics for Language Teachers;* Laurence Wylie, Else M. Fleissner, Juan Marichal, Donald Pitkin, and Ernest J. Simmons, "Six Cultures (French, German, Hispanic, Italian, Luso-Brazilian, Russian): Selective and Annotated Bibliographies," in *Reports of Surveys and Studies in the Teaching of Modern Foreign Languages, 1959-1961*, pp. 253-275; Edward Hall, *Silent Language*, and *Hidden Dimension;* Howard Lee Nostrand, "A Second Culture: A New Imperative for American Education," in the College Entrance Examination Board *Curricular Change in the Foreign Languages: A Language Teacher's Handbook;* and Francis Debyser. "The Relation of Language to Culture and the Teaching of Culture to Beginning Language Students," *The CCD Language Quarterly: The Chilton-Didier Foreign Language Newsletter*, Vol. VI, Nos. 1 and 2 (Spring/Summer, 1968).

CHAPTER VIII

BILINGUAL SCHOOLING
IMPLICATIONS FOR EDUCATION AND SOCIETY

Bilingual schooling represents a bold new attempt to remedy serious defects in our way of educating children who enter school with a limited knowledge of English. Stated affirmatively, it aims to equalize the education of all children, whether from English-speaking or non-English-speaking homes. All normal children speak at least one language and are equipped with a usual complement of concepts and affects when they enter school. By taking full advantage of this "readiness" to expand their learning, first in their dominant language and then in their second, proponents of bilingual education aspire to provide all children with an opportunity to learn some or all the subjects through two languages. Such an audacious undertaking cannot be expected to succeed completely overnight. The basic principles of bilingual education need further clarification, curricular designs need to be tested, methods and materials developed, teachers prepared, and the public fully informed. This being so, what results can resonably be expected of this new educational venture—in five years or in twenty-five?

Short-Term Implications for Education

In five years, or shall we say six, in order to consider the whole span of elementary grades, there will have been time to test the soundness of the rationale on which bilingual schooling is based. Programs beginning in 1969-1970 will have had time to prove themselves, and there will be other programs from six to twelve years old. Still others, benefiting from the experience of these, will have started in the interim. Thanks to the Bilingual Education Act, to the genuine interest on the part of many educators, and to the solid support given by some communities, there is assurance of a sufficient *number* of bilingual programs to yield the needed answers.

The question is: Will the *quality* of these programs demonstrate the advantages which their proponents predict? An affirmative answer to this question is by no means assured. For one thing, the establishment of a bilingual program is costly. The cost of all schooling is increasing, and there is no reason to suppose that the establishment of a bilingual program would be an economy as far as money is concerned. Money cost may be the least expensive kind of cost, however, in a society like ours. After a trial period of five or six years, during which a local education agency has received generous federal support, how many communities will be willing to continue successful programs with local taxes? How many school districts will decide that the difficulties of finding enough competent teachers, of locating and assembling adequate teaching and testing materials, of winning community support are impossibly great? How many, after the first blush of enthusiasm has passed, will be willing to keep on?

Given the whims of public opinion, the present writers believe that nothing short of undeniable success will assure bilingual schooling of more than temporary public favor. But we also believe that this promising young movement has in it an educational reform so urgently needed that fears lest we fail cannot bc permitted to stand in the way of the most strenuous attempts to succeed.

If bilingual programs are to be of quality to match their promise, it seems reasonable to expect that within six years the following educational benefits can be demonstrated:

1) That non-English-speaking children entering a sound bilingual program in the nursery, kindergarten, or first grade can within the first year build a healthy and confident self-image and can maintain and strengthen this image throughout the years.

2) That the normal non-English-speaking child can learn to read and write his mother tongue in the first grade at the latest and can begin to acquire a permanent taste for reading and learning from books.

3) That this same child can by the end of the first grade have learned enough English to understand nearly everything that is said in English by his teachers and by the English-speaking children; that by the end of the second he will have learned to speak English quite freely; by the end of the third he will be able to read and write English in addition to his first language; and by the end of the sixth he will have reached grade level in English reading and writing and will be able to speak English without an accent.

4) That he will be able to carry the full load of learning in all the subjects of the curriculum first through his home language and gradually through English also, reaching grade level by the end of the grade six, at the latest, in every subject in at least one language, and in two languages in some subjects if not all.

5) That, through the study of his own specific history and culture as well as United States history and culture in general, he will acquire cultural awareness and a sympathetic cross-cultural understanding.

6) That he will feel free to participate in the mainstream of American culture or in both that and his ancestral culture.

7) That the normal English-speaking child in a bilingual program will maintain grade level standing in all subjects conducted in English.

8) That this same child will, in addition, learn to understand and speak language X at level appropriate to his age by the end of grade three; and by the end of grade six, will be able to speak X without an accent and to read and write X, again at a level appropriate to his age.

9) That he will be able, in addition to carrying in English the full load of learning in all subjects of the elementary curriculum, to learn at least some subjects of the curriculum through his second language, and by the end of the sixth grade to have achieved a degree of proficiency adequate for pursuing a broad general education.

10) That by studying his own history and culture as well as that of the other ethni group he will acquire cultural awareness and a sympathetic cross-cultural understanding.

11) That, though belonging to the American cultural mainstream, he will feel comfortable in associating with representatives of the other cultural stream.

12) That the school administration and teachers will succeed in getting the activ participation of parents and other members of the community in the program.

Short-Term Implications for Society

In view of the time it takes to accomplish changes in society, expected improvement within a period of five or six years are likely to be very modest indeed. If any perceptible advances at all are observed, a program can be counted as successful.

Within this period of time it is to be hoped

1) That a community, if it has assured itself of the positive educational achievements of its bilingual program, will decide to support it with or without federal assistance.

2) That a community, responding to the informational efforts of the school administration and teaching staff, will begin to understand and therefore support bilingual schooling.

3) That the Bilingual Education Act will have clearly demonstrated its benefits not only for the lower-income strata of our society but also its effectiveness in maintaining and cultivating valuable language and cultural resources of all socioeconomic levels, and that as a result of this demonstration Congress will be moved to broaden the Act in order to help conserve these resources in the national interest.

Long-Term Implications for Education

If all goes well, what educational benefits may reasonably be expected, say twenty-five years from now, near the end of our century? Let us suggest the following, among many:

1) That a variety of curricular designs appropriate to diverse local conditions will have been developed and tested.

2) That the shortage of instructional materials and of testing instruments will have been overcome through the cooperative efforts of teams of specialists and through the unhampered importation of foreign books and materials.

3) That educators will by then have learned, by experience and through research, effective ways of conducting bilingual schooling.

4) That procedures will have been perfected for the identification of special talents in teachers (e.g., special education, materials development, research, public relations, evaluation) and for flexible scheduling to make the best use of such special talents.

5) That teacher-preparing institutions will have found ways of preparing competent teachers or of assessing competencies already possessed by teacher candidates and means of complementing these to complete their preparation to teach.

6) That state departments of education will have worked out a nationwide system of teacher-certification based on demonstrated qualifications, however acquired.

7) that a regular system of teacher exchanges with other countries will have been perfected by federal, state, and local agencies.

8) That satisfactory procedures for school-community cooperation will have been worked out to consist of full accounting by the school to the community and involvement and participation—without interference—by the community in the school's educational program.

9) That an effective system of reporting and disseminating significant information will have been developed, involving local and state newsletters and the use of ERIC (Educational Resources Information Center) on the national level.

10) That the difficult problems of articulation will have been solved, so that the junior and senior high schools can effectively build on a bilingual program in the elementary grades.

11) That colleges and universities will have made the necessary educational adjustments to such a serious change in the schools, that they will have recongized the importance of language—any language—both as a subject and as a medium of study and research; and that languages will have been recognized as leading to advanced study not only in literature but also in other fields, notably the social sciences.

12) That bilingual schooling will have been recognized not merely as a new kind of language learning but as a new educational mode and that as such it will have been widely adopted in many monolingual as well as bilingual parts of the United States.

Long-Range Implications for Society

Just as a single bilingual program is expected to have an impact on the local community, so a national expansion of bilingual schooling has certain implications for society as a whole. As suggestive of others, we mention the following:

1) General understanding of the proposition that English is not threatened by the presence of other languages, nor American culture by the presence of other cultures, but rather that our American culture can be greatly enriched by cultural variety.

2) The beginning of a national acceptance of and respect for speakers of other languages and representatives of other cultures or sub-cultures, resulting in wide acceptance of linguistic and cultural pluralism. How desperate the need is for this kind of acceptance and understanding is suggested by the many present social alienations between blacks and whites, rich and poor, old and young, ingroups and outgroups. Remedy of these societal tensions is a top national priority.

3) Wide appreciation of the national need of educated American specialists in many fields who are native or near-native speakers of other languages to help maintain our dialogue and cooperate with other nations, thus protecting our national interests.

4) A concern by all Americans for the elimination of poverty, based on the realization that the educational improvement of the poor (which include many speakers of other languages who are presently handicapped in English) helps to raise the socioeconomic level of the population. A higher income level can in turn benefit education, setting an upward spiral.

5) The improvement of our image at home and abroad, the resulting better cooperation with other nationals, in all fields, and the further development of our many international enterprises.

There has been much talk in recent years of the "explosion of knowledge" and at the same time specialists operating near the frontiers of knowledge complain that the more they learn the more inadequate is their ability to cope with problems that seem to increase at the same accelerating rate.

Let us take a single example. Looking back over our twenty-five years of national experience in the field of foreign aid—the length of time we are now trying to look ahead—Neil H. Jacoby points out[1] that although our efforts have been joined to those of other relatively prosperous nations and though these efforts have had some effect, in about 100 countries of the world, having two thirds of the world's population, the per capita annual income is still under $500. Although 45 less developed countries show an average annual growth of about five percent in the real gross national product (G.N.P.), a rate similar to that of 22 advanced countries, the spiraling population increase cuts the per capita G.N.P. growth rate in half (2.6%).

"The sheer enormity of the problem and a new awareness of its complexities have bred a sense of despair about its solution. Hope for the future has diminished as powerful voices from both the political Left and Right counsel a retreat, if not a withdrawal, from the effort. Not surprisingly, advanced nations have sharply reduced their economic aid and will continue to do so unless a new approach can be found."[2]

Jacoby defines "development" as "a complex socio-politico-economic process whereby the people of a country progress from a static traditional mode of life toward a modern dynamic society."[3] The similarities between this complex problem and the educational problem with which we are concerned in this book are striking. Jacoby points out that underdeveloped countries are free not to enter into an agreement for outside assistance, just as bilingual communities are free not to apply for federal aid under Title VII. Jacoby also defines progress as acceptance of the dynamics of a modern society. Similarly, Miles Zintz contends, as we have seen,[4] that educational progress in our bilingual areas means the acceptance by those who belong to culture X of the cultural values of culture E (e.g., competition, aggressiveness) if they want to join the mainstream. Fortunately this can be done without abandoning traditional values if, as we believe, the human being is versatile and flexible enough to master two sets of values as well as two languages.

Our problem of educational development, like that of international socio-politico-economic development, is complex. It too has its political, social, and economic aspects in addition to the purely educational one. It involves dozens of cultures and sub-cultures in various states of mix with the predominant American culture. The elements we have selected for study are only samples of many problems in need of study. For the problem of international development Jacoby proposes "a new approach" based on a partnership between developed and underdeveloped nations from which both may derive benefits.

The present writers feel that bilingual education represents "the new approach" which gives hope of helping to solve some of the complex problems of American education. As with international development, the chances of success are greatly increased if this new educational venture is conceived and carried out as a partnership in which all parties profit.

NOTES

[1]In an Occasional Paper published by the Center for the Study of a Demoncratic Institutions under the title of *The Progress of Peoples: Toward a Theory and Policy of Development with External Aid*. Santa Barbara, California, June 1969.

[2]Ibid., p. 3.

[3]Ibid, p. 5.

[4] See note 50 under Methods and Materials.

CHAPTER IX

CONCLUSION

In concluding our study we feel that we have written only an introduction—a very tentative one.

About some aspects of our study we feel confident; the evidence seems conclusive. Our past methods of educating children suffering linguistic handicaps in English have clearly been ineffective. The chief reasons for this seem to be that we have not taken advantage of the child's best instrument of learning—his mother tongue—and that we have failed to create in him a sense of dignity and confidence. In a word, we have not put first things first: We have thought it more important from the outset to teach the non-English-speaking child English than to educate him. We have in short been more interested in assimilating than in educating.

Everyone agrees that in the education of American children English is indispensable. Those who do now know it must learn it. Disagreement comes over the order and method of learning. As we have seen, the mass of evidence shows that, everything being equal, children learn to read and write faster and better in their dominant tongue than they do in a second language. There is also ample evidence that children can learn to read and write a second language more easily and better if they have built confidence in themselves by having become literate first in their native tongue. If, in addition, their English-speaking playmates and teachers treat them with respect and affection, their understanding of themselves, of the meaning of their language, and of their cultural heritage will grow, as will their motivation for further learning.

The new educational vista that the Bilingual Education Act opens is that it obviates the disintegrative choice that millions of "nonstandard" children have faced in our public schools: a choice between the language of their mothers and the language of their country and its schools. That mother-and-country has become cliché should not blind us to the fact that, especially in dealing with young children, we drive a wedge between them at our own peril. When certain identifiable ethnic groups among our people have been confronted with the choice, it has been the schools that have lost. But if the hopes extended by the Bilingual Education Act are realized, our ethnic children can not only maintain and develop their mother tongues but can also learn English better than they have in the past. Results of early bilingual schooling demonstrate that, when a child's learning is properly guided by competent teachers, he can acquire in both languages unaccented spoken command, grade-level literacy, and the means of continuing his education "toward the farthest edge of his talents and dreams."

In this work we have tried to summarize present knowledge concerning bilingual education and to define a point of view, essentially that suggested by the Bilingual Education Act and the Guidelines. A year from now, after the accumulation of experience in a hundred or more bilingual programs, some of which will have been in operation for as long as six years, a preliminary report will be needed on their achievement. Such a report should record essential progress made, and, in the year 1970, redefine the state of bilingual schooling in the United States.

BIBLIOGRAPHY

This bibliography is far from exhaustive. It lists only some of the more relevant items—books, articles, bibliographies, official documents, bulletins, dissertations, theses, manuals, papers, pamphlets, etc., both published and unpublished, that our staff has consulted during its research. Included also are some titles which seemed important but which we were not able to examine. A short annotation follows some entries. A comprehensive bibliography of some 12,000 items is being compiled and computerized by the International Center for Research on Bilingualism in Quebec. We have marked with an asterisk (*) a few of the titles that seem to us most useful to program planners.

BIBLIOGRAPHY

1. Aaronson, A. A. "The Pecan Tree." *Common Ground,* Vol. X, No. 1 (Autumn 1949), pp. 75-88.
   Life of Sicilian immigrants in New Orleans, Louisiana.

2. Abou, Sélim. *Le bilinguisme arabe-français au Liban: Essai d'anthropologie culturelle.* Paris: Presses Universitaires de France, avec le concours du Centre National de la Recherche Scientifique, 1962. 502 pp. Bibliography, pp. 485-491.
   A comprehensive study of French-Arabic bilingualism in Lebanon.

3. Abraham, Willard. "The Bi-Lingual Child and His Teacher." *Elementary English*, Vol. XXXIV, No. 7 (November 1957), pp. 474-478.
   Describes the educational situation of Spanish-speaking children in Arizona.

4. ____. "The Bilingual Child, His Parents and THEIR School." *Exceptional Children*, Vol. XXIII, No. 2 (November 1956), pp. 51-52, 80.
   A plea to the school, parents, and community to take better care of bilingual children, an important category of "exceptional children."

5. Adamic, Louis. *A Nation of Nations.* New York: Harper & Brothers, 1945. 399 pp. Bibliography pp. 353-362.
   Story of Americans from some fourteen countries.

6. Aellen, Carol, and Wallace E. Lambert. "Ethnic Identification and Personality Adjustments of Canadian Adolescents of Mixed English-French Parentage." Montreal, Canada: McGill University, 1967. 36 pp. Mimeographed. 26 references.
   The study concludes that in spite of dual ethnic loyalities, the mixed-ethnic boys showed no sign of personality disturbance, anomie, or feelings of alienation relative to the homogeneous background groups. Their specific attitudes and values suggest a process of cultural fusion rather than a clearcut preference for one or the other system of values.

7. Ainsworth, C. L., ed. *Teachers and Counselors for Mexican American Children.* Austin, Texas: Southwest Educational Development Corporation, 1969. 137 pp. Bibliographies and notes, pp. 61-137.
   Report on a feasibility study conducted at Texas Technological College. The areas of research described and interpreted include characteristics of Mexican Americans (including migrants), sociological implications of their culture, the role of linguistics, the guidance needs of Mexican American youth, and competency patterns of teachers who work with youths of other cultures.

8. Allen, Harold B. *A Survey of the Teaching of English to Non-English Speakers in the United States.* Champaign, Illinois: National Council of Teachers of English, 1966. 158 pp.
   Report based on 810 questionnaires sent to administrators in colleges, schools, and other agencies regarding the teaching of English as a second language. Describes the teacher, teaching situation, aids and materials, and problems and needs in this area.

9. ____. "What English Teachers Should Know About Their Language." See Temple University, The NDEA National Institute for Advanced Study in Teaching Disadvantaged Youth.

10. American Anthropological Association. "Multilingualism and Socio-Cultural Orgnaization." A symposium presented at the 1961 meeting. *Anthropological Linguistics*, Vol. IV, No. 1 (January 1962), 64 pp. Short bibliographies at the end of each article.

    Contents: Henry M. Hoenigswald, "Bilingualism, Presumable Bilingualism and Diachrony;" Uriel Weinreich, "Multilingual Dialectology and the New Yiddish Atlas;" Charles A. Ferguson, "The Language Factor in National Development;" John J. Gumperz, "Types of Linguistic Communities;" A. Richard Diebold, Jr., "A Laboratory for Language Contact;" Joan Rubin, "Bilingualism in Paraguay;" and Robert R. Solenberger, "The Social Meaning of Language Choice in the Marianas."

11. American Council of Learned Societies. Bulletin No. 34, March 1942. *Conference on non-English Speech in the United States, Ann Arbor, Michigan, August 2-3, 1940.* Washington, D. C., 1942. 89 pp.

    Papers read: (1) Hans Kurath. "Pennsylvania Germans." (2) R. M. S. Heffner. "German Settlements in Wisconsin." (3) Alfred Senn. "Swiss Dialects in America." Discussion. (4) Einar Haugen. "Scandinavian." Discussion (5) George L. Trager. "The Slavic-Speaking Groups." Discussion. (6) Hayward Keniston. "The Spanish in the United States." (7) T. Navarro Tomas. "The Linguistic Atlas of Spain and the Spanish in the Americas." Discussion. (8) Walter von Wartburg. "An Atlas of Louisiana French." (9) Ernest F. Haden. "French-Speaking Areas in Canada." Discussion.

12. American Council on Education. Inter-American Schools Service. *Minutes of the First General Conference of American-Sponsored Binational Schools in Latin America, April 10-12, 1957, Washington, D. C.* Washington, D.C., 1957. 185 pp.

    A verbatim report of the proceedings of the Conference together with a list of the official delegates and observers present, the schools and companies represented, etc. Binational schools are schools that provide educational facilities of two nations, namely those characteristic of the United States, and those required by the host country. They include children of both nationalities.

13. Amsden, Constance. *A Reading Program for Mexican-American Children: First Interim Report.* Los Angeles, California: California State College, 1966. 157 pp.

    A preliminary developmental program in beginning reading in English established in an East Los Angeles school to develop oral language skills and to reinforce traditional Mexican cultural values. The emphasis is on parent participation, individual instruction, self-instruction, and cultural awareness.

14. Anastasi, Anne, and Fernando A. Cordova. "Some Effects of Bilingualism Upon the Intelligence Test Performance of Puerto Rican Children in New York City." *The Journal of Educational Psychology*, Vol. XLIV, No. 1 (January 1953), pp. 1-19. 32 references.

    "Whether or not bilingualism constitutes a handicap, as well as the extent of such a handicap, depends upon the way in which the two languages have been learned...."

15. Anderson, James G., and Dwight Safar. "The Influence of Differential Community Perceptions on the Provision of Equal Educational Opportunities," *Sociology of Education*, Vol. XL (Summer 1967), pp. 219-230.

    A study of the perceptions of Mexican American families concerning the ability of their own children in contrast to Indian and Anglo children.

16. ____, and William H. Johnson. *Sociocultural Determinates of Achievements Among Mexican American Students: An Interim Report of the Mathematics Education Program.* Prepared for: National Conference of Educational Opportunities for Mexican-Americans. Southwest Educational Development Laboratory. Las Cruces, New Mexico: ERIC Clearinghouse on Rural Education and Small Schools, March 1968. 41 pp.

"The design of the overall project reflects extensive emphasis upon identifying cultural and social factors and variations among sub-groups of the [Mexican Americans] and relating these cultural characteristics to success in mathematics. The major purpose of this pilot study was to identify distinctive background variables and to study differences among four generations of Mexican-Americans and between this ethnic group and Anglo students." (p. 1)

17. Andersson, Theodore. "Bilingual Elementary Schooling: A Report to Texas Educators." *The Florida FL Reporter*, Vol. VI, No. 2 (Fall 1968), pp. 3-4, 6, 25.

A concise statement on the principles of bilingual education and suggesting guidelines for bilingual programs.

18. ____. "The Bilingual in the Southwest." *The Florida FL Reporter,* Vol. V, No. 2 (Spring 1967), p. 3.

A brief statement written in support of the Bilingual Education Act having to do with the Mexican American child, often called a "bilingual," and "thoughtlessly, sometimes disparagingly, referred to by his teachers as a person 'who knows neither Spanish nor English.'"

19. ____. "FLES for Bilingualism." *The Florida FL Reporter*, Vol. IV, No. 1 (Fall 1965), pp. 15-16.

Examines the relation of FLES to bilingualism, with the thought that bilingualism has implications in monolingual as well as in bilingual societies.

20. ____. *Foreign Languages in the Elementary School: A Struggle Against Mediocrity.* Austin, Texas: The University of Texas Press, 1969.

The FLES movement in the United States: origin, evolution, present status, prospects, recommendations, and evaluation.

21. ____. "A New Focus on the Bilingual Child." *The Modern Language Journal,* Vol. XLIX, No. 3 (March 1965), pp. 156-160. Paper presented at the Conference for the Teacher of the Bilingual Child, University of Texas, June 9, 1964.

Suggests need to correct present miseducation of Spanish-speakers of the Southwest by the means of bilingual education, the principles of which could then be applied to language education in general.

22. ____. "The Optimum Age for Beginning the Study of Modern Languages." *International Review of Education*, Vol. VI, No. 3 (1960).

23. Angel, Frank. "Cognitive Development: A Neglected Aspect of Bilingual Education." From a book in preparation: *Toward a Theory of Transcultural Education.* 26 pp. 11 references.

Argues that the neglect of cognitive education is due to an almost exclusive emphasis on ESL for bilingual Spanish-speaking and Indian pupils.

24.____. "Program Content to Meet the Educational Needs of the Mexican-American." Prepared for the National Conference on Educational Opportunities for Mexican-Americans, April 25-26, 1968, Commodore Perry Hotel, Austin, Texas. Las Cruces, New Mexico: ERIC Clearinghouse on Rural Education and Small Schools, New Mexico State University, March 1968.

25. Ainsfeld, Elizabeth, and Wallace E. Lambert. "Evaluational Reactions of Bilingual and Monolingual Children to Spoken Language." *Journal of Abnormal and Social Psychology,* Vol. LXIX, No. 1 (July 1964), pp. 89-97. 6 references.

"Monolingual and bilingual French-Canadian children listened to tape recordings of children's voices, some in English, some in French, and rated each speaker's personality on 15 traits. Differences between the ratings assigned French and English voices of the subgroups were interpreted as indicative of differences in stereotyped reactions." (Authors' summary)

26. Anthony, J. Garner. *Hawaii Under Army Rule.* Stanford, California: Stanford University Press, 1955.

27. Apsler, Alfred. "'Little Norway' on the Columbia River." *American-Scandinavian Review,* Vol. XLIV, No. 1 (Spring 1956), pp. 63-68.

Description of the Norwegian settlement on Puget Island.

28. Arsenian, Seth. *Bilingualism and Mental Development: A Study of the Intelligence and the Social Background of Bilingual Children in New York City.* Contributions to Education, No. 712. New York: Columbia University, Teachers College, Bureau of Publications, 1937. 164 pp. Bibliography, pp. 155-164. 171 references.

A thorough study. Summarizes available material on bilingualism both in the U.S. and in the world. Sections on language, thought, and background as they relate to bilingualism. Concludes that "bilingualism does not influence–favorably or unfavorably –the mental development of children aged 9 through 14."

*29.____. "Bilingualism in the Post-War World." *Psychological Bulletin*, Vol. XLII, No. 2 (February 1945), pp. 65-68. 46 references.

An important older article. Treats a variety of problems related to this "widespread phenomenon": (1) Its measurement, (2) Its relation to mental development, (3) Its relation to language development, (4) Its relation to school achievement, (5) Its relation to speech and other motor functions, (6) Its relation to personal and social adjustment, (7) Its relation to learning a second language, and (8) Its relation to the political state.

30. Asher, James J. "The Strategy of the Total Physical Response: An Application to Learning Russian." *IRAL* (International Review of Applied Linguistics in Language Learning), Vol. III, No. 4 (December 1965), pp. 291-300.

31. ASPIRA. *Hemos Trabajado Bien.* A Report on the First National Conference of Puerto Ricans, Mexican-Americans, and Educators on "The Special Educational Needs of Urban Puerto Rican Youth." New York City: Aspira, Inc., May 14 and 15, 1968. 74 pp.

Discussion and recommendations regarding bilingual education, teacher and student attitudes, curriculum and textbooks, community involvement, positive self-identity, public politics, etc., with reference to Puerto Rican children.

32. Aucamp, A. J. *Bilingual Education and Nationalism, With Special Reference to South Africa*. Pretoria, South Africa: Van Schaik, 1926. 247 pp. Bibliogrpahy, pp. 242-247.
Includes description of bilingual education in Wales, Scotland, Ireland, Canada, Belgium, and South Africa.

33. Avila, Lilian E., and Alice R. Stewart. "French in Maine." *The French Review*, Vol. XXVII, No. 6 (May 1954), pp. 460-466.
A brief description of the present status of the teaching of French in Maine, Franco-American bilingualism, and the French-Canadian dialect of New England.

34. Axelrod, Joseph. *The Education of the Modern Foreign Language Teacher for American Schools: An Analysis of Ends and Means for Teacher-Preparation Programs in Modern Foreign Languages Based on a Study of NDEA Foreign Language Institutes*. New York: The Modern Language Association of America, March 1966. 55 pp.

35.____. and Donald N. Bigelow. *Resources for Language and Area Studies: A Report on an Inventory of the Language and Area Centers Supported by the National Defense Education Act of 1958*. Washington, D. C.: American Council on Education, 1962. 97 pp. Bibliographical footnotes.
A descriptive inventory of the forty-seven language and areas centers,bringing together information about how the cneters are organized, the number of students enrolled in language and area disciplines, the methods of teaching languages, and the relation between language and area studies.

36. Babin, Partick. "Bilingualism–A Bibliogrpahy." Cambridge, Massachusetts: Harvard Graduate School of Education, May 8, 1968. 30 pp. Unpublished.
A selected listing of books, monographs, journal articles, and bibliographies focusing on bilingualism.

37. Babington, Mima, and E. Bagby Atwood, "Lexical Usage in Southern Louisiana." *Publications of the American Dialect Society*, No. 36 (November 1961), pp. 1-24. 27 bibliographical notes.
Primarily concerned with present lexical usage in six Louisiana parishes centering about Bayou Lafourche. Limited observations of the New Orleans usage for purposes of comparison.

38. Bagster-Collins, E. W., et al. *Studies in Modern Language Teaching: Reports Prepared for the Modern Foreign Language Study and the Canadian Committee on Modern Languages.* Publications of the American and Canadian Committees on Modern Languages, Vol. XXVII. New York: The Macmillan Company, 1930. 491 pp. Bibliographies.

39. Baïche, Marcel. "Le bilinguisme naturel: auxiliaire méprisé." *Les Langues Modernes,* Vol. LIX, No. 2 (March-April 1965), pp. 150-153.
Argument in favor of preserving natural bilingualism in French in the "national interest."

40. Band, Arnole J. "Jewish Studies in American Liberal-Arts Colleges and Universities." *The American Jewish Yearbook,* Vol. LXVII (1966), pp. 3-30.
A comprehensive list of American institutions of higher learning offering courses in Jewish studies, including Hebrew or Yiddish.

41. Barbeau, Marius. "Louisiana French." *Canadian Geographical Journal,* Vol. LIV, No. 1 (January 1957), pp. 2-11.
Brief discussion of the Acadian settlements, their origins, customs, and language.

42. Barker, George C. "Growing Up in a Bilingual Community." *The Kiva*, Vol. XVII, Nos. 1-2 (November-December 1951), pp. 17-32. 7 references.
Examines the role of the home, school, and mass media on the acculturation of children of Mexican descent in a bilingual community: Tucson, Arizona.

43.——. "The Social Functions of Language." *Etc., A Review of General Semantics*, Vol. II, No. 4 (Summer 1945), pp. 228-234. 26 references.
Describes and classifies the functions of spoken language as it relates to social position and organization.

44. Barrett, Donald N., and Julian Samora. *The Movement of Spanish Youth from Rural to Urban Settings*. Washington, D. C.: National Committee for Children and Youth, September 1963. 20 pp.
Contributes information and recommendations relative to the needs of the Spanish-speaking in the Southwest. Presents demographic, historical, and cultural background information; patterns of housing, family life, education, and economics.

45. Barron, Milton L., ed. *American Minorities: A Textbook of Readings in Intergroup Relations*. New York: Alfred A. Knopf, 1957. 518 pp.
An intensive survey of minority groups in the U.S., containing much information. Special treatment is reserved for Indians, Italians, Poles, Japanese, and Spanish-speaking communities.

46.——,ed. *Minorities in a Changing World.* New York: Alfred A. Knopf, 1967. 481 pp. Bibliography, pp. 475-481.
A selection of 33 articles on minority groups in America and other societies.

47. Barry, Colman James. *The Catholic Church and German Americans.* Catholic University of America, Studies in American Church History, Vol. XL. Washington, D. C.: Catholic University of America Press, 1953. 348 pp. Bibliography, pp. 329-337.

48. Bastian, Jarvis. "The Biological Background of Man's Languages." In C. I. J. M. Stuart, ed., "Report of the Fifteenth Annual (First International) Round Table Meeting of Linguistics and Language Studies," Georgetown University *Monograph Series on Languages and Linguistics*, No. 17 (1964), pp. 141-148.
Studies concerning the "profound relation" between human biology and man's languages, particularly to those culture traits associated with technologies.

49. Bauer, Evelyn. "Teaching English to North American Indians in B.I.A. Schools." *The Linguistic Reporter*, Vol. X, No. 4 (August 1968), pp. 1-3.
Outlines the B.I.A. programs of the teaching of English as a second language, and stresses the need for and progress toward bilingual education.

50. Beatty, Willard W., et al. *Education for Action*. Washington, D. C.: U.S. Department of the Interior, Bureau of Indian Affairs, 1944. 347 pp.

Reprints of selected articles in *Indian Education* between 1936 and 1943, setting forth the educational philosophies, policies, and practices of the Bureau. This periodical contains many pertinent articles dealing with Indian language problems.

51. ____, et al. *Education for Cultural Change*. Washington, D.C.: U.S. Department of the Interior, Bureau of Indian Affairs, 1953.
Reprints of selected articles which appeared in *Indian Education* for the years 1944-1951. (See annotation for Beatty, *Education for Action*.)

52. Beck, Magnus Olaf. *Becks of Normanna*. San Antonio, Texas: The Naylor Co., c1964. 198 pp.
History of the Norwegian community in Normanna (Bee County), Texas.

53. Bell, Paul W. "Bilingual Education in an American Elementary School." In H. H. Stern, ed., *Languages and the Young School Child*, London: Oxford University Press, 1969, pp. 112-118.
A description of the Coral Way Elementary School in Miami, Florida.

54. Benoit, Josaphat T. *L'âme franco-américaine.* Montreal, Canada: A. Lévesque, 1935. 245 pp. Bibliography, pp. 235-245.
A classic on the subject of "the Franco-American soul."

55. Benson, Adolph B., and Naboth Hedin. *Americans from Sweden*. The Peoples of America Series edited by Louis Adamic. Foreword by Carl Sandburg. New York: J. B. Lippincott Company, 1950. 448 pp. Bibliography, pp. 427-434.
History, religious life, "denominational" education, activities, and other aspects of the life of Swedish Americans in the United States.

56. Bergman, Robert L. "Boarding Schools and the Psychological Problems of Indian Children." Paper read in Washington, D.C., to Pediatrics Convention, June 19, 1967. 15 pp. Bibliography, p. 15. 9 references.
A thorough analysis of the problems caused by the lack of respect for Indian language and culture and lack of parental substitution. Constructive suggestions as to possible changes.

57. Berney, Tomi D., Robert L. Cooper, and Joshua A. Fishman. "Semantic Independence and Degree of Bilingualism in Two Puerto Rican Communities." *Revista Interamericana de Psicología,* Vol. II (1968), pp. 289-294. 6 references.
A study of semantic independence and relative proficiency as related to independent dimensions of the bilingual's language systems.

58. Berry, Brewton. "The Education of American Indians: A Survey of the Literature." Prepared for the Special Senate Subcommittee on Indian Education of the Committee on Labor and Public Welfare. Washington, D.C.: U.S. Government Printing Office, February 1969. 121 pp.
An 83-page survey precedes the bibliography of 708 references. Both deal with the history, problems, and causes of the problems in Indian education.

59. Besso, Henry V. "Judeo-Spanish in the United States." *Hispania*, Vol. XXXIV (1951), pp. 89-90.

60. Bez, Khaim, "Loyalty to Yiddish." *Kultur un Dertsiung*, Vol. XXXII, No. 7 (1962), pp. 7-8. Written in Yiddish.

61. Bird, Thomas E., ed. See Gaarder and Richardson.

62. Bishop, G. Reginald, Jr., ed. *Foreign Language Teaching: Challenges to the Profession*. See Northeast Conference on the Teaching of Foreign Languages.

63. Bjork, Kenneth. "Early Norwegian Settlements in the Rockies." *Norwegian-American Studies and Records*. Vol. XVIII (1954), pp. 44-81.

64. Blanc, Haim. *Communal Dialects in Baghdad*. Harvard Middle-Eastern Monograph Series, No. 10. Cambridge, Massachusetts: Harvard University Press, 1964. 204 pp. Bibliography, pp. 173-180.

A general introduction of communal dialects in the Arab world with phonology, morphology, syntax, lexical features of communal dialects in Baghdad, Iraq.

65. Blegen, Theodore C. *Norwegian Migration to America 1825-1860*. Northfield, Minnesota: The Norwegian-American Historical Association, 1931. 413 pp.

The classic and oft-cited source of historical information on the immigration of Norwegians to the United States.

66. Bloomfield, Leonard. *Language*. New York: Holt, 1933. 564 pp. Bibliography, pp. 525-545.

A classic text on language, on which most American works have been based.

67. Blossom, Grace A. "A New Approach to an Old Problem." *Journal of American Indian Education*, Vol. I, No. 2 (January 1962), pp. 13-14.

Discusses the relationship between the shift from "speaking" to "comprehension" vocabulary in uppergrade texts and the widespread belief that retardation for many bilingual Indian students starts at the fourth-grade level.

68. Boas, Frank. "The Classification of American Languages." *American Anthropologist*, Vol. XXII (1920), pp. 367-376.

69. Boileau, A. "Le problème du bilinguisme et la théorie des substrats." *Revue des Langues Vivantes,* Vol. XII (1946), pp. 113-25, 169-93, and 213-24.

70. Bolek, Rev. Francis. *The Polish American School System*. New York: Columbia Press Corp., 1948. 108 pp.

A brief survey of Polish programs in American public and parochial schools.

71. Borowitz, Eugene B. "Problems Facing Jewish Educational Philosophy in the Sixties." *American Jewish Yearbook*, Vol. LXII (1961), pp. 145-153.

Discusses the relationship of modern Hebrew study, its goals, objectives, relativity, decision makers, and implications for the majority of American Jewish children.

72. Boudreaux, Elia. "Some Aims and Methods in Teaching French in the Elementary Schools in Louisiana: The Oakdale Elementary School Experiment." *The Modern Language Journal*, Vol. XXIV, No. 6 (March 1940), pp. 427-430.

A FLES program for Louisiana French children during the 1930's.

73. Bovet, Pierre. "Bilingualism and Education." *New Era in Home and School*, Vol. XIV (July 1933), pp. 161-163.
Briefly discusses the pro and con of bilingualism and its educational problems.

74.____. *Les problèmes scolaires posés par le bilinguisme.* Zürich, Switzerland: Pour l'Ere Nouvelle, No. 105, 1935.

75. Boyer, Mildred V. "Bilingual Schooling: A Dimension of Democracy." *Texas Foreign Language Association Bulletin.* Vol. II, No. 2 (December 1968), pp. 1-6.
An address to the Texas Foreign Language Association, Fort Worth. Answers such questions as: What is bilingual education, and what and whom is it for?

76.____. "Poverty and the Mother Tongue." *Educational Forum*, Vol. XXIX, No. 3 (March 1965), pp. 290-296.
Advocates a free, pluralistic development of languages and cultures in the U.S. for theoretical and practical reasons: the conservation and development of potential human wealth otherwise wasted, and the improvement of the non-English-mother-tongue individuals.

77.____. "Texas Squanders Non-English Resources." *Texas Foreign Language Association Bulletin*, Vol. V, No. 3 (October 1963), pp. 1-8.
Concludes that it is of national interest to conserve and cultivate Spanish in the Spanish-speaking population through a bilingual curriculum. Statistical data on the foreign-born Texas population are provided.

78. Brameld, Theodore. *Minority Problems in the Public Schools: A Study of Administrative Policies and Practices in Seven School Systems.* Bureau for Intercultural Education Problems of Race and Culture in American Education, Vol. IV. New York and London: Harper & Brothers, 1946. 264 pp.
A cross-section of American problems of intercultural education with suggestions for a self-survey of a school system.

79. Brault, Gérard J. "L'attitude des participants de l'Institut franco-américain de Bowdoin College." *Le Canado-Américain,* Vol. II, No. 12 (April-May 1962), pp. 33-39. Paper read before the French VIII (North American) Group of the MLA at the Annual Meeting held in Chicago, December 29, 1961.
Outlines the attitude of the participants of the Franco-American NDEA Institute of 1961.

80.____. "Comment doit-on enseigner le français aux jeunes franco-américains?" *Le Canado-Américain,* Vol. II, No. 6 (April-May 1961), pp. 30-34.
Empahsizes the need of *modern* methods and of materials of contemporary interest.

81.____, ed. *Les conférences de l'Institut franco-américain de Bowdoin College.* Brunswick, Maine: Bowdoin College, 1962. Published privately with funds provided by four Franco-American cultural organizations: L'Association Canado-Américaine, La Société d'Assomption, L'Union Saint-Jean-Baptiste d'Amérique, and Le Comité de Vie Franco-Américaine.
Integral text of the lectures given at the 1961 NDEA Franco-American Institute.

82.____. "Le mythe de la langue de Louis XIV." *Assumption Preparatory School Alumnus*, Vol. XXV (Winter 1957-1958), pp. 4-6.
Some thoughts on Franco-American or "popular French," which is spoken everywhere in France, with a few typically French-Canadian differences.

83.____. "New England French Vocabulary." *The French Review*, Vol. XXXV, No. 2 (December 1961), pp. 163-175.
Illustrates the lexical strengths and weaknesses of the French spoken by Franco-Americans.

84.____. "Some Misconceptions About Teaching American Ethnic Children Their Mother Tongue." *The Modern Language Journal*, Vol. XLVIII, No. 2 (February 1964), pp. 67-71.
Points out that mother-tongue teachers of the same ethnic background are regarded with sympathy by their students; yet they rarely recognize or appreciate an immigrant child's linguistic heritage.

85.____. "The Special NDEA Institute at Bowdoin College for French Teachers of Canadian Descent." *PMLA*, Vol. LXXVII, No. 4, Part 2 (September 1962), pp. 1-5.
Describes the essentials of the Institute program and curriculum, as well as its effect on the participants.

86.____. *A Transcript of Interviews with Franco-Americans*. 2 parts. Brunswick, Maine: Bowdoin College, 1960.
These interviews are designed to illustrate the chief features of French spoken by New England Franco-Americans and to provide useful information for facilitating instruction in standard spoken French.

87.____, Alexander Hull, Solange Duboff, Emmanuel Jacquart, and Norman D. Deschênes. *Cours de langue française destiné aux jeunes franco-américains.* ("Bowdoin Materials"). Texts, dialogues, and oral excerises. Photo-offset. Manchester, New Hampshire: Association des Professeurs Franco-Américains, 1965. 261 pp.

Also: "A Manual for Franco-Americans." With tape recordings. Brunswick, Maine: Bowdoin College, 1960. Mimeographed, 82 pp.

And: "Workbook for Franco-Americans." With tape recordings. Brunswick, Maine: Bowdoin College, 1960. Mimeographed, 61 pp.
Instructional materials developed at Bowdoin College for the teaching of standard French "in the new key" to Franco-Americans.

88. Brogan, D. W. *The American Character*. New York: Alfred A. Knopf, 1944. 168 pp.

89. Bronner, Hedin and Gösta Franzén. "Scandinavian Studies in Instutitions of Learning in the United States, Seventh Report: 1966-67." *Scandinavian Studies*, Vol. XXXIX, No. 4 (November 1967), pp. 345-367.
Lists high schools, colleges, and universities that teach Scandinavian languages and studies including enrollment figures.

90. Brooks, Nelson H. *Language and Language Learning: Theory and Practice*. 2nd ed. New York and Burlingame: Harcourt, Brace & World Inc., 1964. 250 pp. Bibliographies.

91._____. "The Meaning of Bilingualism Today." *Foreign Language Annals*, Vol. II, No. 3 (March 1969), pp. 304-309.

Defines bilingualism as the habitual use of two languages by the same person and emphasizes the fact that in its purest form the two languages are quite separate.

92. Brophy, William A., and Sophie Aberle. *The Indian: America's Unfinished Business*. Report of the Commission on the Rights, Liberties, and Responsibilities of the American Indian. Norman: University of Oklahoma Press, 1966.

Regarding language problems emphasizes meaning of words in relation to culture and calls attention to the problem the Indian faces in trying to comprehend our tenses, grammar, inflection, and grammatical categories.

93. Brouillette, Benoît. *La pénétration du continent américain par les Canadiens-Français, 1763-1846: Traitants, explorateurs, missionnaires*. Preface by Mr. L'Abbé Lionel Groulx. Collection de l'Association Canadienne-Française pour l'Avancement des Sciences, No. 1. Montréal, Canada: Librairie Granger Frères Limitée, 1939. 242 pp. Bibliographies and notes at end of each chapter.

Historical sketch of the penetration of the American continent by French-Canadians.

94. Broussard, James F. *Louisiana Creole Dialect*. Louisiana State University and Agricultural and Mechanical College Romance Languages Series, No. 5. Baton Rouge, Louisiana: Louisiana State University Press, 1942. 134 pp. Bibliography, pp. 130-134.

Study of Louisiana Creole phonetics, grammar, idioms, folklore, proverbs and ditons, medical prescriptions, poetry, tales, and a glossary.

95. Brown, Francis J., and Joseph Slabey Roucek, eds. *One America: The History, Contributions, and Present Problems of Our Racial and National Minorities*. New York: Prentice-Hall, Inc., 1952. 718 pp. Selected bibliography, pp. 660-701. Revised post-war edition of *Our Racial and National Minorities: Their History, Contributions, and Present Problems*, New York: Prentice-Hall, Inc., 1937. 877 pp. Selected bibliography, pp. 781-847.

A comprehensive, although theoretical and now outdated, study of American minority groups. Consists of short articles on each ethnic group followed by a discussion of the activities of minority groups, racial and cultural conflicts, educational problems, and cultural democracy in America.

96. Browning, Harley L., and S. Dale McLemore. *A Statistical Profile of the Spanish-Surname Population of Texas*. Population Series No. 1. Austin, Texas: Bureau of Business Research, The University of Texas, 1964. 83 pp.

Number, growth, geographical distribution, basic population characteristics, education and employment opportunities, occupation and income of the Spanish-surname population of Texas, with comparisons with four other southwestern states.

97. Bruneau, Charles. "Quelques considérations sur le français parlé aux Etats-Unis d'Amérique." *Conférences de l'Institut de Linguistique de l'Université de Paris*, Vol. IV, pp. 21-35. Paris: Librairie C. Klincksieck, 1936.

98. Brussell, Charles B. *Disadvantaged Mexican American Children and Early Educational Experience*. Edited by J. A. Forester and E. E. Arnaud. Austin, Texas: Southwest Educational Development Corporation, 1968. 105 pp. Bibliographies, pp. 89-105.

"The study is divided into four major areas of interest—history and demography, social characteristics, intelligence and intellectual functioning of Spanish-speaking children, and implications for early educational experiences for disadvantaged Mexican American children. A fifth section contains brief descriptions of a number of current projects designed for Mexican American children. A bibliography is included for each section." (p. 85)

99. Buffington, Albert F., and Preston A. Barba. *A Pennsylvania German Grammar*. Allentown, Pennsylvania: Schlechter, 1954. 167 pp.

100. Burger, Henry G. *"Ethno-Pedagogy": A Manual in Cultural Sensitivity, with Techniques for Improving Cross-Cultural Teaching by Fitting Ethnic Patterns*. Albuquerque, New Mexico: Southwestern Cooperative Educational Laboratory, Inc., June 1968. 193 pp. Bibliography, pp. 167-180.
Based on a review of around 1500 publications, inspection of some three dozen Southwestern ethnic schools, projects, and laboratory activities, this manual offers a systematic, theoretical, and practical approach to the school as a major institution of culture. Attempts to present the basic information that the teacher-leader must know for an inter-ethnic classroom.

101. Burma, John Harmon. *Spanish-Speaking Groups in the United States*. Durham, North Carolina: Duke University Press, 1955. 214 pp. Bibliography, pp 199-209.
A survey of Mexican Americans, Filipinos, and Puerto Ricans in the United States. A panoramic view of these minorities and their problems of assimilation and adjustment in American culture, and an analysis of their demography, history, and contemporary sociological, cultural, educational, and economic conditions.

102. Burns, Donald. "Niños de la sierra peruana estudian en quechua para saber español." *Anuario Indigenista*, Vol. XXVII (December 1968), pp. 105-110.
Quechua-Spanish bilingual education programs in Peru.

103. Cahman, Werner J. "The Cultural Consciousness of Jewish Youth." *Jewish Social Studies*, Vol. XIV, No. 3 (July 1952), pp. 195-208.
Presents results from a study of a group of non-orthodox but otherwise ideologically undefined and unaffiliated Jewish teen-agers in the Brownsville section of Brooklyn, in order to contribute to the reformulation of the values of Judaism and Jewish culture in the new frame of reference developed since the creation of Israel.

104. California State Department of Education. *Prospectus for Equitable Educational Opportunities for Spanish-Speaking Children.* Sacramento, California: California State Department of Education, 1967.

105. Callard, J. A. "Bilingualism and the Pre-School Child." *Proceedings of the World Federation of Education Associations*, 1933, pp. 56-58.
Observations based on experiences with English-Welsh bilingualism.

106. Canada. Royal Commission on Bilingualism and Biculturalism. Preliminary Report. Ottawa: Queen's Printer, February 1, 1965. 211 pp.
Summary of the Commission's experience in personal contact with the public and a setting forth of its provisional conclusions.

*107.____. *Book I: General Introduction: The Official Languages.* Ottawa: Queen's Printer, October 8, 1967. 212 pp.
Origins, background development, and various forms of bilingualism and biculturalism in Canada.

*108.____. *Book II: Education.* Ottawa: Queen's Printer, May 23, 1968. 350 pp.
Linguistic and cultural aspects of education in Canada.

109. Canada. Royal Commission on Education. (Parent Commission) Report in 5 vols. Quebec, Canada: Ministry of Education, 1963-1966.

*110. Canadian Commission for UNESCO. *The Description and Measurment of Bilingualism/Description et mesure du bilinguisme,* edited by Louis Kelley. Pre-prints for the Moncton Seminar (6-14 June, 1967) Proceedings. Toronto, Canada: University of Toronto Press, In Press. 159 pp.
The most worldwide review of interdisciplinary problems and progress in research of bilingualism.

111. Carman, Justice Neale. *Foreign Language Units of Kansas: Historical Atlas and Statistics.* Lawrence, Kansas: The University of Kansas Press, 1962. Maps, tables, bibliography.

112.____. "Germans in Kansas.", *American-German Review,* Vol. XXVII, No. 4 (1961), pp. 4-8.

113. Carrière, Joseph M. "Creole Dialect of Missouri." *American Speech,*Vol. XIV, No. 2 (April 1939), pp. 109-119.
Focuses on the English influence and English loanwords in the Colonial French of Old Mines, Missouri.

114. Carroll, John B. "The Contributions of Psychological Theory and Educational Research to the Teaching of Foreign Languages." *The Modern Language Journal,* Vol. XLIX, No. 5 (May 1965), pp. 273-281.
An address delivered at the International Conference on Modern Foreign Language Teaching, Kongresshalle, Berlin, Germany, September 5, 1964.

115. Carrow, Sister Mary A. "Linguistic Functioning of Bilingual and Monolingual Children." *Journal of Speech and Hearing Disorders,* Vol. XXII (1957), pp. 371-280.

116. Carter, Thomas P. "A Negative Self-Concept of Mexican-American Students." *School and Society,* Vol. XCVI, No. 2306 (March 30, 1968), pp. 217-219.

117.____. *Preparing Teachers for Mexican American Children.* Las Cruces, New Mexico: ERIC Clearinghouse on Rural Education and Small Schools; and Washington, D. C.: ERIC Clearinghouse on Teacher Education, February 1969. 15 pp. Notes, pp. 14-15.
Stresses need for "a new breed of educators–one equipped to make objective appraisals of problems, and to take rational and appropriate steps to encourage their elimination." (p. 14)

*118.____. *Mexican Americans in School: A Study of Educational Neglect* (tentative title). To be published in 1969 or early 1970 by the College Entrance Examination Board, New York.

119. Caskey, Owen L., and Jimmy Hodges. *A Resource and Reference Bibliography on Teaching and Counseling the Bilingual Student.* Prepared and printed through funds provided by Southwest Educational Development Laboratory to the Mexican American Teacher and Counselor Education Programs. School of Education, Texas Technological College, Lubbock, Texas, March 1968. 733 references.

120. Cebollero, Pedro Angel. *La política lingüístico-escolar de Puerto Rico.* Consejo Superior de Enseñanza de Puerto Rico, Publicaciones Pedagógicas, Vol. II, No. 1. Revised, second edition. San Juan, Puerto Rico: Impr. Baldrich, 1945. 145 pp. Bibliography, pp. 142-143.

Contains a brief history of the language problem in Puerto Rico with a review of the studies related to this problem, an analysis of the social necessity of English.

121.___. *A School Language Policy for Puerto Rico.* Educational Publication Series II, No. 1. San Juan, Puerto Rico: Superior Educational Council, 1945.

See Spanish version for annotation.

122. Center for Applied Linguistics. *International Conference on Second Language Problems. Report on Eighth Meeting. Heidelberg, April 26-29, 1967.* Washington, D.C.: Center for Applied Linguistics, February 1968. 47 pp.

Contains the recommendations, resolutions, and agenda of the conference; with appendices dealing with research, teaching, and the linguistic situations in countries all over the world.

123.___. *Styles of Learning Among American Indians: An Outline for Research.* Report and Recommendations of a Conference held at Stanford University, August 8-10, 1968. Washington, D. C.: Center for Applied Linguistics, February 1969. 36 pp. References at the end of several chapters.

Proceedings of a meeting of specialists in Psycholinguistics, study of child language, child psychology, Indian cultural anthropology, and related fields, organized to outline feasible research projects to investigate the ways in which the styles of learning employed by Indian groups may be related to the school achievement of the Indian student.

124. Cervenka, Edward J. *The Measurement of Bilingualism and Bicultural Socialization of the Child in the School Setting: The Development of Instruments.* Section IV, *Final Report on Head Start Evaluation and Research: 1966-1967* (Contract No. 66-1), to the Institute for Educational Development, by the Staff and Study Directors: Child Development Evaluation and Research Center. Austin, Texas: The University of Texas, August 31, 1967. Mimeographed.

125.___. *Administration Manual for the Inventory of Socialization for Bilingual Children, Ages Three to Ten.* "Administration Manual for Tests of Basic Language Competence in English and Spanish," Levels I and II. Prepared for the Child Development Evaluation and Research Center (Southwest). Parts of the Final Report to the Office of Economic Opportunity (Contract No. OEO-4115). Austin, Texas: The University of Texas, August 1968. Mimeographed.

Set of three batteries of experimental instruments developed for use in the study of bilingual programs and other compensatory education programs in Texas.

126. Charles, Edgar B., ed. *Mexican-American Education: A Bibliography.* Prepared for: National Conference on Educational Opportunities for Mexican-Americans, April 25-26, 1968. Las Cruces, New Mexico: ERIC Clearinghouse on Rural Education and Small Schools, March 1968. 22 pp.
A selected listing of 90 books, monographs, journal articles, and unpublished papers on the education of the Mexican American, with annotations.

127. Child, Irvin L. *Italian or American? The Second Generation in Conflict.* New Haven, Connecticut: Yale University Press, for the Institute of Human Relations; London: Humphrey Milford, Oxford University Press, 1943. 208 pp. Bibliography, pp. 201-202.
A comprehensive study of the acculturation of Italian immigrants.

128. China Project, Stanford University. *Central South China.* New Haven, Connecticut: Human Relation Area Files, 1956. 874 pp. Bibliography, maps, charts.
A conscientious and quite exhaustive compilation of relevant facts and information.

129. China, Republic of. Ministry of Education, National Institute for Compilation and Translation. *A Study of the Most Frequently Used Vocabulary at the Elementary School Level.* Taipei, Taiwan: Chung Hwa Book Co., 1967. 50 pp. text, 244 pp. charts and tabulations, 36 pp. indices.
The most recent vocabulary study of written literature and exercises at this level. No claim cf validity regarding oral vocabulary.

130. Chomsky, Noam. "Language and the Mind." *Psychology Today*, Vol. I, No. 9 (February 1968).

131. Chou, Fa-kao. *A Study of the Chinese Language.* Taipei, Taiwan: Chung-hwa Cultural Publication Enterprises, 1966. 168 pp. Bibliographical footnotes.
This work, by one of the leading Chinese linguists, gives a scholarly overview of the Chinese language, its characteristics, and an introduction to the various approaches to Chinese linguistics.

132. Christian, Chester C., Jr. "The Acculturation of the Bilingual Child." *The Modern Language Journal*, Vol. XLIX, No. 3 (March 1965), pp. 160-165.
Here the effect that insistence on spoken English has on bilingual children is studied. The problem of confusion and frustration which exists when a child learns one language and culture from his parents and then must learn another language and culture when he enters school is discussed.

133.___, ed. *Reports: Bilingual Education: Research and Teaching.* See Southwest Council of Foreign Language Teachers.

134.___, and Robert Lado, eds. *Reports: Our Bilinguals: Social and Psychological Barriers; Linguistic and Pedagogical Barriers.* See Southwest Council of Foreign Language Teachers.

135. Christian, Jane M. *The Navajo: A People in Transition.* Part One. *Southwestern Studies*, Vol. II, No. 3 (Fall 1964), pp. 3-35; Part Two. *Southwestern Studies*, Vol. II, No. 4 (Winter 1965), pp. 39-71.

An anthropologist-linguist studies sympathetically the Navajo effort to live in two worlds at once, and to try to integrate the best in both into a living whole.

136.___, and Chester C. Christian, Jr. "Spanish Language and Culture in the Southwest." In Joshua A. Fishman, et al. *Language Loyalty in the U.S.: The Maintenance and Perpetuation of the Non-English Mother Tongue by American Ethnic and Religious Groups.* London, The Hague, Paris: Mouton & Co., 1966, pp. 280-317.
Contains a history of Spanish-speaking peoples in the development of the Southwest; a profile of the contemporary Mexican Americans; a sociocultural analysis with emphasis on language and its relationship to society and culture.

137. Christophersen, Paul. *Bilingualism.* An Inaugural Lecture delivered on Foundation Day, November 17th, 1958, University College, Ibadan, Nigeria. Published for the University College, Ibadan, by Methuen & Co. Ltd., London, 36 Essex Street, W. C. 2. 16 pp.
A study of the nature of bilingualism, with advantages and disadvantages, especially in the individual.

138. Ciarlantini, Franco. "Italian in American Schools." *Atlantica*, Vol. IX, No. 5 (July 1930), pp. 14-15.
Discusses the teaching of Italian in American public and private schools.

139. Cohen, Marcel. *Pour une sociologie du langage.* Sciences d'Aujourd'hui. Paris: Albin Michel, 1956. 396 pp. Bibliographies.

140. Cole, Desmond. "School for Tommorrow–A Dissent." *VISTA*, Vol. IV, No. 4 (January–February 1969), pp. 59-64.
The philosophy of the United Nations International School is described and its implications considered for future mutual understanding and world peace.

141. Coleman, James S., et al. *Equality of Educational Opportunity.* U.S. Department of Health, Education and Welfare, Office of Education. A publication of the National Center for Educational Statistics. Washington, D.C.: U.S. Government Printing Office, 1966. 737 pp.
This survey is addressed to four major questions: extent to which racial and ethnic minorities are segregated in schools, availability of factors regarded as good indicators of educational quality, achievement as measured by standardized tests, and relationships between achievement and the kinds of schools attended. Six groups were studied: Negroes, American Indians, Oriental Americans, Puerto Ricans, Mexican Americans, and the "majority" or simply "white" Americans.

142. Colorado Commission on Spanish-Surnamed Citizens. *Report to the Colorado General Assembly: The Status of Spanish-Surnamed Citizens in Colorado.* Denver: State of Colorado, January 1967. 125 pp. Notes and bibliography, pp. 121-125.
Contains statistical, sociological, and psychological data; and makes recommendations in the areas of education, income, poverty, health, housing, and consumer problems.

143. Columbia University. Teachers College. The International Institute of Teachers College. *A Survey of the Public Educational System of Puerto Rico.* Columbia University, Teachers College, New York Bureau of Publications, 1926.

144. Comité Permanent de la Survivance Française en Amérique. *La Vie Franco-Américaine,* published annually from 1938 to 1952.
References on the political, intellectual, and social aspects of life among the French-speaking population of New England.

145. Commission de Coopération Technique en Afrique/Committee for Technical Co-operation in Africa. Colloque sur le miltilinguisme/Symposium on Multilingualism. Deuxième Reunion du Comité Interafricain de Linguistique/Second Meeting of the Inter-African Committee on Linguistics. Brazzaville, 16-21, VII 1962. London: Bureau des Publications CCTA/CTCA Publications Bureau, February 1964.
Discusses educational aspects of multilingualism and linguistic problems of multilingualism, including John B. Carroll's "Some Psychological Considerations Relevant to Bilingualism and Second Language Acquisition: Recent Approaches" and Malcolm Guthrie's "Multilingualism and Cultural Factors." Also includes articles on creole and pidgin languages with emphasis on the African linguistic situation.

146. Conwell, Marylin J., and Alphonse Juillaud. *Louisiana French Grammar. Vol. I: Phonology, Morphology, and Syntax.* Janua Linguarum, Series Practica, No. 1. The Hague: Mouton & Co., 1963. 207 pp. Bibliography, pp. 202-207.
A technical study of the three French dialects of Louisiana, with an introduction giving a picture of the history and education of the Acadians, and a long and up-to-date bibliography on dialectal description and Louisiana French.

147. Cook, Katherine M., and Florence E. Reynolds. *The Education of Native and Minority Groups: A Bibliography, 1923-1932.* United States Department of the Interior, Office of Education, Bulletin No. 12 (1933). Washington, D.C.: U.S. Government Printing Office, 1933.
A 573-item classified bibliography with succinct annotations, a subject and author index. Puerto Rico, Hawaii, the Virgin Islands, the Philippines, the Canal Zone, Samoa, and Guam are included.

148. Coombs, L. Madison. *Doorway Toward the Light: The Story of the Special Navajo Education Program (Lawrence, Kansas, 1962).* Washington, D.C.: U.S. Department of the Interior, Bureau of Indian Affairs, 1962.

149.___, et al. *The Indian Child Goes to School: A Story of Interracial Differences.* Washington, D.C.: Department of the Interior, Bureau of Indian Affairs, 1958.
This important study involved administering California Achievement Tests to 23,608 pupils attending federal, mission, and public schools, in 11 states. It offered further evidence that Indian pupils do not achieve as well in the basic skill subjects as white pupils and that they fall progressively behind the national norms as they continue in school.

150. Cooper, James G. "Predicting School Achievement for Bilingual Pupils." *The Journal of Educational Psychology,* Vol. XLIX, No. 1 (February 1958), pp. 31-36. 8 references.
This study demonstrated that the six intelligence tests examined predicted school success with a degree of accuracy ranging from moderate to high for the Territory of Guam's bilingual pupils.

151. Cordasco, Frank M. "The Challenge of the Non-English-Speaking Child in American Schools." *School and Society,* Vol. XCVI, March 30, 1968, pp. 198-201. Bibliographical footnotes.

Advocates bilingual schooling for preservation of cultural identity.

152.___. "The Puerto-Rican Family and the Anthropologist." *Teachers College Records*, Vol. LXVIII, No. 8 (May 1967), pp. 672-674.
Review of Oscar Lewis' *A Puerto-Rican Family in the Culture of Poverty: San Juan and New York*, New York: Random House, Inc., 1966. 669 pp.

153.___. "Puerto-Rican Pupils and American Education." *School and Society*, Vol. XCV (February 18, 1967), pp. 116-119. Bibliographical footnotes.
Strongly recommends that immediate and effective steps be undertaken to provide special educational programs to meet the needs of the Puerto Rican population of American schools.

154. Cornwell, Elmer E., Jr. "Party Absorption of Ethnic Groups: The Case of Providence, Rhode Island." *Social Forces*, Vol. XXXVIII, No. 3 (March 1960), pp. 205-210.
Confirms the hypothesis that the American political party has been an important factor in the integration of successive waves of immigrants into the American political community.

155. Cotnam, Jacques. "Are Bilingualism and Biculturalism Nothing But a Lure?" *Culture*, Vol. XXVIII, No. 2 (June 1967), pp. 137-148.
Discusses the French-Canadians' desire for cultural survival.

156. Covello, Leonard. "The Italians in America." *Italy-America Monthly*, Vol. I, No. 7 (July 15, 1934), pp. 11-17.

157.___. *The Social Background of the Italo-American School Child: A Study of the Southern Italian Family Mores and Their Effect on the School Situation in Italy and America.* Edited and with an introduction and notes by Francesco Cordasco. Leiden, The Netherlands: E. J. Brill, 1967. 488 pp. Bibliography, pp. xxv-xxx.
A valuable study by an experienced educator giving a deep insight into the way of life of a major ethnic group and the educational opportunities given to it in the context of poverty and tradition.

158.___, with Guido D'Agostino, *The Heart is the Teacher.* New York: McGraw-Hill Book Company, Inc., 1958. 275 pp.
The romanticized autobiography of Leonard Covello, who has devoted his talent and experience to solving the educational problems of migrant children in New York, Italians and Puerto Ricans in particular.

159. Cumberland, Charles C. *The United States-Mexican Border: A Selective Guide to the Literature of the Region.* Supplement to *Rural Sociology*, Vol. XXV, No. 2 (June 1960). Ithaca, New York: Rural Sociological Society, 1960. 236 pp.

160. Dadabhay, Yusuf. "Circuitous Assimilation Among Rural Hindustanis in California." *Social Forces*, Vol. XXXIII, No. 2 (December 1954), pp. 138-141.
Shows that the assimilation of East Indian immigrants follows the pattern of that of Mexican Americans, whose subculture is more immediately accessible to them than is the dominant American culture.

161. *Daedalus*, Vol. XC, No. 2 (Spring 1961). Special issue dedicated to "Ethnic Groups in American Life." 211 pp.
A collection of ten articles dealing with the problems of assimilation and education of minority groups.

162. Dakin, Julian, Brian Tiffen, and H. G. Widdowson. *Language in Education; the Problem in Commonwealth Africa and the Indo-Pakistan Sub-Continent.* The Language and Language Learning Series, Vol. XX. London: Oxford University Press, 1968. 177 pp.
Three studies about the choice of the medium of instruction. The first two deal with the evolution of an educational language policy. The third study suggests an alternative approach to the teaching of English as a second language in Africa and India.

163. D'Amours, Ernest R. "Le Collège de l'Assomption de Worcester: son origine et son évolution." *Le Canado-Américain,* Vol. II, No. 4 (1960-1961), pp. 10-17.
Origin and evolution of Franco-American Assumption College in Worcester, Massachusetts.

164. Darcy, Natalie T. "Bilingualism and the Measurement of Intelligence: Review of a Decade of Research." *The Journal of Genetic Psychology,* Vol. CIII, Second Half (December 1963), pp. 259-282. 43 references.
A highly critical review of literature on bilingualism as related to intelligence, 1953-63. Discusses studies related to age and background of students, instruments, verbal and non-verbal language, and teaching methods.

165.___. "The Performance of Bilingual Puerto Rican Children on Verbal and Non-Language Tests of Intelligence." *Journal of Educational Research,* Vol. XLV, No. 7 (March 1952), pp. 499-506.
Discusses the importance of administering both the verbal and the non-language type to yield a valid intelligence score of a bilingual population.

166.___. "A Review of the Literature on the Effects of Bilingualism Upon the Measurement of Intelligence." *The Pedagogical Seminary and Journal of Genetic Psychology,* Vol. LXXXII, First Half (March 1953), pp. 21-57. 110-item bibliography.
Emphasizes the importance of the bilingual student's background in interpreting intelligence tests.

167. Dartigue, Esther. "Bilingualism in the Nursery School," *The French Review,* Vol. XXX, No. 4 (February 1966), pp. 577-587. 10 references.
A report on the United Nations Nursery School in Paris. French and English are used as mediums of instruction, but there is no effort to *produce* bilinguals in these languages.

168. Dawes, T. R. *Bilingual Teaching in Belgian Schools.* Cambridge, England: University of Wales Press, 1902. 63 pp.

169. Dawidowicz, Lucy S. "Yiddish: Past, Present and Perfect." *Commentary,* Vol. XXXIII, No. 5 (May 1962), pp. 375-385.
An account of the Yiddish language in the world and its importance in the United States.

170. Diebold, A. Richard, Jr. "The Consequences of Early Bilingualism in Cognitive Development and Personality Formation." In Edward Norbeck, Douglass Price-Williams,

and William M. McCord, eds., *The Study of Personality: An Interdisciplinary Appraisal*, Holt, Reinhart and Winston, Inc., 1968, pp. 218-245. Bibliography, pp. 239-245.

Focuses on the emotional and intellectual psychology of the bilingual.

171.___. "Incipient Bilingualism." *Language*, Vol. XXXVII, No. 1 (January-March 1961), pp. 97-112.

Reexamines two premises of language contact: (1) that the production of "complete meaningful utterances" is the minimal skill necessary in a second language for bilingual status, and (2) that "the form assumed by interference is determined by the structures of the two languages in contact." Proposes that certain sociological factors are equally crucial in determining the form of interference phenomena. The research uses a Spanish-Huave language contact situation.

172. Diehl, Kemper. "San Antonio Classes Uses Two Languages." *Southern Education Report*, Vol. III, No. 3 (October 1967), pp. 16-19.

Describes Spanish-English bilingual education in Carvajal Elementary School of the San Antonio Independent School District.

173. Diekhoff, John S. *NDEA and Modern Foreign Languages.* New York: The Modern Language Association of America, 1965. 148 pp.

Critical study of the NDEA Language Development Program. Contains a summary of NDEA achievements up to that time and a summary of recommendations.

174. Diller, Karl C. "'Compound' and 'Coordinate' Bilingualism–A Conceptual Artifact." A paper presented to the Linguistic Society of America, Forty-Second Annual Meeting, Chicago, Illinois, December 19, 1967. Revised version to be published in *Word*. 13 pp. 9 references.

Argues that compound and coordinate bilingualism are poorly defined notions; that the experimental evidence does not support these concepts; and that there are strong linguistic reasons why these concepts cannot stand.

175. Dimitrijević, J. R. "A Bilingual Child." *English Language Teaching*, Vol. XX, No. 1 (October 1965), pp. 23-28.

Some observations regarding a child with whom one parent spoke English and one parent Serbian.

176. Dinin, Samuel. "The Curriculum of the Jewish School." *American Jewish Yearbook*, Vol. LXIII, 1962, pp. 214-225. 105-item bibliography.

Presents recent trends tending to modernize and update the curriculum of Jewish schools with increasing emphasis on the study of Hebrew. A selected bibliography of Jewish education curricula follows.

177. Ditchy, Jay K., ed. *Les acadiens louisianais et leur parler.* Paris: Librairie E. Droz; Baltimore, Maryland; The Johns Hopkins Press; London: Oxford University Press, 1932.

Author unknown. Contains brief notes on morphology, phonology, extensive glossary, short history (somewhat sentimental); and a list of original Acadian families. See review by William A. Reed, Louisiana French scholar, in *Zeitschrift für neufranzösische Sprache und Literatur*, Vol. LVII (1934), pp. 257-295.

178. Divine, Robert A. *American Immigration Policy, 1924-1952.* Yale Historical Publication, Miscellany, No. 66. New Haven, Connecticut: Yale University Press, 1957. 220 pp. Bibliographical essay, pp. 195-209.

179. *Doble.* Digest of Bilingual Education published by the Early Childhood Bilingual Education Project Office, Ferkauf Graduate School of Humanities and Social Sciences, Yeshiva University, 55 Fifth Avenue, New York City, New York 10003.

180. Dodson, C. J. *Language Teaching and the Bilingual Method.* London: Sir Isaac Pitman & Sons, Ltd., 1967. 182 pp.
Offers practical help to the modern-language teacher through the "bilingual method."

181. Doran, Thomas A. "Spanish-Biology: Final Report." Report No. NDEA–VI–69. Folsom, California: Folsom Unified School District, January 1, 1965. 32 pp.
Report of the effect on achievement of integrating the elementary and secondary studies of Spanish and Biology.

182. Dorrance, Ward Allison. "The Survival of French in the Old District of Sainte-Genevieve." *The University of Missouri Studies: A Quarterly of Research*, Vol. X, No. 2 (April 1935). 134 pp. Bibliography, pp. 130-133.
An extensive study of the Creole French Dialect of Missouri, with an analysis of the historical and social background of the French peasants living in the district, followed by an extensive glossary and some characteristic aspects of their folklore.

183. Downs, James F. "The Cowboy and the Lady: Models as a Determinant of the Rate of Acculturation Among the Piñon Navajo." *Kroeber Anthropological Society Papers*, No. 29 (Fall 1963), pp. 53-67.
Describes the ideals to which these Navajo subscribe which break with their cultural heritage.

184. Dozier, Edward P. "Two Examples of Linguistic Acculturation: The Yaqui of Sonora and Arizona and the Tewa of New Mexico." *Language*, Vol. XXXII, No. 1 (1965), pp. 146-157.
"These two contrasting acculturative situations, in both linguistic and non-linguistic aspects, appear to be due to the contact situation, one permissive [Yaqui has exhaustive borrowing from Spanish] and the other forced [the Tewa have resisted acculturation]." (pp. 156f)

185. Drotning, Phil. "Norway in Wisconsin." Reprinted from *The Saturday Evening Post* (copyright 1945) in *American-Scandinavian Review*, Vol. XXVIII, No. 2 (Summer 1950), pp. 149-154.

186. Ducharme, Jacques. *The Shadows of the Trees: The Story of the French-Canadians in New England.* New York: Harper & Brothers, 1943. 258 pp. Bibliography of Franco-American literature, pp. 245-258.
A romanticized history of the Franco-Americans.

187. Dulong, Gaston. *Bibliographie linguistique du Canada Français.* Quebec, Canada: Les Presses de l'Université Laval, 1966. 166 pp.

188. Dusel, John P., ed. *What Next in Foreign Languages?* A Planning Conference for Improving Instruction and Articulation in Foreign Languages in California Public Schools, October 4, 5, and 6, 1967. San Diego, California: Foreign Language Council, April 1968.

189. Dushkin, Alexander M., and Uriah Z. Engelman. *Jewish Education in the United States: Report of the Commission for the Study of Jewish Education in the United States.* Vol. I. New York: American Association for Jewish Education, 1959. 265 pp.
A comprehensive seven-year study of Jewish education in the United States.

190. Edelman, Martin, Robert L. Cooper, and Joshua A. Fishman. "The Contextualization of Schoolchildren's Bilingualism." *The Irish Journal of Education*, Vol. II, No. 2 (1968), pp. 106-111.
The contextualized degree of bilingualism measures, one designed to assess the extent to which each language is used, the other to assess relative proficiency in the two languages, were administered to 34 bilingual children of Puerto Rican background.

191. Eichorn, Dorothy H., and Harold E. Jones. "Bilingualism." In "Development of Mental Functions." *Review of Educational Research*, Vol. XXII, No. 5 (December 1952), Chapter II, p. 425.
A general report on the adverse effect of bilingualism on I.Q. taken from two studies: one on New York children of Puerto Rican parentage and the other by Jones and Stewart in Wales.

192. Eikel, Fred, Jr. "New Braunfels German." *American Speech*, Part I: Vol. XLI, No. 1 (February 1966), pp. 5-16; Part II: Vol. XLI, No. 4 (December 1966), pp. 254-260; Part III: Vol. XLII, No. 2 (May 1967), pp. 83-104.
Part I gives a brief history of German settlements in Texas; Part II deals with the phonology of the New Braunfels dialect; and Part III is concerned with its morphology and syntax.

193. Elkholy, Abdo A. *The Arab Moslems in the United States: Religion and Assimilation.* New Haven, Connecticut: College & University Press, Publishers, 1966. 176 pp. Bibliography, pp. 161-172.
Analyzes the historical background as well as the present situation of Arab Moslems in the United States, with detailed statistical data on their number, distributions, activities, characteristics, etc.

194. Ellis, Frances H. "Historical Account of German Instruction in the Public Schools of Indianapolis, 1869-1919." *The Indiana Magazine of History*, Vol. L, Part I: No. 2 (June 1954), pp. 119-138; Part II: No. 3. (September 1956), pp. 251-276; Part III: No. 4. (December 1954), pp. 357-380.

195. Elwert, W. Theodor. *Das zweisprachige Individuum: Ein Selbstzeugnis.* Weisbaden, Germany, in Kommission bei F. Steiner, 1960. 80 pp.
Translation: *The Bilingual Individual: An Autobiographical Statement.*

196. Ernst, Robert. *Immigrant Life in New York City, 1825-1863.* New York: King's Crown Press, 1949. 331 pp. Bibliography, pp. 297-319.

197. Ervin-Tripp, Susan. "Becoming a Bilingual." Working Paper No. 9, Language-Behavior Research Laboratory. Funded by a grant from the Institute of International Studies, University of California, Berkeley. March 1968. Mimeographed. 28 pp.

The author brings to bear some of the considerations affecting age of learning and the milieu to suggest new directions for research.

198.___. "An Issei Learns English." See *The Journal of Social Issues.*

199.___. "Language and TAT Content in Bilinguals." *Journal of Abnormal and Social Psychology*, Vol. LXVIII, No. 5 (May 1964), pp. 500-507. 17 references.

200.___. "Learning and Recall in Bilinguals." *American Journal of Psychology*, Vol. LXXIV, No. 3 (September 1961), pp. 446-451.

Italian bilinguals were tested for recall of pictorial material using English and Italian during learning and during recall.

201.___. "Semantic Shift in Bilingualism." *American Journal of Psychology*, Vol. LXXIV, No. 2 (June 1961), pp. 233-241.

Semantic shift was examined in the color-naming of Navajo bilinguals in comparison with two monolingual groups.

202. Estes, Dwain M., and David W. Darling, eds. *Improving Educational Opportunities of the Mexican-American*. Proceedings of the First Texas Conference for the Mexican-American, April 13-15, 1967, San Antonio, Texas. Austin, Texas: Southwest Educational Development Laboratory, Inter-American Education Center, Texas Education Agency, 1967.

*203. Ferguson, Charles A. "Diglossia." *Word*, Vol. XV, No. 2 (August 1959), pp. 325-340.

Presents the linguistic aspects of a situation where "two varieties of a language exist side by side throughout the speech community, with each having a different role to play."

204.___. "Variant Approaches to the Acquisition of Literacy." Paper presented at the Ninth International African Seminar, University College, Dar es Salaam, Tanzania, in December 1968.

205. Fishman, Joshua A. "Bilingualism, Intelligence, and Language Learning." *The Modern Language Journal*, Vol. XLIX, No. 4 (April 1965), pp. 227-236.

206.___. "Bilingualism With and Without Diglossia; Diglossia With and Without Bilingualism." See *The Journal of Social Issues.*

207.___. "Childhood Indoctrination for Minority-Group Membership." *Daedalus*, Vol. XC, No. 2 (Spring 1961), pp. 329-349. 49 references.

Examines the effects of formal education in minority-group schools on the attitudes and behavior of the pupils.

208.___. "Degree of Bilingualism in a Yiddish School and Leisure Time Activities." *Journal of Social Psychology*, Vol. XXXVI (1952), pp. 155-65.

Considers Yiddish bilinguality, and how it affects the play and other leisure activities of a school population.

209.____. *Hungarian Language Maintenance in the United States.* Bloomington, Indiana: Indiana University Press, 1966. The Uralic and Altaic Series, Vol. LXII, 58 pp. Bibliography, pp. 54-58.

An up-to-date appraisal of past and present Hungarian language maintenance efforts in the United States.

210.____. "Language Maintenance and Language Shift as a Field of Inquiry: A Definition of the Field and Suggestions for Its Further Development." *Linguistics*, No. 9 (1964), pp. 32-70. 90-item bibliography.

Analyzes habitual language use at more than one point in time or space under conditions of intergroup contact.

211.____. "National Languages and Languages of Wider Communication in the Developing Nations." Prepared for delivery as the keynote address at the Regional Conference on Language and Linguistics, Dar es Salaam, Tanzania, December 1968. Mimeographed. 23 pp.

Reviews six factors or dimensions which could be used in differentiating between the language problems of three different types or clusters of new nations.

212.____, ed. *Readings in the Scoiology of Language.* The Hague: Mouton & Co., 1968. 808 pp. Bibliographies.

Contains seven readings related to small-group interaction, social strata and sectors, socio-cultural organization, multilingualism, maintenance and shift, and social contexts.

213.____. "Sociolinguistic Perspective on the Study of Bilingualism." *Linguistics, An International Review*, No. 39 (May 1968), pp. 21-49. 51-item bibliography.

Socio-linguistic study of bilingualism focusing upon the functionally different contexts of verbal interaction in diglossic speech communities.

214.____. "Socio-linguistics and the Language Problems of the Developing Countries." *International Social Science Journal*, Vol. XX, No. 2 (1968), pp. 211-225. Bibliography, pp. 222-225.

Analyzes the social and linguistic components of the problems of developing nations, and suggests some socio-linguistic research methods.

215.____. "Some Contrasts Between Linguistically Homogeneous and Linguistically Heterogeneous Polities." *Sociological Inquiry*, Vol. XXXVI (1966), pp. 146-158.

216.____. "The Status and Prospects of Bilingualism in the United States." *The Modern Language Journal*, Vol. XLIX, No. 3 (March 1965), pp. 143-155.

Discusses cultural pluralism, bilingualism, and biculturalism. Suggests that a commission on bilingualism and biculturalism be established at the federal, state, and local levels.

217.____. "Varieties of Ethnicity and Varieties of Language Consciousness." In Charles W. Kreidler, ed., "Report of the Sixteenth Annual Round Table Meeting on Linguistics and Language Studies." Georgetown University *Monograph Series on Language and Linguistics*, No. 18 (1965), pp. 59-79.

Studies "parallelism between social complexity and complexity of linguistic situations."

218.___. "Who Speaks What Language to Whom and When?" *La Linguistique*, Vol. II (1965), pp. 67-88. 29 references.

Presents the concept of "domains of language choice" in an "attempt to provide socio-cultural organization and socio-cultural context for consideration of variance in language choice in multilingual settings." (p. 86)

219.___. "Yiddish in America: Socio-Linguistic Description and Analysis." *International Journal of American Linguistics*, Vol. XXXI, No. 2, Part 2, April 1965, 94 pp. Bloomington: Indiana University, 1965. Publication of the Indiana University Research Center in Anthropology, Folklore and Linguistics, No. 36. Bibliography pp. 87-94.

Appendix: The Hebrew Language in the United States, pp. 77-85. A systematic study examining all facets of Yiddish language maintenance in the United States.

220.___, et al. *Bilingualism in the Barrio*. 2 vols. Final Report, Contract No. OEC-1-062817-0297. U.S. Department of Health, Education, and Welfare, Office of Education; Bureau of Research, 1968. 1,209 pp. References.

Presents a variety of techniques for the measurement and description of bilingualism, derived separately from the disciplines of linguistics, psychology, and sociology.

*221.___, et al. "Bilingualism in the Barrio." *The Modern Language Journal*, Vol. LIII, No. 3 (March 1969). Special issue on bilingualism, with a preface by Joshua A. Fishman and the following articles:

Fishman, Joshua A. "The Measurement and Description of Widespread and Relatively Stable Bilingualism," pp. 152-156.

Fishman, Joshua A., and Heriberto Casiano. "Puerto Ricans in our Press," pp. 158-162.

Cooper, Robert L.,and Lawrence Greenfield. "Word Frequency Estimation as a Measure of Degree of Bilingualism," pp. 163-166.

Cooper, Robert L., and Lawrence Greenfield. "Language Use in a Bilingual Community," pp. 166-172.

Cooper, Robert L. "Two Contextualized Measures of Degree of Bilingualism," pp. 172-178.

Edleman, Martin. "The Contextualization of Schoolchildren's Bilingualism," pp. 179-182.

Berney, Tomi D., and Robert L. Cooper. "Semantic Independence and Degree of Bilingualism in Two Communities," pp. 182-185.

Fishman, Joshua A., et al. "Bilingualism in the Barrio (continued)." *The Modern Language Journal*, Vol. LIII, No. 4 (April 1969). Contents:

Findling, Joav. "Bilingual Need Affiliation and Future Orientation in Extragroup and Intragroup Domains," pp. 227-231.

Ronch, Judah, Robert L. Cooper, and Joshua A. Fishman. "Word Naming and Usage Scores for a Sample of Yiddish-English Bilinguals," pp. 232-235.

Cooper, Robert L., Barbara L. Fowles, and Abraham Givner. "Listening Comprehension in a Bilingual Community," pp. 235-241.

Silverman, Stuart H. "The Evaluation of Language Varieties," pp. 241-244.

Fertig, Shelton, and Joshua A. Fishman. "Some Measures in the Interaction Between Language Domain and Semantic Dimension in Bilinguals," pp. 244-249.

Silverman, Stuart H. "A Method for Recording and Analyzing the Prosodic Features of Language," pp. 250-254.

Terry, Charles E., and Robert L. Cooper. "A Note on the Perception and Production of Phonological Variation," pp. 254-255.

Fishman, Joshua A. "Some Things Learned; Some Things Yet to Learn," pp. 255-258.

222.___, and Valdimir C. Nahirny. "The Ethnic Group School and Mother Tongue Maintenance in the United States." *Sociology of Education*, Vol. XXVII, No. 4 (Summer 1964), pp. 306-317.

Sketches some of the general characteristics of the schools sponsored by or on behalf of ethnic groups in the United States: their size, auspices, faculty, student body, curricula, and activities; and presents data pertaining to language maintenance efforts of ethnic group schools.

223.___, et al. "Guidelines for Testing Minority Group Children." *Journal of Social Issues,* Vol. XX, No. 2 (April 1964), pp. 129-145. 24 references.

*224.___, et al. *Language Loyalty in the United States; The Maintenance and Perpetuation of Non-English Mother Tongues by American Ethnic and Religious Groups.* With an introduction by Einar Haugen. The Hague: Mouton & Co., 1966. 478 pp. Bibliographies at the end of each chapter.

A basic document for the "study of the self-maintenance efforts, rationales, and accomplishments of non-English speaking immigrants on American shores." (p. 15.) Includes histories of language maintenance efforts on the part of broadcasting, the press, ethnic parishes and schools, and general community organizational and leadership interest. Focuses on the German, French, Spanish, and Ukrainian groups.

225.___, Charles A. Ferguson, and Jyotirindra Das Gupta, eds. *Language Problems of Developing Nations.* New York: John Wiley & Sons, Inc., 1968. 521 pp. Select bibliographies or notes at the end of each chapter.

Provides "examples of the diverse societal and national functions of language varieties,...of the changes in these functions as the roles and statuses of their speakers change, and...of the changes in the language varieties per se that accompany their changed uses and users." (p. x.)

226.___, and Heriberto Casiano. "Puerto Ricans in Our Press." *The Modern Language Journal,* Vol. LIII, No. 3 (March 1969), pp. 157-162.

"This study reports on the treatment of Puerto Ricans in four New York City dailies, two published in English and two in Spanish." It seeks to answer certain questions dealing with attitude and language maintenance. (p. 157.)

227.___, comp., William W. Brickman, and Stanley Lehrer, eds. "Subsidized Pluralism in American Education." Supplement to *School and Society*, Vol. LXXXVII, No. 2154 (May 23, 1959), pp. 245-268.

A collection of seven papers representing the attempts of a philosopher, an educational administrator, an educator, an intergroup relations specialist, a sociologist, and a social psychologist to clarify the concept of publicly subsidized pluralism and to relate it to the reality of American social structure and American democratic values.

228. Fitch, Michael John. "Verbal and Performance Test Scores in Bilingual Children." Research Study No. 1. Unpublished Ed.D. dissertation, Colorado State College, 1966. 70 pp. *Dissertation Abstracts*, Series A, Vol. XXVII, No. 6 (December 1966), pp. 1654-1655.

The purpose of this study is to evaluate the effects of increased exposure to the English language on verbal and non-verbal measures in bilingual children.

229. Foerster, Robert F. *The Italian Emigration of Our Time*. Harvard Economic Studies, Vol. XX. Cambridge, Massachusetts: Harvard University Press, 1919. 556 pp. Bibliographical footnotes.
The standard work on Italian emigration to all countries.

230. Fogel, Walter. *Education and Income of Mexican-Americans of the Southwest*. Mexican-American Study Project, Advance Report No. 1. Los Angeles, California: University of California, 1965. 30 pp.

231. Fogelquist, Donald F. "The Bilingualism of Paraguay." *Hispania*, Vol. XXXII, No. 1 (February 1950), pp. 23-27. Bibliographical notes.
A brief description of the true bilingualism that exists in Paraguay, "the only bilingual country of the new world."

232. Forbes, Jack D. *Mexican-Americans, A Handbook for Educators*. Berkeley: Far West Laboratory for Educational Research and Development, 1967. 41 pp.
Presents sixteen suggestions for the teacher and administrator of the Mexican American to begin acquiring insights into the background of Mexican culture and thinking.

233. Ford, Richard Clyde. "The French-Canadians in Michigan." *Michigan History Magazine*, Vol. XXVII, No. 2 (Spring 1943), pp. 243-257.
Describes the factors which have led to the disappearance of French in Michigan more than a century ago under press of Anglo-Saxon contact.

234. "The 'Fourth Faith.'" *Newsweek*, Vol. LXIV, No. 2 (July 13, 1964), p. 52.
Brief statement on the importance of Orthodoxy in the United States and the Western Hemisphere.

235. Frender, Robert, Bruce Brown, and Wallace E. Lambert. "The Roles of Speech Characteristics, Verbal Intelligence and Achievement Motivation in Scholastic Success." Unpublished paper. Montreal, Canada: McGill University, November 1968. 20 pp. 12 references.

236. Frey, J. William. "Amish 'Triple Talk'" *American Speech* Vol. XX, No. 2 (April 1945), pp. 85-98.
Technical discussion of the Pennsylvania Dutch-High German-English trilingualism existing among the Amish communities of Lancaster County, Pennsylvania, among others.

237. Friedmann, R. *Hutterite Studies*. Goshen, Indiana: Mennonite Historical Society, 1961.

238. Fucilla, Joseph G. *The Teaching of Italian in the United States: A Documentary History*. New Brunswick, New Jersey: American Association of Teachers of Italian, 1967. 300 pp.
A history of the role of the Italian language in American schools and universities from colonial times to the present. Contains a list of elementary and high schools, colleges and universities where Italian is still taught today, with enrollment figures.

239. Gaarder, A. Bruce, "Beyond Grammar and Beyond Drills." *FL Annals*, Vol. I, No. 2 (December 1967), pp. 109-118.
The teacher should be conscious of the points being displayed, but the learner's focus should concentrate on significant meaning. Sample drills in Spanish.

*240.___. "Bilingualism." In Donald D. Walsh, ed., *A Handbook for Teachers of Spanish and Portuguese*. Lexington, Massachusetts: D. C. Heath and Company, A Division of Raytheon Education Company, 1969, pp. 149-172. Bibliography, pp. 170-172.

This authoritative summary deals with the "relationship between natural and artificial bilingualism, and the extent to which the teacher of foreign language must concern himself with more and more aspects of the total phenomenon of bilingualism...." (p. 149)

*241.___. "The Challenge of Bilingualism." In G. Reginald Bishop, ed., *Foreign Language Teaching: Challenges to the Profession.* Reports of the Working Committees of the Northeast Conference on the Teaching of Foreign Languages, 1965, pp. 54-101. 9 references.

242.___. "Conserving Our Linguistic Resources." *PMLA*, Vol. LXXX, No. 2B (May 1965), pp. 19-23.

An appeal in favor of bilingual education for bilingual children in an attempt to preserve the ethnic heritage of non-English-mother-tongue children in the U.S.

*243.___. "Organization of the Bilingual School." *The Journal of Social Issues*, Vol. XXIII, No. 2 (April 1967), pp. 110-120. 13 references.

Directed toward sociologists and school administrators interested in bilingual education. Emphasis on teacher training and full consideration of school organization and classroom practices.

*244.___. "Teaching the Bilingual Child: Research, Development, and Policy." *The Modern Language Journal*, Vol. XLIX, No. 3 (March 1965), pp. 165-175.

Use of mother tongue as language of instruction in beginning school recommended.

245.___, and Mabel W. Richardson. "Two Patterns of Bilingual Education in Dade County, Florida." In Thomas E. Bird, ed., *Foreign Language Learning: Research and Development: An Assessment.* Reports of the Working Commitees of the 1968 Northeast Conference on the Teaching of Foreign Languages. Menasha, Wisconsin: George Banta Co., Inc., 1968, pp. 32-44.

A short description of the Spanish for Spanish-Speakers Program started in Dade County in 1961 and of the Coral Way Bilingual School Program begun in 1963.

246. Gans, Herbert J. *The Urban Villagers: Group and Class in the Life of Italian-Americans.* Foreword by Erich Lindemann. New York: Free Press of Glencoe. 1962. 367 pp. Bibliography, pp. 351-358.

Italian immigrants in Boston.

247. Garvin, Paul L., and Madeleine Mathoit. "The Urbanization of the Guaraní Language—A Problem in Language and Culture." In Anthony F. C. Wallace, Ed., *Men and Cultures: Selected Papers of the Fifth Congress of Anthropological and Ethnological Sciences.* Philadelphia, September 1-9, 1956. Philadelphia, Pennsylvania: University of Pennsylvania Press, 1960, pp. 783-790. 20 bibliographical notes.

248. Gehrke, William H. "The Transition from the German to the English Language in North Carolina." *North Carolina Historical Review*, Vol. XII (1935), pp. 1-19.

249. Gel, Walter Local Emerald. "Education and Income of Mexican-Americans in the Southwest." Mexican-American Study Project Advance Report No. 1. Los Angeles, California: University of California, Division of Research, Graduate School of Business Administration, 1965.

250. Georges, Robert A. "The Greeks of Tarpon Springs: An American Folk Group." *Southern Folklore Quarterly*, Vol. XXIX, No. 2 (June 1965), pp. 129-141.

*251. Georgetown University. *Monograph Series on Languages and Linguistics*, No. 7 (September 1954). Report of the Fifth Annual Round Table Meeting on Linguistics and Language Teaching, edited by Hugo J. Mueller. "Bilingualism and Mixed Languages," pp. 9-56. Contents:
Haugen, Einar. "Problems of Bilingual Description," pp. 9-19.
Leopold, Werner F. "A Child's Learning of Two Languages," pp. 19-30.
Haden, Ernest F. "The Phonemes of Acadian French," pp. 31-40.
Weinreich, Uriel. "Linguistic Convergence in Immigrant America," pp. 40-49; "Discussion," pp. 49-56.

252.___. No. 15 (1962). Report of the Thirteenth Annual Round Table Meeting on Linguistics and Language Studies, edited by Elizabeth D. Woodworth and Robert J. Di Pietro. "Bilingualism," pp. 53-84. Contents:
Diebold, A. Richard, Jr. "Code-Switching in Greek-English Bilingual Speech," pp. 53-62.
Haugen, Einar. "Schizoglossia and the Linguistic Norm," pp. 63-73.
O'Huallacháin, Colmán, O.F.M., "Bilingualism in Education in Ireland, pp. 75-84.
McQuown, Norman A. "Indian and Ladino Bilingualism: Sociocultural Contrasts in Chiapas, Mexico," pp. 85-106.
"National Languages and Diglossia," pp. 109-177. Contents:
Householder, Fred W., Jr. "Greek Diglossia," pp. 109-132.
Moulton, William G. "What Standard for Diglossia? The Case of German Switzerland," pp. 133-148.
Stewart, William A. "The Functional Distribution of Creole and French in Haiti," 149-162.
Ferguson, Charles A. "Problems of Teaching Languages With Diglossia," pp. 165-177.
Each paper is followed by a "discussion."

253. Gerhard, E. S. "The History of Schwenkfelder Schools." *Schwenkfeldiana*, Vol. I, No. 3 (1943), pp. 5-21.

254. Gilbert, Glenn G. "The German Dialect Spoken in Kendall and Gillespie Counties, Texas." Unpublished Ph.D. dissertation, Harvard University, 1963.

255.___. *Texas Studies in Bilingualism.* Studia Linguistica, Vol. I. Berlin: Walter de Gruyter and Co., In Press.

256. Giles, W. H. "Mathematics in Bilingualism: A Pragmatic Approach." *ISA Bulletin: The International Schools Association*, No. 55 (February 1969), pp. 19-26.
A discussion of the bilingual teaching of mathematics in the Toronto French School, where, although the students are basically English-mother-tongue, 75-80 percent of all instruction is carried on in French.

257. Giroux, Marc-Yvain, and Dormer Ellis. "Apprenticeship in Bilingualism in Welland's Public Elementary Schools." Translated from an unpublished paper prepared for the Tenth Annual Conference of the Ontario Educational Research Council. Toronto, Canada, December 7, 1968. 8 pp. 8 references.

Results of a project undertaken in bilingual schools in Welland.

258. Gisolfi, Anthony M. "Italo-American: What it Has Borrowed From American English and What it is Contributing to the American Language." *Commonweal*, Vol. XXX, No. 13 (July 21, 1939), pp. 311-313.

Traces the general lines of the evolution of the dialect of Italian immigrants in America.

259. Gittler, Joseph B., ed. *Understanding Minority Groups.* New York: John Wiley & Sons, Inc.; London: Chapman & Hall, Limited, 1956. 140 pp. Bibliography, pp. 138-139.

Contains valuable articles on the Indians, the Japanese, and the Puerto Ricans in the U. S.

260. Glazer, Nathan, and Daniel Patrick Moynihan. *Beyond the Melting Pot: The Negroes, Puerto-Ricans, Jews, Italians, and Irish of New York City*. Cambridge, Massachusetts: The M.I.T. Press and Harvard University Press, 1963. 360 pp.

Combines quantitative and impressionistic data to consider the melting of ethnicity today.

261. Gleason, H. A., Jr. "The Grammars of English." See Temple University, The NDEA National Institute for Advanced Study in Teaching Disadvantaged Youth.

262. Gobetz, Giles E. "The Tragic Abandonment of our Ethnic Heritage," *Ohio Schools*, October 1965, pp. 26 ff.

263. Goldhagen, Eric. *Ethnic Minorities in the Soviet Union*. New York: Frederick A. Praeger, Inc., 1968. 351 pp. Bibliographies.

Essays read at a symposium held in Fall 1965, at the Institute of East European Jewish Studies of Philip W. Lown School of Near Eastern and Judaic Studies of Brandeis University.

264. González, Nancie L. "The Spanish Americans of New Mexico." Advance Report No. 9, Mexican-American Study Project, Los Angeles, California: University of California, September 1967.

265. Good Samaritan Center, 1600 Saltillo, San Antonio, Texas 78207. "The Crucial Years."

A film strip with synchronized commentary describing bilingual pre-school program for educationally disadvantaged Spanish-speaking children between the ages of three and six.

266. Goodson, W. R., ed. *Addresses and Reports Presented at the Conference on Development of Bilingualism in Children of Varying Linguistic and Cultural Heritages*. See Texas Education Agency.

267. Gordon, Milton Myron. *Assimilation in American Life: The Role of Race, Religion, and National Origins*. New York: Oxford University Press, 1964. 276 pp. Bibliographical footnotes.

268. Gould, Ketayun H. "Social-Role Expectations of Polonians by Social Class, Ethnic Identification, and Generational Positioning." Unpublished Ph.D. dissertation, University of Pittsburgh, 1966. *Dissertation Abstracts*, Series A, Vol. XXVII, No. 3 (1966), p. 3140.

269. Goulet, Alexandre. *Une Nouvelle-France en Nouvelle-Angleterre.* Preface by Emile Lauvrière. Paris: E. Duchemin, 1934. 158 pp. Bibliography, pp. 153-158.
"A New France in New England." The history of the Franco-Americans.

270. Govorchin, Gerald Gilbert. *Americans from Yugoslavia.* Gainesville, Florida: The University of Florida Press, 1961. 352 pp. Bibliography, pp. 283-297.
A comprehensive study of Yugoslav immigration to America. Detailed statistics are given as appendices.

271. Grebler, Leo. "The Schooling Gap: Signs of Progress." Mexican-American Study Project, Advance Report No. 7. Los Angeles, California: University of California, Division of Research, Graduate School of Business Administration, 1967.

272. "Greek Emigration: Keeping the Poor at Home." *Economist* (London), Vol. CCXI (June 13, 1964), p. 1266.

273. Green, Shirley E. *The Education of Migrant Children.* Washington, D. C.: National Education Association, Department of Rural Education, 1954. 179 pp.
This book, written under the sponsorship of the National Council of Agricultural Life and Labor, studies migrant education in various parts of the United States. In the Southwest, conditions among migrant children of Seguin, Texas, receive special study.

274. Grieve, D. W., and A. Taylor. "Media of Instruction: A Preliminary Study of the Relative Merits of English and an African Vernacular as Teaching Media." *Gold Coast Education*, No. 1 (May 1952), pp. 36-52.
Report of a pilot bilingual program conducted in Ghana, in which Twi, a local vernacular, was used as a medium of instruction to teach general subjects to Senior Primary School students.

275. Gross, Feliks. "Language and Value Changes Among the Arapaho." *International Journal of American Linguistics*, Vol. XVII (1951), pp. 10-17.
Discusses language as an index of culture change, the functional distribution of language, the distribution of the use of Arapaho and English within the family, and the transformation of values as these factors pertain to this Indian group.

276. Grueningen, John Paul von, ed. *The Swiss in the United States: A Compilation Prepared for the Swiss-American Historical Society as the Second Volume of its Publications.* Madison, Wisconsin: Swiss-American Historical Society, 1940. 153 pp.
A general study based on a statistical survey of Swiss immigration to the United States, with special attention given to the Italian-Swiss of California.

277. Gudschinsky, Sarah C. "Recent Trends in Primer Construction." *Fundamental and Adult Education*, Vol. XI, No. 2 (1959), pp. x-xxxix.
Describes a program being carried out by members of the Summer Institute of

Linguistics. Deals with primer planning, analysis procedures for primer construction; and examples of complete primer series in 19 different languages including several American Indian languages.

278. Gumperz, John. "On the Linguistic Markers of Bilingual Communication." See *The Journal of Social Issues.*

279. Gurren, Louise. "A Special Project for Teaching Speech to Transitional Puerto Rican High School Students in the City of New York." *Speech Teacher*, Vol. VII (1958), pp. 148-150.

280. Gzowski, Peter. "The B. and B.'s Desperate Catalogue of the Obvious: "What We Got For Our One and a Half Million Dollars." *Saturday Night*, Vol. XXC (April 1965), pp. 17-19.
A reaction to the Laurendeau-Dunton Royal Commission on Bilingualism and Biculturalism in Canada report.

281. Hagwood, J. A. *The Tragedy of German Americans in the Unites States.* New York and London: Putnam, 1940.

282. Hakes, David T. "Psychological Aspects of Bilingualism." *The Modern Language Journal*, Vol. XLIX, No. 4 (April 1965), pp. 220-227.

283. Halich, Wasyl. *Ukrainians in the United States.* Chicago, Illinois: The University of Chicago Press, 1937. 174 pp. Bibliography, pp. 163-168.
The history of Ukrainian immigration to the United States and their life in their new homeland: organizations, churches, press, social activities, civic enterprises, etc., with detailed tables and maps showing their distribution in the country.

284. Hall, Robert A., Jr. *Linguistics and Your Language.* Anchor Books, No. A201. Garden City, New York: Doubleday, 1960. 265 pp. Bibliography, pp. 260-263. Second revised edition of *Leave Your Language Alone!*, Ithaca, New York: Linguistica, 1950.
A brief, non-technical discussion of a number of problems related to language and linguistics.

285.___. *Pidgin and Creole Languages.* Ithaca, New York: Cornell University Press, 1966. 188 pp. "Selected bibliography," pp. 163-177.
Emphasizes nature and history, structure and relationships, linguistic, social, and political significance.

286. Ham, Edward Billings. "French National Societies in New England." *New England Quarterly*, Vol. XII, No. 2 (June 1939), pp. 315-332.
Outlines one aspect of the Franco-Americans' struggle "to preserve some semblance of racial integrity": the Franco-American fraternal societies.

287.___. "French Patterns in Quebec and New England." *New England Quarterly*, Vol. XVIII, No. 4 (December 1945), pp. 435-447.

288.___. "Journalism and the French Survival in New England." *New England Quarterly*, Vol. XI (March-December 1938), pp. 89-107.
An extensive survey of the Franco-American press.

289. Hamon, E. *Les Canadiens-Français de la Nouvelle-Angleterre*. Quebec, Canada: N. S. Hardy, 1891. 483 pp.
"French-Canadians of New England."

290. Handlin, Oscar. *The American People in the Twentieth Century*. Cambridge, Massachusetts: Harvard University Press, 1954. 244 pp.
A historical account since 1900, with a separate discussion of each ethnic group.

291.___. *Children of the Uprooted*. New York: G. Braziller, 1966. 551 pp. Bibliographical references.

292.___, ed. *Immigration as a Factor in American History*. Englewood Cliffs, New Jersey: Prentice-Hall, Inc., 1959. 206 pp.

293.___. *The Uprooted: The Epic Story of the Great Migrations that Made the American People*. Boston, Massachusetts: Little, Brown, 1951. 310 pp.

294. Handschin, Charles Hart. *The Teaching of Modern Languages in the United States*. United States Bureau of Education, Bulletin No. 3. Whole No. 510 (1913). Washington, D.C.: U.S. Government Printing Office, 1913. 154 pp. Bibliographies, pp. 101, 105-149.

295. Haney, George E. *Selected State Programs in Migrant Education*. Washington D.C.: Office of Education, 1963. 45 pp.
Presents a survey of the programs for the education of migrant children in California, Colorado, New Jersey, New York, Ohio, Oregon, and Pennsylvania.

296. Hans, N. "Learning Languages in the U.S.S.R." *Education*, Vol. CXIV (1959), pp. 746-748.

297. Hansen, Marcus Lee, and John Bartlet Brebner. *The Mingling of the Canadian and American Peoples*. New Haven, Connecticut: Yale University Press, 1940. 274 pp. Bibliographical footnotes.

298. Harrigan, Joan, comp. "Materiales tocante los latinos: A Bibliography of Materials on the Spanish-Americans." Denver, Colorado: Colorado Department of Education, Division of Library Services, October 1967. 36 pp.

299. Harris, Dixie Lee. "Education of Linguistic Minorities in the United States and the U.S.S.R." *Comparative Education Review*, Vol. VI, No. 3 (February 1963), pp. 191-199.
Compares general and educational treatment by the U.S.S.R. of its linguistic minorities, and the United States native Indian and Eskimo tribes. Provides a thorough comparison of two schools, one in each country.

300. Harrison, Selig S. *The Most Dangerous Decades: An Introduction to the Comparative Study of Language Policy in Multi-lingual States*. New York: Language and Communication Research Center, Columbia University, 1957. Mimeographed. 102 pp. Bibliographies, pp. 35-69, 75-102.
The study is concerned with the influence of multilingualism on national unity. The comprehensive classified bibliography focuses on the Soviet Union, Switzerland, the Philippines, and Sub-Saharan Africa.

301. Haugen, Einar. "Bilingualism: Definition and Problems." Unpublished paper. Cambridge, Massachusetts: Harvard University, February 1968. 16 pp. 34 references.

*302.___. *Bilingualism in the Americas: A Bibliography and Research Guide*. Second printing. University, Alabama: The University of Alabama Press, 1964. First printing: Gainesville, Florida: The American Dialect Society, November 1956. Publication No. 26. 160 pp.

A thorough analysis of language plurality in America followed by a description of the bilingual individual and the bilingual community, and an extensive bibliography.

303.___. "Language and Immigration." *Norwegian-American Studies and Records*, Vol. X (1938), pp. 1-43.

304.___. *Language Conflict and Language Planning: The Case of Modern Norwegian*. Cambridge, Massachusetts: Harvard University Press, 1966. 393 pp. Bibliography (1. General and 2. Norwegain), pp. 325-353.

A scholarly study of the Norwegian language in the twentieth century.

305.___. *The Norwegian Language in America: A Study in Bilingual Behavior*. 2 vols. Publications of the American Institute, University of Oslo, in cooperation with the Department of American Civilization, Graduate School of Arts and Sciences, University of Pennsylvania. Philadelphia, Pennsylvania: The University of Pennsylvania Press, 1953. 695 pp. Bibliographical footnotes.

Vol. I: *The Bilingual Community,* with footnote references, pp.295-317.

Contains a history of immigration, demographic data, organizations, schools, role of the Lutheran Church, language mixing, controversy over the orthography of Norwegian, etc.

Vol. II: *The American Dialects of Norwegian,* with footnote references, pp. 645-664.

Contains linguistic data on the American dialects of Norwegian.

306.___. *The Norwegians in America: A Student's Guide to Localized History*. Localized History Series, Clifford L. Lord, editor. New York: Teachers College Press, Columbia University, 1967. 40 pp.

A brief account of Norwegian settlement, daily life, churches, and contributions.

307.___. "Problems of Bilingual Description." *General Linguistics*, Vol. I (1955), pp. 1-9.

A concise statement on the problems of description and on its place in aiding linguistic research.

Example: comparison of Norwegian and English.

308.___. "Problems of Bilingualism." *Lingua (International Review of General Linguistics)*, Vol. II, No. 3 (Ausust 1950), pp. 271-290.

Contains valuable information about Pennsylvania Germans, New England Portuguese, American Indians, English loanwords in Norwegian, and general commentary on the bilingual in the U.S.

309.___. "Some Pleasures and Problems of Bilingual Research." *International Journal of American Linguistics*, Vol. XX, No. 2 (April 1954), pp. 116-122.

Suggestions on how to conduct research in bilingualism.

310.___. "The Struggle Over Norwegian." *Norwegian-American Studies and Records.* Vol. XVII (1952), pp. 1-35.

311. Hawaii. Department of Education. Office of Research. "Survey of Non-English Speaking Students Attending the Public Schools in Hawaii." Research Report No. 58. Honolulu, Hawaii: Department of Education, May 23, 1968.

312. Heller, Celia S. *Mexican-American Youth: Forgotten Youth at the Crossroads.* Studies in Sociology, No. 20. Fourth printing. New York: Random House, December 1968. 116 pp. 14 references.

    A sociological analysis of the way of life of Mexican American youth in the U.S., the opportunities offered to them and the obstacles placed in their way.

313. Henninger, Daniel, and Nancy Esposito. "Regimented Non-Education, Indian Schools." *The New Republic*, February 15, 1969, pp. 18-21.

    Paints a depressing picture of the B.I.A. schools today including the more negative data regarding educational failure and environmental rigidity.

314. Hense-Jensen, W., and E. Bruncken. *Wisconsin Deutsch-Amerikaner.* 2 vols. Milwaukee, Wisconsin: Deutsche Gesellschaft, 1902.

315. Herskovits, Melville J. "Some Comments on the Study of Culture Contact." *American Anthropologist*, new series, Vol. XLIII, No. 1 (January-March 1941), pp. 1-10.

    Describes contact studies stating that the "concept of acculturation is beginning its cycle of development."

316. Hickman, John M. "Barreras lingüísticas y socioculturales a la comunicación." *América Indígena,* Vol. XXIX, No. 1 (January 1969), pp. 129-141.

    Presents cardinal rules for teachers of a second language to take into account as they fulfill their function as "cultural change agents" in order that the student become truly bicultural.

317. Hill, Archibald A. "The Typology of Writing Systems." In William M. Austin, ed., *Papers in Linguistics in Honor of Léon Dostert.* The Hague, Paris: Mouton, 1967, pp. 92-99.

    Classifies writing systems in three main divisions (discourse systems, morphemic systems, and phonemic systems) according to the size of the unit of utterance on which each is based.

318. Hill, Faith "Using the Reading of Navajo as a Bridge to English for Unschooled Adults (A Proposed Program)." Unpublished paper. Summer 1968. 14 pp. Bibliography, pp. 12-14.

    Presents the rationale and some possible means of implementing a program where the vernacular is used as a bridge to reading in a second language.

319. Hill, Henry Segner. "The Effects of Bilingualism on the Measured Intelligence of Elementary School Children of Italian Parentage." *The Journal of Experimental Education*, Vol. V. No. 1 (September 1936), pp. 75-78. Doctors's Thesis; Rutgers University, 1935.

    Concludes that the effect of bilingualism on the intelligence of Italian children who hear and speak either English or Italian at home may be disregarded.

320. Hilliard, Asa G. "Cross-Cultural Teaching." *Journal of Teacher Education*, Vol. XVIII (Spring 1967), pp. 32-35.

321. Hobart, Charles W. "Underachievement Among Minority Group Students: An Analysis and a Proposal." *Phylon*, Vol. XXIV, No. 2 (Summer 1963), pp. 184-196.
Explains wastage of resources among minority groups in the American society. Advocates special programs with special attention and unusual enrichment experiences.

322. Hodnefield, Jacob. "Norwegian-American *Bygdelags* and Their Publications." *Norwegian-American Studies and Records*, Vol. XVII (1954), pp. 163-232. 33-item bibliography (all but one item in Norwegian).

323. Hoffman, Moses N. H. *The Measurement of Bilingual Background*. New York: Columbia University, Teachers College, 1934. Contributions of Education, No. 623. 76 pp. 51-item bibliography. Ph.D. Thesis, Columbia University, 1934.
Describes a strong measuring instrument, the "Bilingual Schedule," helping the educator deal more intelligently with many of the problems confronting bilingual children in school.

324. Hoffman, Virginia. *Oral English at Rough Rock: A New Program for Navaho Children.* Rough Rock, Arizona: Navaho Curriculum Center, Rough Rock Demonstration School, Diné, Inc., 1968. 58 pp. 27-item bibliography.
An illustrated presentation of the language program at Rough Rock with its rationale and examples of their materials.

325. Hofman, John E. "The Language Transition in Some Lutheran Denominations." In Joshua A. Fishman, et al., *Language Loyalty in the United States*, Chapter 10. Final report to the U.S. Office of Education, Language Research Section, under contract SAE-8729, c. 1964.
Language transition in German- and Norwegian-speaking Lutheran parishes.

326. Hoglund, A. William. *Finnish Immigrants in America, 1880-1920.* Madison, Wisconsin: The University of Wisconsin Press, 1960. 213 pp. "Sources," pp. 196-203.

327. Holland, William R. "Language Barrier as an Educational Problem of Spanish-Speaking Children." *Exceptional Children*, Vol. XXVII, No. 1 (September 1960), pp. 42-44.

328. Holmes, Graham, William J. Benham, and Walter M. Stepp. "Rationale of Navajo Area's English-as-a-Second-Language Program." June 1966. Mimeographed, 16 pp. With appendices.
An important background paper, which traces the history of government- and religion-sponsored educational developments among the Navajos. Contains materials and philosophy.

329. Holtzman, Father Jerome. "An Inquiry Into the Hutterian Dialect." Unpublished master's thesis, University of South Dakota, 1961.

330. Holtzman, Wayne H. "Cross-Cultural Studies in Psychology." *International Journal of Psychology*, Vol. III (1968), pp. 83-91.

331. ___, R. Díaz-Guerrero, J. D. Swartz, and L. Lara Tapia. "Cross-Cultural Longitudinal Research on Child Development: Studies of American and Mexican School Children." In

J. P. Hill, ed., *Minnesota Symposia on Child Psychology*, Vol. II Minneapolis: University of Minnesota Press, 1968.

332. Hopkins, Thomas R. *Bureau of Indian Affairs Summer Program.* University of Alaska, June 24 to August 2, 1963. Juneau, Alaska: Bureau of Indian Affairs, September 1963. 58 pp.
Describes in detail a six-week college orientation program geared to aid Alaskan native students in overcoming the cultural differences between their world view and that which would be expected of them in college.

333.___. "Educational Provisions for the Alaskan Native Since 1867." M.Ed. Thesis, The University of Texas, 1959. 117 pp. Includes bibliographies.
Provides an overview of the development of the Alaskan native and of schools in this area, analyzes curriculum problems and the administrative structure of Alaskan native education under the Bureau of Indian Affairs.

334.___. *Language Testing of North American Indians.* Washington, D. C.: Department of the Interior, Bureau of Indian Affairs, 1967.

335. Horn, Thomas D. *A Study of the Effects of Intensive Oral-Aural English Language Instruction, Oral-Aural Spanish Language Instruction and Non-Oral-Aural Instruction on Reading Readiness in Grade One.* Cooperative Research Project No. 2648. Austin, Texas: The University of Texas, 1966. 58 pp. plus appendices. Bibliography.
The effectiveness of three methods were compared for developing reading readiness in Spanish-speaking first grade children.

336. Hoyt, Anne K. *Bibliography of the Cherokees.* Northeastern State College Division of Library Science, Tahlequah, Oklahoma. Bilingual Family School, Florence McCormick, Program Specialist. Little Rock, Arkansas: South Central Region Educational Laboratory, 1969. 64 pp.
Intended for those working with Cherokee young people. Contains a comprehensive listing of children's books about Cherokees and selective listings of other related subjects such as folklore, education, history, and language.

337. Hutchinson, Edward P., ed. "The New Immigration." *The Annals of the American Academy of Political and Social Sciences*, Vol. CCCLXVII (September 1966). Special issue.
Up-to-date review of quota, non-quota, and refugee immigration to the United States to 1966.

338. Hymes, Dell. *Language in Culture and Society: A Reader in Linguistics and Anthropology.* New York: Harper & Row, Publishers, 1964. 764 pp. Bibliography, pp. 711-749.
Contains useful articles on linguistic anthropology; linguistic equality, diversity, and relativity; grammatical categories; cultural focus and semantic field; speech; social structure and speech community; processes and problems of change; relationships in time and space; historical perspective.

339.___. "Models On Interaction of Language and Social Setting." See *The Journal of Social Issues.*

*340.*___, and William E. Bittle, eds. *Studies in Southwestern Ethnolinguistics: Meaning and History in Language of the American Southwest.* Studies in General Anthropology, No. 3. The Hague: Mouton & Co., 1967. 467 pp. Bibliographies.

341. Ianni, Francis A. J. "Residential and Occupational Mobility as Indices of Acculturation of an Ethnic Group." *Social Forces*, Vol. XXXVI, No. 1 (October 1957), pp. 65-72.
The Italo-American community of Norristown, Pennsylvania, from 1900 to 1950.

342. Ibarra, Herbert. "Teaching Spanish to the Spanish Speaking." *Foreign Language Annals*, Vol. II, No. 3 (March 1969), pp. 310-315.
Story of a typical Mexican immigrant family in the Southwest with emphasis on the educational opportunities offered to the children.

343. International Bureau of Education, Geneva, and UNESCO. *Organization of Pre-Primary Education: Research in Comparative Education.* XXIVth International Conference on Public Education, Publication No. 230. Geneva, Switzerland, 1961. 288 pp.
Comparative study in 15 topics such as: Language of Instruction and the Teaching of a Foreign Language, Supervision and Inspection, etc. Individual studies of 65 countries, including the U.S.A., the U.K., Canada, Belgium, and Ceylon.

344. Iverson, O. B. "From the Prairie to Puget Sound." Edited by Sverre Arestad. *Norwegian-American Studies and Records.* Vol. XVI (1950), pp. 91-119.

345. Jacoby, Neil H. *The Progress of Peoples: Toward a Theory and Policy of Development With External Aid.* With a Center Discussion. "A Center Occasional Paper," Vol. II, No. 4 (June 1969). For the Center for the Study of Democratic Institutions. Santa Barbara, California: Fund for the Republic, Inc., 1969. 36 pp.

346. James, C. B. E. "Bilingualism in Wales: An Aspect of Semantic Organization." *Educational Research*, Vol. II (1960), pp. 123-136.

347. Jameson, Gloria R. *The Development of a Phonemic Analysis for an Oral English Proficiency Test for Spanish-Speaking School Beginners.* Ph.D. dissertation. Oral English Language Proficiency Test I, The San Antonio, Texas, Language Research Project, Thomas D. Horn, Director. Austin, Texas: The University of Texas, January 1967. 189 pp. Bibliography, pp. 185-187.

348. Jensen, Arthur R. "Learning Abilities in Mexican-American and Anglo-American Children." *California Journal of Educational Research*, Vol. XII, No. 4 (September 1961), pp. 147-159.
Discusses special teaching methods required by Mexican American children who are native Spanish-speakers.

349. ___. "Patterns of Mental Ability and Socio-Economic Status." *Proceedings of the National Academy of Sciences*, Vol. LX, No. 4 (August 1968), pp. 1330-1337.
Suggests a positive correlation between socioeconomic status and scholastic aptitude, and more significantly, that these socioeconomic differences in intelligence are due largely to genetic factors.

*350. Jensen, J. Vernon. "Effects of Childhood Bilingualism." *Elementary English,*
I: Vol. XXXIX, No. 2 (February 1962), pp. 132-143; 200-item bibliography on bilingualism.
II: Vol. XXXIX, No. 4 (April 1962), pp. 358-366.
A study of childhood bilingualism. Compares and illustrates the good and the ill effects of bilingualism on the individual from various points of view.

351. Jespersen, Otto. *Language, Its Nature, Development, and Origin.* London: George Allen & Unwin, Ltd.; New York: Henry Holt and Company, 1922. 448 pp.
A theory of linguistic development beginning with a history of linguistic science, then dealing with the child, the individual in the world, and the development of language.

352. *Jewish Education.* A quarterly published since 1930, by the National Council for Jewish Education with the assistance of the American Association for Jewish Education.

353. John, Vera P. "Language and Education: The Challenge of Pluralism." Paper delivered at American Anthropological Association Conference in Miami, May 1968.
The author is particularly concerned with "communicative competence in children's language, language socialization in the home and at school, and the diversity of situations, especially affecting the poor.

354. Johnson, B. H. *Navajo Education at Rough Rock.* Rough Rock, Arizona: Diné, Inc., 1968. 212 pp.
An illustrated and detailed documentation of the first two years of the Rough Rock Demonstration School operated by the local community.

355. Johnson, Granville B., Jr. "Bilingualism as Measured by a Reaction-Time Technique and the Relationship Between a Language and a Non-Language Intelligence Quotient." *Pedagogical Seminary and Journal of Genetic Psychology*, Vol. LXXXII, First Half (March 1953), pp. 3-10. 17 references.

356.___. "The Relationship Existing Between Bilingualism and Racial Attitude." *The Journal of Educational Psychology*, Vol. XLII, No. 6 (October 1951), pp. 357-365. 6 references.
Many of the younger Spanish-speaking subjects were found to be prejudiced in favor of the Anglo.

357. Jonassen, Christen T. "Cultural Variables in the Ecology of an Ethnic Group." *American Sociological Review*, Vol. XIV, No. 1 (February 1949), pp. 32-41.
A tracing of the movement of the Norwegian communities in New York City from the mid-1800's to the last known settlement in Bay Ridge.

358. Jones, Frank E., and Wallace E. Lambert. "Some Situational Influences on Attitudes Toward Immigrants." *British Journal of Sociology*, Vol. XVIII, No. 4 (December 1967), pp. 408-424. 22 bibliographical notes.
An analysis of the attitudes of Canadian adults toward immigrants, which reveals that variations in attitudes to immigrants are significantly related to certain dimensions of the interaction systems in which immigrants and natives participate.

359. Jones, William Richard. *Bilingualism and Intelligence.* Cardiff, Wales: University of Wales Press, 1959. 68 pp. 45 references.
The report discusses monoglot vs. bilingual groups, social and economic status, and concludes that bilingualism need not be a source of intellectual disadvantage.

360.___. *Bilingualism and Reading Ability in English.* Cardiff, Wales: University of Wales Press, 1955. 45 pp. 33 references.

Compares Welsh-speaking and English-speaking children in respect of reading ability in English, particularly in relation to their intelligence and linguistic background.

361.___ *Bilingualism in Welsh Education.* Cardiff, Wales: University of Wales Press, 1966.

362.___. "A Critical Study of Bilingualism and Non-Verbal Intelligence." *British Journal of Edicational Psychology*, Vol. XXX, Part 1 (February 1960), pp. 71-77. 18 references.
Discusses findings that bilingualism need not be a source of intellectual disadvantages, and stresses the importance of a thorough examination of socioeconomic factors in any comparative study of monoglot and bilingual children.

363.___. "The Influence of Reading Ability in English on the Intelligence Test Scores of Welsh-Speaking Children." *British Journal of Education Psychology*, Vol. XXIII, Part 2 (June 1953), pp. 114-120. 6 references.
Compares bilingual and monoglot groups in both the verbal intelligence test and the silent reading test.

364.___. "The Language Handicap of Welsh-Speaking Children: A Study of Their Performance in an English Verbal Intelligence Test in Relation to Their Non-Verbal Mental Ability and Their Reading Ability in English." *The British Journal of Educational Psychology*, Vol. XXII, Part 2 (June 1952), pp. 114-123. 21 references.

365.___, and W. A. C. Stewart. "Bilingualism and Verbal Intelligence." *The British Journal of Psychology, Statistical Section*, Vol. IV, Part 1 (March 1951), pp. 3-8. 16 references.
A comparative study of tests administered to 11-year-old monoglot and bilingual children in each child's native language (English or Welsh). Resulted in a highly significant difference in favor of the monoglot group.

366.___, J. R. Morrison, J. Rogers, and H. Saer. *The Educational Attainment of Bilingual Children in Relation to Their Intelligence and Linguistic Background.* Cardiff: University of Wales Press, 1957. 52 pp. 20 references.
A rigorous investigation undertaken by the Collegiate Faculties of Education at Aberystwyth and Bangor, Wales, England, at the request of the Welsh Joint Education Committee.

367. Joos, Martin. *The Five Clocks.* Bloomington, Indiana: Indiana University Research Center in Anthropology, Folklore, and Linguistics, 1962. 41 pp.

368. Jordan, Riverda H. "Retention of the Foreign Language in the Home." *Journal of Educational Research*, Vol. III (1921), pp. 35-42.
Reveals that the Germans and Danes are foremost in the acquisition of the English language and that the disposition on the part of the parents to use the native language among themselves is less marked among Danish, German, and Jewish families than among the Slavs, Spaniards, Greeks, and Hungarians.

369. *The Journal of Education*, No. 9 (January 1964). Special issue: Biculturalism and Education. 112 pp.
A collection of 15 articles on French-English bilingualism in Canada and its educational implications.

*370. *The Journal of Social Issues*, Vol. XXIII, No. 2 (April 1967), 138 pp. Special issue: "Problems of Bilingualism," edited by John Macnamara. Contents:
Hymes, Dell. "Models on Interaction of Language and Social Setting," pp. 8-28.
Fishman, Joshua A. "Bilingualism With and Without Diglossia; Diglossia With and Without Bilingualism," pp. 29-38.
Kloss, Heinz. "Bilingualism and Nationalism," pp. 39-47.
Gumperz, John. "On the Linguistic Markers of Bilingual Communication," pp. 48-57.
Macnamara, John. "The Bilingual's Linguistic Performance–A Psychological Overview," pp. 58-77.
Ervin-Tripp, Susan. "An Issei Learns English," pp. 78-90.
Lambert, Wallace E. "A Social Psychology of Bilingualism," pp. 91-109.
Gaarder, A. Bruce. "Organization of the Bilingual School," pp. 110-120.
Macnamara, John. "Effects of Instruction in a Weaker Language," pp. 120-134.
A collection of articles, each illustrating a different aspect of the problems of bilingualism.

371. Katsh, Abraham I. "Current Trends in the Study of Hebrew in Colleges and Universities." *The Modern Language Journal*, Vol. XLIV, No. 2 (February 1960), pp. 64-67.

372. Kehlenbeck, Alfred P. *An Iowa Low German Dialect*. Publication of the American Dialect Society, No. 10. Greensboro, North Carolina: American Dialect Society, November 1948. 83 pp.
Historical background, phonology, morphology, syntax, loan-words, vocabulary, and other characteristics of the Low German dialect spoken by the trilingual (Low German-High German-English) people of four townships of Iowa.

373. Keith, Mary T. "From K Through 3 Successfully: A Progress Report of the Sustained Primary Program for Bilingual Students." Title III, ESEA Application 1967-1968. Las Cruces, New Mexico: Las Cruces School District No. 2. Mimeographed.

374. Kelley, Louis. See Canadian Commission for UNESCO.

375. Kennedy, John Fitzgerald. *A Nation of Immigrants*. Introduction by Robert F. Kennedy. Revised and enlarged edition. New York: Harper & Row, 1964. 111 pp. Bibliography, pp. 95-101.

376. Kennedy, Stetson. *Jim Crow Guide to the U.S.A.: The Laws, Customs and Etiquette Governing the Conduct of Nonwhites and Other Minorities as Second-Class Citizens*. London: Lawrence & Wishart Ltd., 1959. 230 pp.

377. Keston, Morton J., and Carmina Jiménez. "A Study of the Performance on English and Spanish Editions of the Stanford-Binet Intelligence Test by Spanish-American Children." *The Journal of Genetic Psychology*, Vol. LXXXV, Second Half (December 1954), pp. 263-269. 15 references.
Concludes that since bilingual children are able to perform better in the language in which they have received formal instruction, only the English edition should be used to better measure the children's intelligence.

378. King, Paul E. *Bilingual Readiness in Primary Grades: An Early Childhood Demonstration Project*. Project No. D-107, Contract No. OE-4-10-101. New York: Hunter College of the City University of New York, December 1966.

379. Kittell, Jack E. "Bilingualism and Language–Non-Language Intelligence Scores of Third-Grade Children." *Journal of Educational Research*, Vol. LII, No. 7 (March 1959), pp. 263-268. 13 references.

380.___. "Intelligence-Test Performance of Children from Bilingual Environments." *Elementary School Journal*, Vol. LXIV, No. 2 (November 1963), pp. 76-83. 6 references.
In an experiment controlled on all levels, 33 monolingual and 33 bilingual children were tested in three areas in the third and fifth grade.

*381. Kloss, Heinz. *The Bilingual Tradition in America*. Publications of the International Center for Research on Bilingualism. Rowley, Massachusetts: Newbury House, In Press.

382.___. "Bilingualism and Nationalism." *The Journal of Social Issues*, Vol. XXIII, No. 2 (April 1967), pp. 39-47.
An analysis of the relationship between nationalism and bilingualism with many examples taken from various parts of the world.

383.___. *Das Nationalitätenrecht der Vereinigten Staaten von Amerika*. Vienna, Austria: Braumüller, 1963.

384.___. *Das Volksgruppenrecht in den Vereinigten Staaten von Amerika*. Essen, Germany: Essener Verlagsanstalt, 1940 (Part I) and 1942 (Part II).

385.___. "Deutscher Sprachunterricht im Grundschulalter in den Vereinigten Staaten." *Auslandskurier*, Vol. VIII (August 1967), pp. 22-24.

386.___. "Die deutschamerikanische Schule." *Jahrbuch für Amerikastudien* (Heidelberg), Vol. II (1962), pp. 141-175.

387.___. "Experts from the National Minority Laws of the United States of America." Translated from the German by Ulrich Hans R. Mammitzsch. Occasional papers of Research Translations, Institute of Advanced Projects, East-West Center, Honolulu, Hawaii. Mimeographed, 72 pp. 123 bibliographical notes.
Concludes that non-English-speaking ethnic groups in the United States were Anglicized not *because* of nationality laws which were *unfavorable* toward their languages but *in spite* of nationality laws *favorable* to them.

388.___. *FLES: Zum Problem des Fremdsprachenunterrichts an Grundschulen Amerikas und Europas*. Bad Godsberg: Verlag Wissenschaftliches Archiv, 1967.

389.___. "Types of Multilingual Communities: A Discussion of Ten Variables." *Sociological Inquiry*, Vol. XXXVI, No. 2 (Spring 1966), pp. 135-145.
The variables discussed herein are: types of speech communities, number of languages used by individuals, types of personal and impersonal bilingualism, legal status, segments involved, type and degree of individual bilingualism, prestige of languages involved, degree of distance, indigenousness of speech communities, and attitude toward linguistic stability.

390.___. "Uber die mittelbare Kartographische Erfassung der jüngeren deutschen Volksinseln in den Vereinigten Staaten." *Deutsches Archiv für Landes und Volksforschung*, Vol. III (1939), pp. 453-474.

391.___. *Um die Einigung des Deutschamerikanertums: Die Geschichte einer unvollendeten Volksgruppe*. Berlin, Germany: Volk und Reich Verlag, 1937.

392. Kolers, Paul A. "Bilingualism and Bicodalism." *Language and Speech*, Vol. VIII (1965), pp. 122-126.

393.___. "Reading and Talking Bilingually." *American Journal of Psychology*, Vol. LXXIX, No. 3 (September 1966), pp. 357-376.
Report of an experiment in which French-English bilinguals were tested in several linguistic tasks, including how well bilinguals comprehend material in their native language and in the foreign language.

394. Kollmorgen, Walter M., and Robert W. Harrison. "French-Speaking Farmers of Southern Louisiana." *Economic Geography*, Vol. XXII, No. 3 (July 1946), pp. 153-160.
Studies the agricultural problems and socioeconomic situation of the Cajun and shows how cultural considerations have conditioned his economic adjustment.

395. Konvitz, Milton R. *The Alien and the Asiatic in American Law*. Cornell Studies in Civil Liberty. Ithaca, New York: Cornell University Press, 1946. 299 pp.

396. Kosinski, Leonard Vincent. "Bilingualism and Reading Development: A Study of the Effects of Polish-American Bilingualism Upon Reading Achievement in Junior High School." Unpublished Ph.D. dissertation, University of Wisconsin, 1963. (*Dissertation Abstracts* Vol. XXIV, No. 2 (1963), pp. 2462-2463.)
A comparison of reading achievement among three groups of junior high students with Polish and English backgrounds.

397. Kreidler, Carol J., ed. *On Teaching English to Speakers of Other Languages:* Series II, Papers read at the TESOL Conference, San Diego, California, March 12-13, 1965. Champaign, Illinois: National Council of Teachers of English, 1966.
A set of articles on TESOL as a professional field, reports on special programs, some key concepts and current concerns, and the preparation and use of materials and aids.

398. Kreusler, Abraham. "Bilingualism in Soviet Non-Russian Schools." *Elementary School Journal*, Vol. LXII, No. 2 (November 1961), pp. 94-99. 8 references.
A description of the new school programs in the Soviet Union tending to extend the Russian language throughout the country and at the same time preserve the cultural heritage of its minority groups, thus producing bilinguals.

399.___. *The Teaching of Modern Foreign Languages in the Soviet Union*. Leiden, The Netherlands: E. J. Brill, 1963. 129 pp.
A report covering the period from 1917 to date. Includes chapters on teacher-training schools, the school reform of 1958, bilingualism in Soviet non-Russian schools, and the Decree of the Council of Ministers in 1961.

400. Kreighbaum, Hillier, and Hugh Rawson. *To Improve Secondary School Science and Mathematics Teaching (A Short History of the First Dozen Years of the National Science Foundation's Summer Institutes Program, 1954-1965)*. Washington, D. C.: U. S. Government Printing Office, 1968. 41 pp.

401. Labov, William. "The Non-Standard Vernacular of the Negro Community: Some Practical Suggestions." See Temple University, The NDEA National Institute for Advanced Study in Teaching Disadvantaged Youth.

402. Lado, Robert. *Annotated Bibliography for Teachers of English as a Foreign Language.* United States Department of Health, Education, and Welfare, Office of Education. Bulletin 1955, No. 3. Washington, D.C.: U.S. Government Printing Office, 1955. 224 pp. 730 items.

Covers the period from 1946 to 1953 and lists materials for the teacher and the student, broken down according to the native language background of the student.

403.___. *Linguistics Across Cultures: Applied Linguistics for Language Teachers.* With a foreword by Charles C. Fries. Ann Arbor, Michigan: University of Michigan Press, 1957. 141 pp. Bibliography, pp. 124-141.

Written in non-technical language, this book demonstrates the role that descriptive linguistics can play in practical language teaching including comparison of sound systems, grammatical structures, vocabulary systems, and values of contrastive studies.

404.___, Wallace Lambert, and Theodore Andersson. "Relación entre el aprendizaje de una lengua extranjera y el vernáculo." *Educación,* Vol. XI, No. 3 (1962), pp. 11-41.

Three papers presented in Spanish at the *Conferencia sobre la enseñanza de lengua* held at San Juan, Puerto Rico, discussing the relation between the native tongue and the acquisition of a second language.

405. La Fontaine, Hernán, and Muriel Pagan. "A Model for the Implementation of the Elementary School Curriculum through Bilingual Education." Produced by Hernán La Fontaine, 1969. 10 pp. Mimeographed.

A theoretical model presented to the staff of the Bilingual School (P.S. 25, Bronx, New York) for discussion, modification and implementation beginning September 1968.

406. Laird, Charlton. *The Miracle of Language.* Cleveland, Ohio, and New York: World Publishing Company, 1953. 308 pp. Bibliographical notes, 293-295.

An original attempt to present the miraculous aspect of language.

407. Lambert, Wallace E. "Behavioral Evidence for Contrasting Norms of Bilingualism." In Michael Zarechnak, ed., "Report of the Twelfth Annual Round Table Meeting on Linguistics and Language Studies," Georgetown University *Monograph Series on Languages and Linguistics,* No. 14 (1961), pp. 73-80. 11 references.

Psychological approach to bilingualism, to complement the traditional linguistic approach.

408.___. "Developmental Aspects of Second-Language Acquisition." *Journal of Social Psychology,* Vol. XLIII, First Half (February 1956), pp. 83-104. 13 references.

Discusses some of the variables in the linguistic behavior of those who are at different levels of development in the French language.

409.___. "Measurement of the Linguistic Dominance of Bilinguals." *The Journal of Abnormal and Social Psychology,* Vol. L, No. 2 (March 1955), pp. 197-200. 14 references.

A reaction-time method for measuring the extent of bilingualism using three groups of French-English bilinguals.

410.___. "Psychological Approaches to the Study of Language." Part I: "On Learning, Thinking, and Human Abilities." *The Modern Language Journal*, Vol. XLVII, No. 2 (February 1963), pp. 50-62; Part II: "On Second-Language Learning and Bilingualism." *The Modern Language Journal*, Vol. XLVII, No. 3 (March 1963), pp. 114-121.

Part I: Contains a brief sketch of two contrasting learning theories, one dealing with meaning, the other with verbal behavior.

Part II: The first section deals with a social psychology of second-language learning. The second part traces some of the most definitive research work done in the field of the psychology of bilingualism.

411.___. "Social-Psychological Approaches to the Cross-National Study of Values." Unpublished paper. Montreal, Canada: McGill University, March 1969. 41 pp. 33 references.

Demonstrates how the social psychologist approaches and contributes to the cross-cultural study of human values and personality styles.

412.___. "A Social Psychology of Bilingualism." *The Journal of Social Issues*, Vol. XXIII, No. 2 (April 1967), pp. 91-109.

Descirbes distinctive behavior of the bilingual individual, the social influences that affect his behavior, and its consequences.

413.___. "A Social Psychology of Bilingualism." Paper presented at the Ninth International African Seminar of University College in Dar-es-Salaam (Tanzania). International African Institute, December 1968.

A revised and shortened version of an earlier paper with the same title (see the foregoing item).

414.___, and Peal; see Peal and Lambert.

415.___, Maria Ignatow, and Marcel Krauthamer. "Bilingual Organization in Free Recall." *Journal of Verbal Learning and Verbal Behavior*, Vol. VII (1968), pp. 207-214. 20 references.

Two groups of bilinguals, one French-English and the other English-Russian were tested individually. Various results suggest that organization according to semantic categories is a more useful schema than is language for bilinguals.

416.___, and Chris Rawlings. "Bilingual Processing of Mixed-Language Associative Networks." Unpublished paper. Montreal, Canada: McGill University, 1969. 14 pp. 14 references.

Compound and coordinate bilinguals, equally skilled in French and English, were compared for their ability to search out "core concepts" when given mixed-language clues.

417.___, and Otto Klineberg. "The Development of Children's Views of Foreign Peoples." *Childhood Education* (January 1969), pp. 247-253.

A ten-year study to determine how adults effect children's prejudices.

418.___, J. Havelka, and C. Crosby. "The Influence of Language Acquisition Contexts on Bilingualism." *The Journal of Abnormal and Social Psychology*, Vol. LVI, No. 2 (March 1958), pp. 239-244. 9 references.

It was found that if the bilingual has learned his two languages in culturally distinctive contexts, "the semantic differences between translated equivalents are comparatively increased."

419.___, Hannah Frankel, and G. R. Tucker. "Judging Personality Through Speech: A French Canadian Example." *The Journal of Communication*, Vol. XVI (December 1966), pp. 305-321.

420.___, J. Havelka, and R. C. Gardner. "Linguistic Manifestations of Bilingualism." *American Journal of Psychology*, Vol. LXXII, No. 1 (March 1959), pp. 77-82.

A study to develop a series of behavioral measures of bilingualism. Helpful research in determining which is the dominant language in the individual.

*421.___, and J. Macnamara. "Some Cognitive Consequences of Following a First-Grade Curriculum in a Second Language." *Journal of Educational Psychology*, (1969). In press.

Examines "the effects of a year's schooling conducted exclusively in a foreign language on the linguistic and mental development of first-grade children, giving equal attention to possible retardation in native language skills, to progress made in the foreign-language skills, and to relative achievement made with the content of the actual program of study."

*422.___, M. Just, and N. Segalowitz. "Some Cognitive Consequences of Following the Curricula of Grades One and Two in a Foreign Language." Mimeographed. McGill University, 1969. 82 pp. Bibliography, pp. 81-82.

The second report of the Lambert and Macnamara study of a similar title. Follows essentially the same plan.

423. Lancey, Livingstone de. "The French Influence in New Orleans." *The French Review*, Vol. XIII, No. 6 (March 1940), pp. 483-487.

Retraces the history, from colonial times to the present, of the "only remaining city in...the United States whose French origins are still apparent."

424. Landes, Ruth. *Culture in American Education: Anthropological Approaches to Minority and Dominant Groups in the Schools*. New York: John Wiley & Sons, Inc., 1965. 330 pp. Bibliography, pp. 317-324.

A highly stimulating description of an experiment held in Claremont, California, conceived to train public-school educators to understand the social complexities of culture clash in the schools.

425. Landry, Stuart O., ed. *Louisiana Almanac and Fact Book*, New Orleans, Louisiana: Louisiana Almanac and Fact Book.

Contains occasional notes on the French-speaking population of the state.

426. Lang, Gerhard. "Jewish Education." *American Jewish Yearbook*, Vol. LXIX (1968), pp. 370-383.

Latest statistical data on enrollment in American Jewish Schools. Eight tables provided.

427. "Language Usage in Italian Families." *Atlantica,* November 1934.

428. Lauvrière, Emile. *La tragédie d'un peuple: histoire du peuple acadien de ses origines à nos jours.* 2 vols. New edition, revised and completed. Paris: H. Goulet, 1924. 518 + 597 pp. References at end of each chapter.
History of the expulsion of the Acadians from Nova Scotia in 1755.

429. La Violette, Forrest E. *Americans of Japanese Ancestry: A Study of Assimilation in the American Community.* Toronto, Canada: The Canadian Institute of International Affairs, 1945. 185 pp.

430. Lee, Rose Hum. "The Stranded Chinese in the U.S." *Phylon,* Vol. XIX, No. 2 (Summer 1958), pp. 180-194.

431. Lefevre, Carl A. "Values in the Teaching of English and the Language Arts." See Temple University, The NDEA National Institute for Advanced Study in Teaching Disadvantaged Youth.

432. Lehrer, L. "Yiddish in the Yiddish School." *Yiddisher Kemfer,* Vol. XLII (1962), pp. 3-5. (In Yiddish.)

433. Leighton, Alexander H. *The Governing of Men: General Principles and Recommendations Based on Experience at a Japanese Relocation Camp.* Princeton, New Jersey: Princeton University Press, 1946.

434. Leighton, Roby E. *Bicultural Linguistic Concepts in Education.* Tucson: University of Arizona, 1964.
A handbook of suggestions for the administrator, instructor, and guidance counselor interested in the problems of the culturally different student.

435. Lemaire, Hervé B. "Franco-American Efforts on Behalf of the French Language in New England." In Joshua A. Fishman, et al., *Language Loyalty in the United States: The Maintenance and Perpetuation of Non-English Mother-Tongues by American Ethnic and Religious Groups,* The Hague: Mouton & Co., 1966, Chapter 10, pp. 253-279. 24-item bibliography. Revised version of an unpublished study for the Language Resources Project, United States Office of Education, 1964.
An up-to-date description of the status of French in New England, with a full analysis of the elements that have contributed to their cultural survival.

436. Lemoine, Adelard. *L'évolution de la race française en Amérique.* Montreal, Canada: Librairie Beauchemin, Ltd., 1921.
The evolution of the French "race" in America.

437. Lenneberg, Eric H. *Biological Foundations of Language.* With appendices by Noam Chomsky and Otto Marx. New York: John Wiley & Sons, Inc., August 1967. 489 pp.
Perhaps the most comprehensive study to date on the biological bases of speech and language in the light of evolution and genetics and in the context of growth and maturation including a complete biological theory of language development.

438. Leopold, Werner F. *Bibliography of Child Language.* Northwestern University Studies, Humanities Series, No. 28. Evanston, Illinois: Northwestern University Press, 1952. 115 pp.

*439.——. *Speech Development of a Bilingual Child: A Linguist's Records.* 4 vols. Northwestern University Studies, Humanities Series, Nos. 6, 11, 18, and 19. Evanston and Chicago, Illinois: Northwestern University Press, 1939-1949.

An observation and recording of the development of speech in a child to whom German and English were spoken with equal frequency from age two. The first three volumes contain reports of vocabulary growth, sound learning, grammar, and general problems in the first two years, and Vol. 4 contains the author's diary of the study.

440.——. "The Study of Child Language and Infant Bilingualism." *Word*, Vol. IV, No. 1 (April 1948), pp. 1-17. 98 bibliographical footnotes.

441. Le Page, Robert B. *The National Language Question: Linguistic Problems of Newly Independent States.* Issued under the auspices of the Institute of Race Relations, London. London, New York: Oxford University Press, 1964. 82 pp. 9 references.

Writing on the assumption that "no universal solution of the national language question exists," the author discusses the variables involved and then develops the possibilities and consequences of these factors.

442. Lerea, Louis, and Suzanne Kohut. "A Comparative Study of Monolinguals and Bilinguals in a Verbal Task Performance." *Journal of Clinical Psychology*, Vol. XVII, No. 1 (January 1961), pp. 49-52.

In a study involving two experiment groups, 30 bilinguals and 30 monolinguals, matched in age, sex, intelligence, and socioeconomic status, they found bilinguals superior in the micro-utterance association (relearning) task and concluded that "bilinguals may possess a unique potential unacknowledged in past research."

443. Lesser, George S., Gordon Fifer, and Donald H. Clark. *Mental Abilities of Children from Different Social-Class and Cultural Groups.* Monograph of the Society for Research in Child Development, Serial No. 102, Vol. XXX, No. 4. Chicago: University of Chicago Press, 1965.

444. Levi-Everest, K. A. "Geographical Origin of German Immigration to Wisconsin." *Collections of the Wisconsin State Historical Society*, Vol. XIV (1898), pp. 341-398.

Describes the dialect variation of the post-colonial language islands.

445. Levinson, B. M. "A Comparison of the Performance of Bilingual and Monolingual Native-Born Jewish Preschool Children of Traditional Parentage on Four Intelligence Tests." *Journal of Clinical Psychology*, Vol. XV, (1959), pp. 74-76.

446. Lewis, D. G. "Bilingualism and Non-Verbal Intelligence: A Further Study of Test Results." *British Journal of Educational Psychology*, Vol. XXIX (1959), pp. 17-22.

447. Lewis, E. Glyn. *Foreign and Second Language Teaching in the USSR.* ETIC Occasional Papers, No. 1. London: British Council English-Teaching Information Center, 1962. 16 pp.

Report of foreign-language teaching and bilingualism in the Soviet educational system. Includes comments on type of schools, language policy, and attitudes toward foreign language teaching; teacher training; methodology; audio-visual aids; and bilingual education in the USSR.

448. Lewis, Hilda P., and Edward R. Lewis. "Written Language Performance of Sixth-Grade Children of Low Socioeconomic Status from Bilingual and Monolingual Backgrounds." *The Journal of Experimental Education*, Vol. XXXIII, No. 3 (Spring 1965), pp. 237-242.
The study shows that bilingualism did not appear to have an adverse affect upon written language performance.

449. Lewis, Oscar. *A Puerto-Rican Family in the Culture of Poverty: San Juan and New York.* New York: Random House, Inc., 1966. 669 pp.

450. Lieberson, Stanley. "Bilingualism in Montreal: A Demographic Analysis." *The American Journal of Sociology*, Vol. LXXI, No. 1 (July 1965), pp. 10-25.
Census data and linguistic indices are used to examine trends in the ability of Montreal's population to communicate with one another between 1921 and 1961.

451.___. *Ethnic Patterns in American Cities.* New York: Free Press of Glencoe, 1963. 230 pp. 54 references.

452.___. "National and Regional Language Diversity," *Acts of the 10th International Congress of Linguistics*, Academy of the S.R. of Roumania, 1968. 8 pp.
Presents several theoretical propositions about the relationship between linguistic diversity within a nation and within its subparts or regions.

453. Liu, Kwang-Ching. *Americans and Chinese: A Historical Essay and a Bibliography.* Cambridge, Massachusetts: Harvard University Press, 1963. 211 pp.

454. Livingood, F. G. "Eighteenth Century Reformed Church Schools." *Proceedings of the Pennsylvania German Society*, Vol. XXXVIII (1930), p. 199.

455. Locke, William N. "The French Colony at Brunswick, Maine–A Historical Sketch." *Les Archives de Folklore*, Vol. I, pp. 97-111. Montreal: Editions Fides, 1946.

456.___. "Notes on the Vocabulary of the French-Canadian Dialect Spoken in Brunswick, Maine." *The French Review*, Vol. XIX, No. 6 (May 1946), pp. 420-422.

457.___. *Pronunciation of the French Spoken at Brunswick, Maine.* With a preface by J. M. Carrière. Greensboro: University of North Carolina, American Dialect Society, November 1949. Publication of the American Dialect Society, No. 12. 202 pp. 38-item bibliography, pp. 21-22.
An important contribution to the study of Franco-American speech.

458. Logan, J. L. "Coral Way: A Bilingual School." *TESOL Quarterly*, Vol. I, No. 2 (June 1967).
A description of the curriculum, background, and reasons for success for this model bilingual program.

459. Louisiana Legislative Council. *Louisiana: Its History, People, Government and Economy*. Second edition. Research Study No. 7. Baton Rouge, Louisiana, November 1955. 285 pp.

460. Louisiana State Department of Education. *Project for French-Speaking Elementary Teachers*. Baton Rouge, Louisiana: Louisiana State Department of Education, 1967.

461. Love, Harold D. "Bilingualism in South West Louisiana." *Journal of Educational Research*, Vol. LVI, No. 3 (November 1962), pp. 144-147.
Concludes that French-speaking children in Southwest Louisiana can discriminate between the *th* sound, which they have difficulty in uttering, and the *t* sound only if the examiner has an English language background exclusively.

462. Lowie, Robert H. "A Case of Bilingualism." *Word*, Vol. I, No. 3 (December 1945), pp. 249-259.
Autobiography of a German-English bilingual immigrant from Austria.

463. Lucas, Henry S. *Netherlanders in America: Dutch Immigration to the United States and Canada, 1789-1950*. University of Michigan Publications, History and Political Science, Vol. XXI. Ann Arbor, Michigan: The University of Michigan Press; London: Geoffrey Cumberlege, Oxford University Press, 1955. 744 pp. Bibliographical notes, pp. 651-720.
The study of Dutch-Americans, from the time of the early settelements of Michigan and Iowa to date. See especially pp. 579-635 ("Education and Character") and 641-647 (demographic data). The lengthy footnotes provide a rather exhaustive bibliography on the subject.

464. Lyra, Franciszek. "English and Polish in Contact." Unpublished Ph.D. dissertation, Indiana University, 1962. (*Dissertation Abstracts*, Vol. XXIII, No. 2 (1962), p. 2128.)

465.____. "Integration of English Loans in U. S. Polish." *Slavic and East European Journal*, Vol. X, No. 3 (Fall 1966), pp. 303-312.

466. Macdonald, John S., and Leatrice D. Macdonald. "Urbanization, Ethnic Groups and Social Segmentation." *Social Research*, Vol. XXIX (Winter 1962), pp. 433-448.
The authors study the processes by which prospective Southern Italian immigrants to the United States learned of opportunities, were provided with passage money, and had initial accommodation and employment arranged through previous immigrants.

467. Mackey, William F. "Bilingual Interference: Its Analysis and Measurement." *Journal of Communication*, Vol. XV, No. 4 (December 1965), pp. 239-249.
A thoughtfully written study which includes a helpful section on types of language behavior. Describes not only the meaning of interference and language borrowing but also a method for analyzing and measuring bilingual interference.

468.____. "Bilingualism." *Encyclopedia Britannica*, Vol. III (1965), pp. 610-611.
A description of bilingualism and its effects on the individual, the community, and language.

469.____ "Bilingualism and Education." *Revue Trimestrielle Pédagogie-Orientation*, Vol. VI (1952), pp. 135-147. 22 bibliographical footnotes.

The article questions some definitions of bilingualism and discusses in detail the degrees of bilinguality, the bilingual school, and the bilingual child.

470.____. "Bilingualism and Linguistic Structure." *Culture*, Vol. XIV (1953), pp. 143-149.
The study describes the basic changes in linguistic structure due to bilingualism.

*471.____. *Bilingualism as a World Problem.* (E. R. Adair Memorial Lectures.) Montreal, Canada: Harvest House, 1967. Bibliography and works by author. Bilingual French-English edition. 62 + 58 pp.
Seeks the causes and consequences of bilingualism.

472.____. "The Description and Measurement of Bilingualism/Description et Mesure du Bilinguisme." *The Linguistic Reporter*, Vol. IX, No. 5 (October 1967), pp. 1-2.
Briefly sets forth the problems yet to be solved and research yet to be done in this area.

473.____. "The Description of Bilingualism." *Candian Journal of Linguistics*, Vol. VII, No. 2 (1962), pp. 51-85.
The author extends further the definition of bilingualism and, encouraged by his colleagues at the 1960 International Seminar on Bilingualism in Education, held in Aberystwyth, he provides a framework for describing bilingualism.

474.____. "The Description of Bilingualism." In Joshua A. Fishman, ed., *Readings in the Sociology of Languages*, The Hague: Mouton & Co., 1968, pp. 554-584.

475.____. "Les exigences du bilinguisme pour l'immigrant." *Citoyen*, Vol. IV (September 1959), pp. 21-29.
Analyzes in simple language the difficulties of second-language learning, especially by an adult.

476.____. *Language Teaching Analysis*. Indiana University Studies in the History and Theory of Linguistics. Bloomington, Indiana: Indiana University Press, 1967. 562 pp. 1,741-item topical bibliography, pp. 465-550.
A comprehensive general work on foreign language pedagogy.

477.____. "The Lesson to Be Drawn from Bilingualism." *Applied Linguistics and the Teaching of French*. Montreal, Canada: Centre Educatif et Culturel, 1967.
"On the one hand, we have students being taught without learning; and on the other, we have people who are learning without being taught." The author analyzes five ways in which the two groups differ with respect to language learning.

478.____. "The Measurement of Bilingual Behavior." *The Canadian Psychologist*, Vol. VIIa, No. 2 (April 1966), pp. 72-92.
This paper is an attempt to supply a technique for the analysis and measurement of bilingual behavior.

479.____. "Method Analysis: A Survey of Its Development, Principles, and Techniques." In Charles W. Kreidler, ed., "Report of the Sixteenth Annual Round Table Meeting on Linguistics and Language Studies," Georgetown University *Monograph Series on Languages and Linguistics*, No. 18 (1965), pp. 149-162. 10 references.

Gives a general idea of what has been done in the field of method analysis with specific reference to the field of language didactics.

*480.____. "Toward a Redefinition of Bilingualism." *Journal of the Canadian Linugistic Association*, Vol. II, No. 1 (March 1956), pp. 4-11.
An incorporation and elaboration of his article on "Bilingualism and Education," (1952), with an expansion of definitions.

481.____. "The Typology, Classification and Analysis of Language Tests." *Language Learning*, Special issue No. 3, (August 1968), pp. 163-166.
Discusses the above topics as they relate to the work of the International Center for Research on Bilingualism. See especially p. 166, where the Center's Thesaurus of Bilingualism project is briefly described.

482.____, and James A. Noonan. "An Experiment in Bilingual Education." *English Language Teaching*, Vol. VI, No. 4 (Summer 1952), pp. 125-132.
Describes a successful experiment in teaching Polish children aged 6-15 an academic subject in English after only 15-35 hours of instruction in English.

483.____, and Jean-Guy Savard. "The Indices of Coverage: A New Dimension in Lexicometrics." *IRAL (International Review of Applied Linguistics in Language Teaching)*, Vols. II-III (1967), pp. 71-121. 15 references.
Using dictionaries and other materials, the authors attempt to obtain a measure for the capacity of definition, inclusion, extension, and combination of 3,626 French words.

484. Mackun, Stanley. "The Changing Patterns of Polish Settlements in the Greater Detroit Area: Geographic Study of the Assimilation of an Ethnic Group." Unpublished Ph.D. dissertation, University of Michigan, 1964. (*Dissertation Abstracts*, Vol. XXV, No. 4 (1964), pp. 4644.)

485. MacMillan, Robert W. *A Study of the Effect of Socioeconomic Factors on the School Achievement of Spanish-Speaking School Beginners*. Ph.D. dissertation. Supplement No. 1 to Thomas D. Horn's *A Study of the Effects of Intensive Oral-Aural English Language Instruction, Oral-Aural Spanish Language Instruction and Non-Oral-Aural Instruction on Reading Readiness in Grade One*. Cooperative Research Project No. 2648. Austin, Texas: The University of Texas, 1966. 259 pp. Bibliography, pp. 251-258.

*486. Macnamara, John. *Bilingualism and Primary Education: A Study of Irish Experience*. Chicago, Illinois: Aldine Publishing Company; Edinburgh, United Kingdom: Edinburgh University Press, 1966. 173 pp. Bibliography, pp. 151-161. Reviewed by Joshua A. Fishman in *The Irish Journal of Education*, Vol. I, No. 1 (Summer 1967), pp. 79-83.
An up-to-date study of bilingualism in the elementary grades, based on scientific research and extensive surveys.

487.____. "The Bilingual's Linguistic Performance–A Psychological Overview." *The Journal of Social Issues*, Vol. XXIII, No. 2 (April 1967), pp. 58-77.
Mainly six topics are discussed: the measurement of bilingualism, the distinction between coordinate and compound bilinguals, linguistic interference, language switching, and translation. Suggestions for future research.

488.____. "The Effects of Instruction in a Weaker Language." *The Journal of Social Issues*, Vol. XXIII, No. 2 (April 1967), pp. 121-135. 17 references.
A discussion of the attainment of bilingual students in general subjects taught through their second language.

489.____. "How Can One Measure the Extent of a Person's Bilingual Proficiency?" *Preprints*, International Seminar on the Description and Measurement of Bilingualism. Ottawa, Canada: Canadian National Commission for UNESCO, 1967.

490.____, ed. "Problems of Bilingualism." See *The Journal of Social Issues*.

491.____. "Successes and Failures in the Movement for the Restoration of Irish." Unpublished paper presented at the Conference on Comparative Studies of Language Planning, Honolulu, Hawaii, 1969. 29 pp. 61 bibliographical notes.

492.____. "The Use of Irish in Teaching Children from English-Speaking Homes: A Survey of Irish National Schools." Unpublished Ph.D. dissertation, University of Edinburgh, 1963.

493.____, Marcel Krauthammer, and Marianne Bolgar. "Language Switching in Bilinguals as a Function of Stimulus and Response Uncertainty." *Journal of Experimental Psychology*, Vol. LXXVIII, No. 2, Part 1 (October 1968), pp. 208-215. 19 references.
Studied number-naming by French-English bilingual college students, and found that language switching in the bilinguals's speech production takes an observable amount of time.

494. Macrae, L. "The Problem of Bilingualism in Ceylon." *The Year Book of Education*, 1939, pp. 457-468.

495. Madaj, M. J. "Poles in the U.S." *New Catholic Encyclopedia*, 1967.

496. Madsen, William. *Mexican-Americans of South Texas*. Case Studies in Cultural Anthropology. New York: Holt, Reinhart and Winston, October 1965. 112 pp. 12 references.
Gives details on the aspects of behavior and beliefs that make the Mexican American way of life distinctive and then describes the resulting culture conflict.

497. Magnan, D. M. A. *Histoire de la race française aux Etats-Unis*. Paris: C. Amat, 1912. 356 pp.
"History of the French 'race' in the United States."

498. Makaroff, Julian. "America's Other Racial Minority: Japanese-Americans." *Contemporary Review*, Vol. CCX, No. 1217 (June 1967), pp. 310-314.

499. Malan, Gladys. "Realism in Bilingual Teaching." *Transvaal Education News*, Vol. XL (1944), pp. 13-14.

*500. Malherbe, Ernst Gedeon. *The Bilingual School: A Study of Bilingualism in South Africa*. Second edition. With an introduction by T. J. Haarhoff. London and New York: Longmans, Green, and Company, 1946. First edition: Johannesburg, South Africa: The Bilingual School Association, 1943. 127 pp.

An important work on bilingual schooling. Although confined to Afrikaans-English bilingual programs in South Africa, it has far-reaching implications and conclusions.

501.____. Inaugural Address, International Seminar on Bilingualism in Education, Aberystwyth, Wales, 20 August - 2 September 1960, published by the United Kingdom, National commission for UNESCO, in *Bilingualism in Education,* London: Her Majesty's Stationery Office, 1960, pp. 3-20.

Authoritative guidelines for bilingual schooling by an international expert in the field.

502.____. *The New Education in a Changing Empire.* Address delivered before the British Commonwealth Education Conference, London, July 1931. Pretoria, South Africa: J. L. Van Schaik, Ltd., 1933. 14 pp.

Deals with Afrikaans-English bilingual education in South Africa.

503. Manning, Clarence A. *A History of Slavic Studies in the United States.* Milwaukee, Wisconsin: The Marquette University Press, 1957. 69-item bibliography.

Slavic language studies in the U.S. in the 19th and 20th centuries.

504. "Manpower: Emigration from Greece in 1961-62." *International Labour Review,* Vol. LXXXVI, No. 5 (November 1962), pp. 488-491 and Vol. LXXXVIII, No. 5 (November 1963), pp. 518-521.

Reports on the number of temporary and permanent emigrants from Greece. High emigration rates have been a cause of national concern.

505. Manuel, Herschel T. *Development of Inter-American Test Materials.* Austin, Texas: The University of Texas, 1966. 109 pp.

Two new tests were developed in parallel English and Spanish editions: the preschool test of general ability, and Level 1 test of reading Spanish; the editions of earlier tests were revised.

506.____. "Recruiting the Training Teachers for Spanish-Speaking Children in the Southwest." *School and Society,* Vol. XCVI, No. 2036 (March 30, 1968), pp. 211-214.

*507.____. *Spanish-Speaking Children in the Southwest: Their Education and the Public Welfare.* Austin, Texas: The University of Texas Press, 1965. 222 pp. References, pp. 209-215.

An authoritative study of the many educational problems of the Mexican Americans.

508.____. *Tests of General Ability and Reading. Inter-American Series.* Austin, Texas: The University of Texas, 1963. 636 pp. Spanish and English editions.

Conclusions indicated that the new series of Inter-American tests of general ability and reading were successfully developed.

509. Marckwardt, Albert H., ed. *Language and Language Learning.* Papers relating to the Anglo-American Seminar on the Teaching of English at Dartmouth College, New Hampshire, 1966, Champaign, Illinois: National Council of Teachers of English, 1968. 74 pp.

See especially Joshua A. Fishman's "The Breadth and Depth of English in the United States," pp. 43-53.

510. Marden, Charles F. *Minorities in American Society*. New York: American Book Company, 1952. 494 pp.

The focus is primarily on the relations between minority and majority groups: native-foreigner, white-colored, ward-wardship, Jewish-gentile, etc.

511. Margolis, Richard J. *The Losers: A Report on Puerto Ricans and the Public Schools*. New York: Aspira, Inc., May 1968. 17 pp.

This report identifies many of their unique educational problems ranging from language deficiencies and cultural differences to the virtual absence of Puerto Rican professionals from the school system.

512. Mariano, John Horace. *The Second Generation of Italians in New York City*. Boston, Massachusetts: The Christopher Publishing House, 1921. 317 pp. Bibliography, pp. 311-317.

513. Maurer, C. L. "Early Lutheran Education in Pennsylvania." *Proceedings of the Pennsylvania German Society*, Vol. XL (1932), p. 200.

514. Mayer, Kurt. "Cultural Pluralism and Linguistic Equilibrium in Switzerland." *American Sociological Review*, Vol. XVI, No. 2 (April 1951), pp. 157-163.

A comprehensive study of cultural pluralism and its implications in multilingual (French-German-Italian-Romansch) Switzerland. Detailed statistical data as well as a language chart are provided.

515. McCanne, Roy."A Study of Approaches to First-Grade English Reading Instruction for Children from Spanish-Speaking Homes." Denver, Colorado: Colorado State Department of Education, 1966. 270 pp.

Comparisons made among three approaches to developing English arts skills, particularly in basal, second language, and language-experimental reading.

516. McCarthy, Dorothea. "LanguageDevelopment in Children." In Leonard Carmichael, ed., *Manual of Child Psychology*. New York: John Wiley and Sons, Inc.; London: Chapman & Hall, Limited, 1946, pp. 476-581. Bibliography, pp. 568-587.

A review emphasizing the ontogenetic development of spoken language in normal children. The author attempts "to show the setting of this aspect of language development in the broader relationships which are involved, and to show something of the relationships of normal speech development to the acquisition of the secondary forms of language development in reading and writing." (p. 476.)

517. McConkey, W. G. "An Experiment in Bilingual Education." *Journal for Social Research, Pretoria*, Vol. II (1951), pp. 28-42.

A 1949 study inquiring into the time allocated to second language instruction (either English or Afrikaans) in the Natal schools and into the measure of success which had attended the giving of lessons on other subjects through the medium of the pupil's second language.

518. McDermott, John Francis. ed. *The French in the Mississippi Valley*. Urbana, Illinois: University of Illinois Press, 1965. 247 pp. Bibliographical footnotes.

519.——. *A Glossary of Mississippi Valley French, 1673-1850*. Washington University Studies, New Series, Language and Literature, No. 12. St. Louis, Missouri: Washington University,

December 1941. 161 pp. Bibliography, pp. 149-161.

520. McDowell, Neil A. *A Study of the Academic Capabilities and Achievements of Three Ethnic Groups: Anglo, Negro, and Spanish-Surname in San Antonio, Texas*. Ph.D. dissertation. Supplement No. 2 to Thomas D. Horn's *A Study of the Effects of Intensive Oral-Aural English Language Instruction, Oral-Aural Spanish Language Instruction, and Non-Oral-Aural Instruction on Reading Readiness in Grade One.* Cooperative Research Project No. 2648. Austin, Texas: The University of Texas, 1966. 175 pp. Bibliography, pp. 169-173.

521. McKenney, J. Wilson. "The Dilemma of the Spanish Surname People of California." *California Teachers Association Journal*, Vol. LXI (March 1965), pp. 17, 38, 40.

522. McWilliams, Carey. *North From Mexico: The Spanish-Speaking Peoples of the United States*. The Peoples of America Series. Philadelphia, Pennsylvania: J. B. Lippincott Co., 1949. 324 pp. Bibliographical notes, pp. 307-313.

One of the best all-round statements of the problems of the acculturation of the Spanish-speaking peoples of the Southwest, with broad perspectives including historical background and social origins.

523.___. *Prejudice: Japanese-Americans, Symbol of Racial Intolerance*. Boston: Little Brown and Company, 1945. 337 pp.

A comprehensive study of our treatment of the Japanese before and during World War II.

524. Melaragno, Ralph J., and Gerald Newmark. "Final Report: A Pilot Study to Apply Evaluation-Revision Procedures in First-Grade Mexican-American Classrooms." Santa Monica, California: System Development Corporation, May 17, 1968.

525. Menarini, Alberto. "L'italo-americano degli Stati Uniti." *Lingua Nostra*, Vol. I, Nos. 5-6 (October-December 1939), pp. 152-160.

A thorough technical study of the dialects spoken by Italian immigrants in the U.S.

526.___. "Sull'italo-americano degli Stati Uniti." In his *Ai margini della lingua* (Biblioteca de Lingua Nostra, Vol. VIII), Florence, Italy: Sansoni Editore, 1947, pp. 145-208. Reviewed by Robert A. Hall, Jr., in *Language*, Vol. XXIV, No. 2 (April-June 1948), pp. 239-241.

Deals with the transformation which Italian has undergone in this country, particularly in respect to vocabulary, and the influence of Italo-American speech on Italian dialects.

527. Meriam, Lewis, et al. *Problem of Indian Administration*. Baltimore, Maryland: John Hopkins Press, 1928.

Since its publication, this work, which covers many areas of concern with respect to Indian affairs in existence at that time, was the instigator of many new programs and policies effecting Indian economics, schooling, etc., down to the present day.

528. Messinger, Milton A. "The Forgotten Child: A Bibliography, with Special Emphasis on Materials Relating to the Education of Spanish-Speaking People in the United States." The University of Texas, Department of History and Philosophy of Education, Austin, Texas, July 15, 1967.

*529. Mexican-American Study Project. Los Angeles, California: University of California, Graduate School of Business Administration, 1967. Includes:
1. *Education and Income of Mexican-Americans of the Southwest.*
2. *Mexican Immigration to the United States.*
3. *Bibliography.*
4. *Residential Sergregation in the Urban Southwest.*
5. *The Burden of Poverty.*

530. Meyerstein, Ruth G. "Selected Problems of Bilingualism Among Immigrant Slovaks." Unpublished Ph.D. dissertation, University of Michigan, 1959. 208 pp. (*Dissertation Abstracts*, Vol. XX (1959), p. 1774.)
Applies principles of modern linguistic science and bilingualism to the description of some speech features characteristic of Slovak immigrants in the U.S.

531. Meynen, Emil. *Bibliography on German Settlements in Colonial North America, Especially on the Pennsylvania Germans and Their Descendants, 1683-1933*. Leipzig: O. Harrassowitz, 1937. 636 pp.

532. Miljan, Toivo. *Bilingualism in Finland*. Comparative Studies. Data Book on Finland. Vol. I, by Toivo Miljan, including a statistical chapter by John G. Gordon. Prepared under the general supervision of Prof. Kenneth D. McRae, with the research assistance of John G. Gordon, and the editorial assistance of Miss Judy M. C. Dibben. A background study prepared for the Canadian Royal Commission on Bilingualism and Biculturalism.

533. Miller, George A., and Frank Smith, eds. *The Genesis of Language: A Psycholinguistic Approach*. Proceedings of a conference on "Language Development in Children," sponsored by the National Institute of Child Health and Human Development, National Institute of Health. Cambridge, Massachusetts, and London, England: The M.I.T. Press, 1966. 400 pp. References at end of each chapter.
A penetrating analysis of the mystery of language development in children.

534. Miller, Robert L. *The Linguistic Relativity Principle and Humboldtian Ethnolinguistics: A History and Appraisal*. The Hague, Paris: Mouton & Co., 1968. 127 pp. Bibliography, pp. 120-127.

535. Mills, C., Clarence Senior, and Rose Kohn Senior. *The Puerto-Rican Journey*. New York: Harper & Bros., 1950. 238 pp.
A report on the Puerto Rican migration to New York and of the migrants' colonies in Spanish Harlem, with resulting problems of acculturation.

536. Mitchell, A. J. "The Effect of Bilingualism in the Measurement of Intelligence." *The Elementary School Journal*, Vol. XXXVIII, No. 1 (September 1937), pp. 29-37.
Concludes that Spanish-speaking children suffer from an inferiority in ability to think accurately in the adopted language.

537. "Modern-Day Vikings in New Jersey." *Christian Science Monitor* (Magazine section), February 4, 1950, pp. 8-9.
Description of the picturesque town of Telemark, New Jersey.

538. Modern Language Association of America. "Childhood and Second Language Learning." FL [Foreign Language] *Bullettin*, No. 49 (August 1956).

*539. *The Modern Language Journal*, Vol. XLIX, Nos. 3 and 4 (March and April 1965). "Bilingualism and the Bilingual Child: A Symposium." Contents:
Foreword by Robert F. Roeming.
Fishman, Joshua A. "The Status and Prospects of Bilingualism in the United States," pp. 143-155.
Andersson, Theodore. "A New Focus on the Bilingual Child," pp. 156-160.
Christian, Chester. "The Acculturation of the Bilingual Child," pp. 160-165.
Gaarder, Bruce A. "Teaching the Bilingual Child: Research, Development and Policy," pp. 165-175.

Hakes, David T. "Psychological Aspects of Bilingualism," pp. 220-226.
Fishman, Joshua A. "Bilingualism, Intelligence, and Language Learning," pp. 227-237.
Rojas, Pauline M. "Instructional Materials and Aids to Facilitate Teaching the Bilingual Child," pp. 237-239.

*540. Modiano, Nancy. "National or Mother Tongue in Beginning Reading: A Comparative Study." *Research in the Teaching of English*, Vol. II, No. 1 (April 1968), pp. 32-43. Bibliographical footnotes.
Report of an experiment conducted among several Indian tribes in the Highlands of Mexico.

541. Moreland, Lilian. *A Select Bibliography on Bilingualism.* Capetown, South Africa: University of Capetown, December 1948. 37 pp. 161 items, partially annotated.
A fine, but old, resource, with the countries of Belgium, Canada, Finland, Ireland, South Africa, Switzerland, and Wales emphasized.

542. Morrison, John R. "Bilingualism: Some Psychological Aspects." *The Advancement of Science*, Vol. XIV, No. 56 (March 1958), pp. 287-290.
Concerned with evaluation and research. Reviews types of useful tests, examples of good evaluation and research, and stresses the need for much more of both.

543. Mousset, Paul. "Un îlot de vieille France en Nouvelle-Angleterre: 1,200,000 franco-américains, parfaits citoyens des U.S.A., conservent pieusement la langue et la foi de leurs pères." *France-Illustration*, Vol. IX, No. 384 (February 21, 1953), pp. 249-252.
An optimistic appraisal of Franco-American ethnicity.

544. ____. "La Louisiane, qui fête son cent-cinquantenaire, compte 700,000 habitants de langue francaise." *France-Illustration*, Vol. IX, No. 382 (February 7, 1953), pp. 186-189.
A Parisian magazine publishes an article, with illustrations, in order for the French living in France to remember their "language brothers" in Louisiana.

545. Mueller, Hugo J., ed. See Georgetown University *Monograph Series on Languages and Linguistics*, No. 7 (September 1954).

546. Mulder, Arnold. *Americans from Holland.* The Peoples of America series, edited by Louis Adamic. Philadelphia, Pennsylvania, and New York: J. B. Lippincott Company, 1947. 320 pp. Bibliography, pp. 309-313.
Detailed account of Dutch-American life in the United States. See Chapter XXIV, "A Bilingual Culture."

547. Muller, Seigfried H. *The World's Living Languages: Basic Facts of Their Structure, Kinship, Location, and Number of Speakers*. New York: Frederick Ungar Publishing Co., 1964. 21 pp. Bibliography, pp. 191-194.

A useful book for quick reference, although many of the figures cited are only rough estimates.

548. Munch, Peter A. "Segregation and Assimilation of Norwegian Settlements in Wisconsin." *Norwegian-American Studies and Records,* Vol. XVIII (1954), pp.102-140.

A detailed sociological study of Norwegian Settlements in Dune and Vernon counties, Wisconsin. Describes primarily the interaction between Norwegian and Anglo residents of these counties. Findings are applicable to settlements in other areas.

549. ___. "Social Adjustment Among Wisconsin Norwegians." *American Sociological Review*, Vol. XIV, No. 6 (December 1949), pp. 780-787.

550. Musmanno, Michael A. *The Story of the Italians in America.* Garden City, New York: Doubleday & Company, Inc., 1965. 300 pp. Bibliography, pp. 279-285.

551. Myers, Jerome K. "Assimilation in the Political Community." *Sociology and Social Research*, Vol. XXXV, No. 3 (January-February 1951), pp. 175-182.

Studies the assimilation of the Italians in New Haven, Connecticut, in order "to determine the rate at which ethnic groups are incorporated into American society."

552. Nadeau, Gabriel. "Notes pour servir à une bibliographie franco-américaine." *Bulletin de la Société Historique Franco-Américaine,* Année 1952, pp. 64-65. Manchester, New Hampshire, 1953. Paper read before the French VIII Group of the MLA at the Annual Meeting in 1952.

Bibliographical notes on the Franco-Americans.

553. Naert, Pierre, Halldór Halldórsson, et al. "Appel d'un ensemble de professeurs des universités scandinaves en faveur de groupes ethniques et de langues menacées de disparition." *Revue de Psychologie des Peuples,* Vol. XVII (1962), pp. 350-358.

A fervent appeal made by forty-nine Scandinavian professors in favor of preserving the languages which are in danger of becoming extinct.

554. Nahirny, Vladimir C., and Joshua A. Fishman. "American Immigrant Groups: Ethnic Identification and the Problem of Generations." *Sociological Review*, Vol. XIII, No. 3 (November 1965), pp. 311-326. 35 bibliographical notes.

555. The National Advisory Committee on Mexican American Education. *The Mexican American: Quest for Equality: A Report*. Albuquerque, New Mexico: Southwestern Cooperative Laboratory, 1968.

States in brief form the educational and social priorities for this group.

556. National Conference on Social Work. *Minority Groups: Segregation and Integration*. Papers presented at the 82nd annual forum of the National Conference of Social Work. New York: Columbia University Press, 1955. 110 pp.

Discusses the relations between the migrant and the community, the citizen's role toward migrants, school desergregation and youth programs. Short section on Indians.

557. National Education Association, Department of Rural Education. *The Invisible Minority...Pero No Vencibles*. Report of the NEA-Tucson Survey on the Teaching of Spanish to the Spanish-Speaking. Joseph Stocker, editor. Washington, D. C.: National Education Association, 1966. 39 pp.

This report initially presents a brief survey of the background of the Mexican American in the five-state Southwest area and the problems he encounters, followed by details of some innovative programs for Spanish-speaking children.

558.____. *Las Voces Nuevas del Sudoeste*. Third National NEA–PR&R Conference on Civil and Human Rights in Education. Symposium: "The Spanish-Speaking Child in the Schools of the Southwest," Tucson, Arizona, October 30-31, 1966. Elinor Hart, editor. Washington, D.C.: National Education Association.

A "blueprint for action" in six areas ranging from the individual classroom to the federal government.

559. Nelson, E. Clifford, and Eugene L. Fevold. *The Lutheran Church Among Norwegian-Americans: A History of the Evangelical Lutheran Church*. Vol. I, 1825-1890; Vol. II, 1890-1959. Minneapolis, Minnesota: Augsburg Publishing House, 1960.

560. Nelson, Helge. *The Swedes and the Swedish Settlements in North America*. 2 vols. (I: *Text* and II: *Atlas*). Skrifter Utgivna av Kungl. Humanistika Vetenskapssamfundet i Lund, XXXVII. New York: Albert Bonnier, 1943. 441 and 70 pp. Bibliography, Vol. I, pp. 410-418.

A classic in the literature dealing with Swedish-Americans. This exhaustive study contains practically all the available information on American Swedes to date.

561. Nelson, Lowry. "Speaking of Tongues." *American Journal of Scoiology*, Vol. LIV, No. 3 (November 1948), pp. 202-210.

Retention rates for various foreign languages spoken in the U.S.

562. Nesiah, K. *The Mother Tongue in Education*. Colombo, Ceylon: Ola Book Company, 1950.

563. "New Ground Rules for Immigration to the U.S." *Out of Many*....Published by the American Council for Nationalities Service, Vol. I, No. 1 (March 1969), pp. 1-2.

Presents a brief, clear picture of the new immigration policies with their inherent problems and positive changes from past legislation.

564. Newman, Louis. "Jewish Education." *American Jewish Yearbook*, Vol. LXV, 1964, pp. 84-92.

Describes recent trends in American Jewish Education: summer study programs, the day-school movement, teacher-training courses, curriculum developments, etc.

565. New York City, Board of Education. *The Puerto-Rican Study 1953-1957: A Report on the Education and Adjustment of Puerto-Rican Pupils in the Public Schools of the City of New York*. New York, 1958. 265 pp. Bibliography, pp. 260-265.

A volume summarizing, evaluating, and setting further goals for the program for Puerto-Rican children in New York schools.

566. New York City Mayor's Committee on Puerto Rican Affairs. *The Puerto Rican Pupils in the Public Schools of New York City*. New York, 1951.

567. Noreen, Sister, D. C. "A Bilingual Curriculum for Spanish-Americans: A Regional Problem With Nation-Wide Implications." *Catholic School Journal*, Vol. LXVI, No. 1 (January 1966), pp. 25-26.

*568. Northeast Conference on the Teaching of Foreign Languages. *The Challenge of Bilingualism*, report of Working Committee II. In G. Reginald Bishop, Jr., ed., *Foreign Language Teaching: Challenges to the Profession:* Reports of the Working Committee, Northeast Conference on the Teaching of Foreign Languages, 1965, pp. 54-101. 9 references.

This report is essential for information concerning the rationale behind bilingual schooling. A group of recognized experts analyze bilingualism problems in the U.S. and unanimously advocates bilingual education for bilingual children, and proposes guidelines for the realization of bilingual programs.

569. Nostrand, Howard Lee. "Report on a Level-II Standard for Understanding of the Sociocultural Context." In Jerrold L. Mordaunt, ed., *Proceedings of the Pacific Northwest Conference on Foreign Languages*, Nineteenth Annual Meeting, Carroll College, April 19-20, 1968, Vol. XIX, pp. 8-18. Victoria, British Columbia, Canada: The University of Victoria, 1968.

Proposes a standard for an understanding of the people's culture and social structure after two senior-high-school years of a language or whatever length of time the student may need at a lower or a high age to reach the same proficiency.

570.___. *Understanding Complex Structures: A Language Teacher's Handbook*. Waltham, Massachusetts: Blaisdell Publishing Company, a division of Ginn and Company. In press.

571. Nova Scotia, Department of Education. *Program of Studies in the Schools of Nova Scotia: 1968-1969*. Published by authority of the Minister of Education. Halifax, Nova Scotia: Publication and Information, and Curriculum Divisions, 1968. 123 pp.

572. O'Doherty, E. F. "Bilingual School Policy." *Studies*, Vol. XLVII (Autumn 1958), pp. 259-268.

The author questions the effectiveness of bilingual schooling in Ireland.

573.___. "Bilingualism: Educational Aspects." *The Advancement of Science*, Vol. XIV, No. 56 (March 1958), pp. 282-287.

Distinguishes the "pseudo-bilingual" from the genuine bilingual.

574. Officer, James E. *Indians in School: A Study of the Development of Educational Facilities for Arizona Indians*. Tucson, Arizona: University of Arizona, Bureau of Ethnic Research, 1956.

Includes the language situation and Indian attitudes toward education. Also contains a brief history of the then current educational situation among Arizona's Indian tribes.

575. Oficina Internacional de Educación. *El bilingüismo y la educación*. Trabajos de la *Conférence Internationale sur le Bilinguisme* celebrada en Luxemburgo del 2 al 5 de abril de 1928. Translated from English by Vicente Valls Anglés. Ediciones de "La Lectura." Madrid, Spain: Espasa-Calpe, S.A., 1932. 226 pp.

576. Oftedal, Magne. "The Vowel System of a Norwegian Dialect in Wisconsin." *Language*, Vol. XXV, No. 3 (July-September 1949), pp. 261-267.

577. Ohannessian, Sirarpi. "Patterns of Teacher Preparation in the Teaching of English to Speakers of Other Languages." In Robert B. Kaplan, ed., *Selected Conference Papers of the Association of Teachers of English as a Second Language (A Section of the National Association for Foreign Student Affairs), 1966*. Los Angeles, California: The University of Southern California Press, 1966, pp. 8-14. NAFSA Studies and Papers, English Language Series, No. 12.

578.____. *Planning Conference for a Bilingual Kindergarten Program for Navajo Children: Conclusions and Recommendations, October 11-12, 1968*. Washington, D. C.: Center for Applied Linguistics, April 1969. 16 pp.

579.____. *The Study of the Problems of Teaching English to American Indians: Report and Recommendations*. Washington, D. C.: Center for Applied Linguistics, July 1967. 40 pp. 27 references.

A group of specialists in fields related to these problems assessed the learning and teaching of English in several specified areas in elementary and secondary schools sponsored by the B.I.A. and in selected public schools having American Indian students. The main problem areas dealt with administration, teachers, student performance, and instructional materials.

580.____, ed., with assistance of Carol J. Kreidler, Beryl Dwight, and Julia Sableski. *Reference Lists of Materials for English as a Second Language*. 2 vols. Washington, D. C.: Center for Applied Linguistics, 1964-1966. (See Pedtke, Dorothy for 1968 Supplement.)

A comprehensive annotated bibliography covering materials on the teaching of English as a second language produced between 1953 and 1963. Contents:
Part I: *Texts, Readers, Dictionaries, Tests,*
Part II: *Background, Materials, Methodology*.

581. Oittinen, R. H. "The Finish School System." *UNESCO Education Abstracts*, Vol. XII, No. 2 (1960), pp. 3-8.

582. Olszyk, Edmund G. *The Polish Press in America*. Milwaukee, Wisconsin: Marquette University Press, 1940. Bibliography, pp. 92-95.

583. Ornstein, Jacob. "The Development and Status of Slavic and East European Studies in America Since World War II." *American Slavic and East European Review*, Vol. XVI, No. 3 (October 1957), pp. 369-388.

584.____. "Patterns of Language Planning in the New States." *World Politics*, Vol. XVII, No. 1 (October 1964), pp. 40-49.

Discusses the acute language problems of the great number of recently independent states (especially in Africa) where a wide variety of vernaculars coexist, with none being predominant.

585.____. "Soviet Language Policy: Theory and Practice." *Slavic and East European Journal*, Vol. XVII, No. 1 (Spring 1959), pp. 1-24. 71 bibliographical footnotes.

A study of Soviet patterns of Russification after World War II, the progressively intensified teaching of the Russian language in the schools, and the high degree of bilingualism attained by minority groups in multilingual Soviet Union.

586. Osborn, Lynn R. "A Bibliography of North American Indian Speech and Spoken Language." Lawrence, Kansas: The University of Kansas, Communication Research Center, 1968. Mimeographed. 55 pp.

This very comprehensive bilbiography draws together citations to relevant materials concerning the spoken language of the North American Indian. It includes 132 theses and dissertations and 500 articles, books, and published reports from both domestic and foreign sources.

*587. Osgood, Charles E., and Susan M. Ervin. "Second Language Learning and Bilingualism." Supplement to *The Journal of Abnormal and Social Psychology*, Vol. XL, No. 4, Part 2 (October 1954), pp. 139-146. (Psycholinguistics: A Survey of Theory and Research Problems; Report of the 1953 Summer Seminar Sponsored by the Committee on Linguistics and Psychology of the Social Science Research Council, edited by Charles E. Osgood and Thomas A. Sebeok. Baltimore, Maryland: Waverly Press, Inc., 1954.)

Technical treatment of the psychological aspects of the acquisition and utilization of two linguistic codes. Distinction made between *compound* and *coordinate* language systems.

588. O'Shea, A. B. "How Egypt Solves Its Language Problems." *Studies*, Vol. XXXVIII, No. 151 (September 1949), pp. 318-324.

A clear picture of the multilingualism that existed in Egypt when foreign influence in the country was still strong.

589. Osterberg, Tore. *Bilingualism and the First School Language: An Educational Problem Illustrated by Results from a Swedish Dialect Area*. Umea, Sweden: Västerbottens Tryckeri AB, 1961. 158 pp. Bibliography, pp. 139-151.

A report of research findings which focuses on the connection between bilingualism and language progress, motor functions, personal and social adaptation, school performance, teaching method, etc., as they relate to the Pitea dialect area in Sweden.

590. Ott, Elizabeth H. "Organizing Content for the Bilingual Child." In Carol J. Kreidler, ed., *On Teaching English to Speakers of Other Languages*, Series II, Champaign, Illinois: National Council of Teachers of English, 1966, pp. 55-59.

Description of a curriculum designed to meet the particular needs of the non-English-speaking child.

591. ____ . *A Study of Levels of Fluency and Proficiency in Oral English of Spanish-speaking School Beginners.* Ph.D dissertation. Oral English Language Proficiency Test II, The San Antonio, Texas, Language Research Project, Thomas D. Horn, Director, Austin, Texas: The University of Texas, 1967. 149 pp.

592. Overbeke, Maurits van. "La description phonétique et phonologique d'une situation bilingue." *La Linguistique*, No. 2 (1968), pp. 93-109.

A phonetic and phonological description of bilingualism, with emphasis on French-Flemish bilingualism in Belgium.

593. *PACE Report*. 201 Taylor Education Building, College of Education, University of Kentucky, Lexington, Kentucky 40506.

A new periodical publication, started in January 1968, whose prime purpose is to provide Title III project directors with a continuing source of news and information on educational innovation.

594. Padilla, Elena. *Up from Puerto Rico*. Morningside Heights, New York: Columbia University Press, 1958. 317 pp.
A documentary story written for the general reader providing a detailed description of the ways of life and changing culture of Puerto Ricans in a New York City slum.

595. Palisi, Bartolomeo J. "Ethnic Patterns of Freindship." *Phylon*, Vol. XXVII, No. 3 (Fall 1966), pp. 217-225.
Concludes that second-generation people are likely to have more intimate friends than first-generation persons.

596.____. "Patterns of Social Participation in a Two-Generation Sample of Italian-American." *Sociological Quarterly*, Vol. VII, No. 2 (Spring 1966), pp. 167-178.

597. Pap, Leo. *Portuguese-American Speech: An Outline of Speech Conditions Among Portuguese Immigrants in New England and Elsewhere in the United States*. New York: King's Crown Press, 1949. 223 pp. Bibliography, pp. 193-199.
Provides an outline of Portuguese language history, economic conditions, culture, and social traits in America.

598. Parenton, Vernon J. "Notes on the Social Organization of a French Village in South Louisiana." *Social Forces*, Vol. XVII, No. 1 (October 1938), pp. 73-82.
Describes the essential social characteristics of the French-speaking people along Bayou Lafourche.

599.____. "Socio-Psychological Integration in a Rural French-Speaking Section of Louisiana." *Southwestern Social Science Quarterly*, Vol. XXX, No. 3 (December 1949), pp. 188-195.
A description of the social adaptation of the Acadians of Bayou Lafourche.

600. Parker, William Riley. *The National Interest and Foreign Languages*. Third edition. Department of State publication No. 7326. International Organization and Conference Series, No. 26. Washington, D. C.: U.S. Government Printing Office, September 1961, released March 1962. 159 pp. References at end of each chapter.
Discusses whether or not the national interest would be served by increased study of modern foreign languages in the United States including how much and what sort of language study would best serve the country and the individual citizen.

601. Passow, A. Henry, Miriam Goldberg, and Abraham J. Tannenbaum, eds. *Education of the Disadvantaged: A Book of Readings*. New York: Holt, Rinehart and Winston, Inc., 1967. 503 pp. Bibliographies.
A group of 31 articles on the education of disadvantaged children in the United States. Emphasis is put on the Negroes, but Indians and immigrants are also treated.

602. Paulston, Christina Bratt. "Las escuelas bilingües: The Peruvian Experience." Paper read at the National TESOL Convention, Chicago, Illinois, March 7, 1969. 13 pp. 13 references.
A brief description of the public bilingual schools in Peru, the role of the Summer Institute of Linguistics, as well as an overall picture of education in Peru.

603. Pavlovitch, Milivoïe. *Le langage enfantin: acquisition du serbe et du français par un enfant serbe*. Paris: Librairie Ancienne Honoré Champion, Editeur, 1920. 203 pp. Bibliography, pp. 181-189.

A study of the development of language in a bilingual (French-Serbian) child. As a conclusion, a whole theory of child language is presented.

*604. Peal, Elizabeth, and Wallace E. Lambert. "The Relation of Bilingualism to Intelligence." *Psychological Monographs: General and Applied*, Vol. LXXVI, No. 27, Whole No. 546 (1962), pp. 1-23 References, pp. 22-23.

A study of the effect of bilingualism on intellectual functioning. This famous paper marks a new period in bilingual research.

605. Peate, Iorwerth C. "The Welsh Language as a Medium of Instruction in the University of Wales." *Lochlann, A Review of Celtic Studies*, Vol. I (1958), pp. 261-262.

Reports eight recommendations to inquire into the advisability of establishing as one of the constituent Colleges of the University of Wales a College in which the medium of instruction would be the Welsh language.

606. Pedtke, Dorothy, ed. *Reference List of Materials for English as a Second Language: Supplement*. Washington, D. C.: Center for Applied Linguistics, 1968. (See Ohannessian, Sirarpi, ed., with the assistance of Carol J. Kreidler, Beryl Dwight, and Julia Sableski for original.)

607. Pellegrini, Angelo M. *Americans By Choice*. New York: The Macmillan Company, 1956. 240 pp.

The history of a group of Italian immigrants presented as a novel.

608. Peña, Albar A. "A Comparative Study of Selected Syntactical Structures of the Oral Language Status in Spanish and English of Disadvantaged First Grade Spanish-Speaking Children." Austin, Texas: The University of Texas, 1967.

609. Penfield, Wilder G. "A Consideration of the Neurophysiological Mechanisms of Speech and Some Educational Consequences." *Proceedings of the American Academy of Arts and Sciences*, Vol. LXXXII, No. 5 (May 1953).

610.____ . "The Uncommitted Cortex: The Child's Changing Brain." *The Atlantic Monthly*, Vol. CCXIV, No. 1 (July 1964).

*611.____ , and Lamar Roberts. *Speech and Brain-Mechanisms*. Princeton, New Jersey: Princeton University Press, 1959.

612. Perren, G. E. "Bilingualism, or Replacement? English in West Africa." *English Language Teaching*, Vol. XIII, No. 1 (October-December 1958), pp. 18-22.

Suggests that in Kenya, where English is an official language and there is no common vernacular, bilingualism is "a necessity which cannot be avoided," and its advantages should be extended.

613. Phillips. T. A. "Laboratory Experiences for Cuban Refugees." *Teachers College Journal*. (Terre Haute: Indiana State University), January 1965.

614. Pieris, Ralph. "Bilingualism and Cultural Marginality." *British Journal of Sociology*, Vol. II, No. 4 (December 1951), pp. 328-339. Bibliographical footnotes.
Valuable thoughts on languages and bilingualism as related to culture, with examples taken mainly throughout the British Commonwealth.

615. Pierson, Oris Emerald. *Norwegian Settlements in Bosque County, Texas.* Unpublished Master's Thesis, The University of Texas, June 1947.

616. Pietrzyk, Alfred, et al. *Selected Titles in Sociolinguistics: An Interim Bibliography of Works on Multilingualism Language Standardization, and Languages of Wider Communication.* Washington, D.C.: Center for Applied Linguistics, 1967. 226 pp.
The primary emphasis is on language in its relation to sociological phenomena. There is a listing of bibliography relevant to the field and general reference works are included.

617. Pike, Kenneth L. "Toward a Theory of Change and Bilingualism." *Studies in Linguistics*, Vol. XV, Nos. 1-2 (Summer 1960), pp. 1-7. Bibliographical notes.
Discusses setting up a frame of reference to discuss the relationships between change of system in general and the status of the languages of the bilingual or the dialects or styles of the monolingual.

618. Pines, Maya. *Revolution in Learning: The Years from Birth to Six.* New York: Harper & Row, Publishers, 1967. 244 pp. Bibliography, pp. 232-237.
Deals with how a child learns with special emphasis on language development.

619. Pintner, Rudolf. "The Influence of Language Background on Intelligence Tests." *Journal of Social Psychology*, Vol. III (1932), pp. 235-240. 3 references.
Suggests that a bilingual environment may prevent some individuals from ever really indicating their maximum intelligence on a verbal group intelligence test.

620. ——, and Seth Arsenian. "The Relation of Bilingualism to Verbal Intelligence and School Adjustment." *The Journal of Educational Research*, Vol. XXXI, No. 4 (December 1937), pp. 255-263. 11 references.
Discusses the bilingual (Yiddish/English) children of New York.

621. Pisani, Lawrence Frank. *The Italian in America: A Social Study and History.* An Exposition University Book. New York: Exposition Press, 1957. 293 pp. Includes bibliographies.
Attempts to show the part played by Italian immigrants in American history.

622. *Planning for Non-English Speaking Pupils.* Miami: Dade County Public Schools, 1963. 34 pp.
Presents the necessary guidelines for the development of an adequate bilingual program, including a summary of the guiding principles underlying the program, the details of the administration, and techniques used in teaching.

623. Pochmann, H., comp., and A. Schultz, ed. *Bibliography of German Culture in America to 1940.* Madison, Wisconsin: University of Wisconsin Press, 1953. 483 pp.
A very useful bibliography on German Americans, whose index lists 170 entries under the single heading "German American Schools."

624. Poirier, Pascal. *Le parler franco-acadien et ses origines.* Quebec, Canada: Imprimerie Franciscaine Missionnaire, 1928. 339 pp.
Origins, description, and evolution of the French-Acadian dialect.

625. Politzer, Robert L. "Problems in Applying Foreign Language Teaching Methods to the Teaching of Standard English as a Second Dialect." Stanford Center for Research and Development in Teaching, Research and Development, Memorandum No. 40. Stanford, California: Stanford University, December 1968. 21 pp. Bibliography, pp. 19-21.
A series of insights into the second dialect teaching situation with special emphasis on the differences between this and foreign language teaching with specific reference to the role of the native dialect, the definition of the standard, special factor affecting the pupil, teaching methodology, and teacher training.

626. Post, P. "Over de Woordenschat van Zesjarige kindered in tweetalig Friesland." Groningen.
A study in Dutch-Frisian bilingualism, summarized in *UNESCO Education Abstracts*, Vol. X, April-May 1958.

627. Potts, Alfred M., II. *Knowing and Educating the Disadvantaged – An Annotated Bibliography*. Alamosa, Colorado: Adams State College, The Center for Cultural Studies, 1965. 462 pp.
An inclusive bibliography describing the agricultural migrant and his family in many accounts of their factual circumstances and programs designed to benefit them.

628. Pousland, Edward. *Etude sémantique de l'anglicisme dans le parler franco-américain de Salem (Nouvelle-Angleterre).* Société de Publications Romanes et Françaises, Vol. XII, Paris: Librairie E. Droz, 1933. 309 pp. Bibliography, pp. 287-295.
Semantic study of Anglicisms in the Franco-American Dialect of Salem, Massachusetts.

629. Powers, Francis, and Marjorie Hetzler. *Successful Methods of Teaching English to Bilingual Children in Seattle Public Schools.* Project in Research in Universities. Pamphlet No. 76. Washington, D.C.: U.S. Government Printing Office, 1937. 17 pp. "A Review of Studies on Bilingualism," pp. 9-16.

630. Prator, Clifford H., Jr. *Language Teaching in the Philippines: A Report.* Manila, Philippines: U.S. Educational Foundation in the Philippines, 1956. 96 pp.
The author covers the language situation in the islands and the possibilities of improving the teaching of English, including the Iloilo experiment in the use of the vernacular for the first stages of elementary instruction.

631. Prezzolini, Giuseppe. *Tutta l'America.* Florence, Italy: Vallecchi Editore, 1958. 836 pp.
America as seen by an Italian-American.

632. Prior, G. "The French Canadians in New England." Unpublished master's thesis, Brown University, 1932.

633. Pryor, Guy C. "Evaluation of the Bilingual Project of Harlandale Independent School District, San Antonio, Texas, in the First Grade of Four Elementary Schools During 1966-1967 School Year." For Harlandale Independent School District. San Antonio,

Texas: Our Lady of the Lake College, June 1967. 70 pp. Mimeographed.

The purpose of this experiment was to provide competent instruction in both Spanish and English by a bilingual teacher and to compare the learning, behavior, personal adjustment of pupils and attitude of parents with these same aspects of growth and learning. The result was that in the bilingual sections of all four schools pupils could speak, read, and write two languages at the end of the *first grade*.

634. Radin, Paul. *The Italians of San Francisco: Their Adjustment and Acculturation*. n.p., 1935. Monograph No. 1. Multigraphed abstract from the SERA Project 2-F2-98 (3-F2-145): Cultural Anthropology.

635. Raffler-Engel, Walburga von. "Investigation of Italo-American Bilinguals." *Zeitschrift für Phonetik Sprachwissenschaft und Kommunikationsforschung*, Vol. XIV, No. 2 (1961), pp. 127-130.

A technical analysis of the speech patterns of Italian Americans.

636. ——. *Il prelinguaggio infantile*. Studi grammaticali e linguistici, No. 7. Brescia, Italy: Paideia, 1964.

This study of childhood language concludes that the initial stage of infant speech is purely a melodic expression.

637. Raisner, Arnold. "New Horizons for the Student of Spanish-Speaking Background." *High Points*, Vol. XLVIII, No. 2 (February 1966), pp. 19-23.

An experimental program of 18 classes devised to teach Science in Spanish to junior high school pupils in New York.

638. ——, Philip Bolger, and Carmen Sanguinetti. *Science Instruction in Spanish for Pupils of Spanish-Speaking Background: An Experiment in Bilingualism.* Final Report, Project No. 2370, Contract No. 407-9, U.S. Department of Health, Education, and Welfare, Office of Education, Bureau of Research, June 1967. 180 pp. 49 references.

An experiment in bilingual schooling to improve self-image.

639. Rapier, Jacqueline L. "Effects of Verbal Mediation Upon the Learning of Mexican-American Children." *California Journal of Educational Research*, Vol. XVIII, No. 1 (January 1967), pp. 40-48. 4 references.

These experiments support Jensen's earlier findings (1961) that the low IQ of Mexican Americans is of a different nature than the low IQ of Anglo-Americans and thus Mexican Americans require different kinds of educational treatment.

640. Raubicheck, Letitia. "Psychology of Multilingualism." *Volta Review*, Vol. XXXVI, No. 1 (January 1934), pp. 17-20, 57-58.

Some thoughts on language, culture, second-language learning, and bilingualism.

641. Read, Allen Walker. "Bilingualism in the Middle Colonies, 1725-1775." *American Speech*, Vol. XXI, No. 2 (April 1937), pp. 93-99.

In an attempt to learn about the "melting pot" in the colonial era, the author uses material drawn from newspaper advertisements for runaway slaves and indentured servants to build a picture of the linguistic conditions of the time in Pennsylvania and New York.

642. Read, William A. *Louisiana French*. Revised edition. Baton Rouge, Louisiana: Louisiana State University Press, 1963. 263 pp. Bibliography, pp. 223-245. First published in 1931.
An all-time classic in the literature on French dialects in Louisiana. Traces the history and evolution of the language in Louisiana, analyzes thoroughly the foreign elements in it (Indian, German, English, African, Spanish, and Italian words).

643. Reed, Carroll E., and L. W. Seifert. *A Linugistic Atlas of Pennsylvania German*. Marburg: Lahn, 1954.

644. Rice, Frank A., ed. *Study of the Role of Second Languages in Asia, Africa, and Latin America*. Washington, D.C.: Center for Applied Linguistics, 1962. 123 pp.
The results of a survey to investigate the nature and extent of the problem of second-language learning as a factor in national development of these countries. This document represents essentially the reaction of half a dozen specialists to some of the problems dealt with in the survey.

*645. Richardson, Mabel Wilson. "An Evaluation of Certain Aspects of the Academic Achievement of Elementary Pupils in a Bilingual Program: A Project." Coral Gables, Florida: The University of Miami, January 1968. Mimeographed. 72 pp. 43-item bibliography. Also published as a D.Ed. dissertation, The University of Miami, January 1968.
A study of the Coral Way Elementary School (Dade County, Florida) bilingual program, with a review of previous literature on the philosophy of language teaching.

646.___ , and A. Bruce Gaarder. See Gaarder and Richardson.

647. Riessman, Frank. *The Culturally Deprived Child*. New York: Harper & Row, Publishers, 1962. 140 pp. Bibliography, pp. 131-133.
Provides information concerning disadvantaged children in the United States and the problems they present.

648. Robinett, Betty Wallace, ed. *On Teaching English to Speakers of Other Languages*. Series III. Papers read at the TESOL Conference, New York City, March 17-19, 1966. Washington, D.C.: Teachers of English to Speakers of Other Languages, 1967. 189 pp.
Contains articles on the teaching of English as a second language in Eastern Europe, Japan, France; reports on special programs (language policy in the primary schools of Kenya, education of the Spanish-speaking child in Florida, ESL for Alaska natives, ESL for pupils of FL background, especially Chinese and Arabic, the training of ESL teachers).

649. Rodgers, Raymond. "Prepared Text of Remarks at the (First) French-Acadian Conference of the Louisiana Department of Education, January 20, 1968." Unpublished paper, 6 pp.
Explores the implications of the proposed Quebec-Louisiana Agreement on Cultural Cooperation. Expresses hope for the establishment of French-English bilingual programs in Louisiana.

650. Roessel, Robert A., Jr., et al. "An Overview of the Rough Rock Demonstration School." *Journal of American Indian Education*, Vol. VII, No. 2 (January 1968), pp. 1-6.

651. Rojas, Pauline M. "Instructional Materials and Aids to Facilitate Teaching a Bilingual Child." *The Modern Language Journal*, Vol. XLIX, No. 4 (April 1965), pp. 237-239.

652. ——. "The Miami Experience in Bilingual Education." In Carol J. Kreidler, ed., *On Teaching English to Speakers of Other Languages: Series II*, Champaign, Illinois: National Council of Teachers of English, 1966, pp. 43-45.

A brief description of the Dade County Public Schools' Spanish-English bilingual programs, their administrative policy, their curriculum, and the Ford Foundation Project.

653. Romanides, John S. "The Orthodox: Arrival and Dialogue." *The Christian Century*, Vol. LXXX, No. 46 (November 13, 1963), pp. 1399-1403.

Brief statement on the number of Orthodox parishes and parishioners in the United States.

654. Rona, José Pedro. "The Social and Cultural Status of Guaraní in Paraguay." Unpublished paper, given at the Sociolinguistics Conference, University of California at Los Angeles, May 1964.

655. Ronjat, Jules. *Le développement du langage observé chez un enfant bilingue.* Paris: Librairie Ancienne H. Champion, 1913. 155 pp.

A classic study of the linguistic progress of a child to whom two languages, French and German, were spoken with equal frequency. Emphasizes the facility of children to learn more than one language at the same time.

656. Rose, Arnold M., and Caroline B., eds. *Minority Problems: A Textbook of Readings in Intergroup Relations*. New York: Harper and Row, Publishers, 1965. 438 pp.

A sequence of studies analyzing the nature of minority problems in the United States as well as in other parts of the world, types of tension and discrimination, group identification and minority adjustment, and the causes of prejudice, with proposed techniques for eliminating minority problems.

657. Rosenthal, Robert, and Lenore Jacobson. *Pygmalion in the Classroom: Teacher Expectation and Pupils' Intellectual Development*. New York: Holt, Rinehart and Winston, Inc., 1968. 240 pp. Bibliography, pp. 219-229.

658. Rossi, Peter H., and Alice S. "Some Effects of Parochial School Education in America." *Daedalus*, Vol. XC, No. 2 (Spring 1961), pp. 300-328. References.

One of the very rare studies devoted exclusively to the parochial school situation in America. Historical roots are discussed, as well as doctrinal basis, organization structure, and social context.

659. Rosten, Leo. *The Joys of Yiddish*....New York: McGraw-Hill Book Company, 1968.

660. Roucek, Joseph S. "The Contributions of Japanese to the U.S." *The Study of Current English*, Vol. XIX (August 1964), pp. 6-9; Vol. XIX, No. 9 (September 1964), pp. 14-20; Vol. XIX, No. 10 (October 1964), pp. 6-13; Vol. XIX, No. 11 (November 1964), pp. 16-21.

661. ——. *Poles in the United States of America*. The Baltic Pocket Library. Gdynia, Poland: The Baltic Institute, 1937. 121-item bibliography, pp. 56-64.

Comprehensive description of the immigration, location, religion, education, and organizations of Poles in the U.S. until the 1930's.

662.——. "The Story of the American Japanese." *The Study of Current English.* Part I: Vol. XIX, No. 4 (April 1964), pp. 6-13; Part II: Vol. XIX, No. 5 (May 1964), pp. 6-11.

663. Royal Commission on Bilingualism and Biculturalism, or Royal Commission on Education. See Canada.

664. Rubel, Arthur J. *Across the Tracks, Mexican-Americans in a Texas City.* Austin and London: University of Texas Press, for the Hogg Foundation for Mental Health, 1966. 166 pp. Bibliography, pp. 247-254.

Provides an account of the social life of Mexican Americans in South Texas; considers those characteristics of their social and belief systems which impede full utilization of available professional health services; and develops an explanation for the prominence of anxiety and disaffection in Mexiquito, the Mexican American section of the town.

*665. Rubin, Joan. *National Bilingualism in Paraguay.* Janua Linguarum, series practica, No. 60. The Hague: Mouton & Co., 1968. 135 pp. Bibliography, pp. 131-135.

A sociolinguistic study of a bilingual nation which focuses on the historical background as well as on the political and cultural factors which direct and enhance Spanish-Guaraní bilingualism: attitudes, stability, usage, acquisition, and proficiency.

666. Ruiz, Ramón Eduardo. "Mexico: The Struggle for a National Language." *Social Research*, Vol. XXV, No. 3 (Autumn 1958), pp. 346-360.

Analyzes the problems caused by the language barrier which for four centuries has plagued Mexico, where roughly 15 percent of the population speaks exclusively one of the fifty or more Indian languages.

667. Rūke-Dravina, Velta. *Mehrsprachigkeit im Vorschulalter.* Travaux de l'Institut de Phonétique de Lund, No. 5. Lund, Sweden: Gleerup, 1967. 104 pp.

A study of infant and pre-school bilingualism based on a careful review of the literature in more than a hundred sources, supplemented by personal observations of the author's own bilingual (Latvian-Swedish) child. This monograph deals in particular with such questions as how long it takes a child to learn a second language, how many languages he can master, the age at which he can distinguish between two language systems, the process of acquisition, and contacts between children speaking different languages.

668. Rumilly, Robert. *Histoire des Franco-Américains.* Montreal, Canada: Publié sous les auspices de l'Union Saint-Jean-Baptiste d'Amérique, 1958. 552 pp.

Complete and up-to-date history of the Franco-Americans.

669. Saer, D. J., F. Smith and John Hughes. *The Bilingual Problem.* Aberystwyth, Wales: The University College of Wales, 1924. 112 pp.

An examination of the educational, psychological, and sociological results of bilingualism as seen in Wales.

670. Salisbury, Lee H. "Communication for Survival–the COPAN Program." Paper prepared for the Intercultural Communication Conference sponsored by the National Society for the Study of Communication at the Speech Association of America Convention, Los Angeles, California, December 30, 1967. Mimeographed. 13 pp.

On the rationale behind the College Orientation Program for Alaska Natives, with good information on culture traits and educational problems.

671.___ . "Cross Cultural Communication and Dramatic Ritual." In Lee Thayer, ed., *Communication: Concepts and Perspectives*, Washington, D. C.: Spartan-Macmillan, 1967, pp. 77-95.

Describes the cultural confrontation taking place in Alaska. A thorough and interesting analysis of problems in the classroom as they relate to cultural differences.

672.___. "The Speech Education of the Alaskan Indian Student as Viewed by the Speech Educator." *Journal of American Indian Education,* Vol. IV, No. 3 (May 1965), pp. 1-7

Suggests, among other things, that the language problem may be a "symptom" rather than the cause of scholastic failure.

673.___ . "Teaching English to Alaska Natives." *Journal of American Indian Education*, Vol. VI, No. 2 (January 1967), pp. 1-13.

Reports that Indians, Eskimos, and Aleuts make up 20 percent of the freshman class at the University of Alaska, but predicts that "over 50 percent of them are likely to drop out" before the end of the year, and "less than 2 percent" will eventually graduate. A major reason, he suspects, is their failure to develop what he calls "a conceptual knowledge of English."

674. Sallet, R. "Russlanddeutsche Siedlungen in den Vereinigten Staaten." *Jahrbuch, Deutsch-Amerikanische historische Gesellschaft*, Vol. III (1931), pp. 5-126.

675. Saloutos, Theodore. *The Greeks in the United States.* Cambridge, Massachusetts: Harvard University Press, 1964. 445 pp. Bibliography, pp. 389-400.

676.___ . *They Remember America: The Story of the Repatriated Greek-Americans.* Berkeley and Los Angeles, California: University of California Press, 1956. Annotated bibliography, pp. 143-149.

677. Samora, Julian. "The Educational Status of a Minority." *Theory Into Practice*, Vol. II, No. 3 (June 1963), pp. 144-150.

A discussion of the educational situation of the Spanish-speaking population in the Southwest.

678.___ . *La Raza: Forgotten Americans.* South Bend, Indiana: University of Notre Dame, 1966.

Contains a series of essays and articles directed toward achieving an understanding of contemporary Mexican American affairs.

679. Sánchez, George I. *Concerning Segregation of Spanish-Speaking Children in the Public Schools.* Inter-American Education Occasional Papers, No. 9. Austin, Texas: The University of Texas Press, 1951. 75 pp.

A pamphlet which sets forth in summary form the various aspects of the segregation of Spanish-speaking children: legally, educationally, and morally.

680. ——. "The Crux of the Dual Language Handicap." *New Mexico School Review*, Vol. XXXVIII, (March 1954), pp. 13-15.
Fallacies about bilingualism are analyzed. The basic handicap is lack of skill in any language.

681. ——. *Forgotten People: A Study of New Mexicans*. Albuquerque, New Mexico: C. Horn, 1967. First edition: Albuquerque, New Mexico: The University of New Mexico Press, 1940. 98 pp.
A study of New Mexico's people and their background, emphasizing three groups: the Indians, the 270,000 descendants of original Spanish settlers, and the Anglos; with special treatment of the problems of land and of education.

682. ——, and Howard Putnam. *Materials Relating to the Education of Spanish-Speaking People in the United States: An Annotated Bibliography*. Latin-American Studies, Vol. XVII. Austin, Texas: The Institute of Latin American Studies, The University of Texas, 1959. 76 pp. 882-item bibliography.
A comprehensive list of books, articles, monographs, bulletins, courses of study, bibliographies, and unpublished theses and dissertations having a bearing on the topic.

683. Saporta, Sol, ed., with the assistance of Jarvis R. Bastian. *Psycholinguistics: A Book of Readings*. New York: Holt, Rinehart and Winston, 1961. 551 pp. References.
A collection of articles on the nature and function of language, approaches to the study of language, speech perception, the sequential organization and semantic aspects of linguistic events, and the relation of linguistic processes to perception and cognition.

684. Saussure, Ferdinand de, in collaboration with Albert Reidlinger. *Cours de linguistique générale*. Edited by Charles Bally and Albert Sechehaye. Paris: Payot, 1916. 331 pp. Translated by Wade Baskin under the title *Course in General Linguistics*, New York: Philosophical Library, 1959. 240 pp.
Gives insight into various technical aspects of linguistics: principles of phonology; graphic representation of language; synchronic, diachronic, geographical, and retrospective linguistics; among others.

685. Savard, Jean-Guy. "A Proposed System for Classifying Language Tests." *Language Learning*, Special Issue No. 3 (August 1968), pp. 167-174.
Describes four stages needed in the development of an open classification system.

686. ——. "La valence lexicale." *Les Sciences de l'Education Pour l'Ere Nouvelle*, Nos. 3-4 (July-December 1968), pp. 124-134.
Factors to be taken into account in selecting second-language vocabulary.

687. Schenker, Alexander M. *Beginning Polish I and II*. Yale Linguistic Series. New Haven and London, Connecticut: Yale University Press, 1966. Reviewed in *Slavic and East European Journal*, Vol. XII, No. 2 (Summer 1968), pp. 222-227.

An intensive one-year course. Vol. I contains classroom or self-instruction text; Vol. II has drills for the lessons in Vol. I.

688. Schermerhorn, Richard A. *These Our People: Minorities in American Culture*. Boston: D.C. Heath and Company, 1949. Heath's Social Relations Series. 635 pp. Bibliographical notes, pp. 579-628.
Separate studies of Japanese, Spanish-speaking communities, Poles, Italians, Czechs and Slovaks, Hungarians, Yugoslavs, Jews, and Negroes.

689. Schiavo, Giovanni Ermenegildo. *Italian-American History*. New York: The Vigo Press, 1947-1949.
A series of fifteen books dealing with the history of the Italians in America from Columbus to present.

690. Schiff, Alvin Irwin. *The Jewish Day School in America*. New York: The Jewish Education Committee Press, January 1966. 294 pp. Bibliography, pp. 273-284.
Discusses the "growth," the "essence," the "impact," and the "challenge" of the Jewish day school in the United States.

691. Schreiber, William I. *Our Amish Neighbors*. Drawings by Sybil Gould. Chicago, Illinois: The University of Chicago Press, 1963. 227 pp. Bibliography, pp. 215-221.
Life of the Amish in America.

692. Schrieke, B. *Alien American: A Study of Race Relations*. New York: The Viking Press, 1936. 208 pp. Bibliography, pp. 197-203.
The Chinese and Japanese in California, the Mexicans, the Indians, the Filipinos, and especially the Negroes are gathered together in this unbaised account of race relations in America written by a foreigner from Java.

693. The Scottish Council for Research in Education. *Gaelic-Speaking Children in Highland Schools*. Publication No. XLVII. London: University of London Press, 1961. 95 pp.

694. Seaman, Paul David. "Modern Greek and American English in Contact: A Socio-Linguistic Investigation of Greek-American Bilingualism in Chicago." Ph.D. dissertation, Indiana University, 1965. 451 pp.
Besides the thorough linguistic analysis of the speech of Greek-Americans, a demographic analysis gives a brief history of Greek immigration to the United States, and outlines the geographical distribution of the half-million Americans of Greek descent.

695. Senior, Clarence. *The Puerto-Ricans: Strangers—Then Neighbors*. Foreword by Hubert H. Humphrey. Chicago, Illinois: Quadrangle Books, 1965. 128 pp. Bibliography, pp. 112-123.

696. Sexton, Patricia Cayo. *Spanish Harlem*. New York: Harper & Row, Publishers, 1965. 208 pp.
The woeful plight of the Puerto Ricans in New York.

697. Shedd, William B. "Italian Population of New York." *Atlantica*, September 1934.

698. Shelson, Edward S. "Some Specimens of a Canadian French Dialect Spoken in Maine." *Transactions of the Modern Language Association of America*, Vol. III (1887), pp. 210-218.

699. Shtarkman, M. "Yiddish Literature in the United States, 1942-1955." *General Jewish Encyclopedia*, Vol. Yidn V, pp. 130-144. New York: Jewish Encyclopedic Handbooks, 1957. (In Yiddish.)

700. Shuy, Roger W. "A Selective Bibliography on Social Dialects." Washington, D.C.: Center for Applied Linguistics, June 1968. 5 pp. (Published in the June 1968 issue of *The Linguistic Reporter* by CAL.)

Presents 46 annotated items to serve as a representative selection of linguistically oriented readings on the availability theory, design, research, and pedagogical applications in the area of social dialects.

701. Sibayan, Bonifacio P. "Language Planning Processes and the Language Policy Survey in the Philippines." Unpublished paper. Manila, Philippines, 1968. 73 pp. References, pp. 71-73.

Discussed the language situation and the (bilingual) educational system of the Philippines.

702. Simirenko, Alex. *Pilgrims, Colonists, and Frontiersmen: An Ethnic Community in Transition*. London: The Free Press of Glencoe, Collier-Macmillan Limited, 1964. 232 pp. Bibliography, pp. 213-224.

Examines the dynamics of social and cultural change that accompanied the formation and transformation of the Minneapolis, Minnesota, Russian community.

703. Simmons, Donald C. "Anti-Italian–American Riddles in New England." *Journal of American Folklore*, Vol. LXXIX, No. 313 (July-September 1966), pp. 475-478.

A collection of some 26 riddles illustrating the hostile attitude of some New Englanders toward Italian-Americans.

704. Singer, Harry. "Bilingualism and Elementary Education." *Modern Language Journal*, Vol. XL, No. 8 (December 1956), pp. 444-458.

Analyzes the meaning of bilingualism, the language proficiency of bilinguals, their mental development, school achievement and emotional adjustment; then advocates the teaching of foreign languages in the elementary schools.

705. Sizemore, Mamie. "Project Head Start for Indian Students: A New Focus on the Teaching of English as a Second Language." *Sharing Ideas*, Vol. V, No. 6. Phoenix, Arizona: Division of Indian Education, 1333 W. Camelback Rd., 1965. 8 pp. 14 references.

Emphasizes the need for new, exciting methods of teaching the Indian child and describes the advantages of fostering and developing the native tongue.

706. Skramstad, Marie. "Norwegian Teachers' Conference." *Scandinavian Studies*, Vol. XXXVIII, No. 3 (August 1966), pp. 276-279.

707. Smith, M. Estellie. "The Spanish-Speaking Population of Florida." In June Helm, ed., *Spanish-Speaking People in the United States. Proceedings of the 1968 Annual Spring Meeting of the American Ethnological Society*. Seattle and London: University of Washington Press, 1968, pp. 120-133. 4 references.

Focuses on the cultural characteristics of this language group.

708. Smith, T. Lynn, Homer L. Hitt. *The People of Louisiana.* Baton Rouge, Louisiana: Louisiana State University Press, 1952. 272 pp. Bibliography on Louisiana population studies, pp. 263-264.

A population study providing information and statistical data on the people of Louisiana, including the French-speaking communities.

709. ____, and Vernon J. Parenton. "Acculturation Among the Louisiana French." *American Journal of Sociology*, Vol. XLIV, No. 3 (November 1938), pp. 355-364.

Examines how and why the white elements in the "extremely heterogeneous" mass of European settlers have been absorbed in particular into the French-Acadian culture of South Louisiana.

710. Smith, William C. *Americans in the Making: The Natural History of the Assimilation of Immigrants.* New York: Appleton-Century-Crofts, 1939.

Discusses the causes of immigration, the disorganization and reorganization of the immigrant, factors in and agencies of assimilation, immigrant heritages, second generation problems, indices of degree of assimilation, etc.

711. *Société Historique Franco-Américaine, Bulletin de la.* Old and new series. Manchester, New Hampshire: Imprimerie Ballard Frères.

Yearly bulletin on Franco-American life.

712. Soffietti, James P. "Bilingualism and Biculturalism." *The Journal of Educational Psychology*, Vol. XLVI, No. 4 (April 1955), pp. 222-227. 9 references.

Attempts to solve the problem of the definition of bilingualism and proposes that the research worker be able to distinguish between four basic culture-language types.

713. Solnit, Albert J. *Bilingual Education and Community Development.* Lima, Peru: Summer Institute of Linguistics and Ministry of Public Education, 1968.

714. Soriano, Jesse M., and James McClafferty. "Spanish-Speakers of the Midwest: They Are American Too." *Foreign Language Annals*, Vol. II, No. 3 (March 1969), pp. 316-324.

A study of the educational problems of the Spanish-speaker of the Midwest, which are different from those of his Southwest counterpart. A description of the Title III, ESEA, Program in developing bilingual and bidialectal instructional materials in Ann Arbor, Michigan.

*715. Southwest Council of Foreign Language Teachers. *Reports: Bilingual Education: Research and Teaching.* Edited by Chester Christian. Fourth Annual Conference, November 10-11, 1967. El Paso, Texas, 1967. 88 pp. Bibliographies.

An account of contemporary bilingual education in the United States. The first report deals with areas of needed research and a description of bilingual programs in American schools abroad; the second analyzes the problem of reading content in a foreign language; the third is an account of bilingual programs operating in the Southwest or of the need of them.

716. ____. *Reports: Bilingualism.* Edited by Charles Stubing. Third Annual Conference, November 4-5, 1966. El Paso, Texas, 1966. 62 pp. Bibliographies.

An important booklet containing useful information on the feasibility of bilingual schooling and reports on the programs, methods, and materials from the viewpoint of the administrator and counselor. Analyzes the problems of recruitment and preparation of bilingual teachers.

*717.____ . *Reports: Our Bilinguals: Social and Psychological Barriers; Linguistic and Pedagogical Barriers.* Edited by Chester Christian and Robert Lado. Second Annual Conference, November 13, 1965. El Paso, Texas, 1965.

718. Southwest Council on the Education of Spanish-Speaking People. *Proceedings. Fifth Annual Conference.* Los Angeles, California: George Pepperdine College, January 18-20, 1951. 101 pp.
Covers problem areas of Spanish-speaking groups including education, sociology, business opportunities, culture patterns, etc.

719. Southwest Educational Development Laboratory. *Bilingual Bylines.* Newsletter of the Southwest Educational Development Laboratory Language-Development-Bilingual Education Program, Austin, Texas.

720.____ . *Evaluation of Migrant Education in Texas: Final Report.* A research report from the Texas Migrant Educational Development Center operated under a contract with the Texas Education Agency, Contract Period March 7–August 31, 1968. Austin: Southwest Educational Development Laboratory, June 24, 1968. 163 pp.
Based on on-site observations at 90 schools throughout Texas, this report determines the educational opportunities available for children of migratory agricultural workers in Texas and evaluates the educational programs for migrants in Texas schools.

721.____ . *New Priorities: Educating Children of the Disadvantaged.* Austin, Texas: Southwest Educational Development Laboratory, through the support and cooperation of the Texas Education Agency and the Louisiana State Department of Education, 1968. 26 pp.
The major objective of this study is to determine the nature and extent of efforts in colleges, universities, and public schools to help elementary teachers and prospective elementary teachers deal with the problems of educating disadvantaged children.

722. Spicer, Edward H. *Cycles of Conquest; The Impact of Spain, Mexico and the U.S. on the Indians of the Southwest, 1533-1960.* Tucson: University of Arizona Press, 1962. 609 pp. Bibliographical notes, pp. 507-609.
An important work in terms of historical perspective, which includes chapters on linguistic unification and processes of acculturation.

723. Spoerl, Dorothy Tilden. "The Academic and Verbal Adjustment of College Age Bilingual Students." *The Journal of Genetic Psychology,* Vol. LXIV, First Half (March 1944), pp. 139-157. 16 references.
Concludes that at college level there are no lasting effects due to bilingualism in childhood which are apparent in academic records, vocational choices, or English ability: if there was a handicap, it has been stabilized by the first year of college.

724.____ . "Bilinguality and Emotional Adjustment." *The Journal of Abnormal and Social Psychology,* Vol. XXXVIII, No. 1 (January 1943), pp. 37-57.
It is suggested that, although at the college level bilingualism as such does not affect the students' expressive power, there is in his mental organization a residual effect of

the emotional turmoil and mental effort which might have been present in the early days of his school career when English was not, for him, a facile medium of expression.

725. Stella Maris, Sister, C.S.S.J. "A Note on the Pronunciation of New England French." *The French Review*, Vol. XXXII, No. 4 (February 1959), pp. 363-366.
A technical study of the Franco-American dialect.

726. Stern, H. H. *Foreign Languages in Primary Education: The Teaching of Foreign or Second Languages to Younger Children*. Report on an international meeting of experts, April 9-14, 1962. Hamburg: UNESCO Institute for Education, 1963. 103 pp. Bibliography, pp. 97-103.
Reports of FLES experiments throughout the world, arguments for early second language practice, and recommendations for practice and research.

*727.____, ed. *Languages and the Young School Child*. With a Research Guide by John B. Carroll. Language and Language Learning Series. London: Oxford University Press, 1969. 270 pp. Bibliography, pp. 261-267.
A useful collection of some 17 articles on the teaching of foreign languages in the primary school. (See Bell, Paul W.)

728. Stubing, Charles, ed. *Reports: Bilingualism*. See Southwest Council of Foreign Language Teachers.

729. Stycos, J. Mayone. "The Spartan Greeks of Bridgetown: Community Cohesion." *Common Ground*, Vol. VIII, No. 3 (Spring 1948), pp. 24-34.

730.____. "The Spartan Greeks of Bridgetown: The Second Generation." *Common Ground*, Vol. VIII, No. 4 (Summer 1948), pp. 72-86.

731. Summer Institute of Linguistics. See Wares, Alan C., comp.

732. Swansen, H. F. "The Norwegian Quakers of Marshall County, Iowa." *Norwegian-American Studies and Records*, Vol. X (1938), pp. 127-134.

733. Szy, Tibor, ed. *Hungarians in America*. New York: Hungarian University Association, Inc., 1963. 606 pp.
Directory of outstanding people of Hungarian-American descent and of Hungarian-American organizations.

734. Tabouret-Keller, Andrée. "Problèmes psychopédagogiques du bilinguisme." *International Review of Education*, Vol. VI, No. 1 (1960), pp. 52-66.
Describes the Alsacian situation in France: at school the language of instruction is French whereas outside the school the Alsacian dialect is spoken.

735. Taillon, Léopold. *Diversité des langues et bilinguisme*. Third edition. Collection Bilinguisme. Montréal, Canada: Les Editions de l'Atelier, 1967. 166 pp. 37-item bibliography.
An informally written account of the status of bilingualism in the world, with emphasis on the Canadian situation, by an educator concerned particularly with the education of French Speakers.

736. Tan, G. L. "Bilingual Education and its Inherent Problems, With Special Reference to Burma." Ph.D. dissertation, University of California, 1947.

737. Teel, D. "Preventing Prejudice Against Spanish-Speaking Children." *Educational Leadership*, Vol. XII (November 1954), pp. 94-98.
Suggests a school program to eliminate prejudice against Spanish-speaking people, with emphasis on basic principles of curriculum making.

738. Temple University. The NDEA National Institute for Advanced Study in Teaching Disadvantaged Youth. *Position Papers from Language Education for the Disadvantaged.* Report/Three, June 1968. Published by The American Association of Colleges for Teacher Education, 1126 Sixteenth Street, N. W., Washington, D. C. 20036. 16 pp.
Contents:
Allen, Harold B. "What English Teachers Should Know About Their Language," pp. 2-4.
Labov, William. "The Non-Standard Vernacular of the Negro Community: Some Practical Suggestions," pp. 4-7.
Gleason, H. A., Jr. "The Grammars of English," pp. 7-11.
Lefevre, Carl A. "Values in the Teaching of English and the Language Arts," pp. 11-16.

739. Texas Conference for the Mexican-Americans. See Estes, Dwain M., and David W. Darling, eds.

740. Texas Education Agency. Regional Educational Agencies Project in International Education. *Addresses and Reports Presented at the Conference on Development of Bilingualism in Children in Varying Linguistic and Cultural Heritages.* W. R. Goodson, ed. Austin, Texas: Texas Education Agency, January 31–February 3, 1967. 123 pp. 220-item bibliography, pp. 111-123.
Includes reports on various Texas cities, Guatemala, New Mexico, Germany, etc. With addresses and statements by several experts in this field.

741. ____. *Preschool Instructional Program for Non-English Speaking Children.* Bulletin No. 642. Austin, Texas, March 1964. 132 pp. Bibliography, pp. 125-132.

742. ____. Division of Research. "Report of Pupils in Texas Public Schools Having Spanish Surnames, 1955-56." Austin, Texas, August 1957.

743. Thériault, George F. "The Franco-Americans in Nashua, New Hampshire: An Experiment in Survival." Ph.D. dissertation, Harvard University, 1951.

744. ____. "The Franco-Americans of New England." In Mason Wade, ed., *Canadian Dualism: Studies of French-English Relations/La dualité canadienne: essais sur les relations entre Canadiens français et Canadiens anglais*, pp. 392-411. Toronto, Canada: University of Toronto Press; Quebec, Canada: Presses Universitaires Laval, 1960.
Describes how Franco-Americans have managed to keep their cultural heritage alive.

745. Thériot, Maria del Norte. "French in the Public Elementary Schools of Louisiana." *The French Review*, Vol. XIII, No. 4 (February 1940), pp. 344-346.
A description of the steps undertaken by a group of French teachers to start FLES programs in the public schools of Louisiana.

746. Therriault, Sister Mary Carmel, S.M. *La littérature française de Nouvelle-Angleterre.* Brunswick, Maine: Bowdoin College Bureau for Research in Municipal Government, 1961.
Discusses the contribution of Franco-Americans to French literature and culture.

747. Thompson, Frank V. *Schooling of the Immigrant.* New York and London: Harper & Brothers, 1920. 408 pp.

748. Thompson, Hildegard, et al. *Education for Cross-Cultural Enrichment.* Lawrence, Kansas: Haskell Institute, 1964.
Reprints of selected articles which appeared in *Indian Education* for the years 1952-1964. (See annotation for Beatty, *Education for Action*).

749. Thompson, Kenneth. "Recent Greek Emigration." *Geographical Review*, Vol. LVII, No. 4 (October 1967), pp. 560-562.

750. Thonis, Eleanor. "Bilingual Education for Mexican-American Children: A Report of an Experiment Conducted in the Marysville Joint Unified School District, Marysville, California, October 1966-June 1967." Prepared for the Mexican-American Education Project of the California State Department of Education. Sacramento, California: California State Department of Education, 1967.

751. Tiffany, Warren I. *Education in Northwest Alaska.* Revised Edition. Juneau, Alaska: Bureau of Indian Affairs, 1966. 71 pp. Bibliography, pp. 36-71.
This account deals not only with this specific geographic section, but reflects the economic, political, social as well as educational development of the whole state from the era of Russian occupation to the period of young statehood.

*752. Tireman, Lloyd S. *Teaching Spanish-Speaking Children.* Albuquerque, New Mexico: The University of New Mexico Press, 1951. 252 pp. Bibliographical footnotes.
A survey of bilingualism in the world studied separately in different countries and in general as a social phenomenon. Conclusions of studies applied to design a pattern for the education of Spanish-speaking children.

753. Tisch, Joseph LeSage. *French in Louisiana: A Study of the Historical Development of the French Language of Louisiana.* New Orleans, Louisiana: A. F. Laborde and Sons, 1959. 68 pp. Bibliography, pp. 66-68.
A study of the evolution of the Acadian-French, Creole-French, and *patois nègre* French dialects of Louisiana, with an analysis of the factors leading toward a unified "Louisiana French" in the future. A sampler of Louisiana French is provided.

754. Tits, Désiré. *Le mécanisme de l'acquisition d'une langue se substituant à la langue maternelle chez une enfant espagnole âgee de six ans.* Brussels, Belgium, 1948. 102 pp.

755. Tomanio, Antonio, J., and Lucille B. LaMacchia. *The Italian-American Community in Bridgeport.* University of Bridgeport Area Studies, Student Monograph No. 5. Bridgeport, Connecticut: University of Bridgeport, Sociology Department, 1953. 44 pp.
Studies the social institutions of Italian Americans in Bridgeport, their acculturation to the community, and the extent to which they have preserved elements of their original Italian culture.

756. Toussaint, N. *Bilinguisme et éducation.* Preface by Tobie Jonckheere. Brussels, Belgium: Maurice Lamertin, 1935. 200 pp. Long annotated bibliography.

A thorough study, emphasizing the irreparable harm done to a child in instructing him in any language other than his vernacular. Detailed analysis of bilingualism in the schools of most European countries individually.

757. Treudley, Mary Bosworth. "Formal Organization and the Americanization Process, With Special Reference to the Greeks of Boston." *American Sociological Review*, Vol. XIV, No. 1 (February 1949), pp. 44-53.

*758. Treviño, Bertha Alicia Gámez. "An Analysis of the Effectiveness of a Bilingual Program in the Teaching of Mathematics in the Primary Grades." Ph.D. dissertation, The University of Texas, 1968. 116 pp. Bibliography, pp. 106-116.

759. Truesdell, Leon E. *The Canadian Born in the United States: An Analysis of the Statistics of the Canadian Element in the Population of the United States, 1850 to 1930.* New Haven, Connecticut: Yale University Press; Toronto, Canada: The Ryerson Press, for the Carnegie Endowment for International Peace, Division of Economics and History, 1943. 263 pp.

A thorough study. Especially relevant is Chapter XI: "Ability to Speak English Among French-Canadians in the United States."

760. Turano, Anthony M. "The Speech of Little Italy." *American Mercury*, Vol. XXVI, No. 103 (July 1932), pp. 356-359.

A brief description of the "peculiar patois" spoken by Italian communities in the United States.

761. Ulibarrí, Horacio. *Educational Needs of the Mexican-American.* Prepared for the National Conference on Educational Opportunities for Mexican-Americans, April 25-26, 1968, Austin, Texas. Las Cruces, New Mexico: ERIC Clearninghouse on Rural Education and Small Schools, March 1968. 20 pp. 32 references.

Examines the educational needs of the Mexican American in relation to occupational success, citizenship participation, and personality factors.

762.____. *Interpretive Studies on Bilingual Education.* Final Report, Project No. 80609, Grant No. HEW-OEC-O-080-609-4531 (010). U.S. Department of Health, Education, and Welfare, Office of Education, Bureau of Research. Albuquerque, New Mexico: University of New Mexico, College of Education, March 1969. 154 pp.

Following an analysis of literature on bilingual education, the author has prepared a summary of research and drawn implications for education and for research. Contains an annotated bibliography, a selected bibliography, and a list of projects and on-going programs.

763.____. "Social and Attitudinal Characteristics of Migrant and Ex-Migrant Workers–New Mexico, Colorado, Arizona, and Texas." *ERIC.* Ed. 011 215, 1964.

A study of the feelings of the migrant worker or the bilingual person who has not acquired a great deal of formal education. Was conducted with migrant workers in regard to family, health, economics, government, children, religion, and recreation.

*764. United Kingdom. National Commission for UNESCO, Department of Education and Science. *Bilingualism in Education.* Report on an International Seminar, Aberystwyth,

Wales, 20 August-2 September 1960. London: Her Majesty's Stationery Office, 1965. 234 pp. 267-item bibliography.

Contains valuable papers by well-known specialists throughout the world illustrating the linguistic, social, psychological, cultural, historical, and above all educational aspects of bilingualism.

*765.____. Ministry of Education, Central Advisory Council for Education (Wales). *The Place of Welsh and English in the Schools of Wales.* London: Her Majesty's Stationery Office, 1953. 112 pp. Bibliography on bilingualism, pp. 107-110.

A comprehensive study of bilingualism in Wales taking most previous studies into consideration, an examination of the desirability of bilingual schooling, and a discussion on what policies to follow.

766. United Nations Educational, Scientific, and Cultural Organization. *African Languages and English in Education.* UNESCO Educational Studies and Documents, No. 2. Paris, 1953. 91 pp.

A report of a meeting held at Jos, Nigeria; includes discussions of the place of African languages and English both in and out of school, problems in the use of African languages in education, and the teaching of English as a second language in African territories.

*767.____. *The Use of Vernacular Languages in Education.* Monographs on Fundamental Education, VIII. Paris: UNESCO, 1953.

Report of 12 international experts describing the status of education in bilingual areas in all parts of the world, and strongly recommends use of learner's mother tongue in beginning formal education.

768. United States Bureau of the Census. See United States Department of Commerce, Bureau of the Census.

769. United States Bureau of Indian Affairs. See United States Department of the Interior, Bureau of Indian Affairs.

770. United States Congress. House of Representatives. *Hearings Before Subcommittee No. 1 of the Committee on the Judiciary. 89th Congress. First Session on H.R. 2580 To Amend the Immigration and Nationality Act and For Other Purposes.* Serial No. 7. Washington, D.C.: U.S. Government Printing Office, 1965.

Papers, presentations, arguments for and against, statistics, and statements concerning the new immigration legislation are presented.

*771.____. Senate. Bilingual Education. Hearings Before the Special Subcommittee on Bilingual Education of the Committee on Labor and Public Welfare, United States Senate, Ninetieth Congress, First Session, on S. 428. Two parts. Washington, D.C.: U.S. Government Printing Office, 1967.

"A bill to amend the Elementary and Secondary Education Act of 1965 in order to provide assistance to local education agencies in establishing bilingual American education programs, and to provide certain other assistance to promote such programs." An extremely important collection of data, information, materials, discussions, and statements by scholars, responsible persons, and experts in the field.

*772.——. *Bilingual Education Programs.* Hearings Before the General Subcommittee on Education of the Committee on Education and Labor, House of Representatives, Ninetieth Congress, First Session on H.R. 9840 and H.R. 10224. Hearings Held in Washington D.C., June 28 and 29, 1967. Washington, D.C.: U.S. Government Printing Office, 1967.

Bills to amend the Elementary and Secondary Education Act of 1965 in order to assist bilingual education programs.

*773.——. Committee on Labor and Public Welare. *Committee Print, Elementary and Secondary Education Act Amendments of 1967, With Background Materials and Tables.* Prepared for the Subcommittee on Education. Washington, D. C.: U.S. Government Printing Office, March 1968.

774.——. *Cuban Refugee Problem.* Hearings before the Subcommittee to Investigate Problems Connected with Refugees and Escapees of the Committee on the Judiciary, 89th Congress, Second Session, Part 1: Washington, D.C., March 23, 24, 29, and 30, 1966; Part 2: New York, New York, April 13, 1966; Part 3: Newark, New Jersey, April 15, 1966. Washington, D.C.: U.S. Government Printing Office, 1966. 304 pp.

Part 1 presents testimony and statistics dealing with the resettlement problem; the memorandum of understanding between Cuba and the U.S.; conditions in Cuba; effectiveness of the refugee program; issues reflected in the mail to Congress; and the inability of Cubans to practice their profession or skill. Part 2 focuses on the New York situation and Part 3 on the New Jersey situation (Part 3 is entitled *Cuban Refugee Program.*)

775.——. *Hearings Before the Subcommittee on Immigration and Naturalization of the Committee on the Judiciary. 89th Congress. First Session on S. 500 to Amend the Immigration and Naturalization Act. Part I.* Washington, D.C.: U.S. Government Printing Office, 1965.

Papers, presentations, arguments for and against, statistics, and statements concerning the new immigration legislation are presented.

776.——. "Quality Education for American Indians, A Report on Organizational Location." Subcommittee on Education of the Committee on Labor and Public Welfare. Washington, D.C.: U.S. Government Printing Office, May 1967. 11 pp.

Gives details concerning the responsibility for Indian education within the federal government. Contains a description of past and present governmental educational policies with pertinent data as to school enrollment, legislation, financing, etc. The report also makes a series of recommendations regarding research, planning, and programs.

777. United States Department of Commerce. Bureau of the Census. *Census of Population, 1960: Subject Reports, Persons of Spanish Surname.* Final Report PC(2)1B. Washington, D.C.: U.S. Government Printing Office, 1963.

778.——. *Historical Statistics of the United States, Colonial Times to 1957.* Washington, D.C.: U.S. Government Printing Office, 1960.

779.——. *Historical Statistics of the United States, Colonial Times to 1957; Continuation to 1962 and Revisions.* Washington, D.C.: U.S. Government Printing Office, 1965.

780.____. *Mother Tongue of the Foreign-Born: Selected Characteristics of Foreign-Born by Language Spoken Before Coming to U.S.* Final Report PC(2)1E, 1960. 26 pp.
A basic, official document frequently used throughout the monograph.

781. United States Department of the Interior. Bureau of Indian Affairs. *English for American Indians.* Prepared by the Center for Applied Linguistics under contract with the B.I.A. Washington, D.C., first issue Fall 1968.
A newsletter intended for teachers and other educators who are involved with the teaching of English in the educational system of the Bureau of Indian Affairs.

782.____. Division of Education. *Fiscal Year 1968, Statistics Concerning Indian Education.* Lawrence, Kansas: Haskell Institute, 1968. 40 pp.

783.____. *Indians of the Eastern Seaboard*, 1967, 28 pp.; *Indians of the Great Lakes Area*, revised edition, 1968, 24 pp.; *Indians of the Gulf Coast States*, 1968, 20 pp.; *Indians of the Lower Plateau*, 1968, 24 pp. Washington, D.C.: U.S. Government Printing Office.

784.____. *Report to the Senate Appropriations Committee on the Navajo Bordertown Dormitory Program by the Commissioner of Indian Affairs.* Washington, D.C.: U.S. Government Printing Office, 1965. 72 pp.

785. United States Department of Justice. Immigration and Naturalization Service. *Annual Report of the Immigration and Naturalization Service, 1967.* Washington, D. C.: Government Printing Office, 1967.

786. United States Department of State. Inter-Agency Committee on Mexican American Affairs. *The Mexican American: A New Focus on Opportunity.* Testimony presented at the Cabinet Committee Hearings on Mexican American Affairs, El Paso, Texas, October 26-28, 1967. Washington, D. C.: U.S. Government Printing Office, 1968. 253 pp.
Over fifty men and women presented statements on agriculture; labor; health, education, and welfare; the war on poverty and the general improvement in the economic and social condition of the Mexican American. Bilingual education was given support by several persons.

787. United States Federal Writers' Project, Work Progress Administration of the City of New York. *The Italians of New York: A Survey.* With 24 plates by the WPA Federal Art Project of the City of New York. Sponsored by the Guilds' Committee for Federal Writers' Publications, Inc. The American Guides Series. New York: Random House, 1938. 241 pp. Bibliography, pp. 227-230.
A study of the greatest concentration of Italians in the United States: their religious, recreational, social, and cultural life, problems of adjustment and integration, share in building and developing New York, creative work and intellectual influence, role in business and industry, etc.

788. United States House of Representatives. See United States Congress. House of Representatives.

789. United States Senate. See United States Congress. Senate.

790. University College of Wales. *Llyfryddiaeth. Dwyietheg: Bilingualism: A Bibliography With Special Reference to Wales.* Aberystwyth, England: University College of Wales,

Faculty of Education, 1960. Pamphlet No. 7. 55 pp.

A research guide for bilingualism throughout the world. 784 items listed in alphabetical order.

791. University of Southwestern Louisiana. "Disadvantaged Youth: Reading and Language Arts for Elementary Teachers and Supervisors of French-English Speaking Children." Proposal to the U.S. Office of Education for an Institute for Advanced Study. Lafayette, Louisiana: College of Education, University of Southwestern Louisiana, 1967.

792.____ . "The Role of Education and Government in the Regional Preservation of French: A Colloquy." Lafayette, Louisiana, December 4, 1968. 28 pp.

A collection of papers discussing the problem of French language maintenance in Louisiana.

793. Upham, W. Kennedy, and David E. Wright. "Poverty Among Spanish Americans in Texas: Low-Income Families in a Minority Group." Departmental Information Report No. 66-2. College Station, Texas: Department of Agricultural Economies and Sociology, Texas A&M University, Texas Agricultural Experiment Station, April 1967. 55 pp. Bibliography, pp. 39-41.

Poverty is abnormally prevalent among Spanish American families, especially in Texas as compared with Anglo-white families. Also, a large number of Mexican American families fall in the extreme poverty classification. Moreover, given the size of Spanish American families, the number of *persons* in need is greater than the family unit figures would indicate.

794. Valdman, Albert, ed. *Trends in Language Teaching*. Foreword by Alfred S. Hayes. New York: McGraw-Hill Book Company, 1966. 298 pp. Bibliographies.

Articles reporting the search for progress in foreign language education during the years since the passage of the National Defense Education Act of 1958.

795. Valette, Rebecca M. "Some Reflections on Second-Language Learning in Young Children." *Language Learning*, Vol. XIV, Nos. 3-4 (1964), pp. 91-98.

796. Valls Anglés, Vicente. See Oficina Internacional de Educación.

797. Vander Zanden, James W. *American Minority Relations: The Sociology of Race and Ethnic Groups*. Second edition. New York: The Ronald Press Company, 1966. 550 pp. Bibliography, pp. 515-538.

A report of various theories dealing with the sources of prejudice and discrimination. Special treatment is reserved for Negroes, Puerto Ricans, Hispanos, Mexican Americans, Chinese, Japanese, Jews, and Amish.

798. Vanstone, James W. *Point Hope: An Eskimo Village in Transition*. Edited by Viola E. Garfield, The American Ethnological Society. Seattle, Washington: The University of Washington Press, 1962. 177 pp. Bibliography, pp. 169-172.

Concerned with the functioning of a contemporary Eskimo community of Western Alaska. Historical materials are utilized to provide a background but the study is functional and acculturational rather than historical.

799. Vaughan, Herbert H. "Italian and Its Dialects as Spoken in the United States." *American Speech,* Vol. I, No. 8 (May 1926), pp. 431-435.

800. Vecoli, R. J. "Contadini in Chicago: A Critique of the Uprooted." *Journal of American History*, Vol. LI (December 1964), pp. 404-417.

801. Velikonja, Joseph. "The Italian-Born in the United States, 1950." *Association of American Geographers, Annals*, Vol. LI, No. 4 (December 1961), p. 426. Paper presented at the 57th annual meeting of the American Association of Geographers, East Lansing, Michigan, August 28–September 1, 1961.

A study of the distribution of Italians in the U.S.

802.____. *Italians in the U.S.: Bibliography*. Department of Geography Occasional Papers No. 1. Carbondale, Illinois: Southern Illinois University, 1963. 90 pp. 793 references.

The most extensive and up-to-date classified bibliography on Italian-Americans. Lists items related to all aspects of their life in the U.S. Of special relevance is Part A7, "Education and Language, Teaching of Language."

803.Verdoort, Albert. *Zweisprachige Nachbarn*. Vienna, Austria: Braumüller, 1968. 355 pp.

804. Verrette, Adrien. "La mutualité chez les Franco-Américains." *Le Canada Français,* Vol. XXVIII (January 1941), pp. 477-496.

805. Viatte, Auguste. "Les franco-américains de Nouvelle-Angleterre." *Renaissance*, Vol. II-III (1944-1945), pp. 322-335.

A thorough description of the Franco-American ethnic group.

806. Viereck, Louis. "German Instruction in American Schools." In *Report of the Commissioner of Education for 1900-1901*, Washington, D.C.: U.S. Government Printing Office, 1902, pp. 531-708. (German edition: *Zwei Jahrhunderte der Unterricht in den Vereinigten Staaten*, Braunschweig, Vieweg, 1903.

807. Viereck, Wolfgang. "German Dialects Spoken in the United States and Canada: A Bibliography." *Orbis*, Vol. XVI (1967), pp. 549-568.

*808. Vildomeć, Věroboj. *Multilingualism*. Leyden, The Netherlands: A. W. Sythoff, 1963. 262 pp. Bibliography, pp. 242-256.

A study of the psychological and linguistic aspects of multilingualism, with pertinent remarks on its influence on the mother tongue, and on the mutual interference of languages. Analysis of the relation between speech and thought. Conclusions based on surveys and experiments.

809. "The Village People." Anchorage, Alaska: Anchorage Daily News, 1966. 53 pp.

Offers a panorama of the life of the present day Alaskan native with information on schooling, B.I.A. policies and practices, etc.

810. Vogelin, C. F., and F. M. "Indo-European Fascicle One." *Anthropological Linguistics*, Vol. VII, No. 8 (November 1965), pp. 1-294.

Classification of Indo-European languages and demographic data on number of speakers.

811. ___. "Languages of the World: Native America Fascicle One." *Anthropological Linguistics*, Vol. VI, No. 6 (June 1964), pp. 1-149.

Classification of American Indian languages and various estimates of number and location of speakers.

812. ___, and Noel W. Schutz, Jr. "The Language Situation in Arizona as Part of the Southwest Culture Area." In Dell H. Hymes and William E. Bittle, eds., *Studies in Southwestern Ethnolinguistics: Meaning and History in the Languages of the American Southwest.* The Hague: Mouton & Co., 1967, pp. 403-451.

A well researched study which includes a section on bilingualism among the Indian groups in the Southwest.

813. Vogt, Evon Z., and Clyde Kluckhohn. *Navajo Means People.* Photos by Leonard McCombe. Cambridge, Massachusetts: Harvard University Press, 1951. 159 pp.

814. Vygotsky, L. S. *Thought and Language.* Edited and translated from Russian by Eugenia Hanfmann and Gertrude Vakar. Cambridge, Massachusetts: The M.I.T. Press; New York: John Wiley & Sons, Inc., 1962. 168 pp. Bibliography, pp. 157-159.

A study of the interrelation of thought and language with a critical analysis of the two most influential theories about the development of language and thinking.

815. Wagley, Charles, and Marvin Harris. *Minorities in the New World: Six Case Studies.* New York: Columbia University Press, 1958. 320 pp. Bibliography, pp. 297-304.

Based in part upon studies prepared for UNESCO by social scientists of five different countries. Studies minorities in the Americas: the American Indian (Brazil, Mexico); the Negro in the Americas (Martinique, United States), and European immigrants in U.S. (French Canadians, Jews).

816. Walker, D. B. *Politics and Ethnocentrism: The Case of the Franco-Americans.* Brunswick, Maine: Bowdoin College Bureau for Research in Municipal Government, 1961. 48 pp.

Discusses the political aspect of Franco-American life.

817. Walker, Willard. "An Experiment in Programmed Cross Cultural Education: The Import of the Cherokee Primer for the Cherokee Community and for the Behavioral Sciences." Unpublished paper presented at Tahlequah, Oklahoma, March 1965, in connection with the Carnegie Corporation Cross-Cultural Education Project of the University of Chicago. Mimeographed. 10 pp.

Presents the rationale for the design of the Cherokee primer by noting such variables as the factors influencing motivation, the presentation of the information to be learned, the native learning and teaching patterns, etc.

818. Walsh, Donald D. "Bilingualism and Bilingual Education: A Guest Editorial." *Foreign Language Annals*, Vol. II, No. 3 (March 1969), pp. 298-303.
A foreign language teacher advocates progressive bilingual education in order to have "brighter, more tolerant" children, who would be "more preceptive about their own culture and the other than are otherwise comparable monolinguals."

819.——, ed. *A Handbook for Teachers of Spanish and Portuguese*. Lexington, Massachusetts: D. C. Heath and Company, 1969.

820.——. *What's What: A List of Useful Terms for the Teacher of Modern Languages*. Third edition. New York: Modern Language Association, 1965. 34 pp. Bibliography, pp. 7-9.
Explanatory information on about 300 items dealing with fields whose special lexicon perplexes the language teacher: culture, linguistics, programmed instruction, the language laboratory, psychometry, psycholinguistics, etc.

821. Wapple, Robert J., and Alvin A. Fodor. "Bilingual Education for Mexican-American Children: An Experiment." Marysville, California: Marysville Joint Unified School District, September 30, 1967.

822. Wares, Alan C., comp. *Bibliography of the Summer Institute of Linguistics: 1935-1968*. Santa Ana, California: Summer Institute of Linguistics, 1968. 124 pp.
Contains 2514 entries dealing with close to 300 languages (not including separate dialects) and representing the work of more than 670 different authors. Basically three types of output: general works, articles and monographs on specific languages, and educational materials written in a specific language.

823. Warner, W. Lloyd, and Leo Srole. *The Social Systems of American Ethnic Groups*. Yankee City series, Vol. III. New Haven, Connecticut: Yale University Press, 1945. 318 pp.
A study of ethnic groups, including the Irish, French-Canadians, Jews, Armenians, and Poles. See especially Chapter VII, pp. 220-253, "Language and the School: (1) Generation Shift in Language Usage; (2) The Catholic Parochial Schools; (3) The Hebrew School; and (4) The Greek Schools."

824. Warriner, Helen P. *The Effectiveness of the Use of Foreign Languages in Teaching Academic Subjects: A Research Contribution to Education Planning*. Richmond, Virginia: Division of Educational Research, State Department of Education, September 1968. 40 pp.
Report of an experiment in which a language foreign to the students was used as a medium of instruction.

825. Webster, D. H. "On Cross-Cultural Communication." Fairbanks, Alaska: Summer Institute of Linguistics, n.d. Mimeographed. 11 pp.
A helpful guide to the teacher of Eskimo and Athabaskans in developing his presentation in English to parallel the thought patterns of the student's native language. He presents insights into these languages, contrasting them with English. Both parts of the paper emphasize the value of a coordinate language system.

826. Weinberg, George. "School in Transition." *Journal of Educational Sociology*, Vol. XXV (November 1951), pp. 140-145.

827. Weinberg, Roy D. *Eligibility for Entry to the United States of America.* Based on *Immigration Laws in the United States*, by Carol M. Crosswell. Revised third edition. Oceana Legal Almanac series, No. 5. Dobbs Ferry, New York: Oceana Publications, Inc., 1967. 116 pp.

The introduction contains a helpful presentation of the history of immigration legislation in the United States.

828. Weinreich, Max. "History of the Yiddish Language: The Problems and Their Implications." *Proceedings of the American Philosophical Society*, Vol. CIII, No. 4 (August 15, 1959), pp. 563-570.

829.____. "Internal Bilingualism in Ashkenazic Jewry to the Enlightenment Period: Facts and Concepts." *Goldene Keyt*, Vol. XXXV (1959), pp. 3-11. (In Yiddish.)

*830. Weinreich, Uriel. *Languages in Contact: Findings and Problems.* With a preface by André Martinet. The Hague: Mouton and Co., 1967. 150 pp. 658-item bibliography.

One of the deepest, most technical, and most comprehensive accounts ever written on bilingualism from primarily two angles: its linguistic consequences and its relation to intelligence and personality.

831.____. "Research Problems in Bilingualism, With Special Reference to Switzerland." Unpublished Ph.D. dissertation, Columbia University, 1951. 568 pp. 572 references. *Dissertation Abstracts*, series A, Vol. XII, No. 4 (1952), pp. 418-419.

Contains a critical review of the pertinent research literature on bilingualism (done in 10 languages) entitled "Approaches to Bilingualism," followed by a study of the quadrilingualism that exists in Switzerland.

832.____. "The Russification of Soviet Minority Languages." *Problems of Communism*, Vol. II, No. 6 (1953), pp. 46-57.

833. Weir, Ruth Hirsch. *Language in the Crib.* Janua Linguarum, series maior, Vol. XIV, The Hague: Mouton & Co., 1962. 216 pp. Bibliography, pp. 213-216.

A study of the linguistic development in children. The presence or absence of structural signals in the language of a child aged 2-3 gives the author valuable clues to the identification of linguistic universals.

834. Weiss, Andreas von. *Hauptprobleme der Zweisprachigkeit: Eine Untersuchung auf Grund deutsch/estnischen Materials.* Heidleberg, Germany: Winter 1959.

835. Welsh, Peter, et al. *Plurilingualism in Switzerland.* Comparative Studies, Data Book on Switzerland. Vol. I by Peter Welsh, with a statistical chapter by John G. Gordon. Prepared under the general supervision of Prof. K. D. McRae, and with the editorial assistance of Mireille Desjardais. Information Services, Royal Commission on Bilingualism and Biculturalism, Room 609, 88 Metcalfe St., Ottawa, Ontario, Canada. Part II—International Research Report of the Royal Commission on Bilingualism and Biculturalism, Peter Welsh, August 1966.

836. Wessel, Bessie Bloom *An Ethnic Survey of Woonsocket, Rhode Island.* Chicago, Illinois: The University of Chicago Press, April 1941. 263 pp. Bibliography, pp. 246-262.

An exhaustive sociological study. The bibliography is an impressive, though now somewhat outmoded, research tool on the Franco-Americans.

837. West, Michael. "Bilingualism." *English Language Teaching*, Vol. XII, No. 3 (April-June 1958), pp. 94-97.
Suggests that bilingualism is an inevitable disadvantage and points out its ill effects. Suggests measures mitigating its evils.

838.____. *Bilingualism* (with special reference to Bengal). Bureau of Education Occasional Reports, No. 13. Calcutta, India: Government of India Central Publication Branch, 1926. 356 pp.
A discussion of the nature and origin of the problems of bilingualism, the history of the policy of bilingualism in the educational system of Bengal, and the Bengali's need of English, followed by experiments on the teaching of English to Bengali boys.

839.____. "Bilingualism in Gibraltar." *Overseas Education*, Vol. XXVII (1956), pp. 148-153.

840. Whyte, William Foote. *Street Corner Society: The Social Structure of an Italian Slum*. Second, enlarged edition. Chicago, Illinois: The University of Chicago Press, 1955. First edition, 1943. 276 pp.
A study of the sociological phenomena of the gang as found among first- and second-generation Italian-Americans.

841. Wieczerkowski, Wilhelm. *Bilingualismus in frühen Schulalter: Gruppenprüfungen mit Intelligenztests und mit dem Helsingforstest*. Societas Scientiarum Fennica, Commentationes Humanarum Litterarum, Vol. XXXIII, No. 2. Helsinki, Finland, 1963. 194 pp.

842. Williams, Frederick, and Rita C. Naremore. "Language and Poverty: An Annotated Bibliography." Madison, Wisconsin: The University of Wisconsin, 1968. 42 pp. Mimeographed.
On the basis of literature cited in this 124-item annotated bibliography, the two researchers have reached the following conclusion: "A poverty environment has a socializing influence upon its population, an influence which manifests itself in distinctions of language and cognition, and these distinctions in turn serve in the definition and perpetuation of that population as a poverty culture." (p. iv.)

843. Williams, Jac L. "Bilingual Wales: Lessons for the Language Teacher." *Times Educational Supplement*, February 15, 1963, p. 299.
The author discusses experiences in Wales in teaching both English and Welsh as second languages, which emphasize the importance of early exposure in the second language for effective progress toward bilingualism.

844.____. "A Welsh View of Bilingualism and Primary Education." *Irish National Teacher*, Vol. XI, No. 7 (September 1966), pp. 25, 27, 32.
A criticism of Fr. John Macnamara's *Bilingualism and Primary Education: A Study of the Irish Experience*.

845. Wislon, Herbert B. "Evaluation of the Influence of Educational Programs on Mexican-Americans." Prepared for the National Conference on Educational Opportunities for

Mexican-Americans, April 25-26, 1968, Commodore Perry Hotel, Austin, Texas. Las Cruces, New Mexico: ERIC Clearinghouse on Rural Education and Small Schools, New Mexico State University, March 1968.

846. Wilson, J. "The Teaching of English in a Bilingual Partnership." *Teacher Education*, Vol. I, No. 1 (May 1960), pp. 9-17.
Suggests that the need of emerging African nations for English as a lingua franca and as an aid to higher education requires improved and more extensive training of teachers of English. Also surveys the various techniques in use.

847. Wilson, Robert D. "A Bilingual Academic Program for the Early Grades of the Schools of the Bureau of Indian Affairs in the Navajo Area." A proposal sent to Dr. William J. Benham, 1968. Mimeographed. 8 pp.
Defines the implementation and guidelines for this project.

848.____ . "Bilingual Education for Navaho Students: Strategies for Teaching the Nature of Coordinate Bilingualism as Part of the General Objective, Learning How to Learn." Unpublished paper delivered at the Conference of Teaching English to Speakers of Other Languages, Chicago, March 7, 1969.
Presents the rationale and general objectives for the curriculum materials the author is developing with the Bureau of Indian Affairs.

849. Winter, Nathan H. *Jewish Education in a Pluralist Society: Samson Benderly and Jewish Education in the United States*. New York: New York University Press, 1966. 262 pp.

850. Wise, Mary Ruth. "Utilizing Languages of Minority Groups in a Bilingual Experiment in the Amazonian Jungle of Peru." Unpublished paper. n.p., 1965. 16 pp.
Description of a program in bilingual education initiated in 1952 by the Peruvian Ministry of Public Education in cooperation with the Summer Institute of Linguistics.

851. Wittke, Carl. *We Who Built America: The Saga of an Immigrant*. Revised edition. Cleveland, Ohio: The Press of Western Reserve University, 1964. Chapter 15, "The Poles, Jugoslavs [sic], Russians, Hungarians, and Other Minor [sic] Groups," and Chapter 17, "The Greeks, Americans, Portuguese, Spanish, Mexicans, Puerto Ricans."

852. Wolcott, Harry. *A Kwakiutl Village and School*. New York: Holt, Rinehart and Winston, 1967.
States that he embarked upon his research hoping to discover why Indian pupils fail so badly in school, but after living and working in the community, he began to pose a different question, "How do the schools fail their Indian pupils?"

853. Wollfradt, K. W. "Die Statistik des Deutsch-Amerikanischen Schulwesens." *Deutscher Pionier* (Cincinnati), Vol. XVIII (1886), pp. 50-55.

854. Wonder, John P. "The Bilingual Mexican-American as a Potential Teacher of Spanish." *Hispania*, Vol. XLVIII, No. 1 (March 1965), pp. 97-99.

855. Wood, Arthur Evans. *Hamtramck Then and Now*. New York: Bookman Associates, 1955.

A comprehensive sociological description of Polish-Americans in their role as the local majority in Hamtramck, Michigan.

856. Wood, Ralph C., ed. *The Pennsylvania-Germans.* Princeton, New Jersey: Princeton University Press, 1942. 299 pp. Bibliography, pp. 285-286.
Contains a good article by Clyde S. Stine on the educational situation at the time, "The Pennsylvania Germans and the School," pp. 103-127.

857. Woodworth, Elizabeth D., and Robert J. Di Pietro, eds. See Georgetown University *Monograph Series on Languages and Linguistics,* No. 15 (1962).

858. Wranosky, Ernest J., et al. *Teaching the Bilingual Child: A Handbook for Teachers.* Edited by Dorothy T. Arnold. Corpus Christi, Texas: Flour Bluff Public Schools, 1953. Mimeographed. 67 pp. Bibliography, pp. 61-62.

859. Wuorinen, John H. *Nationalism in Modern Finland.* New York: Columbia University Press, 1931. 302 pp. Bibliography, pp. 281-294.
"Describes some of the main forces and tendencies which served to bring the people of Finland, in the course of the nineteenth century, to nationalist-conscious citizenship, enabled them to withstand the attempts at Russification which were made... and contributed to the attainment of political independence...." (p. v.) Contains sections on language policies and problems.

860. Wysocki, Boleslaw, A., and Aydin Cankardas. "A New Estimate of Polish Intelligence." *Journal of Educational Psychology*, Vol. XLVIII, No. 8 (December 1957), pp. 525-533.
Rebuttal of the misconception that Poles have an inferior intelligence.

861. Wytrwal, Joseph A. *America's Polish Heritage: A Social History of the Poles in America.* Detroit, Michigan: Endurance Press, 1961. 294-item bibliography, pp. 295-309.
A basic, comprehensive study of the Poles in the U.S., their organizations, assimilation, language maintenance, religious affiliation, etc.

862. Yamamoto, Kaoru. "Bilingualism: A Brief Review." *Mental Hygiene*, Vol. XLVIII, No. 3 (July 1964), pp. 468-477. 10 references.
A general summary and review of the literature dealing with bilingualism: bilingualism and verbal intelligence, studies of English-Yiddish, -Gaelic, -Italian, -Chinese, -Spanish bilingual children, bilingualism and later emotional development.

863. Yarborough, Ralph M. "Bilingual Education As a Social Force." *Foreign Language Annals*, Vol. II, No. 3 (March 1969), pp. 325-327.
Discusses the implications of the Bilingual Education Act. Based on an address before the joint conventions of the Modern Language Association and the American Council on the Teaching of Foreign Languages, New York, 28 December, 1968.

864. Yefroikin, S. "Jewish Education in the United States." *General Encyclopedia in Yiddish*, Vol. Yidn V, pp. 166-219. New York: Jewish Encyclopedia Handbooks, 1957. (In Yiddish.)

865. ———. "Yiddish Secular Schools in the United States." In *The Jewish People: Past and Present*, Vol. II. New York: Central Yiddish Culture Organization and Jewish

Encyclopedic Handbooks, 1948, pp. 144-150.
Briefly describes the three Yiddish school systems in America: their origin, development, and status in 1948.

866. Young, Donald. *American Minority Peoples: A Study in Racial and Cultural Conflicts in the United States.* Harper's Social Science series. New York and London: Harper & Brothers, Publishers, 1932. 621 pp. Bibliography, pp. 594-607.
See especially Chapter XIII, "The Education of American Minorities," pp. 446-466, and Chapter XIV, "Educational Segregation," pp. 467-503.

867. Zallio, A. G. "The Piedmontese Dialects in the United States." *American Speech*, Vol. II, No. 12 (September 1927), pp. 501-504.
A list of Piedmontese-dialect forms, given "for the purpose of affording the reader a general idea of the great differences in vocabulary between [the dialect] and the Italian language." (p. 501.)

868. Zeydel, Edwin H. "The Teaching of German in the United States from Colonial Times to the Present." In *Reports of Surveys and Studies in the Teaching of Modern Foreign Languages.* New York: The Modern Language Association of America, 1961, pp. 285-308. 25 bibliographical notes.
Emphasis on teaching German to English-speaking school and college population. Discussion on (1) colonial era, (2) revolutionary war to 1825, (3) uphill struggle 1826-1876, (4) era of self-examination 1876-1899, (5) first decades of 20th century, and (6) period of recuperation 1917-1957.

*869. Zintz, Miles V. *Education Across Cultures.* Dubuque, Iowa: William C. Brown Co., Inc., 1963. 412 pp.
Utilizing Spanish-speaking and Indian populations for exemplary samplings and illustrations, the content covers the range of educating minority group children from the understanding of environmental influences on child and teacher to problems of meeting educational needs in curriculum.

*870.——. "What Teachers Should Know About Bilingual Education." In Horacio Ulibarrí, and James G. Cooper, *Interpretive Study on Bilingual Education.* Albuquerque, New Mexico: University of New Mexico, College of Education, March 1969. 60 pp.
Special emphasis placed on cross-cultural education, problems in second language learning, classroom methodology, special aspects of vocabulary, and the bilingual school. Several valuable bibliographies included, some annotated.

INDEX TO BIBLIOGRAPHY

Note

Having arranged the bibliography alphabetically by author and numbered the items, we have appended a subject index, which, though incomplete, we hope will be helpful.

INDEX

D